THE GALILEE IN LATE ANTIQUITY

THE GALILEE IN LATE ANTIQUITY

edited by Lee I. Levine

The Jewish Theological Seminary of America
New York and Jerusalem

Distributed by Harvard University Press
Cambridge, Massachusetts and London

The Hebrew version of this volume will be published jointly by
The Jewish Theological Seminary of America and
Yad Izhak Ben-Zvi, Jerusalem.

Library of Congress Cataloging-in-Publication Data

The Galilee in late antiqulty / edited by Lee I. Levine.
    p. cm.
    Includes bibliographical references and index.
    ISBN 0-674-34113-9 : $35.00
    1. Galilee (Israel)--History--Congresses. 2. Jews-
-History--70-638--xCongresses. 3. Judaism--History--Talmudic
period, 10-425--Congresses. 4. Galllee (Israel)--Church history-
-Congresses. I. Levine, Lee I.
DS110.G2G37 1992
933--dc20   92-12475 CIP

Publication of this volume was made possible
by the generous support of
the Alan M. and Katherine W. Stroock Fund.

qʎ

Table of Contents

VI. ARCHEOLOGICAL EVIDENCE IN THE GALILEE

List of Illustrations

Abbreviations

AB	Assyriologische Bibliothek
ADAJ	Annual of the Department of Antiquities of Jordan
AJA	American Journal of Archaeology
AJS Review	Association for Jewish Studies Review
ANRW	Aufstieg und Niedergang der römischen Welt
AOAT	Alter Orient und Altes Testament
ASTI	Annual of the Swedish Theological Institute
b.	*ben*, son of
B	Babylonian Talmud
BA	Biblical Archaeologist
BAR	Biblical Archaeology Review
BASOR	Bulletin of the American Schools of Oriental Research
BJPES	Bulletin of the Jewish Palestine Exploration Society
BSOAS	Bulletin of the School of Oriental and African Studies
BMC	British Museum Catalogue
CBQ	Catholic Biblical Quarterly
CCSL	Corpus Christianorum, Series Latina
CSEL	Corpus Scriptorum Ecclesiasticorum Latinorum
DJD	Discoveries in the Judaean Desert
EAEHL	Encyclopedia of Archaeological Excavations in the Holy Land
EJ	Encyclopaedia Judaica
GCS	Die griechischen christlichen Schriftsteller der ersten drei Jahrhunderte
Ḥ.	*Ḥorvah*, ruin
HSCP	Harvard Studies in Classical Philology
ICC	International Critical Commentary
IEJ	Israel Exploration Journal
IGLS	Inscriptions grecques et latines de la Syrie

IGR	Inscriptiones Graecae ad Res Romanas Pertinentes (R. Cagnat et al.)
INJ	Israel Numismatic Journal
J	Jerusalem Talmud
JAAR	Journal of the American Academy of Religion
JANES	Journal of the Ancient Near Eastern Society
JAOS	Journal of the American Oriental Society
JBL	Journal of Biblical Literature
JE	Jewish Encyclopedia
JJA	Journal of Jewish Art
JJS	Journal of Jewish Studies
JNES	Journal of Near Eastern Studies
JQR	Jewish Quarterly Review
JR	Journal of Religion
JRS	Journal of Roman Studies
JSJ	Journal for the Study of Judaism
JSNT	Journal for the Study of the New Testament
JSS	Journal of Social Studies
JTS	Journal of Theological Studies
Kh.	*Khirbeh*, ruin
LA	Liber Annuus
LCL	Loeb Classical Library
M	Mishnah
MEFR	Mélanges de l'école française de Rome
MGWJ	Monatsschrift für Geschichte und Wissenschaft des Judentums
NT	Novum Testamentum
NTD	Das Neue Testament Deutsch
NTS	New Testament Studies
OTS	Old Testament Studies
PAAJR	Proceedings of the American Academy for Jewish Research
PBSR	Papers of the British School at Rome
PEQ	Palestine Exploration Quarterly
PG	Patrum Graecorum Cursus Completus (J.-P Migne)
PL	Patrum Latinorum Cursus Completus (J.-P Migne)
PRK	Pesiqte de-Rav Kahana
QDAP	Quarterly of the Department of Antiquities of Palestine
R.	Rabbi
RB	Revue Biblique
REJ	Revue des Études Juives

SBL	Society of Biblical Literature
SHA	Scriptores Historiae Augustae
SNTS	Studiorum Novi Testamenti Societas
SVT	Supplementum, Vetus Testamentum
T	Tosefta
TDNT	Theological Dictionary of the New Testament
VT	Vetus Testamentum
YCS	Yale Classical Studies
ZAW	Zeitschrift für die Alttestamentliche Wissenschaft
ZDPV	Zeitschrift des deutschen Palästina Vereins
ZNW	Zeitschrift für die Neutestamentliche Wissenschaft
ZPE	Zeitschrift für Papyrologie und Epigraphik

Introduction

The papers included in this volume were delivered at the First International Conference on Galilean Studies in Late Antiquity held at Kibbutz Hanaton in the Lower Galilee, Israel, on August 13-15, 1989. The conference was held under the auspices of the Center for the Study of the Galilee (המרכז לחקר הגליל) and was sponsored by six academic institutions, three American (the Jewish Theological Seminary, Duke University, and the University of Connecticut) and three Israeli (the Seminary of Judaic Studies, the Hebrew University, and the Izhak Ben-Zvi Institute).

The initiative for the conference was the outcome of a meeting held in Jerusalem the summer before, between Professors Eric Meyers of Duke, Stuart Miller of the University of Connecticut, and myself. Given the enormous proliferation of studies related to the Galilee of late, as well as the increased trend toward regional studies, we felt that the time was ripe to bring together scholars who have related to the Galilee in their various fields of research, asking each to address an issue central to Galilean society and culture in late antiquity. To achieve the most fruitful deliberations as possible, and in order to give full expression to the diversity of interests concerning the Galilee, we decided to invite a wide spectrum of scholars: Americans, Israelis, and Europeans; Jews and Christians; historians and archeologists; scholars of New Testament and rabbinic literature; as well as those who concentrate on the sociological and cultural aspects of the Galilee in late antiquity. Due to the importance of the writings of the New Testament and Josephus for our understanding of the Galilee, we found it necessary to define the term "late antiquity" liberally, to include events and sources from the first century C.E. down to the Arab conquest of the seventh century.

The conference itself was a resounding success. Twenty-two scholars from five countries met for three days of intensive deliberations, with daily field trips to important archeological sites in the area. The exchange of ideas, the mutual fructification of scholar sharing with scholar in a relaxed atmosphere of a kibbutz nestled in the Galilean hills, the opportunity to respond to content and method from one discipline to the other, to be apprised first-hand of the latest developments in a myriad of areas—all these and more contributed to an experience treasured by all.

*   *   *

The fact that the conference focused on the first centuries of the Common Era is not coincidental: practically nothing is known about the Galilee per se up until the first century C.E. so that we cannot even be sure whether Jewish life continued in this region in the post-biblical period. If not, when indeed did Jewish resettlement resume? What was the nature of the Galilee, politically, socially, and religiously, during the Hasmonean and Herodian eras? The debate whether the Galilee was unique vis-à-vis Judea in its nationalistic fervor and religious proclivities has engrossed scholars over the last few generations and is due in part to the severely limited sources and tantalizing shreds of information at our disposal.

The first half of the first millennium C.E., however, has left us with a veritable plethora of information in sources ranging in genre and type over vast areas. As noted, the first century is reflected in the writings of the gospels and Josephus. Some Jewish-Christian writings may date from the second century, as well as not an insignificant part of tannaitic literature (Mishnah, Tosefta, halakhic midrashim, etc.). By the third and fourth centuries, the volume of sources available expands dramatically, with the bulk of rabbinic literature dating from this period. From the third century onward we are likewise inundated by archeological data from synagogues, cemeteries, and cities. The fifty or so ancient Galilean synagogues thus far excavated all date from late antiquity; the extant rural remains also date from the third and fourth centuries.

Byzantine Galilee (fourth to seventh/eighth centuries) has produced much of the Targumic literature, almost all of our epigraphic evidence, thousands of synagogue poems (*piyyutim*) and sermonic midrashim—all attesting to a vibrant Jewish presence in this period. The art, architecture, and epigraphic remains uncovered in Galilean churches testify to the large Christian population there as well.

The striking contrast in the state of the evidence for the Galilee between the first millennia B.C.E. and C.E. is to be generally attributed to the place and importance of the region in Jewish history in each of these periods. In the former, the Galilee was of secondary—if not tertiary—political, institutional, and religious importance; the focus of Jewish life then was to the south, in Judea and Jerusalem.

All this changed as a result of the catastrophes of 70 and 135. With the destruction of Jerusalem and the ravaging of Judea, the Galilee was catapulted into the forefront of Jewish life; from the second century on, and indeed for the next 800 years, this region was the center of the Jewish community in Israel. The relatively large number of sources written or edited in the Galilee during the millennium reflects this reality, and, at the same time, sheds light on almost every aspect of contemporary Galilean life.

*   *   *

The collection of essays in this volume, arranged in six major categories, deals with a wide spectrum of Galilean life. At times complementing one another, at times addressing singular issues, these essays constitute a veritable mosaic attesting to the diversity of areas under investigation today in the study of the Galilee in late antiquity. In the first section, which deals with early Christianity in the Galilee, Kee challenges a number of common assumptions in New Testament research. He claims that the synagogue in the time of Jesus was not a definable structure but a group of people who used private dwellings or small public halls for prayer and reading of Scriptures; Jesus' associations were with a wide range of people, including gentiles and Roman officials, reflecting the heterogeneous society at the time; the cultural background of the gospels was bilingual, reflecting a large degree of Greek and Aramaic influence.

Both Saldarini and Baumgarten suggest that the Galilee may have been the provenance for two of early Christianity's major documents. Saldarini analyzes the gospel of Matthew as the literature of a deviant group that considered itself Jewish but was not regarded as such by the main Jewish community. He claims that the Matthean community and its gospel follow sociological and ideological patterns common to deviant groups generally. Many of the polemics and apologetics in Matthew are what might be expected from a peripheral group. Matthew's positive attitude to many things Jewish, and the fact that the book never finds it necessary to translate Aramaic or Hebrew terms—all point to a Jewish setting, and the Galilee becomes a prime candidate.

Baumgarten addresses himself to the Nazorenes and the Pseudo-Clementine literature, which is widely assumed to have been of Jewish-Christian origin. Noting numerous instances of the work's positive attitude to the Pharisees and certain rabbinic practices, he suggests that the most likely *Sitz im Leben* for the Pseudo-Clementine material would have been the Galilee of the second century.

The second section of the volume treats various dimensions of Galilean society generally. In the light of recent research based on archeological and literary evidence attesting to an economic network between Galilean villages and urban centers, Edwards challenges the notion of a rustic, isolated, "primitive" Galilee of the first century. Our data point to a densely populated region where gentiles and not an insignificant degree of Romanization were in evidence. One can no longer speak of the Galilee as a Semitic enclave surrounded by a sea of Hellenism.

Drawing on sociological theories regarding urban cultures, Freyne discusses four areas of cultural and social roles of cities in general and of the Galilee in particular: dominant social types within Galilean cities; city-rural relations; economic patterns; social unity and dissent. The Galilee related at one and the same time to the surrounding urban culture of the heterogenetic type, and to Jerusalem which was more of an orthogenetic city.

Section Three discusses Roman presence in the Galilee. Rappaport questions one of the major assumptions regarding first-century Galilee, namely, that the region was rabidly nationalistic and anti-Roman. Preferring Josephus' account in *Life* over that in *War*, he concludes that throughout early Roman rule—from Pompey to Bar-Kokhba—the Galilee was one of the most politically stable regions in the country. Safrai traces Roman military presence throughout the country in general, according particular attention to the Galilee. He examines the impact of army units on the local economy, with especial reference to the tax burdens imposed on the native population.

Oppenheimer focuses primarily on the role of city administration in the Galilee and its relationship to the Patriarch (*nasi*), especially R. Judah I. Drawing heavily on talmudic literature for his insights, he also addresses the social and cultural impact of the Roman army on the civilian populations of the cities, thereby nicely supplementing Safrai's remarks.

Goodman explores the status of the *nasi* in Roman eyes. Rejecting several currently accepted definitions (e.g., the *nasi* as a Roman governor of the Galilee), he suggests that the *nasi* was viewed first and foremost as a religious leader of the Jews. As the Romans had supported such people beforehand (for example, the high-priestly families from 6–66 C.E.), and as they were coming to view the Jews more and more in religious terms, so now the *nasi* was understood as playing such a role in Jewish society of late antiquity.

The fourth section of this volume focuses on the rabbis and the Galilee. Schiffman addresses an issue which has vexed scholars for decades: was there a Galilean halakha in the first century which differed from that of Judea to the south? Examining a variety of sources dealing with marriage customs, tithes, festivals, vows, etc., he concludes that there is no essential difference in the halakha of the Galilee and Judea. Whatever differences there were in interpretation of the halakha can be attributed to local variations and a marked stringency in Galilean customs.

Cohen suggests that the sages of the second century—in the Galilee as well as in Judea—were "an insular group which produced an insular literature." Primarily a rural phenomenon, they made few inroads among the masses, focusing on purity laws and personal status—issues of primarily sectarian concern. Only under R. Judah I did rabbinic orientation change dramatically; the sages became urbanized and began penetrating communal institutions, relating to the lower as well as upper classes.

Miller focuses on R. Ḥanina, the most important third-century Sepphorian sage, particularly with regard to the "Zipporaʾei." He concludes that this term carried with it several meanings, referring on occasion to everyday Sepphorians or to those related to the sages—friends, neighbors, students, and even the sages themselves.

Levine attempts to define the relationship between the rabbis and the synagogue. Based in the academy, the sages' involvement in the synagogue was limited, although their role expanded in late antiquity. They, however, never exercised control over the synagogue nor was their influence all-pervasive. The synagogue was primarily a local institution governed by its members, the wealthy or the *nasi*.

The fifth section of the volume is devoted to language and literature in the Galilee. Rendsburg asserts that Mishnaic Hebrew was a colloquial dialect of the Galilee which developed from the northern, Israelian Hebrew of biblical times. He examines twelve cases of this similarity, noting the common traits of this northern dialect with other neighboring languages—Aramaic, Phoenician, and Ugaritic. An interesting by-product of this study is the recognition of linguistic regionalism in ancient Palestine, both in biblical as well as classical times.

Shinan focuses on the Targumic literature created in the Galilee between the fourth and eighth centuries. Noting many of the popular beliefs and customs alluded to in the Targum, as well as popular proverbs and repeated references to the synagogue as a בית—קודשא "a house of holiness," Shinan concludes that this Targumic material may serve as a reliable source for understanding Jewish society in late antiquity.

Fraade reviews rabbinic evidence for the practice of Targum in synagogue and rabbinic academy settings. This leads him to examine bilingualism in Byzantine Palestine in general, and in the Galilee in particular. Contrary to accepted opinion, Fraade claims that Hebrew did not disappear in late antiquity. Aramaic was used in Targum to enhance, facilitate, and deepen the Scriptural-reading experience. The case for bilingualism is attested by rabbinic as well as extra-rabbinic (i.e., epigraphical) evidence.

The final section is devoted to some of the most important archeological finds from Roman and Byzantine Galilee. Foerster discusses in detail the various types of buildings and the architectural and artistic forms regnant in the synagogal remains of the Galilee. Meyers offers a brief history of Sepphoris and describes some of the most significant finds of his excavations at the site, focusing on a detailed description of the recently discovered mosaic depicting scenes from the life of Dionysios. Strange summarizes clearly and concisely his excavation team's work at Sepphoris in the 1980s, offering important insights regarding the development of the city from the early Roman period (the era of Herod Antipas?) to the end of late antiquity. Finally, Weiss draws on the evidence from the famous Beth She'arim necropolis, as well as on rabbinic literature, to discuss burial practices among Jews, the kinds of burial organizations which existed, and the place of the sages in Jewish society as reflected in their burial practices.

*   *   *

Finally, it is a pleasure to acknowledge all those who helped make the conference and this publication possible.

To Professors Eric Meyers and Stuart Miller and their respective institutions, Duke University and the University of Connecticut, for their support of the conference;

To Rabbis Lee Diamond, Eli Havivi, and Michael Goldstein, as well as Irena Petrie, for their part in making the conference a success. The Center for the Study of the Galilee and Kibbutz Ḥanaton did a splendid job of organization and hosting;

To the Jewish Theological Seminary, its Chancellor, Professor Ismar Schorsch, and Vice-Chancellor for Public Affairs, Dr. John Ruskay, who played a major role in support of the Center for the Study of the Galilee, our conference, and the publication of this volume;

To the Izhak Ben-Zvi Institute and its director, Zvi Zameret, for participating in the organization and publicity of the conference and for making available the facilities of the Institute for our concluding symposium;

Finally, to the staff of the Seminary of Judaic Studies in Jerusalem, and especially to Ḥani Davis who helped organize the conference and prepare this manuscript for publication—my deepest gratitude.

Jerusalem   Lee I. Levine
January 1992
Tevet 5752

I. EARLY CHRISTIANITY IN THE GALILEE

Early Christianity in the Galilee: Reassessing the Evidence from the Gospels

HOWARD CLARK KEE

There are three features of the gospels about which there has been broad scholarly consensus in the current century, and all three have a direct bearing on the interpretation of the texts in relation to the religious and cultural setting of early Christianity: (1) the nature of the synagogue in the first century C.E.; (2) the cultural and social make-up of the audience addressed by Jesus in the Galilee; and (3) the linguistic setting of the Galilee in this period. With regard to each of these factors, the dominant history-of-religions school has not only made pronouncements but has developed scholarly tools based on historical assumptions. In each case, the results of recent archeological study of this region, and the ensuing reassessment of the literary evidence, require replacing these assumptions with historical conclusions which are supported by the new insights these discoveries have provided.

1. The Synagogue in First-Century C.E. Galilee

The scholarly assumption since the development of historical-critical methods in the nineteenth century has been that the Judaism in which Jesus was reared and the movement that arose in his name were basically synonymous with the Judaism reflected in the Mishnah and the Talmud. Even before the Common Era, this Judaism had developed a cadre of formally qualified leaders (the rabbis), a distinctive type of building in which its activities were centered (the synagogue), and a stylized mode of scriptural interpretation, which was later systematized in the Mishnah and Talmud. German scholarship of the post-World War I and II eras developed such scholarly tools as the Strack-Billerbeck *Kommentar;*[1] G. Kittel's monumental work[2] shows the direct influence of these assumptions about Judaism in the time of Jesus on the historical reconstruction of the origins of Christianity and interprets the New Testament evidence accordingly. Jesus' controversies with his contemporaries are represented in this scholarly set of assumptions as an ongoing public debate between an upstart amateur rabbi and learned professionals. What is the evidence for this set of assumptions?

Scholars agree that the most important single piece of archeological evidence in support of the picture of the synagogue sketched above is the Theodotus inscription found in Jerusalem just before World War I.[3] The inscription states that the one honored by the tablet was a leader of a synagogue, son and grandson of synagogue leaders; that he built the synagogue for the reading of the Law and the teaching of the commandments; that it served as a lodging for strangers and pilgrims from abroad; that his father, together with elders and one Simonides, had laid the foundation. From this inscription it may be inferred that there was a widespread pattern of synagogue building in the first century and that these structures functioned as places of instruction for local Jewish families and for rabbis-in-training, and also as hostelries for pious pilgrims.

That there were gatherings of Jews in the first century for the reading of the Law, that there were members chosen to guide the affairs of the group that met regularly in the accustomed meeting place, that instruction was carried on under the auspices of the group, and that there were numbers of Jews from the Diaspora who visited Jerusalem as pilgrims are historically established inferences based on both Jewish and early Christian sources. What is not established, however, is that this inscription dates from the first century, or before 70, and that it therefore provides an accurate picture of what constituted a synagogue in the period of the Second Temple, as Deissmann assumed. L. H. Vincent, N. A. Bees, and G. Dalman all dated the inscription to the second century or later, but since Deissmann took Schürer's word that after 70, "for a long period

---

[1] H. Strack and D. Billerbeck, *Kommentar zum Neuen Testament aus Talmud und Midrasch* (4 vols.; Munich, 1922–28).

[2] G. Kittel and G. Friedrich, eds., *TDNT* (10 vols.; Grand Rapids, 1964–76).

[3] A brief account of its discovery and a summary of the early scholarly publications concerning it are conveniently summarized by A. Deissmann, *Light from the Ancient East*, trans. L. R. M. Strachan (London, 1927).

of time," no Jew could settle in the Jerusalem area,[4] he insisted that the inscription must be pre-70. He acknowledged, however, that it was not found *in situ* but had been discarded in a cistern which was part of a bath complex. He quite arbitrarily dated the baths to the Second Temple period, even though it would seem much more likely to have such an architectural development in the City of David after Hadrian had rebuilt the city as Aelia Capitolina. The inscription itself had no connection with the baths, but since it was found in the cistern there it most likely post-dates the baths. The find is in no sense a closed locus, so that to date the inscription on the basis of other rubble associated with it is logically and archeologically precarious. Yet, in spite of the wholly conjectural basis for the date assigned to the inscription by Deissmann, it has been taken as fact by generations of historians and even archeologists. Accordingly, it has been widely used as evidence for the nature of the synagogue in the first part of the first century C.E.

M. Schwabe has attempted to prove the first century origin of the Theodotus inscription.[5] Anyone who has engaged in responsible archeological excavation or analysis knows that dates can be assigned to finds only when they are discovered in a closed locus with datable coins, pottery or other artifacts. This inscription, however, was in a heap of rubble at the bottom of a cistern, together with some other building fragments. This is hardly an appropriate place for laying out remnants of a ruined building for preservation purposes, as Schwabe points out. His sole criterion for dating the inscription, therefore, is the style in which it was carved. A recent survey by epigraphers of the Classical period, however, shows them to be in agreement that this inscription could be as late as the third century. The literary evidence adduced to place this structure among the 480 synagogues of Jerusalem is from a document which achieved its present form only in the fourth century C.E., the Jerusalem Talmud. As in the New Testament, this document is filled with efforts to legitimize later developments by dating them back into the first century or earlier. Far more plausible is the proposal that in the fourth century C.E., as the Christianizing of Jerusalem was in progress, this late second-century synagogue which housed the Theodotus inscription was destroyed.

---

4 E. Schürer, *Geschichte des jüdischen Volkes* (3 vols.; Leipzig, 1901–09; reprint 1970), I, 649, 703.

5 M. Schwabe, "Greek Inscriptions," in: *Sepher Yerushalayim*, ed. M. Avi-Yonah (Jerusalem, 1956), 362–365 (Hebrew).

As the first scholars to see the inscription noted, the epigraphical evidence suggests a second century date.[6] One would expect this inscription to resemble closely the pre-70 inscription from the Jerusalem Temple rebuilt by Herod, but the latter displays a far simpler epigraphical style than the synagogue inscription of Theodotus.[7] It would be difficult to recall another archeological phenomenon which has been the basis for so many historical assumptions and interpretations but which lacks scientific criteria for dating. Deissmann's crucial factor in assigning a date— that Jews were not allowed in Jerusalem for an extended period after 70—may be compared with the judgment of S. Safrai,[8] who shows that, although (according to rabbinic tradition) the emergent rabbinic movement was based in Yavneh in the period between the revolts, by the time of Nerva and Trajan the system of Jewish self-government was confirmed by regional and imperial authorities, including laws dealing with property and criminal matters. Although there was a period of repression following the revolt under Bar-Kokhba (132–135), as early as the reign of Antoninus Pius (138–161) persecutions were relaxed, institutions were revised, and the earlier form of self-government developed at Jamnia (Yavneh) was reestablished. This culminated in the developments under R. Judah the Patriarch in the later second and early third centuries. On the basis of this reading of the historical evidence, the Theodotus inscription would fit best no earlier than the time of Hadrian or Antoninus Pius, when a "Jamnia-based" institutional pattern had been developing over a period of more than half a century.

An indirect but exceedingly significant line of evidence for assigning a second century date to the building erected by Theodotus in Jerusalem comes from the brilliant analyses of synagogue structures in the Galilee by a series of scholars. The conclusions reached by J. Gutmann[9] have been confirmed by more recent discoveries and archeological analyses. The word *synagoge* down into the Flavian period meant an assembly; only in the first century—and I should add *late* first century at the earli-

---

6 The epigraphers I consulted in preparing this paper suggest the mid- to late second century C.E. as the earliest likely date and the late third century as the latest possible date.

7 For a comparison of the two inscriptions, see E. Gabba, *Iscrizioni Greche e Latine per lo Studio della Biblio* (Marietti, 1958), Tables 6 and 7.

8 S. Safrai, "Jewish Self-government," in: *The Jewish People in the First Century*, eds. S. Safrai and M. Stern (2 vols.; Assen, 1974–76), I, 377–419.

9 J. Gutmann, Prolegomena to *The Synagogue: Studies in Origins, Archaeology and Architecture*, ed. J. Gutmann (New York, 1975), ix–xxix.

est—did the term come to be used with reference to an assembly hall. By the third century C.E., Gutmann concludes, there were distinctive buildings known as synagogues in the Galilee, although the oldest structure that can be dated with certainty is from the sixth century.

M. Hengel has shown that the situation in the Diaspora was different from that in Judea or the Galilee.[10] The two oldest synagogue inscriptions in the Diaspora are from Egypt and date from the third century B.C.E. The fact that they are in Greek and mention the Ptolemaic rulers led Hengel to assume that the Jews received royal sanction for developing these community assembly halls, which are referred to as *proseuchai* rather than *synagogai*. Hengel has pointed out that Philo, in keeping with his aim to show the compatibility between Torah and Greek learning, gave emphasis to the instructional function of these places—which very likely served as places of worship as well. From the first century C.E. to the time of Diocletian, in Rome and in inscriptions from the Aegean and Black Sea regions, *synagogē* was used to mean assembly; *proseuchē* was used to signify the buildings where the *synagogē* assembled. According to Hengel, the use of *proseuchē* was avoided in Palestine before 70 C.E. in order to preclude any hint of competition with the Temple. The meeting places of the Jewish communities in Delos and Ostia were originally private homes, which were later expanded to include courtyards and larger public entrances. The synagogue inscription from Stobi is dated to the late third century C.E., and the Dura Europos synagogue from the year 244/245 C.E.

What about the alleged synagogue structures in Judea and the Galilee from the Second Temple period? Regarding the rabbinic tradition about a synagogue within the Temple precincts, S. B. Hoenig has shown that it is likely that scribal discussion and instruction were carried on in the Temple area, but he asserts that synagogues as established religious edifices or houses for standardized and canonical prayer "did not exist in Judea during the Second Commonwealth, and surely not within the Temple precincts."[11] As for the supposed synagogues at Herodium and Masada, Gutmann finds no evidence of special facilities for piety or worship other than the excavators' "wishful thinking"; he further conjectures that the synagogues mentioned by Josephus and the New Testament were "probably indistinguishable from domestic architecture."[12] With

---

10 M. Hengel, "Proseuche und Synagoge: Jüdische Gemeinde, Gotteshaus und Gottesdienst in der Diaspora und in Palästina," ibid., 27.

11 S. B. Hoenig, "The Supposititious Temple Synagogue," ibid., 55.

12 Gutmann, ibid., xiii–xiv.

one exception—which we shall discuss below—references in the New Testament to *synagogē* make perfect sense if understood as meetings rather than meeting places. The same may also be said of nearly all the occurrences of this term in Jewish writings of the time.

Gutmann notes with approval the proposal of S. Zeitlin, that these Jewish assemblies began as a purely secular phenomenon to deal with common social and economic problems shared by expatriate Jews. In the later Maccabean period, however, groups fostered by the Pharisees began meeting in homes or small assembly halls to read the Torah and the Prophets.[13] This theory for the origins of the synagogue is confirmed by the remains of the supposed synagogue at Gamla. Josephus reports that the place was razed by the Romans in 67,[14] which fixes a *terminus ad quem* for the building. According to Z. Maʿoz the Herodian triclinium there had been converted into an assembly hall by introducing benches along the wall. He dismisses the claim that the structure was oriented toward Jerusalem, insisting that it—like the assembly rooms at Herodium and Masada—was positioned and the entrances determined by the terrain and the surrounding structures.[15] Maʿoz goes on to assume, however, that the meeting rooms found at Masada and Herodium were indeed synagogues, noting that early synagogues may have been housed in large unadorned rooms, from which traces of religious use such as a Torah shrine or benches have disappeared, "since they were probably made of wood."[16] Since this argument is not based on any archeological evidence, the conclusions are precarious at best. The most we can say of this room at Gamla, therefore, is that it indicates the transition of *synagogē* from an assembly of general purpose to a special building for wor-

---

13 This view of the rise of the synagogue movement is held by E. Rivkin, ibid., 74, and has been developed in detail by J. Neusner, *The Pharisees: Rabbinic Perspectives* (Hoboken, 1973) and in his extensive studies on formative Judaism. The best summary of his views on the Pharisees is in "The Pharisees in Light of the Historical Sources of Judaism," in: *Formative Judaism (Brown Judaic Studies* 37; Chico, 1982), 71–83.

14 *War* IV, 1, 10, 83.

15 Z. Maʿoz, "The Synagogue at Gamla and the Typology of Second-Temple Synagogues," in: *Ancient Synagogues Revealed*, ed. L. I. Levine (Jerusalem, 1981), 35–41; G. Foerster, "Architectural Models of the Greco-Roman Period and the Origin of the 'Galilean' Synagogue," ibid., 45–48, suggests that the prototype for the Galilean synagogue was the Nabatean temple forecourt, while E. Netzer, "The Herodian Triclinia – A Prototype for the 'Galilean-Type' Synagogue," ibid., 49–51, proposes the Herodian triclinium, as exemplified by Herod's winter palace at Jericho.

16 Maʿoz, "The Synagogue at Gamla," ibid., 35.

ship and study. Yet, one must keep in mind S. Gutman's comment, that there is no conclusive evidence at Gamla for the religious use of the structure.[17] Similarly, M. Dothan writes concerning Level III of the synagogue at Hammath Tiberias (which he dates from the end of the first or first half of the second century C.E.) that, "its plan resembles that of a public building, such as a gymnasium." He adds, however, "it may already have been a synagogue in that early period."[18] We should perhaps alter this to read, "a *synagogē* may have met there earlier."

Terminologically, it is significant that when Josephus mentions the Jewish assembly building at Tiberias in his *Life* he calls it a *proseuchē*, and that in his elaborate description in *Against Apion* of the weekly gatherings for instruction in Torah and the training of children in the tradition he neither uses the term *synagogē* nor refers to the meeting places.[19] It is also noteworthy that these works of Josephus were written at the end of his life, at the close of the first or the beginning of the second century. One might expect that by then the development toward formalization of worship and instruction emanating from Yavneh would have had its terminological effect. In his *War* he describes the brigands raiding the cities and the "holy places" (*hierois*, not *synagogois*;[20] the closest he comes to identifying a synagogue as a place is in *War*,[21] where he relates that offerings taken from the Temple by Antiochus Epiphanes were given to the Jews in Antioch to be placed "in the synagogue"—surely anachronistic for an incident that occurred in the early second century B.C.E.

What does this archeological and literary evidence imply for a reassessment of the gospels? This material corresponds well with the evidence in the gospels, where, with a single exception, *synagogē* refers to Jewish and Christian gatherings rather than to structures.[22] A divergence from this terminology occurs in Luke 7:5, where Luke reports that the centurion who approached Jesus to have his servant healed had built for the Jews a synagogue in Capernaum. Generations of Christian pilgrims to the Galilee have been shown the reconstructed synagogue which is said to be the one where Jesus worshiped and taught. Archeologists

17 S. Gutman, "The Synagogue at Gamla," ibid., 30–34.
18 M. Dothan, "The Synagogue at Ḥammath-Tiberias," ibid., 64.
19 *Life* 54, 276–282; *Ag. Ap.* 2, 17, 175.
20 *War* IV, 7, 2, 408.
21 *War* VII, 3, 3, 44.
22 Regarding terminology for Jewish meeting places, see Acts 16:13, where Luke reports that Paul went outside Philippi to a *proseuchē*, where he met Lydia, his first convert on the mainland of Europe.

have long recognized that the visible structure there dates centuries later than the time of Jesus; S. Loffreda, who has been excavating at the site more recently, dates it as late as the last decade of the fourth century to the mid-fifth century C.E.[23]

The fact that this detail about a synagogue constructed in Capernaum is found only in Luke's version of this incident and is missing from the Q equivalent in Matthew 8:5–13, coupled with the dating of Luke to the turn of the second century (which is indicated on other grounds[24]), point to Luke's having read the post-70 developments back into the first half of the first century C.E. We agree, therefore, with Gutmann's inference from the archeological evidence that no synagogue buildings from Palestine in the first century can be positively identified, and that the synagogue began to develop as an institution housed in a definable structure only after the destruction of the Temple and with the Pharisaic-rabbinic assumption of authority within the Jewish community.[25] Accordingly, Luke seems to have added an anachronistic detail in his reference to the centurion having built the synagogue in Capernaum.

Thus, it would appear that transformation of older domestic property used for the gatherings of Jews in publicly accessible structures began within the synagogue movement no earlier than the Antonine period. This assumption receives important confirmation from the observations offered by L. M. White[26] concerning synagogues in Rome, the Greek islands, and Asia Minor. He has shown that the widespread practice among a range of religious groups was to adapt houses to serve as meeting places: he points out that an inscription on Delos reports that the Roman senate granted the local *thiasoi* of the Serapis cult permission to meet in rented domestic headquarters; at Dura, the worshippers of the Palmyrene goddess fashioned her shrine from two adjoining houses; of 55 mithraea that have been found, only about a dozen were constructed as such. The evidence suggests that all of the early Diaspora synagogues that have been studied were renovations of earlier structures, such as

[23] S. Loffreda, "The Late Chronology of the Synagogue at Capernaum," in: *Ancient Synagogues Revealed*, 52. This late date has been challenged, but the fourth century is the date proposed by others.

[24] See my detailed discussion of the date and origins of Luke-Acts in: *Understanding the New Testament*[4] (Englewood Cliffs, 1983), 173–205.

[25] Gutmann, *Synagogue*, 75.

[26] L. M. White, *Building God's House in the Roman World: Social Aspects of Architectural Adaptation among Pagans, Jews, and Christians* (Baltimore & London, 1990).

warehouses, baths or private homes. Of the synagogues known in the Mediterranean, from Stobi eastward, only in Sardis was the *proseuchē* built initially as a public space rather than as a private house. White concludes "that architectural adaptation of private facilities for religious use was, in fact, part of the social environment into which the earliest Christians moved along with other ethnic and cultic groups. Through multiple stages of renovation we may be able to measure the movement of Christian groups (both locally and translocally) into the public realm of religion in the Roman world."[27]

This has a direct bearing on how one is to understand the frequent references to *synagogē* in the gospels and requires the historian to be sensitive to the fact that the connotations of the term change within the period of the writing of the gospels. A seemingly innocent pronoun in Mark 1:23, for example, has important implications for our historical understanding. There we read of a man with an unclean spirit who was in *their* synagogue. The phrase is repeated in Mark 1:39 with reference to Jesus' preaching tour of the Galilee, where it is reported that he preached in *their* synagogues and performed exorcisms. The fact that this possessive pronoun is used implies unmistakably that from the writer's perspective the early Christians' *our* synagogues or assemblies were perceived by Mark to be in competition with *their* synagogues, i.e., those of the Jews. This competition is explicit in Matthew, where he reports the choice by Christians to use an alternate term, *ekklēsia*, to designate their assemblies, thereby intensifying the contrast with *their* synagogues. In Mark, however—which I assume to have been written in the early sixties C.E., just prior to the first Jewish revolt—synagogue practices are mentioned, as, for example, in his criticism of the scribes who "like to go about in long robes, to have salutations in the marketplaces and the best seats in the synagogues,"[28] in mentioning that Jesus entered a synagogue,[29] and in reporting him teaching in a synagogue.[30]

We have no indications of a formal architectural structure or of a set pattern of spatial or operational arrangements, or of a resident leader of the assembly. One could argue that if such institutional structures had

---

27 Idem, "Building God's House: Social Aspects of Architectural Adaptation among Pagans, Jews, and Christians," *SBL Seminar Papers* (1985), 25.

28 Mark 12:38–39. Cf. my *Community of the New Age: Studies in Mark's Gospel* (rev. ed.; Macon, GA, 1983), 100–105.

29 Mark 3:1; the best mss. lack the definite article, although the parallel in Luke 6:6 includes it at this point.

30 Mark 6:2.

existed, they simply would be presupposed by the writer and need not be mentioned. Countering that assumption, however, is the fact that in the later gospels—Matthew and Luke—we have clear indications that the developments in synagogue practice were added to the older Markan tradition. Even those who would insist that there must have been special buildings and organized processes for synagogue worship and instruction in rabbinic Judaism would not argue that the Christians already had developed their own type of community building with a distinctive architectural style as well as specific roles for the leaders of their communities. As for Christian meeting houses, all the evidence points to house churches. The rare pre-Constantinian church at Dura Europos was adapted from a private dwelling! Similarly, the formalization of organization within Christian communities appears only in the later books of the New Testament, such as the Deutero-Pauline letters. The consistent picture is that the Christian counterpart of the *synagogē*—that is, the *ekklēsia*—is the gathered community of those who saw themselves as God's people.

What seems most plausible, therefore, is the conclusion indicated by a convergence of archeological and literary studies of both Jewish and Christian materials: Jews and Christians in the Galilee in the pre-70 period—and probably down into the second century—met in homes or small public halls for study of the Scriptures, worship, and instruction. Only later did the patterns of worship and leadership begin to take on set forms, and only in subsequent centuries did their respective assembly rooms take on the distinctive architectural features which have been uncovered and analyzed by archeologists. To assign a date prior to the first Jewish revolt for the institutional and architectural features of church and synagogue that are implicit in the rabbinic materials and in the later books of the New Testament is anachronistic.

Anticipations or early stages of these subsequent developments are apparent in the later gospel tradition, especially in Matthew, where the number of references to *their* synagogues markedly increases.[31] But in a unique polemical passage in Matt. 23, which is bitterly critical of the scribes and Pharisees, Jesus is portrayed as directly addressing his antagonists with the announcement, "I [Jesus] will send you [i.e., the scribes and Pharisees] prophets and wise men and scribes, some of whom you will kill and crucify, and some you will scourge in *your* synagogues and

---

[31] Matt. 10:17; 12:9; 13:54.

persecute from city to city."[32] In the same strongly denunciatory Matthean speech, and there alone, the Markan tradition has been expanded to include references to phylacteries and fringes and to seeking public acclaim in the form of the honorific title of Rabbi.[33] I have shown elsewhere that Matthew was written in direct conflict and in competition with the mode of rabbinic Judaism that was emerging from Yavneh, and that we must assume that it dates from the late first century.[34] The lack of archeological and architectural evidence for institutional forms of synagogue life in the pre-70 period is wholly consonant with this interpretation of the literary evidence from the gospels.

Of all the New Testament writers, only the gospel of Luke relates details which have been interpreted as references to organizational categories of officers in the synagogue. In Luke 4:16–30, where Luke greatly expands the report in Mark 6:1–6, Jesus is described as returning the scroll to the *hyperetes* at the conclusion of the formal reading from the prophet Isaiah. *Hyperetes* is a term which has been understood as the formal designation of an assistant to the rabbi in the organizational structure of the synagogue. Some have equated it with *ḥazzan*, but that word seems to be closer in significance to *episkopos*, "overseer." Others have associated it with *shamash*, one who executes orders.[35] *Hyperetes* means simply one who follows instructions, and it is used in Hellenistic Judaism for army paymasters, bankers' assistants, agents who follow the will of another (Josephus) or one who performs the will of God (Philo). A similar range of functions for this term is evident in the New Testament: Mark as assistant to the apostles; Paul as the servant of Christ and agent of God's will; and Jesus is reported as having refused to call in armed protectors to save him from the Roman arresting officers.[36] Thus, there is no clear evidence that Luke uses *hyperetes* as a technical term for a synagogue official. Indeed, he uses it in the proem to his gospel with reference to the original apostles as witnesses and messengers of Jesus.[37] But

---

32 Matt. 23:34.

33 Matt. 23:5–7.

34 H. C. Kee, "The Transformation of the Synagogue after 70 C.E.: Its Import for Early Christianity," *NTS* 36 (1990).

35 As in the Dead Sea scrolls, and in rabbinic literature (e.g., J Sanhedrin 1, 19c).

36 *Mark*: Acts 13:5; *Paul*: Acts 26:16 and I Cor. 4:1; *Jesus*: John 18:36.

37 Similar instances of the transformation of widely used Hellenistic terms for leadership and social structure into technical designations for religious organizational modes and roles can be made: (1) *synedrion*, which was simply a local council set up in territories controlled by Hellenistic and Roman rulers to grant the local dominant group authority to exercise a degree of local autonomy. Only later does

even if Luke did intend this meaning of a special synagogue official or attendant, and if the word had taken on this technical connotation, it would have been anachronistic to use it in describing leadership roles during the lifetime of Jesus. That Luke begins his two-volume work with a term which was to have a functional equivalent in the developing rabbinic tradition, however, may offer further evidence for the crucial competitive transition occurring at the turn of the second century between the two developing movements—rabbinic Judaism and early Christianity. In spite of important internal differences within each movement, both claimed to be the true heirs and the correct interpreters of the biblical tradition.

2. The Clientele Rallied by Jesus

Interpreters of the New Testament have noted that in the first century C.E. Nazareth was a tiny village of no distinction and that Jesus' imagery and metaphors were drawn in large measure from rural life: grain, plows, workers in fields and vineyards, shepherds and flocks—to mention only the most obvious. The considerable distance of the Galilee from the capital city of Jerusalem has served as the basis for an inference that Jesus lived and taught withdrawn from the Greco-Roman cultural mainstream of his era. Accordingly, mention in the gospels of his contacts with gentiles or Roman officials has been attributed by critical scholarship in the German Protestant history-of-religions tradition to the Pauline wing (with gentile orientation) of the early Church. For R. Bultmann, who is perhaps the major figure in this form-critical assessment of the gospel tradition, both the stories of Jesus healing gentiles or visiting gentile sites and the narrative patterns in which such incidents are recounted indicate Hellenistic influences and are therefore declared to be non-Galilean in origin.[38]

Careful analysis of the archeological sites and remains in the Galilee, however, emphatically contradicts these assumptions. Although Nazareth is not mentioned in Jewish sources prior to the third century

---

such a group come to be portrayed as an ancient, long-standing supreme Jewish religious council with the significantly transliterated name, *sanhedrin*; (2) *archisynagogos* was initially the leader of a local meeting; (3) *presbyteros* was originally a respected member of a religious community. Only later does this become a title for a synagogal or ecclesiastical office.

[38] R. Bultmann, *History of the Synoptic Tradition*, trans. J. Marsh (New York, 1963), 179–205, 302–317.

C.E., the village overlooked the main route that led south and west from Sepphoris to Caesarea and was only a short distance from Japhia. E. Meyers and J. Strange have accurately observed that the cities and trade routes of the Galilee in the first century C.E., and especially the Via Maris near where Jesus grew up, were among the busiest in ancient Palestine. They raise the rhetorical question whether anyone living in the Lower Galilee could have escaped the dominant cultural—that is, Greco-Roman—atmosphere of the region, even in a village whose population they estimate to have been between 1,500 and 2,000.[39]

Sepphoris, while not mentioned in the New Testament, lay only a few miles to the northwest of Nazareth and was one of the four major centers of Greco-Roman culture and Roman administration for all of the Galilee. This city was the seat of the *synedrion* of the Galilee under Gabinius in the mid-first century B.C.E.,[40] and following a revolt and desolation after the death of Herod[41] it was rebuilt by Herod Antipas and regarded as "the ornament of all the Galilee."[42] All the features of a Hellenistic city were there, including a theater, hippodrome, and temples. Although the reported occupation of Jesus as a *tekton*[43] has traditionally been rendered as "carpenter," it means "builder" and could well have included masonry. This opens the possibility that Jesus and his father, of similar trade according to Matthew 13:55, may have worked in the building of the adjacent Greco-Roman-style city of Sepphoris. In any case, the physical proximity makes it impossible that there would not have been extensive economic and cultural contact by inhabitants of Nazareth with this important Roman cultural and administrative center. Even though the capital of the Galilee was for a time transferred to Tiberias[44] under Herod Agrippa, it was later restored to Sepphoris. To assume that Jesus and his first followers in the Galilee were unaffected by or out of communication with Hellenistic culture is historically untenable.

Capernaum was the place to which Jesus moved his base of operations early on in his period of public activity.[45] Meyers and Strange have

---

39 E. M. Meyers and J. Strange, *Archaeology, The Rabbis and Early Christianity* (Nashville, 1981), 42–43.

40 *Ant.* XIV, 5, 4, 91; *War* I, 8, 5, 170.

41 *Ant.* XVII, 10, 9, 286–294; *War* II, 5, 1, 66–71.

42 *Ant.* XVIII 2, 1, 27–28.

43 Mark 6:3.

44 *Life* 9, 37.

45 Mark 1:32; 2:1.

estimated the population of this town at 12,000–15,000, although they believe that a considerable portion of the ancient site now lies beneath the
waters of the Sea of Galilee.[46] Its importance as a population center on
the trade route with the territory east of the Sea of Galilee, and its connections with the Mediterranean ports, are attested by the location of a
tax-collector there.[47] The discovery of a milestone at the site dating from
the time of Hadrian confirms the view that this town was located on an
important interregional highway. The excavations carried out there show
that the basic housing structures were built of basalt, one story in height,
consisting of small rooms around a central court and a staircase leading
to a flat roof made of beams, branches, rushes, and compacted mud.
These details fit precisely the account in Mark 2 of the friends of the
paralytic who dug through the roof of Jesus' residence in Capernaum in
order to bring the man to Jesus' attention, in spite of the throng that filled
the house to the door. Significantly, Luke, who was accustomed to
houses with sturdy roofs, reports the friends as removing the tiles in
order to lower their friend down to Jesus.[48] Meyers and Strange believe
that there may have been a place of prayer in a domestic structure underlying the fourth-century synagogue at Capernaum. The discovery of
quantities of fish-hooks among the ruins of this town and the remains of
the ancient harbor confirms the New Testament reports that prominent
among the followers of Jesus were those who made a living from fishing.
The indications of relative prosperity at the site also correspond with the
report in Mark 1:20, that when James and John became followers of Jesus
they left the family fishing business in the hands of their father, who
employed hired servants.

The excavations at these Hellenistic cities and towns or, simply,
scholarly observation at these sites—especially those known in antiquity
as the Decapolis—reveal how thorough and enduring were the efforts of
Hellenistic rulers and their Roman successors to establish well-developed
centers of Greco-Roman culture in this part of the eastern Mediterranean.
To Gerasa and Philadelphia-Amman, the most striking examples of this
aggressive cultural effort, has now been added Caesarea Maritima, with
all the familiar features of this type of city: theater, temples, aqueduct,
and baths. Important for our purposes is the fact that the literary evidence from this period shows that there were sizable segments of Jewish

[46] Meyers and Strange, *Archaeology*, 58.
[47] Mark 2:14.
[48] Luke 5:19.

population in these Hellenized cities. Josephus mentions that at the time of the First Revolt Jews were slaughtered in Scythopolis (one of the four major cities of the Lower Galilee) and were protected and aided by the people of Gerasa in their escape from the Romans.[49] The differing attitudes of Jews in these cities toward the Romans and the Jewish revolutionaries show that the relationships between Jews and non-Jews in the Decapolis were by no means uniformly distant or hostile. There is not the slightest hint in Josephus' reports that there was a linguistic or communications gap between Jews and gentiles in these urban areas.

Josephus' description of the Jews of Tiberias in his *Life* is similar to that of the cities of the Decapolis: built on the shore of the Sea of Galilee to honor the emperor Tiberius, the city was of mixed population and apparently with a predominance of Jews; its constitution was of the Hellenistic type, with a *boule* of 600 members exercising local rule. The populace was split in its attitude toward the Jewish Revolt but opened its doors to Vespasian, thus taking a stand against the revolutionaries. It is worth noting that one of the Jewish leaders at Tiberias is described by Josephus as "not unversed in Greek culture."[50] Although Tiberias is mentioned only once in the New Testament, and then only in passing,[51] the picture related by the gospel writer of easy movement across the Sea of Galilee and from cities of gentile name and origin (such as Tiberias) to those of clearly Jewish character (such as Capernaum) conveys the overall impression that personal and cultural lines between Jews and non-Jews were not always sharply drawn in the Galilee of the first century.

The cultural range of Jesus' activity as reported in the gospels makes perfect sense in light of the reconstruction of life in the Galilee in this period. Jesus is described in the gospels as having extensive dealings with a group of Jews whose occupation would have rendered them outsiders to champions of Jewish nationalism or ritual purity, namely, tax-collectors. Mark and Luke depict Jesus as calling one member of his inner circle of followers "the tax-collector Levi" (named Matthew in Matthew's parallel account).[52] In his response to the questions sent to him by John the Baptist, he quotes his detractors as characterizing him by his associations with tax-collectors and other flagrant violators of the covenantal bound-

---

49 *War* II, 18, 5, 480.

50 See *Life* 9, 40. The evidence is conveniently summarized by E. Schürer, *The History of the Jewish People in the Age of Jesus Christ*, rev. and ed. G. Vermes, F. Millar and M. Goodman (3 vols.; Edinburgh, 1973–87), I, 178–184.

51 John 6:23.

52 Mark 2:13–17; Luke 5:27–32; cf. Matt. 9:9–13.

aries, i.e., "sinners."[53] Far from denying this charge, Jesus is described as defending this policy of association across religious and cultic boundaries. The important feature for our purposes is the evidence of his free association with those who were seen to be violating the ritual and ethnic integrity of the covenant. Similar, but in some ways even more radical, are Jesus' relationships with officers of the despised Roman occupying forces. In a story related only in Luke and Matthew, Jesus complies with the request of a centurion to heal his slave, and then defends having done so, predicting that others will come from all parts of the world to share in the eschatological banquet with God's people.[54]

Jesus' activity is described in the gospels as reaching not merely beyond the ethnic and ritual but even geographical boundaries of the Galilee proper. He travelled to the region on the eastern side of the Sea of Galilee, to the district around Gerasa.[55] That this was not predominantly Jewish territory is clear from the fact that there were herds of swine in the area into which Jesus is said to have driven the demons that possessed the man he found living among the tombs. In this detail as well, the distance between Jewish ritual requirements and Jesus' associations is clear, since physical contact with the dead and with tombs would have been considered a defilement. According to the gospel writer, the effect of this activity of Jesus is confirmed by the evangelization that the former demoniac carried out "in the Decapolis"—apparently reaching beyond the single member of that conglomerate of Hellenistic cities, in or near where the man had been resident.[56] Mark reports the success of Jesus in his healing and exorcism activities which extended to regions far beyond the Galilee, to the districts of Tyre, Sidon, and the Decapolis.[57]

The enduring impact of Jesus' activities may be inferred from the fact that when Paul set out to destroy the Jesus movement his attack was on a community gathered in the name of Jesus, not in the Galilee or even in Jerusalem, but in Damascus, the chief city of the Decapolis.[58] Given the evidence from archeological and literary sources for the common and inescapable interchange between Jews and residents of Hellenistic background and culture in the Galilee and adjoining regions, there is no reason to dismiss out of hand these gospel accounts of Jesus' initiative in

---

53 Matt. 10:3; 11:19; Luke 5:27; 7:34.
54 Luke 7:2–6; Matt. 8:5–13.
55 Mark 5:1–20. "Gerasa" according to the best mss.; others have "Gergesa."
56 Mark 5:20.
57 Mark 7:24–37.
58 Gal. 1:13–17.

reaching people from Hellenistic centers adjacent to the Galilee as later additions to the Jesus tradition, written after the Church had begun to undertake a conscious mission to gentiles.

Although commentators on Mark's gospel uniformly and correctly identify Caesarea Philippi with Paneas (various spellings), the site of the shrine to the god Pan at the source of the Jordan, they do not consider why such a locus should have been chosen (either historically by Jesus or literarily by his biographers) as the setting for one of the most important events in the gospel narratives: the disciples' confession of Jesus as Messiah.[59] Josephus tells how Philip built this place,[60] and that both Vespasian and Titus went there in search of a respite from their struggles with Jewish nationalists during the First Revolt.[61] The fact that at that time Jewish prisoners were offered to the wild animals in characteristically Roman fashion—combining public entertainment and grim warning to potential enemies—demonstrates that Caesarea Philippi was primarily a center of Roman culture and Roman sympathizers. The presence of Jews in the city is attested by Josephus, even though there was a preponderance of non-Jewish Syrians living there as well.[62] The fact that Jesus took his followers there as the crisis with the Jewish religious leadership was beginning to develop suggests not only that it was a place of temporary retreat for him, but also that he felt free to associate with those in the area of Syria-Palestine whose values and perspectives were so strongly influenced by Greco-Roman culture. The picture of the crosscultural mix in this section of the Roman world and of the easy and, perhaps, inescapable contacts of Jews with non-Jews revealed in the literature of this period are now given strong confirmation by the archeological finds of recent decades in the Upper[63] and Lower Galilee.

---

59 Mark 8:27–33 and parallels.
60 *War* II, 9, 1, 168.
61 *War* III, 7, 3, 144; VII, 1, 2, 23.
62 *Life* 2, 52–57.
63 E. M. Meyers, A. T. Kraabel, and J. F. Strange, *Ancient Synagogue Excavations at Khirbet Shemaᶜ, Upper Galilee, Israel, 1970–1972* (*AASOR* 42; Durham, N.C., 1976), 47, have shown that the Jewish population in the Upper Galilee was so low that the earliest evidence of a synagogue at this site dates from the late third and early fourth centuries C.E.

3. The Bilingual Culture of the Galilee

Meyers and Strange have made a persuasive case for the linguistic penetration of Greek into the Galilee in the Greco-Roman period; they suggest that there is evidence for its use there before the coming of Alexander the Great[64] and that ostracon inscriptions found at sites in the region, while predominantly in Aramaic, are also bilingual and in Greek only. From the third century B.C.E. on, public inscriptions were regularly in Greek. The composition of Jewish writings in the Greek language in this period has been well-documented by S. Lieberman's pioneering work[65] and more recently by M. Hengel.[66] The publication of the so-called Apocrypha and Pseudepigrapha by J. H. Charlesworth[67] testifies that many of these important documents of Judaism in the Second Temple period were written originally in Greek or translated into that language early on. Of the latter type, The Wisdom of Ben Sira is the most obvious example, as the prologue to the work attests. The justification for the translation of Jewish writings into Greek is legitimized by the Letter of Aristeas. Major inscriptions of import for Jews in this period were in Greek, from Caesar's decree in the Galilee regarding the sanctity of tombs to the public notice forbidding admission of the *allogenai* into various sections of the Jerusalem Temple.[68] One could argue that this notice was in Greek because it was addressed to non-Jews. As noted earlier, however, when the synagogue movement began to flourish and to take on architectural forms in the second century C.E., the inscriptions were in Greek, even in Jerusalem.

The catacomb inscriptions at Beth She'arim in the Galilee are likewise predominantly in Greek, many of them in highly colloquial language, suggesting that this was the basic tongue used by the departed and their families. The wide prevalence of Greek names among Jews further confirms this impression. Most striking is the fact that, while most of the letters of Bar-Kokhba found near Masada were in Aramaic, one in which he implies that he is in a hurry to get his message written and dispatched is accordingly written in Greek.[69] The conclusion reached by Meyers and Strange is, therefore, that while Greek began as a language of urban peo-

---

64 Meyers and Strange, *Archaeology*, 78.
65 S. Lieberman, *Hellenism in Jewish Palestine* (New York, 1962).
66 M. Hengel, *Judaism and Hellenism* (2 vols.; Philadelphia, 1974).
67 J. H. Charlesworth, ed., *The Old Testament Pseudepigrapha* (2 vols.; Garden City, 1983–85).
68 Meyers and Strange, *Archaeology*, 81, 84.
69 Ibid., 85–87.

ple in Palestine, it penetrated the Aramaic-speaking countryside to such an extent that Aramaic became the minority language, possibly with "small pockets of people . . . who never learned Greek." During the first century B.C.E., Aramaic declined among the educated and the urban dwellers. Hebrew survived only on ossuaries and was decidedly the linguistic feature of a minority, until it was consciously revived by the rabbis in the fifth and sixth centuries for liturgical and inscriptional purposes. On the other hand, in the Upper Galilee, which was cut off from the main lines of social and commercial interchange with the Greco-Roman world by the relative inaccessibility of its mountain and valleys, there was much less impact of Greek than in the Lower Galilee. And it is in the Lower Galilee, of course, where most of the activities reported in the gospels occurred.

This means that for Jesus to have conversed with inhabitants of cities in the Galilee, and especially of cities of the Decapolis and the Phoenician region, he would have had to have known Greek, certainly at the conversational level. The modes and forms of communication deriving from the Greek tradition would not have had to be acquired by Greek editors or writers of a later generation, as the form-critical school assumes. The cultural adjustment that the form-critics posit for the composition of the gospels, and the supposed transformation of Christian preaching and instruction in order to reach non-Palestinians, are not only unnecessary but contrary to the thrust of recent evidence. The spread of Christianity in a very short space of time through the Hellenistic league of cities known as the Decapolis—including its public visibility in Damascus within a year or so of the death of Jesus—makes perfect sense in light of these new insights. At the same time, the basic and traditional Semitic linguistic tradition in the Galilee is evident in the Jesus material through the reports of his use of Aramaic terms at certain crucial points.[70] Nevertheless, the dominant medium of communication in the Jesus tradition seems to have been Greek.

Closely related to these cultural factors is the fact that the Greek version of the Jewish Scriptures instantly became the Bible of the early Church, as is evident not only in the letters of Paul but in the gospels as

---

[70] Examples of this phenomenon are his term of address to God, *Abba*, which appears not only in Mark 14:36 but is also echoed by Paul in Gal. 4:6 and Rom. 8:15. Similarly, Jesus' word of command to a demon is Semitic: *ephaphtha* in Mark 7:34.

well.[71] This preference for the Greek translation was not imposed on the Markan community or on the Church as a whole by gentile Christians or by Diaspora Jewish converts to Christianity, but was an inevitable development of the bilingual, multicultural environment in which the Jesus movement arose in the Galilee.

The subsequent break which occurred between Jews and Christians in the second and later centuries resulted in the sociologically inevitable process of the mutual self-definition of each of these movements. The rabbinic movement turned back to the Semitic linguistic traditions of the Bible, while the Christians preferred the Greek language and modes of communication as essential aids for their outreach to the wider gentile world. The mixed features of the Galilean matrix out of which both movements grew provided this kind of choice, while enabling each to claim continuities with the traditions out of which both developed.[72]

---

[71] For my analysis of Mark's use of Scripture, see "The Function of Scriptural Quotations and Allusions on Mark 11–16," in: *Festschrift for W. G. Kümmel*, eds. E. Grässer and E. E. Ellis (Göttingen, 1975), 165–188.

[72] Two recent studies which describe the context of Jewish life in the Galilee in the first two centuries C.E. are: S. Freyne, *Galilee, Jesus and the Gospels: Literary Approaches and Historical Investigations* (Philadelphia, 1988); and M. Goodman, *State and Society in Roman Galilee A.D. 132–212* (Totowa, N.J., 1983). Both illuminate broader social and political factors, as well as the specific issues addressed here. In contrast to the methodological perspective of this essay, regrettably both draw heavily on the mishnaic and talmudic sources, thereby reading back the evidence anachronistically to the pre-70 C.E. period.

The Gospel of Matthew and Jewish-Christian Conflict in the Galilee

ANTHONY J. SALDARINI

This study views the Matthean community and its spokesperson, the author of the gospel of Matthew, as deviant Jews. They have been labeled deviant by the authorities and by many members of the Jewish community in their city or area. Sociologically, the Matthean community was a fragile minority that still regarded itself as Jewish and that was still identified by others with the Jewish community. Despite sharp conflicts with the leaders of the Jewish community and subjection to standard disciplinary measures, or, better, because of this, the Matthean community was still Jewish. Many of the stigmatizing procedures used by communities against deviants and the countermeasures they provoked can be seen in Matthew's polemics and apologetics.[1] Deviance processes, far from driving a group out of society, often keep them in. Paradoxically, social theory has established that non-conformity, resistance to social structures, and deviance are always part of any functioning society.[2]

---

[1] The charge that Jesus' marvelous birth was illegitimate is answered in 1:18–25, and the charge that his disciples stole his body in 27:62–66; 28:11–15.

[2] The tension between deviance as destructive and formative for society is illustrated well by N. Ben-Yehuda, *Deviance and Moral Boundaries: Witchcraft, the Occult and Deviant Sciences and Scientists* (Chicago, 1985), 3–7. On the positive effects of deviance, see K. T. Ericson, *Wayward Puritans: A Study in the Sociology of Deviance* (New York, 1966), 3–5. On the need for deviance, see E. Durkheim, *The Rules of Sociological Method* (Glencoe, 1958), 67; idem, *The Division of Labor in Society* (Glencoe, 1960), 102. See also G. H. Mead, "The Psychology of Punitive Justice," *American Journal of Sociology* 23 (1918), 577–602, esp. 591.

Viewed in this way, the gospel of Matthew (dating from the 80s–90s C.E.) fits not only into the development of Christian theological thought but also into the post-70 Jewish debate over how Judaism was to be lived and how that way of life was to be articulated in order to insure the survival of the Jewish community without the Temple and its related political institutions. Thus, the gospel of Matthew should be read along with other Jewish post-destruction literature, such as the apocalyptic works 2 Baruch, 4 Ezra and Apocalypse of Abraham, early strata of the Mishnah, and Josephus. All this Jewish literature tries to envision Judaism in new circumstances, reorganize its central symbols, determine the precise will of God, and propose a course of action for the faithful community.

The Identity of Matthew's Community

On the basis of the text of the gospel of Matthew, it will be shown that Matthew's community was a Jewish-Christian group that kept the whole law as interpreted through the Jesus tradition. Matthew considered himself a Jew who had the true interpretation of the Torah and who was faithful to God's will as revealed by Jesus, whom he declared to be the Messiah and son of God. Matthew promoted "a perfected or fulfilled Judaism brought to its goal by the long-awaited Christ."[3] He sought to promote his interpretation of Judaism over that of other Jewish leaders, especially those of emerging rabbinic Judaism,[4] and to legitimize his particular form of Judaism by utilizing the sources of authority prevalent in the Jewish community (see chapters 5–6 and his use of Scripture generally) and by delegitimizing its Jewish leaders (see esp. chapter 23).[5] His

---

3 D. A. Hagner, "*The Sitz im Leben* of the Gospel of Matthew," *SBL Seminar Papers 1985*, ed. K. Richards (Chico, 1985), 256.

4 For the specific nature of Matthew's opponents as early proponents of rabbinic Judaism, see J. A. Overman, *Matthew's Gospel and Formative Judaism: The Social World of the Matthean Community* (Minneapolis, 1990).

5 P. Richardson, *Israel in the Apostolic Church* (*SNTS Monographs* 10; Cambridge, 1969), 194, correctly characterizes Matthew thus:

> In so far as he works toward a theory of the Church as "true Israel," he does it as a Jewish Christian for a Jewish Christian community, as a part of a dispute with a pharisaic Synagogue which is also claiming to be "true Israel." In the post-Jamnian situation where a Jewish Christian church might stand alongside a synagogue, each has a deep need to clarify its thinking about its relationship to the cultus and the law. Each is forced to move beyond the attitude before the fall of Jerusalem towards these matters, and in doing so each is tempted to claim that it fully represents "Israel." The pharisaic com-

motivational accounting system was still Jewish. Significantly, he had no name for his group. He did not call it "Israel" or "the people" (*ho laos*); he used these terms either in their biblical setting or to designate all Jews—without distinguishing among groups within Israel—whom Jesus and the Matthean community had tried to instruct and influence. Matthew did not even use the terms "new" or "true Israel." Rather, members of the Jewish community who rejected Jesus, especially the leaders, were excoriated, in the prophetic mode, as unfaithful members of Israel, but still as members. Israel was the concrete community of Jews from which Matthew had been banned but to which he believed he still belonged.[6]

The conflicts Matthew had with Jewish community leaders, and even his alienation from their assembly, did not affect his Jewishness sociologically or psychologically. He considered himself a Jew and fought for his interpretation of Jewish life. He was regarded as a Jew by the surrounding communities, by the Jewish authorities who disciplined him, and by other believers-in-Jesus. In fact, though this is a minority view, there is no good reason to doubt that Matthew still performed circumcisions.[7] Most interpreters see Matthew as very much a Christian and cannot conceive of a late first-century community of believers-in-Jesus performing

---

munity rested its claim basically on continuous tradition; the Christian on the fulfillment of the old and better obedience through the Messiah.

It should be noted that the claims to both continuous tradition and fulfillment are equally artificial and are creative initiatives at adapting Jewish tradition to new circumstances.

6 This thesis is contrary to Christian salvation-history schemes which claim that Matthew sees the time of Israel as past and Israel as irrevocably lost (except for those Jews who have become members of the Matthean community). See D. R. A. Hare, *The Theme of Jewish Persecution of Christians in the Gospel According to St. Matthew* (*SNTS Monographs* 6; Cambridge, 1967), 153, for a stark presentation of this theme. G. Strecker, *Der Weg der Gerechtigkeit: Untersuchung zur Theologie des Matthäus*[3] (Göttingen, 1971 ; original ed. 1962), 34–35, like Hare, holds that Matthew and his community were gentile. W. Trilling, *Das Wahre Israel: Studien zur Theologie des Matthäus-Evangelium*[3], (*SANT* 10; Munich, 1964), sees the gospel community at midpoint, separated from Israel but claiming to be the true Israel (hence all the Jewish traditions). R. Hummel, *Die Auseindersetzung zwischen Kirche und Judentum im Matthäusevangelium* (Munich, 1963), 156, n. 72, 157–161, correctly stresses the integral connection and close relationship between Matthew's community and other Jewish communities .

7 S . Brown, "The Matthean Community and the Gentile Mission," *NT* 22 (1980), 193–221, esp. 218—against most interpreters, including recently Hagner, "*Sitz im Leben*," 258, and the more traditional typology of R. Brown, "Not Jewish Christianity and Gentile Christianity but Types of Jewish/Gentile Christianity," *CBQ* 45 (1983), 74–79.

circumcisions. This view is influenced by Paul's rejection of circumcision for gentiles, combined with the influx of gentiles who dominated many (most?) communities of believers-in-Jesus by the end of the first century. In the first century, however, the boundaries of Christianity varied greatly. Paul's position that gentiles were free of the law was strongly opposed and only gradually became the majority view, long after Paul's death. Many Christian Jewish communities survived into the second century and some beyond. Matthew fit in with these Christian Jewish communities. He affirmed the validity of Jewish law understood in his way (5:17–20) and the authority of Jewish community leaders, though he denied their practices and legal interpretations (23:1–36, esp. 2–3). He mitigated Christian rejection of purity and dietary laws (15:1–20; cf. Mark 7:1–23, esp. 19) and felt the need to justify letting his disciples pick grain on the Sabbath (12:1–8; cf. Mark 2:23–28). Thus, Matthew seems to have been one of a diminishing number of Christian Jews who accepted as normative the whole Jewish law and way of life through the teaching of Jesus.

Matthew in the Galilee

The Jewish tenor of Matthew's gospel and its strong polemics posit a geographical setting with an established Jewish community. A plausible case can be made that Matthew wrote for a community or group of communities in the Galilee or in an area contiguous to the Galilee.[8] More than the other gospels, Matthew sets Jesus' home, Capernaum (4:13), and his significant work (chapters 3–18) in the Galilee, in the numerous vil-

---

[8] For a review of positions, see G. Stanton, "The Origin and Purpose of Matthew's Gospel: Matthean Scholarship from 1945–1980," in: *ANRW*, II, 25.3, eds. H. Temporini and W. Haase (Berlin/New York, 1985), 1941, and W. D. Davies and D. C. Allison, *The Gospel According to Saint Matthew* (ICC; Edinburgh, 1988), I, 138–147. Antioch is the location most preferred, but without a wealth of evidence. G. D. Kilpatrick, *The Origins of the Gospel According to St. Matthew* (Oxford, 1946), 130–134, makes a plausible case for the Phoenician coast. B. T. Viviano, "Where was the Gospel According to Matthew Written," *CBQ* 41 (1979), 533–546, suggests a more southerly place, Caesarea Maritima. H. D. Slingerland, "The Transjordanian Origin of St. Matthew's Gospel," *JSNT* 3 (1979), 18–28, argues for Transjordan. E. Schweizer, "Matthew's Church," in: *The Interpretation of Matthew*, ed. G. Stanton (Philadelphia, 1983), 129–130, makes a case for the Galilee or contiguous areas. Overman, *Matthew*, 158–159, argues for the Galilee. Antioch remains the preference of most scholars because it provides what the composition of the gospel requires: a city with Greek-speaking Jews and gentiles and enough economic and cultural strength to support literary activity; the Galilee, the coast, and southern Syria provide these factors just as adequately.

lages and cities in the region northwest of the Sea of Galilee. This focus on the Galilee may indicate that the Matthean community lived there. Good-sized cities, such as Sepphoris, Tiberias, Capernaum, and Bethsaida,[9] would have had Jewish and gentile Greek-speakers as well as the community resources to educate and support a leader and writer such as the author of Matthew. In this setting the author would not have had to explain Hebrew or Aramaic words and Jewish customs as Mark and John did.[10] The author's insistence on arguing seriously for the observance of Jewish law (or justifying his alternative interpretations by Scripture and detailed argument) suits best a setting where Jewish culture was dominant and taken for granted. It seems reasonable, then, that the Galilee would have been a place where Matthew came into conflict with the emerging rabbinic movement and its particular mode of Jewish life[11] and where the Jewish community had a powerful opponent and the gentiles were in ultimate control. Thus, there is no need to locate Matthew in Antioch in order to find a literary, linguistic, and cultural milieu rich enough to support the gospel. The Galilee, with its complex and cosmopolitan society and its tightly woven cultural network, could easily have supported the nascent rabbinic Jewish and Christian Jewish movements, as well as the other apocalyptic, priestly, messianic, revivalist, and revolutionary currents running through society.[12]

Deviance as Part of a Functioning Society

The study of deviance is crucial to the understanding of culture and community. What a society considers deviant is intimately related to its identity, showing where it draws its boundaries and exposing key structures and values in its social and symbolic system.[13] To study what a so-

9 Sepphoris and Tiberias were regional capitals at different times; they had garrisons and populations perhaps as high as 40,000. Capernaum and Bethsaida were good-sized cities with populations of up to 20,000.

10 Mark 7:3–4 explains ritual purity customs; Matthew omits this explanation in 15:1–3. John (1:38, 20:16) explains that "rabbi" means teacher; Matthew does not (23:7–8). Matthew, however, translates *Emmanuel* (1:23) and follows Mark in translating *Golgotha* (27:33) and *Eli, Eli, lema sabachthani* (27:46) for his Greek audience. He seems to presume his audience's knowledge of Jewish culture, but not of Hebrew.

11 See W. D. Davies, *The Setting of the Sermon on the Mount* (Cambridge, 1963), and Overman, *Matthew*.

12 See 2 Baruch and 4 Ezra; G. W. E. Nickelsburg, "Enoch, Levi and Peter: Recipients of Revelation in Upper Galilee," *JBL* 100 (1981), 575–600 and G. Stanton, "5 Ezra and Matthean Christianity in the Second Century," *JTS* 28 (1977), 67–83.

13 Ben-Yehuda, *Deviance*, 19–20.

ciety rejects is to study what it is.[14] Thus, consideration of the conflicts
between Matthew and the dominant Jewish community will reveal how
each conceives of and lives life. What Matthew defends is what is crucial
to him and what he attacks is probably important to his opponents' view
of Judaism. Both communities share many values and know each other's
weak points. The struggle to define and sanction some behaviors and
their attendant attitudes as deviant is always political (in the broad
sense) and involves a power struggle for control of society.[15] Therefore,
the study of deviance must be set within this context.

Competing political interest groups promote particular modes of living; they create coherent symbols and condemn those who are different.
Far from being a subjective, foolish debate about preferences, these conflicts concern the basic shape of society, the relationships which hold the
society together, and the symbolic universe which makes sense out of the
flux of life. Recent theories of deviance have stressed the processes
whereby some people, behaviors, and ideas are declared deviant.[16] While
these studies will be used, greater attention will be given to the larger
questions of social order and structure, of how groups interrelate within
a whole system, and of how social conflict and deviance relate to stability
and change in society. I shall work within a broadly functionalist theory
of society, but will give attention to the symbolic interaction and power
struggles analyzed by labeling theory.[17]

Every society has norms, patterns of behavior, and viewpoints which
cluster around a center. The boundaries of a society, which are more or

[14] Ericson, *Wayward Puritans*, 22–23. What we fear is what is likely to emerge as
deviance, probably because our fears are centered around what we value; therefore,
someone who thinks and acts differently does so concerning matters which are important for all in the society.

[15] See recently E. M. Schur, *The Politics of Deviance: Stigma Contests and the Uses of
Power* (Englewood Cliffs, 1980).

[16] Surveys of various sociological theories and a critique of each can be found in S.
J. Pfohl, *Images of Deviance and Social Control: A Sociological History* (New York, 1985)
and N. Davis, *Sociological Constructions of Deviance: Perspectives and Issues in the Field*
(Dubuque, 1975). Labeling theory is ably expounded by E. H. Pfuhl, *The Deviance Process* (New York, 1980). A seminal book is H. S. Becker, *Outsiders: Studies in the Sociology of Deviance* (New York, 1963). Many aspects of deviance theory are based on the
fundamental works of Max Weber and Emile Durkheim.

Recent work stresses the viability of deviant behaviors and the oppressive
causes of deviance. It has often neglected to relate deviance to larger social structures
and the nature of society, a weakness which will be avoided here. The theory that society is only process (Garfinkel) will be avoided here as well.

[17] Davis, *Sociological Constructions of Deviance*, chapter 5, esp. p. 118.

less sharply defined depending on a variety of factors, delineate the normative from the deviant. Deviance is a necessary part of a functioning society in several senses;[18] it is part of the larger social processes associated with stability and change, continuity and adaptation;[19] it prevents the society from rigidifying and failing to fulfill its necessary functions. In the present case, Jews in Palestine and southern Syria had to adapt, or, perhaps better, reconstitute their symbolic worlds, and their social-political worlds as well, in the aftermath of the destruction of the Temple and its leadership. The symbolic and political center of Palestinian Judaism was eliminated, with grave consequences for the community.

Deviance in the Gospel of Matthew

One cannot be deviant unless one is a member of a community. The gospel of Matthew, like the community behind it, is Jewish in that it accepts all the fundamental commitments of first-century Judaism but argues about their interpretation, actualization, and relative importance. In the gospel and in other forms of Judaism God rules (the Kingdom of Heaven), cares for His people (6:25–34), and communicates to them His will. Israel, its special relationship to God, and its history permeate the gospel. The Bible is the authoritative source for knowing God, God's will, and God's purposes. Thus, Matthew quotes the Bible frequently and often solemnly in the formula quotations. Prophets, ancient and contemporary, true and false (Elijah in 11:14 and 17:9–13; true prophets in 23:34; false in 7:15 and 24:11), are invoked, as is Moses (17:3).[20] Numerous biblical Jewish laws and community norms are affirmed or accepted by Matthew as part of his world: the commandments (19:18), alms, prayer and fasting (6:1–18), care for the poor, powerless and sick (preaching and miracles of Jesus), biblical virtues (5:1–12; 11:5; 12:17–21), faith (17:14–20; 21:21–22), observance of the Sabbath (24:20; 12:1–14) and of purity laws (15:1–20; 23:25, 26; 8:1ff.), tithing (23:23), observance of Temple ritual (12:3-5; Passover in 21–27), divorce in case of adultery (1:18–19; 5:32; 19:9),[21] Jewish community leaders, and standard community discipline

---

18   See n. 2 above.

19   Ben-Yehuda, *Deviance*, 1–20, esp. 3.

20   Josephus reports about a number of leaders claiming prophetic or messianic warrants for their leadership in the first century. See R. A. Horsley and J. S. Hanson, *Bandits, Prophets, and Messiahs: Popular Movements at the Time of Jesus* (Minneapolis, 1985).

21   Recently, the Matthean exception allowing divorce because of *porneia* (some kind of immorality) has been interpreted, in the light of Qumran legislation, as mar-

(10:17, 23; 23:2–3) are assumed. Resurrection of the dead, a final judgment, and a typical apocalyptic scenario are woven into the text. Circumcision, however, is not mentioned. Most commentators assume, on the basis of Pauline letters and the influx of gentiles into most Christian communities by the late first century, that no New Testament community practiced circumcision. It is worth considering whether Matthew's silence on the issue implies that his community took circumcision for granted. A strong Jewish Christian community such as Matthew's, which was not afraid to disagree explicitly and vocally with the majority of Jews in many particulars of law, was unlikely to have kept silent on the status of circumcision. Even in the second century Christian authors raised the issue of circumcision, claiming it was not needed or it was ineffective. It is most probable that if circumcision were not practiced, Matthew would have discussed it, as he discusses and justifies many other deviations from common Jewish practice.

Matthew's Jewish community was, nevertheless, a deviant one. Though the list of practices and symbols he shares with his fellow-Jews is long (and more could be added), in most cases Matthew modifies the interpretation or actualization of the law so that it conflicts with that of other Jewish groups.[22] His innovations can be roughly classified under

---

riage within forbidden degrees of kinship. See J. A. Fitzmyer, "The Matthean Divorce Texts and Some New Palestinian Evidence," in: *To Advance the Gospel: New Testament Essays* (New York, 1981), 79–111. Traditionally, *porneia* has been understood to mean adultery. Recently this view has been subsumed into an argument that any sexual interference in a marriage (adultery, rape, etc.) would have forbidden the resumption of that marriage according to first-century norms; M. Bockmuehl, "Matthew 5.32; 19.9 in the Light of Pre-Rabbinic Halakhah," *NTS* 35 (1989), 291–295.

22 Matthew's disputes regarding the interpretation of Jewish law and life should not lead commentators to the conclusion that he was no longer Jewish (in his own eyes or sociologically speaking) nor should a covert notion of a universal "normative" Judaism be introduced. In the first century, especially after the destruction of the Temple, there was no "normative" Jewish teaching, practice or authority, but rather a traditional way of living Judaism with many local variations and some strikingly dissident voices. It was only after a century or two of recruiting followers and gaining community influence that the rabbinic leaders made an impact on Palestinian Judaism and could claim to be normative; it was even longer before talmudic Judaism became normative for all Diaspora Jewish communities. Matthew was deviant not because of disagreement with a "normative" Judaism but because he was a minority against the majority and because he recommended a more fundamental reorientation of the tradition than many other Jewish movements.

Matthew modifies or rejects many specific Jewish practices and teachings which he attributes mostly to the scribes and Pharisees. He is probably responding to the

five headings: core symbols, cosmology, boundaries, laws, and social structure.

Core symbols. A key change from the majority view of Judaism found in the Matthean community and in the text of the gospel is the rising status of Jesus as son of God, authoritative teacher (9:8, etc.), and crucified savior.[23] Though Matthew's community did not believe that Jesus was divine in the way later Christian theologians and councils defined it, the belief in and focus on Jesus escalated to the point where they eventually veered the Jesus communities away from Judaism. As a consequence of this focus on Jesus as central authority and symbol, the Torah became subordinate to both Jesus and his interpretation of its provisions, as articulated by Matthew.

The law as a core symbol has an altered status and role in Matthew's symbolic world. Though the commandments and the law as a whole are affirmed (5:17–19; 19:16–20), in each instance Matthew, through Jesus, counsels a further effort to reach perfection (5:48 [see also 5:20]; 19:21–22) and gives further instructions (5:21–47; 19:23–30) to guide that effort. The commandments themselves, besides being modified (see *Laws* below), are also subsumed under the two greatest commandments—love of God and love of neighbor (22:34–40). Though these commandments are biblical, the apologetic and rhetorical use made of them shifts the emphasis from a careful study of the Torah to a more flexible use and adaptation which fit the needs of Matthew's changing, alienated community. For example, when Matthew criticizes the scribes and Pharisaic practice of tithing, he affirms tithing itself but puts the emphasis on "the weightier matters of the law, justice and mercy and faith" (23:23). All these central symbols and affirmations are Jewish, but Matthew's community has rearranged and reweighted them.

Cosmology. A strong apocalyptic orientation and the promise and threat of divine judgment are a characteristic of a deviant minority group

---

leaders of an early form of rabbinic Judaism who were competing with him for the loyalties of the local Jewish community; Overman, *Matthew.*

23   This usually forms the centerpiece of Christian analyses of Matthew. It has been neglected here in order to get a different perspective on the gospel and community. As noted above, a small amount of deviance can be controlled, qualitatively and quantitatively, by the majority and can strengthen the community boundaries; a large amount is a threat to the community and a sign of significant social change. The growing focus on Jesus and neglect of the Jewish way of life by Christian Jews and their gentile brethren at first tightened Jewish community boundaries and identity, and then led to a deep rupture. Matthew's community stood in the early stages of this process.

under pressure. Divine mandate and sanction justify change and invalidate the current norms in view of the apocalyptic crisis. Future orientation produces a revised version of what society should be. New revelation and the need for conversion[24] become most comprehensible in this situation. It is no accident that the rabbinic leaders who gradually gained control of Jewish society through a very traditional program of reform masked innovations under the guise of immemorial tradition and eschewed apocalypticism as a fundamental organizing principle for their reform of Judaism.

Boundaries. The boundaries of the Matthean community were broadened and membership requirements were modified. Sinners and tax collectors, that is, those marginalized in Jewish society, were welcomed (9:10–11; 11:19; 21:31–32), in conscious opposition to the Jewish community which declared them deviant. Enemies had to be pacified (5:38–48; chapter 9) so that the Matthean community could avail itself of all existing social groups. The chosenness of the larger Jewish community was qualified (chapters 21–22, esp. 21:43; 3:9–10) and non-Jews were systematically included by the Magi in chapter 2 in the command to preach to all nations at the end (28:16–20). Though the Matthean community was very Jewish in tradition, thought, and practice, it, in principle (though perhaps not yet very much in fact), opened its boundaries to non-Jews. Cautiously and tentatively Matthew redefines Israel, even though he reserves the words "Israel" and "people" (*laos*) for the Jewish community alone. He does not declare himself a new or true Israel, nor does he give his community a new name instead of Israel. That will be left to the next generation. Rather, prompted by the inclusion of gentiles and marginal groups, such as the poor, sick, and outcasts, and influenced by biblical passages which include these groups, Matthew constantly defends the gentiles' right to faith in and salvation by Jesus. In Matthew's case this adherence to Jesus seems to involve an acceptance of much of the Jewish way of life as well.

Laws. The reinterpretation of many laws, customs, and outlooks had an aggregate impact on the Matthean community and alienated it from the majority community of Jews. A stress on inwardness rather than adherence to traditional practices, institutions, and leaders (chapters 5, 6, 23, esp. the charge of hypocrisy) opened the way for change, legitimized

---

[24] Strictly speaking, neither Matthew nor his fellow-Jews were converts to another religion. However, as the deviant way of living Judaism became stronger, it also became sociologically legitimate to speak of conversion, that is, of moving from one community to another.

the deviants through appeal to different norms and higher authorities, and undermined the given norms and their defenders (scribes and Pharisees). Specifically, Matthew rejects the washing of hands (15:20) and qualifies the importance of purity regulations without rejecting them totally (15:11; cf. Mark 7:19); he emphatically opposes the use of oaths (5:33–37; 23:16–22) and rejects divorce except for *porneia* (5:31–32; 19:1–12); he modifies the interpretation of the Sabbath (12:1–13) and subordinates it to other values; and, as was noted above, he affirms tithing but puts the emphasis on "the weightier matters of the law, justice and mercy and faith" (23:23).

Social Structure. Matthew moves decisively away from the prevailing modes of leadership and social organization. The Temple and its priestly and aristocratic leadership had already been destroyed and Matthew sheds no tears for them. In the narrative the Temple and its supporting institutions function as part of Judaism, but their legitimacy is severely qualified. The Temple will be destroyed (24:2, 15), must be cleansed (21:12–13), is less important than mercy (Hos. 6:6 quoted in 9:13; 12:7), and is subordinate to something greater—Jesus (12:6). The leaders "sit in the chair of Moses" (23:2) but are hypocrites who set a bad example. The Matthean community has its own inner order (18) and mode of leadership (23:4–12, 34) which clashed with those of the larger Jewish community. Matthew's community, like most new groups, stressed egalitarian relationships with little differentiation and specialization. Fellowship rather than hierarchy bonded the community.

Matthew's disagreements with the dominant forces in the Jewish community were more radical than this list would indicate. The choice and arrangement of materials in Matthew's gospel suggest that the author envisioned a thoroughly reformed Jewish society as the correct response to God's will and that he contrasted it negatively with the mode of Judaism practiced by the Jewish community at large. He expounds his own program and seeks to delegitimize that of his opponents—a typical exercise for the leader of a deviant group. A few examples will suffice. The first of Matthew's five sermons begins with the eight (or nine) beatitudes which propose fundamental attitudes and patterns of behavior for Matthew's community. The final sermon on the end of the world (chapters 24–25) is preceded by seven woes against the scribes and Pharisees who are called hypocrites and blind guides (23:13–36). These blessings and curses define the broad outline of how Matthew conceived of society and what he opposed in the Jewish society surrounding him.[25]

The seven woe oracles are not a random selection of complaints, but a structured series of charges aimed at key aspects of the outlook, practices, and leadership roles in the Jewish community. The first two woes concern membership in the community. The Jewish leaders prevented their members from joining Matthew's community and attracted gentiles to the Jewish community, thus frustrating the recruitment goals of Matthew's community. The next three woes, concerned with oaths, tithes, and purity, attacked the legal system, economy, and customs which held the Jewish community together and gave it its identity. Finally, the last two woe oracles attack the personal ethics and intentions of the leaders with charges of lawlessness and murder. These woes are preceded by a rejection of leadership titles such as "rabbi," "teacher," and "father," knit together by continual charges against the motives and perceptions of the leaders, that is, their inner selves, and concluded with a charge of homicide against the prophets in the past and the leaders of the Matthean community (prophets, wisemen, and scribes—23:34) in the present. Matthew seeks to present the current interpretation of Jewish society as misguided and corrupt in its practices and leadership.

The beatitudes which begin the Sermon on the Mount (chapters 5–7), like the woes in chapter 23, stress the attitudes of the Matthean community and the patterns of its behavior. Its members should be merciful, meek, pure of heart, and peacemakers; they mourn and seek justice; they know suffering for they are poor in spirit and persecuted (the beginning and end of the series). One senses that this community was neither powerful nor established; it sought to make the best of its minority, deviant status. The reward offered both at the beginning and end of the beatitudes (5:3, 10) to those who adhere to this code is the Kingdom of Heaven, that is, life under the rule of God rather than that of the Jewish community excoriated in chapters 6, 23, and elsewhere in the gospel. They will see God, possess the land, and enjoy justice, mercy, peace, and comfort. This is in direct contradiction to the society promoted by the scribes and Pharisees which, according to Matthew, neglects justice and mercy (23:23), places burdens on people (23:4), keeps cups and dishes pure but not their hearts (23:25), appears just but is hypocritical (23:28),

---

25 The relationship between the Sermon on the Mount and the denunciation of the scribes and Pharisees has been noted by Davies, *Sermon on the Mount*, 291–292, and J. Schniewind, *Das Evangelium nach Matthäus* (NTD; Göttingen, 1962), 225.

and kills God's messengers (23:31–32) rather than creating peace and harmony. Thus, Matthew couples his account of Jesus' deeds and teaching with a vision of a new society and an attack on an alternate program (one which has succeeded quite well for almost 2000 years, it must be noted).

Many other sections of Matthew's gospel support this interpretation of Matthew's program and purpose. Chapters 11–12 are paralleled by chapters 14–15 in treating the identity and status of Jesus and John the Baptist, in defending them against attack, and in showing the people's need for their care and leadership. These chapters also reveal the opposition of the Pharisees and the conflicts over food and purity, that is, over the boundaries of the community. The sermons of Jesus, woven out of traditional and new material by the author, mirror the mixed success of this deviant Jewish community in its struggles to recruit new members (chapter 10); it is losing members due to the embattled situation of the community (chapter 13) and is divided by disputes and defections ↙ (chapter 18). Against this depressing scenario Matthew arrays his interpretation of the words and works of Jesus, not as solely a spiritual hope but as a concrete vision of a different society, Jewish but different.

The Matthean Community as a Deviance Association

The changes which Matthew introduced into his interpretation of Judaism are typical of those found in deviant communities and religious sects. Social movements which deviate from the majority usually originate because there are steering problems within a society. They respond to a lack of focus and direction in a society, to a decentering and loss of self and meaning. Movements such as these attempt to resolve contradictions among the social, political, religious, and economic orders and to revitalize the society through reinvigorated central symbols and patterns of behavior.[26] When large numbers of people have been labeled deviant and have been rejected in some effective way by the dominant forces in society, they may organize into voluntary associations aimed at defending and restoring respectability to their "deviant" behavior. Typically, they challenge the conventional standards by which community members are measured, seek to delegitimize the societal leaders who control the definitions of deviance, and ultimately to change the social order.

---

[26] Davis, *Sociological Constructions of Deviance*, 239–240.

The disputes with the leadership of the Jewish community and the changed customs in the Matthean community led Matthew's community to form its own assembly and to compete with the Jewish assemblies for members.[27] It is most probable that Matthew's community viewed itself as authentically and faithfully Jewish but was regarded by its parent community as a deviant form of Judaism. Both these Jewish communities, along with many other Jewish communities, sought to survive and adapt in a changing world. Matthew's community engaged in many of the functions of a deviant association. It recruited members, attempted to develop a coherent worldview and belief system, articulated an ideology and rhetoric to sustain its behavior, and devalued outside contacts and norms. The formation of such a voluntary association requires adjustment to a new situation, the need to assign new community functions and status rankings, and the creation of new community goals.[28] All of these activities are carried out in the narrative through the sermons and other teachings of Jesus.

Deviance associations have been conventionally classified into four types, using two criteria. Those who seek acceptance by society are *conformative* and those who seek societal change are *alienative*; those who focus on the needs of their own members are *expressive* and those who seek to have an impact on society are *instrumental*.[29] Thus, it seems that Matthew's community, at the time the gospel was written, was an *alienative-expressive* group offering its adherents a new Jewish-Christian world as an alternative to the conventional Jewish one. It defended and justified its way of life against opposition and sought to establish a firm and reliable identity. Though the Matthean community had its own assembly, it was not withdrawn from Jewish society as a whole, for it still sought to recruit members from society at large.[30] It continued to operate within a Jewish world according to the interpretation of Judaism attributed to its prophetic teacher, Jesus.

---

[27] Matthew has Jesus referring to "your" or "their synagogue" a number of times, in a way which indicates opposition between him and the teachers in the synagogues or at least distance from the synagogue (4:23; 9:35; 12:9; 13:54; 10:17; 23:34). See also "their scribes" in 7:29. The first two curses against the scribes and Pharisees (23:13, 15) accuse them of preventing Jews from joining Matthew's community and of converting gentiles to their community and thus "stealing" them from Matthew's.

[28] Davis, *Sociological Constructions of Deviance*, 216.

[29] Two standard expositions of this typology can be found in Pfohl, *Images*, 315–317 and Pfuhl, *Deviance Process*, 269–273.

[30] On recruitment, see Pfuhl, *Deviance Process*, 131.

Whether Matthew hoped to replace the Jewish leaders and their interpretation of Judaism is questionable. Probably at an earlier stage in the community's history, before opposition had solidified, the community of Christian Jews was an *alienative-instrumental* group which sought to significantly change the social order and worldview of Judaism.[31] But the gospel of Matthew reads as if it were the literature of a group with a stabilized deviant identity.[32] Because of the conflict and differentiation, the members of Matthew's community found their core identity and "master status" in being believers-in-Jesus.[33] All other aspects of their Jewish life and worldview were filtered through this central commitment, which alienated them from fellow-Jews and colored all their activities and relationships. In the next generation this "master status" would crystallize into a Christian identity and lead them to abandon their Jewish identity. Thus, Matthew's gospel entered the mainstream of the non-Jewish second-century Christian church.

Conclusion

Though many contemporary Christians cannot conceive of Matthew as having retained a Jewish identity, Matthew, in fact, accepted the identity of the Jewish community because of its overwhelming, real presence in his world. (For Justin Martyr, less than a century later, Judaism was patently other and at some distance.) Matthew insisted on his allegiance to Jesus by carving out a deviant Jewish identity for his sectarian Jewish community. This situation was only transitional, however; accepting this deviant status quickly led Matthew's community, and the communities which subsequently used his gospel, to adopt an integral new identity

---

31 It is likely that at an even earlier stage the Palestinian Jesus movement was more like a sub-culture in which the members functioned both as members of their group of believers-in-Jesus and as respectable Jews.

32 Pfuhl, *Deviance Process*, chapters 5–6.

33 The concept "master status" denotes a person's primary trait to which all others are subordinate. Though we all occupy multiple social positions, statuses, and roles, one of them may predominate. In a racially stratified society such as the United States, being black is a "master status"; Pfohl, *Images*, 291; Pfohl, *Deviance Process*, 163–165; E. C. Hughes, "Dilemmas and Contradictions of Status," *American Journal of Sociology* 50 (1975), 353–359.

bearing many secondary deviance characteristics,[34] as well as a Christian interpretation of Matthew's text to go along with it.

Matthew lost the battle for Judaism. Within Christianity his way of following Jesus died out for the most part during the following generation. His gospel was used by later Christians in order to make sense out of Christianity's relationship to Judaism, but fidelity to the Torah in Matthew's sense was non-operative, causing "fulfillment" of the Torah to be understood in a different way.[35] From the viewpoint of deviance theory, Matthew's community or its successors were engulfed by their deviant role and adopted their deviance as a "master status," that is, as the set of values and characteristics which defined and controlled all other aspects of their lives.[36] Within a short time, because of both rejection by the majority of the Jewish community and the dominance of non-Jewish believers-in-Jesus, most communities like Matthew's became sociologically Christian, that is, they lost their identification with Judaism and became a separate, competing group. Late first and early second-century Christian and Roman writings testify to the separate identity of Christians. Yet, the lines of demarcation should not be drawn too sharply. Jewish influence remained so strong that Marcion felt compelled to radically revise Christian symbols and boundaries in the mid-second century, that various churches in the late second century fought over changing the commemoration of Jesus' death and resurrection from 14 Nisan to a Sunday, and that John Chrysostom in the late fourth century excoriated his gentile Christians for worshipping with Jews in the synagogue.[37]

---

[34] Secondary deviance is a set of deviant attitudes and behaviors acquired by a person after being labeled deviant for some primary behavior or trait. See Pfuhl, *Deviance Process*, 201ff., 234-238; Pfohl, *Images*, 291.

[35] E. Massaux, *Influence de l'évangile de Matthieu sur la littérature chrétienne avant sainte Irénée* (Louvain, 1950), traces the literary influence of Matthew in the second century. For the milieu of Matthew and later developments, see G. Stanton, "5 Ezra," and U. Luz, "The Disciples in the Gospel According to Matthew," in: *The Interpretation of Matthew*, ed. G. Stanton (Philadelphia, 1983), 115–119.

[36] Schur, *Politics*, 13; idem, *Labeling Deviant Behavior* (New York, 1971), 69–81.

[37] *Logoi kata Ioudaion* (*Homilies Against the Jews*, or *Discourses Against Judaizing Christians*), most recently translated into English by P. W. Harkins, in: *The Fathers of the Church*, LXVIII (Washington, D.C., 1979).

Literary Evidence for Jewish Christianity in the Galilee

ALBERT I. BAUMGARTEN

The Nazoreans are one of the better known groups on the sometimes hazy borderline between Judaism and Christianity. The principal descriptions of this group were written by Church fathers, such as Epiphanius and Jerome, who lived at least part of their lives in Palestine. The Nazoreans were situated in the eastern part of the Roman empire, with an important concentration in the Galilee.[1] They are noted for their especially unfavorable attitude towards rabbinic Jews and their Pharisaic predecessors. In a survey of comments on the Pharisees in patristic texts, I found the remarks of the Nazoreans to be the most hostile of all.[2] This hatred was mutual; several recent studies have suggested that *Birkat ha-Minim* was formulated specifically against the Nazoreans.[3] The Nazore-

---

[1] See the discussion in R. A. Pritz, *Nazarene Jewish Christianity* (Jerusalem/Leiden, 1988), 120–121. In arguing for a Galilean location, Pritz does not mention one potentially useful piece of data. Jerome notes that the Nazoreans call Hillel the unholy (*Hellel . . . profanus: Comm. in Isa.* 8:14; *CCL* 73A, 116). This interpretation is based on the interchange of ה and ח, a point Pritz discusses at some length, ibid., 61. He does not, however, raise the point of the well-known tendency of Galileans to pronounce these letters identically as the basis for understanding this exchange. See E. Y. Kutscher, *EJ*, XVI, 1595, s.v. "Hebrew Language."

[2] See A. I. Baumgarten, "Josephus and Hippolytus on the Pharisees," *HUCA* 55 (1984), 8–12.

[3] See the summary and survey of the literature in Pritz, *Nazarene Jewish Christianity*, 102–107. For a reason I cannot determine, Pritz omits all reference to the contribution of R. Kimelman, "*Birkat Ha-Minim* and the Lack of Evidence for an Anti-Christian Jewish Prayer in Antiquity," in: *Jewish and Christian Self-Definition*, eds. E. P. Sanders, et al. (3 vols.; Philadelphia, 1980–82), II, 226–244, 391–403.

ans, therefore, rejected Judaism as it was practiced in their day and had harsh things to say about Jewish leaders; in turn, they were cursed by the Jews. While their attitude towards the Church cannot be determined, their status as Christians was denied by leading spokesmen of Christianity, beginning with Epiphanius and Jerome at the very least.[4] The Nazoreans thus represent one side of the relationship between rabbinic Jews and Jewish-Christians, one of mutual rejection and hostility.[5] Do they, however, reflect the whole picture? This question is not meant to be apologetic; rather, it is based on the recognition that a relationship as potentially complicated as that of rabbinic Jews and Jewish-Christians need not have had one and only one dimension.

The most notable scholarly attempt arguing for a more nuanced answer is that of A. Marmorstein.[6] Insisting that his intentions are not apologetic,[7] he cites the rabbinic sources on the "sinners of Israel," who observe the law and, according to some authorities at least, are as full of good deeds as a pomegranate, and suggests that these were Jewish-Christians. He finds confirmation of the existence and nature of these sinners in the Pseudo-Clementine literature, and thus claims that the "sinners of Israel" known to the rabbis were Jewish-Christians whose internal literature has been preserved in the Pseudo-Clementine collections.[8]

---

[4] Epiphanius, *Panarion* 29, 7 (*GCS* 25, 239) calls them "Jews, and nothing else." Jerome, *Ep.* 112, 13 (*CSEL* 55, 382) makes the following observation: *"dum volunt et Iudaei esse et Christiani, nec Iudaei sunt nec Christiani."* See also his remarks in *Comm. in Hiez.* 16:16 (*CCL* 75, 182) and *Comm. in Hier.* 3:14–16 (*CCL* 74, 36). The significance of these and other similar passages is consistently understated by Pritz, who argues that the doctrine of the Nazoreans was suitably orthodox and that their keeping of the law might well have been considered acceptable in an earlier period, even to authorities such as Paul. See, for example, Pritz, *Nazarene Jewish Christianity*, 45, or his comment on p. 109: "Those Fathers of the fourth century who wrote against them could find nothing in their beliefs to condemn; their objections were to matters of praxis." Contrary to Pritz, I would maintain that we should judge the Nazoreans as they were seen by Epiphanius and Jerome, for whom they were beyond the limits of Christianity because of their practice.

[5] See the comment of A. Segal, *Rebecca's Children* (Cambridge, 1986), 162: "the biggest casualty in this religious separation was the group that claimed to be both Jewish and Christian, since it was judged heretical by both sides."

[6] A. Marmorstein, "Judaism and Christianity in the Middle of the Third Century," *HUCA* 10 (1935), 223–263.

[7] "I am not guided by apologetic tendencies"; ibid., 223.

[8] It is worth noting that Marmorstein regards the Galilee as at least one possible locus for the interaction between the rabbis and the "sinners of Israel" he surveyed.

Marmorstein's article, I believe, would be regarded as rather unsophisticated by today's standards. Assuming the identity of all the apostates of Israel, from all sources and all periods,[9] his thesis was implicitly criticized by M. Simon, who wrote: "We ought not to be asking whether all the *posh'im* [sinners] were Jewish Christians but whether the term was ever applied to Christians at all."[10] In addition, there is little, if anything, in the texts Marmorstein cites to identify these sinners as Christians.[11] Marmorstein's case can therefore be dismissed as almost entirely speculative. Furthermore, in spite of the disclaimer that his intentions were not apologetic, he explicitly states that he would like the tolerant attitude he believed was held by the ancient rabbis towards Jewish-Christians to serve as an example for his own time.[12] For all these reasons, I do not believe that Marmorstein's contribution can form the basis for asserting a claim that the hatred between rabbinic Jews and Nazoreans did not exhaust the range of possible responses of Jews and Jewish-Christians to each other.

I

In spite of the criticism levelled against Marmorstein, one essential insight in his article remains valid: the Pseudo-Clementines are a good place to look for attitudes of Jewish-Christians who are more sympathetic to rabbinic Judaism than one might expect. The authors of these texts offer a totally neutral interpretation of the name of the Pharisees,

---

He mentions that this contact could have occurred around the rabbinic centers of Tiberias, Sepphoris, Caesarea and Lydda; ibid., 259.

9 Except when it does not suit his case. Thus, the apostates who deny the existence of God—a belief Jewish-Christians obviously would not have held—are excluded; ibid., 227.

10 M. Simon, *Verus Israel*, trans. H. McKeating (Oxford, 1986), 257.

11 To utilize Simon once again for contrast, the closest reference Simon could find in which the "sinners of Israel" are explicitly Christian is a passage in Midrash Psalms 31:8 (Buber, p. 120b), which even Simon classifies as a discreet contrast (at best) between the "sinners of Israel" and other Jews ; ibid., 258.

12 It is not clear whether he means the example to be one from which Jews of his day are to learn how to relate to Christians, or whether it is Christians who are to learn a tolerance Marmorstein believed they still needed to acquire. In any case, only a page after declaring that he does not mean to write apologetics, he concludes the introduction to his article by stating that the material he will present "should serve as guidance for the problems facing us at present"; Marmorstein, "Judaism and Christianity," 224. In the course of the article (e.g., pp. 223 and 247) he makes a number of remarks about the hatred of Christians towards Jews.

free from the innuendo normally encountered in patristic sources;[13] the Pharisees, in fact, know the law better than others,[14] they sit on the seat of Moses,[15] and their tradition goes back to Moses.[16] The latter belief is particularly important: the tradition of the Pharisees, as I have tried to show elsewhere,[17] was controversial, with non-Pharisaic groups challenging its authority. Responding to these attacks, the Pharisees asserted that their tradition was associated with the great men of the nation of all times, beginning with Moses at Sinai. The Pseudo-Clementines therefore do not merely think well of the Pharisees in this case, but they reflect a Pharisaic point of view on a particularly sensitive issue.

On a more ambivalent note, however, the Pseudo-Clementines acknowledge the charge found in the New Testament that the Pharisees are hypocrites, but they insist that it is true only of *some of them*.[18] Similarly, the Pharisees possess the keys to the Kingdom of Heaven, but are to be faulted for hiding these keys from the people.[19]

The description of the Sadducees in this literature adds a further dimension to the account. The Pseudo-Clementines describe the Sadducees as the real heretics deserving denunciation.[20] This agrees remarkably with the rabbinic view of the Sadducees offered by 'Avot de R. Nathan, according to which the Sadducees "separated themselves off from the law."[21] The Sadducees thus were the genuine separatists, having deliberately chosen to depart from the truth known and acknowledged by all (at least according to this rabbinic version). In a similar vein, the Pseudo-Clementines explain that the Sadducees denied the resurrection of the dead because they did not want to seem as if they were serving God for

---

13 *Homil.* 11, 28, 4 (*GCS* 42, 168). In this section I repeat arguments first presented in my "Josephus and Hippolytus," 13–14. For the usual attitude towards the Pharisees, see there, 11, n. 42.

14 *Homil.* 11, 28, 4 (*GCS* 42, 168). Cf. *Homil.* 3, 51, 1 (*GCS* 42, 75)

15 *Homil.* 11, 29, 2 (*GCS* 42, 169).

16 *Rec.* 1, 54, 7 (*GCS* 51, 39).

17 See A. I. Baumgarten, "The Pharisaic *Paradosis*," *HTR* 80 (1987), 70–77.

18 *Homil.* 11, 29, 1 (*GCS* 42, 168). Cf. *Rec.* 6, 11, 2 (*GCS* 51, 194). This interpretation has been a favorite of apologists for the Pharisees over the centuries, reappearing in the works of a number of modern scholars. See, for example, R. Marcus, "The Pharisees in the Light of Modern Scholarship," *JR* 32 (1952), 162.

19 *Rec.* 1, 54, 7 (*GCS* 51, 39).

20 *Rec.* 1, 54, 2 (*GCS* 51, 39): *Hique ut ceteris justiores segregare se coepere a populi coetu.* Jerome, *Comm. in Matt.* 22:23 (*CCL* 77, 205), knew a similar tradition: the Sadducees *used to believe* in the resurrection of the body and soul, like other Jews, but then rejected these articles of faith.

21 ARN A 5, Schechter, p. 26.

the purpose of reward.[22] This, too, agrees with the above rabbinic account of the Sadducees in ʾAvot de R. Nathan. The Sadducees understood the famous maxim of Antigonus of Socho[23] as requiring the denial of the belief in the resurrection of the dead: if there were a resurrection, they argued, one would always be serving God for the purpose of reward, a service they understood Antigonus as having explicitly denied;[24] hence there can be no resurrection. The picture of the Sadducees in the Pseudo-Clementines thus confirms the above conclusion reached in the discussion of their account of the Pharisees: these texts view the Jewish past in much the same way as the Pharisees and/or their rabbinic heirs did.

The argument can be carried one significant step further on the basis of the analysis of a text which does not deal with the past, but makes its claims directly in the present. *Homilies* opens with a letter ascribed to Peter (EpP), ostensibly the covering letter to the whole collection.[25] Peter

---

[22] *Rec.* 1, 54, 2 (*GCS* 51, 39): *dicentes non esse dignum ut quasi sub mercede proposita colatur Deus.*

[23] M ʾAvot 1:3: "Be not like slaves who serve upon the master on the condition of receiving their daily [food] allowance, but be like the slaves who serve their master not on the condition of receiving their daily [food] allowance, and let the fear of heaven be upon you." In translating and interpreting this saying I follow the suggestions of E. J. Bickerman, "The Maxim of Antigonus of Socho," in: *Studies in Jewish and Christian History* (3 vols.; Leiden, 1976–86), II, 270–289.

[24] This point has been noted by J. Le Moyne, *Les Sadducéens* (Paris, 1972), 147–148. See also S. J. Isser, *The Dositheans* (Leiden, 1976), 54–55.

[25] For the Greek text, see *GCS* 42, 1. The English translation which follows is that of G. Strecker, "The Kerygmata Petrou," in: *New Testament Apocrypha*, eds. E. Hennecke and W. Schneemelcher, trans. R. McL. Wilson (2 vols.; London, 1973–75), II, 111:

I. 1. Peter to James, the lord and bishop of the holy church: Peace be with you always from the Father of all through Jesus Christ. 2. Knowing well that you, my brother, eagerly take pains about what is for the mutual benefit of us all, I earnestly beseech you not to pass on to any one of the Gentiles the books of my preachings which I (here) forward to you, nor to any one of our own tribe before probation. But if some one of them has been examined and found to be worthy, then you may hand them over to him in the same way as Moses handed over his office of a teacher to the seventy. 3. Wherefore also the fruit of his caution is to be seen up to this day. For those who belong to his people preserve everywhere the same rule in their belief in the one God and in their line of conduct, the Scriptures with their many senses being unable to incline them to assume another attitude. 4. Rather they attempt, on the basis of the rule that has been handed down to them, to harmonize the contradictions of the Scriptures, if haply some one who does not know the traditions is perplexed by the ambiguous utterances of the prophets. 5. On this account they permit no one to teach unless he first learn how the Scrip-

writes to James,[26] recommending that he take care not to pass on the books of his preaching to any of the gentiles, but to emulate the practice of the Jews and confine these works to members of his group only. Moses, Peter writes, handed over his "seat" to the seventy elders and the fruits of his caution are evident to this day:[27] "for those who belong to his people preserve everywhere the same rule (*kanona*) in their belief in one God and in their line of conduct, the Scriptures with their many senses being unable to incline them to assume another attitude."[28] The unity and harmony of Jews (an obvious exaggeration of reality), lauded by Jewish apologists and denounced by their detractors,[29] is here introduced as a model for James and his community. The many senses of Scripture might undermine that unity, but Jews are protected against such possible harmful consequences by the one rule they do preserve.

Thus far in EpP the nature of this rule is not clear: it could be a practical regulation (as it preserves a line of conduct) or it could be hermeneutical (as the many senses of Scripture are noted). If the former is intended, this sense of *kanōn* is well attested.[30] The hermeneutical nature

---

tures should be used. Wherefore there obtain amongst them one God, one law and one hope.

26 I recognize, of course, that the letter is Pseudo-Petrine and that the real James was not the recipient. It seems tedious, however, to repeat these facts each time Peter or James is mentioned, hence I have written Peter and James, relying on this note and the reader's understanding.

27 I presume this refers to the time of the author of the letter or his sources. See further the comment of G. Strecker, "On the Problem of Jewish Christianity," in: *Orthodoxy and Heresy in Earliest Christianity*, ed. W. Bauer (trans. of second German edition; Philadelphia, 1971), 260: "there are actual references to contemporary Judaism."

28 EpP 1:3.

29 Best known are the passages by Josephus, *Ag. Ap.* II, 19, 179–181 and II, 39, 283. See also Philo's comments on the unity of the Jews under the leadership of Moses at the time of the Exodus in *Hyp.* 6, 2. Philo noted the unity of native born Jews and proselytes in *Spec. Leg.* I, 52. Pagan detractors of Judaism, on the other hand, wrote of Jewish xenophobia. See, for example, Juvenal, *Sat.* 14, 96–106 (= *Greek and Latin Authors on Jews and Judaism*, ed. M. Stern [3 vols.; Jerusalem, 1974–84], II, 102–106, #301).

30 This usage goes back as far as Archytas of Tarentum (DK 35 B3). It is also attested for Lycurgus, *Leocrat.* 9; Aeschines, *Ktes.* 199; Aristotle, *EN* 14, 1137b27; Chrysippus, *SVF* III, 314; Epictetus, 1, 28,28. See the discussion in H. Oppel, *Kanon* (Leipzig, 1937), 51–57.

Jewish authors also used the word in this sense. See the LXX to Mic. 7:4; Philo, *Quis Rer. Div.* XXXV, 173 and *Spec. Leg.* III, 164. See also Josephus, *Ant.* X, 4, 1, 49 and *Ag. Ap.* II, 17, 174. Paul uses this term with a new Christian meaning in Gal. 6:15–16, a meaning picked up by other Christian authors, such as I Clement 7:2 and Clem. Alex., *Strom.* 4, 15 (*GCS* 52, 292). See further Oppel, *Kanon*, 58–64.

of the rule is, however, specified in the next sentences: Jews harmonize contradictions in Scripture on the basis of the rule (*kanona*) handed down (*paradothenta*) to them.[31] The rule therefore consists of principle(s) for interpreting the Bible. As such, *kanōn* is the perfect literal and contextual translation for the Hebrew *middah*, the term employed by the rabbis for their hermeneutical rules. EpP goes on to explain that someone might need to know this *kanōn* in order to reconcile contradictions in Scripture: "if haply someone who does not know the traditions (*paradoseis*) is perplexed by the ambiguous utterances of the prophets."[32] There can be no doubt of the hermeneutical nature of the *kanōn* we have been considering.

Before discussing the implications of the meaning of *kanōn*, one point should be noted. The term *paradoseis* appears in a favorable sense in this passage from EpP: knowing the *paradoseis* is one way to avoid being misled by the ambiguous utterances of the prophets. Furthermore, the *kanōn* itself was "handed down" (*paradothenta*), raising the possibility that *kanōn* and *paradoseis* are to be identified—an identification which is particularly plausible since *kanōn* and *paradoseis* have the same function (protecting one from being misled by the ambiguous passages in Scripture). If this identification is accepted, it is clear that all the praise lavished on the *kanōn* applies equally to the *paradoseis*, but even if it is not, the favorable evaluation of the *paradoseis* is significant in the light of Christian attacks on the *paradoseis* of the Pharisees referred to above (see pp. 41–42).

To return to the discussion of *kanōn*, our passage has a philological importance which must be considered before passing on to a consideration of its contents. *Kanōn* as a hermeneutical rule is unattested in any other text, and even its meaning here in EpP has not been noted by lexicographers.[33] Since the meaning is unquestionably plausible in the light of attested usages,[34] we must try to determine the source of this unusual

---

31 EpP 1:4.

32 Ibid.

33 I checked LSJ, BAG, *TDNT*, Lampe and Stephanus. Oppel did not discuss this meaning either, perhaps because he did not intend to write an exhaustive analysis of patristic material. See his comment in *Kanon*, vii. I was surprised to note that the hermeneutical sense of *kanōn* in EpP was not noticed even by scholars who cited the passage: see, for example, B. F. Westcott, *A General Survey of the History of the New Testament* (London, 1881), 506, n. 1.

34 See IV Macc. 7:21 (the whole *kanōn* of philosophy) or Cicero, *Off.* 1, 110 and 3, 81, where it refers to an ethical standard; there are numerous similar examples in Seneca. See the discussion in Oppel, *Kanon*, 88ff. In D.H. 1, 174, *kanōn* means the rules for

occurrence. I believe the answer to be obvious in light of the evidence we have considered. *Kanōn*, as noted above, is the perfect literal and contextual translation for the Hebrew *middah*. As such, its use in EpP is virtually perfect.[35] The use of *kanōn* in EpP is therefore dependent on material learned by its author(s) from the rabbis; one of the rabbinic hermeneutical concerns—resolving contradictory verses—is explicitly noted.[36] We therefore have another example in which the Pseudo-Clementine literature adopts as its own a feature characteristic of rabbinic Judaism, thereby praising an aspect of contemporary rabbinic reality.[37]

The conclusion of the passage from EpP which we have been considering holds no surprises. It is a paean in praise of the Jews, who have held fast to their rule in preparing and selecting teachers, obtaining for themselves "one God, one law and one hope."[38] We thus return to the

doing historical research; Oppel, *Kanon*, 67. Authors can be cited as models of specific Greek dialects, as in D.H. *Pomp.* 3 and *Lys.* 2; Oppel, *Kanon*, 45. Cicero uses the word for rules of oratorical style in *Or.* 231; Oppel, *Kanon*, 102–105. The *regulae iuris*—the principles of Roman law which underlie individual cases—are discussed by Oppel, *Kanon*, 98–100. Closest to our case is probably Philo, who uses *kanōn* for the rules of allegorical interpretation in *Spec. Leg.* I, 287 and *Somn.* I, 13, 73; Oppel, *Kanon*, 64–65. On *kanōn* as the equivalent of Hebrew *halakhah*, see S. Lieberman, *Hellenism in Jewish Palestine*² (New York, 1962), 83, n. 3.

35 I have deliberately qualified perfect with "virtually." Normally, in rabbinic contexts, one would talk of rules rather than a rule. In addition, rabbis would use their rules primarily for legal interpretation of the Pentateuch, while EpP writes of using the *kanōn* (in the singular) to resolve the contradictory utterances of Scripture in general, and once explicitly mentions using that rule for interpreting the Prophets. In spite of these difficulties, I would not agree with Strecker, "Problem," 261, who assumes that the discussion of *kanōn* in EpP is based on "heretical" as opposed to "official" Judaism.

36 See L. Jacobs, *EJ*, VIII, 366–372, s.v. "Hermeneutics." The last of R. Ishmael's principles deals with the issue of contradictory verses, but the concern may go back to Hillel. See the list of seven hermeneutical rules attributed to Hillel in Sifra, Finkelstein, II, p. 10, and compare this list with that at the end of chapter 7 of T Sanhedrin. Lieberman, *Hellenism*, 53, understands the latter list in the light of ARN A 37, Schechter, p. 110, but this interpretation of T Sanhedrin 7 may not be correct in the light of the information in Sifra.

37 It seems worth noting that the reality reflected in the comments of the Pseudo-Clementines is one in which the rabbis dominate and control Jewish life. This would suggest a date for the composition of these writings some time after rabbinic rule was firmly established.

38 EpP 1:5. The slogan *heis theos* is frequent in Christian epigraphy. See E. Peterson, *Heis Theos* (Göttingen, 1926). Peterson discusses a number of possible Jewish examples of the use of this slogan, 277–295. While some of his examples are no longer necessarily viewed as Jewish, such as the Amwas inscription (= J.-B. Frey, *Corpus Inscrip-*

theme with which we began—the unity and harmony of the Jews. Such unity was much admired in the ancient world; it was considered a sign of possessing the truth, while disagreement an indication of falsehood.[39] EpP thus repeats a point of which Jews were proudest and praises them in the highest terms possible.

To summarize the analysis of the Pseudo-Clementine passages proposed above, we have seen that these texts view crucial aspects of the Jewish past in ways identical to the rabbis. They know at least one essential feature of the contemporary rabbinic world, the hermeneutical rules by which Scripture is expounded, and assess it most favorably.

II

The Pseudo-Clementine texts therefore exhibit detailed and specific knowledge of rabbinic Judaism. Their awareness is not of commonplaces or of vague generalities which might be based on a shared biblical heritage, but of information uniquely characteristic of the rabbinic world. There can be no doubt that we are dealing with two groups in close proximity that maintained intellectual contact with each other. The authors of the Pseudo-Clementines quite obviously admired rabbinic Jews and their leaders. Before tackling an attempt at understanding and evaluating this position we must ask whether the admiration was mutual.

It seems reasonably certain that the practice of those who lived by the Pseudo-Clementine writings would not have found favor in the eyes of rabbinic Jews. While they opposed Paul,[40] they were probably not circumcised; in the one or two places where that commandment is mentioned it is likely to be a literary fiction.[41] In their system, the authoritative guide to the meaning and application of Scripture is the true

---

tionum Iudaicarum [2 vols.; Rome, 1936–52], II, 1186), other examples have been added since, such as nos. 848 and 1174 (ibid.). All these inscriptions, however, date considerably later than the latest possible date for EpP, hence I do not believe they form part of its background. If one is looking for such a background, biblical verses such as Deut. 6:4 seem more likely. The central place of passages such as Deut. 6:4 in Jewish liturgy would reinforce this possibility.

[39] See above, n. 29 and the discussion in A. I. Baumgarten, "The Torah as a Public Document in Judaism," *Studies in Religion* 14 (1985), 19.

[40] See the discussion in G. Lüdemann, *Paulus der Heidenapostel*, II: *Antipaulinismus im frühen Christentum* (Göttingen, 1983), 251–253.

[41] See Strecker, "Problem," 266, who argues that baptism was their sole rite of initiation. Cf. H. J. Schoeps, *Theologie und Geschichte des Judenchristentums* (Tübingen, 1949), 137–138.

prophet, Jesus;[42] appropriately, the tasks of Moses and Jesus are identified.[43] The law is eternal, not because it is inherently so, but only because Jesus asserted its eternity in the gospels.[44] Furthermore, they believed that the law was transmitted in such a way as to allow for the insertion of false pericopes,[45] which could be detected only by the true prophet Jesus.[46] Some of these false pericopes contain anthropomorphisms and other theologically objectionable material.[47] Furthermore, the Pseudo-Clementines eliminate all passages that discuss the Temple and its sacrificial system from their version of the true revelation of God.[48] It is difficult to conceive of rabbinic Jews having thought well of a group which was not circumcised, denied the divine origin of parts of the Torah, and specifically rejected the Temple and its sacrificial system.[49] I therefore find it difficult to accept Marmorstein's suggestion that the rabbinic descriptions of the "sinners of Israel," who are as full of good deeds as a pomegranate, are references to people who followed the way of life advocated in the Pseudo-Clementine literature.[50] The love shown by the authors of these texts for rabbinic Jews would have been unrequited.

---

[42] See G. Strecker, *Das Judenchristentum in den Pseudoklementinen* (Berlin, 1958), 152, 164.

[43] See *Homil.* 8, 5-7 (*GCS* 42, 123–124).

[44] See Matt. 24:35 and EpP 2:4.

[45] See especially *Homil.* 3, 47, 1-4 (*GCS* 42, 74) and the discussion in Strecker, *Judenchristentum*, 166ff.

[46] See *Homil.* 3, 53, 3 (*GCS* 42, 76).

[47] Some rabbinic Jews might have been embarrassed or troubled by these same places in Scripture, but they would not have eliminated the verses by utilizing a theory of false pericopes.

[48] See the discussion in Strecker, *Judenchristentum*, 179–184. Strecker understands the roots of this view in a more rationalistic conception of religion, combining that approach with a discussion of sources in "late" Judaism and the New Testament which might support these conclusions. Nevertheless, he recognizes that the views expressed in the Pseudo-Clementine literature go beyond the bounds of what could be tolerated in "official" Judaism. See, for example, his remark, *Judenchristentum*, 184: "Im offiziellen Judentum konnte eine Polemik gegen den Tempel naturgemäss nicht geduldet werden." Cf. the discussion in Schoeps, *Theologie und Geschichte*, 220–242.

[49] Rabbinic literature contains at least one passage which explicitly states that the sacrificial system was instituted by God as a means of weaning the Israelites away from the idolatry of Egypt (see Leviticus Rabbah 22:8, Margulies, p. 517) but this is a far cry from denying the divine origin of the sacrificial system and excising all references to it from the "true" and unexpurgated word of God.

[50] In my opinion, the description of these sinners is ultimately both so vague and so diverse that we may not be able to specify their identity (or identities).

Unreciprocated love between groups is a relatively rare phenomenon and requires a special explanation. What led those who wrote the Pseudo-Clementines to praise the rabbis so effusively while they probably did not enjoy a similar status among the rabbinic Jews?

On the social level the answer remains elusive,[51] but on the theological or textual level the answer may be based on an understanding of Matt. 23:2. If the scribes and Pharisees sit on the seat of Moses and one is to accept their authority, one is virtually required to think well of them, at least to some extent. On the other hand, that same gospel passage instructs not to live as do the scribes and Pharisees, "for they preach, but do not practice. They bind heavy burdens hard to bear, and lay them on men's shoulders; but they themselves will not move them with their finger." The ambivalent attitude expressed in this verse suits perfectly and is echoed in a comment on the Pharisees in the Pseudo-Clementine literature noted above: the Pharisees possess the keys to the Kingdom of Heaven, but *are to be faulted* for hiding these keys from the people.[52] In other words, in order to play the role of the real guide to the Kingdom of Heaven designated by the true prophet Jesus one must be like the Pharisees, but with appropriate corrections for the errors of that group. In this sense, the Pseudo-Clementines may have claimed to be the "true" Pharisees, as opposed to their rabbinic heirs.[53] Further support for this conclusion may be found in the fact that *paradosis* and *kanōn*, the two terms which recur in favorable senses in the discussion of the Pharisees and their heirs in EpP, occur later in that same text as important terms in the theological system of the Jewish-Christian group itself.[54] I believe this explanation will account for the unusual combination we have seen of

51 One possible explanation, nevertheless, deserves mention. Perhaps the Jews are being used by the author(s) of the Pseudo-Clementines as a club to hit over the head of opponents within Christianity; that is, perhaps their praise is not intended so much in and for itself but rather as a weapon against others.

52 See above, p. 42.

53 This proposal has been made in the past. See, for example, H. F. Weiss, in: *TDNT*, IX, 48, s.v. "Pharisaios."

54 EpP 3:2; *GCS* 42, 2. It should be noted, however, that when *kanōn* is used in EpP in reference to the belief system of the Jewish-Christian author, it does not have the clear hermeneutical sense discussed above when employed for the Pharisees and their heirs. The pattern, however, is a familiar one. Terms with favorable meanings in the usage of Jews have been adopted and adapted for use by Christians. See above, n. 30 and my discussion of *akribeia*, "The Name of the Pharisees," *JBL* 102 (1983), 416, n. 20; and *paradosis* in "The Pharisaic *Paradosis*," 66, n. 10.

fulsome praise of the Pharisees together with beliefs and practices which that group would not have considered acceptable.

III

The problems posed by the Pseudo-Clementine texts have occupied the attention of several generations of scholars.[55] The already confused picture has been further disturbed by the recent contribution of J. Wehnert, who cast serious doubt on the existence of sources previously believed to have been part of the corpus, utilizing the concordance to the *Homilies* then under preparation.[56] This article does not attempt to resolve these complex issues; rather, it is an analysis of yet another aspect of an already complicated problem.

One point, however, should be noted before concluding. Whatever sources one discerns, and whatever may be their dates, the authors of these texts as a whole are usually understood to have lived in Syria, Coele-Syria, or Palestine.[57] In view of the detailed knowledge of characteristic aspects of the world of rabbinic Judaism which we have been analyzing, I conclude that these groups must have been in close proximity to each other, and propose that we should consider specifying the Galilee as the likeliest place for the encounter between rabbinic Jews and Jewish-Christians, whose traces we have recovered. Only that concentration of rabbinic Jews would have been sufficiently nearby the areas where the Pseudo-Clementine literature is generally believed to have been composed in order to yield the blend of information and praise considered above.

[55] See the extensive account of the history of scholarship by F. Stanley Jones, "The Pseudo-Clementines: A History of Research Part I" and "The Pseudo-Clementines: A History of Research Part II," *The Second Century* 2 (1982), 1–33 and 63–96, respectively.

[56] J. Wehnert, "Literaturkritik und Sprachanalyse: Kritische Anmerkungen zum gegenwartigen Stand der Pseudoklementinen-Forschung," *ZNW* 74 (1983), 268–301.

[57] Ibid., 276. Cf. also above, n. 8.

II. ASPECTS OF GALILEAN SOCIETY

The Socio-Economic and Cultural Ethos of the Lower Galilee in the First Century: Implications for the Nascent Jesus Movement*

DOUGLAS EDWARDS

Rudolph Bultmann's contrast between "primitive Palestinian Christianity" and "Hellenistic Christianity" has few adherents today.[1] Yet, some who examine the first-century Jesus movement often assume ideas reminiscent of Bultmann's thesis, most particularly, that Palestinian Christianity in the first century was village-centered, agrarian-based, and Aramaic-speaking.[2] One prominent interpreter, in fact, has argued that the movement developed among peasants, farmers, and "the simple people of rural Galilee"; the rationale for this view generally stems from the use of agricultural metaphors in sayings material in the New Testament gospels and from the fact that no major urban centers such as Tiberias or Sepphoris are mentioned in early traditions.[3]

* My thanks to Martin Goodman and David Adan-Bayewitz for their valuable comments, and to the National Endowment for the Humanities and the University of Puget Sound, whose grants enabled me to complete this paper while at the Ashmolaean Museum in Oxford and at the W. F. Albright Institute of Archaeological Research in Jerusalem in 1991.

[1] R. Bultmann, *History of the Synoptic Tradition*, trans. John Marsh (New York, 1967), 240f.

[2] M. Hengel, *Judaism and Hellenism* (2 vols.; Philadelphia, 1974), has shown the inadequacy of this paradigm; cf. S. Freyne, *Galilee from Alexander the Great to Hadrian 323 B.C.E. to 135 B.C.E.* (Wilmington, 1980).

[3] G. Vermes, *Jesus the Jew* (Philadelphia, 1973), 48–49; cf. G. E. M. de Ste. Croix, *The Class Struggle in the Ancient Greek World from the Archaic Age to the Arab Conquests*

Such attitudes often have their roots in an adherence to one or more of the following views of the Galilean ethos. The Galilee is viewed as a Jewish enclave in the midst of "unfriendly" gentile seas, causing contact between Galilean Jews and gentiles to be strained, if this contact occurred at all.[4] Almost as axiomatic has become the view that antagonism, alienation, and suspicion dominated relations between inhabitants of urban and rural areas in the Galilee.[5] Thus, peasant hostility brought on by oppressive taxation and land acquisition policies of the local elite and the Roman government were major causes of the first Jewish revolt.[6] Finally, some argue that the urbanization encouraged by the Romans from Augustus onward had little impact on the Galilee, except in the negative sense already noted, because the Galilee was primarily agrarian and village-centered; Roman urbanization was largely limited to the two urban centers, Sepphoris and Tiberias.[7]

Recent archeological research indicates that such assumptions regarding the Galilean ethos (and, by implication, the nature of the Jesus movement) must be reevaluated. The aims of this paper are threefold: to examine the character of urban and rural economic, political, and cultural relations in an effort to clarify the socio-economic and cultural ethos of first-century Lower Galilee; to evaluate the Romanization of the Lower Galilee and its impact on urban and rural relations; and finally, to explore the import of this analysis for understanding the nascent Jesus movement and its Galilean ethos.

Overview of the Lower Galilee

Josephus and rabbinic literature partition the Galilee into two distinct geographical regions, the Upper and the Lower Galilee.[8] The synoptic

---

(Ithaca, 1981), 427, who concludes that Jesus "lived and preached almost entirely outside the area of Graeco-Roman civilization proper."

4 Vermes, *Jesus the Jew*, 44.

5 Ibid., 49; cf. G. Theissen, *Sociology of Early Palestinian Christianity*, trans. J. Bowden (Philadelphia, 1978), 48, who sees antagonistic statements about Jerusalem as a reflection of conflict between city (Jerusalem) and country (the Galilean peasants in the movement).

6 R. Horsley and J. Hanson, *Bandits, Prophets, and Messiahs: Popular Movements at the Time of Jesus* (New York, 1985).

7 S. Freyne, *Galilee, Jesus and the Gospels: Literary Approaches and Historical Investigations* (Philadelphia, 1988), 143–144.

8 The Mishnah defines a third area, the territory of Tiberias (M Shevi'it 9:2). See discussion by S. Freyne, *Galilee from Alexander the Great to Hadrian*, 9ff.

tradition and the gospel of John situate Jesus and his followers primarily in the Lower Galilee and in the rift region around the Sea of Galilee.[9] Even so, it is important not to downplay *a priori* the gospel traditions that depict the movement in the area of the Decapolis, the coast near Tyre and Sidon, and as far as Herod Philip's northern kingdom, the villages of Caesarea Philippi.[10] As we shall see, commercial activity between these areas makes such movement plausible.

E. M. Meyers has noted that the four major valleys in the Lower Galilee that run southwest-northeast provided excellent trade routes to the sea and the coastal seaports of Caesarea, Acco-Ptolemais, and Tyre. Such commercial connections made the Lower Galilee especially open to urban development.[11] Moreover, according to M. Broshi, the Lower Galilee, along with Palestine as a whole, reached a population density in late antiquity largely unsurpassed until the twentieth century. Indeed, the Lower Galilee, Broshi argues, was one of the more densely populated regions of the Roman empire.[12] The Meiron survey of the Galilee and the Golan in 1976 confirms a sharp increase in the number of villages in the late Hellenistic and early Roman period.[13] The Jesus movement, therefore, operated in a relatively small, densely populated area with significant urban centers and a large number of villages.

What was the relationship between this plethora of villages and urban areas? Let us first explore trade and commercial relations.

Trade and Commercial Relations

R. MacMullen once remarked that the exchange of goods that occurred within any given fifteen-mile radius probably accounted for about "three quarters of the value of exchange throughout" the Roman econ-

---

9 Without delving into the complex questions of the historical Jesus, I assume this to have been the primary locus of his ministry. For the boundaries of the Lower Galilee, see ibid. for references and bibliography.

10 *Decapolis*: Mark 5:1, 7:31; Matt. 8:28; Luke 8:26; *near Tyre and Sidon*: Mark 7:24; Matt. 15:21; cf. Mark 3:8; *Caesarea Philippi*: Mark 8:27; Matt. 16:13.

11 E. M. Meyers, "Galilean Regionalism as a Factor in Historical Reconstruction," *BASOR* 221 (1976), 93–102; idem, "Galilean Regionalism: A Reappraisal," in: *Approaches to Ancient Judaism*, V, ed. W. S. Green (Atlanta, 1985), 116–117.

12 M. Broshi, "The Role of the Temple in the Herodian Economy," *JJS* 38 (1987), 32, puts the figure in Palestine at about 1/2 million. Cf. idem, "The Population of Western Palestine in the Roman-Byzantine Period," *BASOR* 236 (1979), 3.

13 E. M. Meyers, J. F. Strange, and D. E. Groh, "The Meiron Excavation Project: Archaeological Survey in Galilee and Golan, 1976," *BASOR* 230 (1978), 18.

omy.[14] I. Hopkins, who draws on central place theory, argues that a similar situation may have existed for Palestine. He provides a theoretical illustration of the economic and administrative interaction between urban areas and villages in Palestine.[15] Large urban and commercial centers in Palestine, such as Scythopolis, he argues, incorporated a network of smaller cities (e.g., Sepphoris and Tiberias) within their trading spheres (usually about a 25-mile radius). In turn, these smaller urban areas had villages associated with them. If the villages were close to the urban area (e.g., Nazareth to Sepphoris), a trade and commercial relationship was likely. If the villages were on the border of a territory, an administrative connection (e.g., judicial, taxation, banking) may have existed.

Hopkins' work indicates a need to acknowledge the close commercial and administrative relations that existed between city and village in the Lower Galilee. Such commercial ties do not mean that cities such as Tiberias or Sepphoris were parasites,[16] draining goods, money, and agricultural produce from the countryside into Herodian, Roman or the local elites' coffers with little offered in return.[17] The Galilean village of Kefar Ḥananya provides material evidence suggesting that reciprocal economic relations were also at work. The village, located on the border between the Upper and Lower Galilee, is mentioned in rabbinic sources as a settlement where pottery was manufactured.[18] D. Adan-Bayewitz has confirmed through neutron activation analysis and excavations both the location of the pottery manufactured at Kefar Ḥananya and the distribu-

---

[14] R. MacMullen, "Market-Days in the Roman Empire," *Phoenix* 24 (1970), 333; cf. M. I. Finley, *The Ancient Economy* (London, 1973), 107, who talks about peasant markets where peasants and village craftsmen came from distances of five-six miles to exchange goods.

[15] I. W. J. Hopkins, "The City Region in Roman Palestine," *PEQ* 112 (1980), 19–32.

[16] Finley, *The Ancient Economy*, 125, argues that cities in the Roman empire were "centres of consumption" and parasitic; in other words, they drew rents and taxes from the country with little returned by way of services or goods. He correctly observes, however, that the economic relationship between rural and urban areas covered a spectrum that ranged from complete parasitism to full symbiosis, the latter depicting both country and urban areas contributing in equal portions to urban production and services; see further the useful discussion by P. Garnsey and R. Saller, *The Roman Empire* (London, 1987), 49ff.

[17] M. Goodman, *State and Society in Roman Galilee A.D. 132–212* (Totowa, N.J., 1983), 13.

[18] For references and discussion, see D. Adan-Bayewitz, "Manufacture and Local Trade in the Galilee of Roman-Byzantine Palestine: A Case Study" (doctoral dissertation, Hebrew University; Jerusalem, 1985).

tion pattern of the village's pottery. The pottery was marketed through-out the Upper and Lower Galilee and even extended into the Golan. Pottery finds indicate that the Sea of Galilee may have served as a trade route for the pottery to the Golan.[19] The village was a major supplier of high quality cooking ware for much of the Galilee, including Sepphoris, the villages around Sepphoris, and numerous other localities, including the Upper Galilean villages of Khirbet Shemaᶜ and Meiron.[20] Moreover, the pottery was traded to predominantly gentile cities and towns, includ-ing Acco-Ptolemais in the west, Tel Anafa in the north, and at or near the Decapolis cities of Hippos, Pella, and Scythopolis.[21]

In short, a Galilean village served as a center for pottery manufacture that was marketed throughout the Galilee, to village and city alike and to both Jewish and gentile enclaves. As D. Adan-Bayewitz and I. Perlman argue, there existed "a network of interrelated settlements of first century B.C. to fourth century A.D. Galilee and Golan."[22]

Kefar Ḥananya lies on the perimeter of several urban areas, including Tiberias and Sepphoris. The volume of its pottery and its distribution ex-plain well the application of central place theory. In other words, it is probable that urban centers such as Sepphoris served as distribution ar-eas for villages within their economic horizons.[23] This suggests the exis-tence of a complex marketing pattern that included travelling craftsmen,

---

19 Several pottery types from Kefar Ḥananya occur in settlements on the Golan, east of the Jordan Valley rift; D. Adan-Bayewitz and I. Perlman, "Local Pottery Provenience Studies: A Role for Clay Analysis," *Archaeometry* 27 (1985), 206; D. Adan-Bayewitz, "Manufacture and Local Trade," 231; idem, "Kefar Hananya 1986," *IEJ* 37 (1987), 178–179; idem, "Kefar Hananya 1987," *IEJ* 39 (1989), 98–99. For pottery found in the Sea of Galilee, idem, "The Pottery," in: S. Wachsmann, *The Excavations of an Ancient Boat in the Sea of Galilee* (ᶜAtiqot 19 [English Series]; Jerusalem, 1990), 89–96; C. Fritsch and I. Ben-Dor, "The Link Marine Expedition to Israel, 1960," *BA* 24 (1961), 57–58.

20 D. Adan-Bayewitz and I. Perlman, "The Local Trade of Sepphoris in the Roman Period," *IEJ* 40 (1990), 153–172. Excavators have found large quantities of pottery identified by Adan-Bayewitz as Kefar Ḥananya pottery at Capernaum, Nazareth, Ke-far Kanna (a large village 3–4 miles northeast of Nazareth), Tiberias, Magdala, and Tel Anafa in the Upper Galilee. See review by J. F. Strange, "The Capernaum and Herodium Publications," *BASOR* 226 (1977), 72; for Tel Anafa, see S. C. Herbert, "Tel Anafa 1978—Preliminary Report," *BASOR* 234 (1979), 82, n. 7; Meyers, Strange, and Groh, "Meiron Excavation Project, 1976," 20; for Nabratein, Capernaum, Magdala, and Khirbet Shemaᶜ, see E. M. Meyers, J. F. Strange, C. L. Meyers, "Preliminary Re-port on the 1980 Excavations at en-Nabratein, Israel," *BASOR* 244 (1981), 21.

21 Adan-Bayewitz, "Manufacture and Local Trade," 231–234.

22 Adan-Bayewitz and Perlman, "Local Pottery Provenience Studies," 217.

23 Adan-Bayewitz, "Manufacture and Local Trade," 243–253.

local merchants, and central distribution areas in urban centers. It parallels areas in Italy where, MacMullen observes, "the exchange of goods between the rural population on the one hand, and urban and itinerant merchants on the other hand" occurred at well-planned and regularly held festivals and bazaars.[24] In fact, this pattern developed across the Roman empire, where cities served as:

> the seat of social, legal and religious amenities, the centre for the processing of primary products and the production of craft goods, and the market centre for the sale and distribution of locally produced and imported commodities.[25]

Villagers no doubt had their markets in which to exchange local goods and crafts.[26] Second-century evidence indicates that various service personnel such as scribes, money changers, entertainers, healers, and even proponents of religious values made their rounds alongside travelling merchants and vendors.[27] Rabbinic sources, for example, suggest that money changers worked daily in the cities but came once a week to village areas in the Lower Galilee.[28] M. Goodman has argued that villages of the Galilee after 135 C.E. were largely independent and relied on city markets to earn coins for Roman taxes, to purchase goods not available (e.g., luxury goods such as gold, glass, pearls, wood products), and to sell surplus produce and goods like olive oil.[29] Yet, villagers also bought common wares such as cooking pots made at Kefar Ḥananya.

The central place market network which allowed the widespread distribution of Kefar Ḥananya pottery indicates a vibrant economic interaction between urban markets and village consumers. The market network brought together merchants and others who provided assorted

[24] MacMullen, "Market-Days," 341. S. Applebaum, "Economic Life in Palestine," in: *The Jewish People in the First Century*, eds. S. Safrai and M. Stern (2 vols.; Assen, 1974–76), II, 680, suggests that some persons obtained their goods from travelling craftsmen who sold their wares (including pottery) from place to place. See, however, the discussion by D. Adan-Bayewitz on itinerant peddlers in rabbinic tradition, "The Itinerant Peddler in Roman Palestine," in: *Jews in Economic Life*, ed. N. Gross (Jerusalem, 1985), 67–85 (Hebrew).

[25] Garnsey and Saller, *The Roman Empire*, 56.

[26] M. Goodman, *State and Society*, 54, lists the pertinent references for later periods in Roman Galilee.

[27] Ibid., 57; cf. Adan-Bayewitz, "The Itinerant Peddler," 67–85.

[28] Goodman, *State and Society*, 57–59. Here may be the "bankers" with whom the financially inept servant was to invest his master's money (Matt. 25:27; Luke 19:23).

[29] Ibid., 60f. Cf. Applebaum, "Economic Life," 672ff.

goods and services (including hawking one's religious or philosophical perspective), binding closely spaced villages and urban areas into a common economic and, to a degree, social fabric. If one takes Mac-Mullen's fifteen-mile radius to market seriously, then nearly every village in the Lower Galilee would fall within range of the two major cities, Sepphoris and Tiberias. The pottery distribution from Kefar Ḥananya indicates that at least one village took full advantage of this fact. Even so, villages outside the political influence of a particular city participated in urban settings and followed the economic "rules" set forth by Roman-aligned personnel, such as Herod Agrippa I in his capacity as *agoranomos* of Tiberias[30] or Gaius Julius, possibly a Jew with Roman citizenship who was *agoranomos* of Tiberias for Herod Antipas in 29–30 C.E.[31] It should come as no surprise, therefore, when the Markan writer portrays the Jesus movement as entering the marketplaces of cities, villages, and country or when the early sayings tradition illustrates theological points with marketplace imagery.[32] It is at the marketplace that urban and rural people gathered to carry on economic, social, and religious discourse. Furthermore, the regional market network reflected in the distribution of Kefar Ḥananya pottery proves that contact between Galilean Jews and gentiles in the surrounding areas existed in the first century. For that reason, the journey depicted in the Markan narrative of the Jesus movement going to the regions of the Decapolis, the villages of Caesarea Philippi, and encountering Greeks such as the Syro-Phoenician woman, Tyrians, or Sidonians need not simply reflect the writer's "gentile interests."[33] Indeed, even the Jesus movement's travel from Tyre to Sidon to the Decapolis depicted in Mark, which has struck some New Testament interpreters as evidence for an ignorance of Galilean geography, is, in fact, quite plausible.[34] Josephus notes that during the reign of Antipas, while Herod Agrippa I was in Syria, a dispute regarding boundaries arose between Sidon and Damascus, a city of the Decapolis.[35] It is therefore conceivable that the movement headed east toward Damascus

30 *Ant.* XVIII, 6, 2, 149.
31 S. Qedar, "Two Lead Weights of Herod Antipas and Agrippa II and the Early History of Tiberias," *INJ* 9 (1986–87), 29–30, 33.
32 Mark 6:53–56; Matt. 11:16; Luke 7:32.
33 Freyne, *Galilee, Jesus and the Gospels*, 143.
34 Mark 7:31; see, for example, Freyne, ibid., 55.
35 *Ant.* XVIII, 6, 3, 153–154. Pliny understands Damascus to have been part of the Decapolis; see *Nat. Hist.* 5, 74.

and then south through the region of the Decapolis, following major roads linking Damascus with either Caesarea Philippi or Hippos.[36]

Import and Export Networks: Long Distance Exchange Systems

The Lower Galilee profited from the *pax Romana*, as its participation in international trade has indicated. According to Josephus, Acco-Ptolemais served as the maritime city of the Galilee;[37] it dominated the Mediterranean coast west of the Galilee in the early part of the first century,[38] although numismatic evidence indicates that its maritime fortunes may have declined with the rise of Caesarea as a major political and commercial city during the reign of Claudius.[39] Archeologically, international trade was most evident in the import of such items as the eastern Terra Sigillata wares,[40] marble, luxury goods, and the numerous small ointment bottles that have been found throughout Palestine dating from the third century B.C.E. to the first century C.E.[41] Additional evidence for the extent of the Galilee's import network is found in the literary texts, some late, and includes such items as Babylonian beer, Egyptian barley beer, smoked fish and lentils from Egypt, cheese from Bythinia, mackerel

---

[36] For maps showing the ancient road system in these areas, see M. Avi-Yonah, "Historical Geography," in: *The Jewish People in the First Century*, I, 100–101; I. Roll, "The Roman Road System in Judaea," in: *The Jerusalem Cathedra*, ed. L. I. Levine (3 vols.; Jerusalem, 1981–83), III, 139.

[37] *War* II, 10, 2, 188.

[38] M. Avi-Yonah, *Gazetteer of Roman Palestine* (*Qedem* 5; Jerusalem, 1976), 89.

[39] D. Ariel, "A Survey of Coin Finds in Jerusalem," *LA* 32 (1982), 292, notes that no coins of Acco-Ptolemais were found in Jerusalem for the period of Claudius-Caracalla, whereas large numbers were found for the period before Claudius. The city became a Roman colony under Nero, which may have caused or have resulted from increasing hostility and decreased commercial interaction between the gentile city and Jewish territories. See Y. Meshorer, *City-Coins of Eretz-Israel and the Decapolis in the Roman Period* (Jerusalem, 1985), 12.

[40] J. Gunneweg, I. Perlman, and J. Yellin, *The Provenience Typology and Chronology of Eastern Terra Sigillata* (*Qedem* 17; Jerusalem, 1983); cf. Adan-Bayewitz, "Manufacture and Local Trade," 263–264.

[41] M. Hershkovitz, "Miniature Ointment Vases," *IEJ* 36 (1986), 50–51. In most cases the ointment bottles were found in household contexts. The bottles apparently held precious ointment used for inflammations and eye infections. These items, possibly imported from Lycia (Tarsus?), were found as far south as the city of Jerusalem and as far north as Gush Ḥalav in the Upper Galilee. Local imitations apparently were also manufactured.

from Spain, imported wines, asses from Lydia, purple dye from Tyre, jewelry from Egypt, as well as parchment and papyrus.[42]

Galilean exports were less numerous. They included vegetables, grain, olive oil, and raw materials such as Galilean rushes for ropemaking.[43] Balsam from Gennesareth may have produced significant revenue.[44] In addition, salted fish was a major export item from Magdala-Tarichaeae and provided a source of revenue for the fishing industry in the area around the Sea of Galilee.[45] It should not surprise us that the father of two early followers of Jesus is portrayed as having hired servants to help with his fishing enterprise.[46]

What does our discussion about pots and fish have to tell us, beyond persons' culinary habits? Exports and imports did not simply benefit a few wealthy individuals. K. Hopkins rightly criticizes the tendency to split the population of the Roman empire into two social and economic strata: a tiny elite and the broad mass of peasants and proletarians who lived near the level of minimum subsistence. This, he argues, neglects the varied and sophisticated market that addressed a large buying public who sought the "best clothes for brides and grooms or for rich peasants or ordinary clothes for respectable school teachers or doctors or for middling landlords."[47]

Trade and industry played a major economic role in the Roman empire; agriculture was not the "sole" significant base for the economy.[48]

---

42   See M. Avi-Yonah, in: *The Herodian Period*, ed. M. Avi-Yonah (*The World History of the Jewish People*, VII; Jerusalem, 1975), 180ff.

43   Examples of other export material from Palestine as a whole include date wine, date honey, perfumes (Pliny, *Nat. Hist.* 13, 44; Tacitus, *Hist.* 5, 6), dried figs, fig honey, and wine; fine olive oil also came from the Galilee. See Applebaum, "Economic Life," 653–656, 667–690 for additional discussion.

44   Strabo notes that balsam was found in the Gennesareth Plain (*Geog.* 16, 2, 16); it was found almost exclusively in Palestine and was no doubt an important source of revenue (*War* I, 6, 6, 138–140). For a discussion on balsam in the Galilee, see Freyne, *Galilee from Alexander the Great to Hadrian*, 172–173.

45   See Goodman, *State and Society*, 24.

46   Mark 1:20; see *Interpreters' Dictionary of the Bible, Supplement* (Nashville, 1976), s.v. "fishermen"; Freyne, *Galilee from Alexander the Great to Hadrian*, 173–174.

47   K. Hopkins, "Economic Growth and Towns in Classical Antiquity," in: *Towns in Societies: Essays in Economic History and Historical Sociology*, eds. P. Abrams and E. A. Wigley (Cambridge, 1978), 55.

48   G. Pucci, "Pottery and Trade in the Roman Period," in: *Trade in the Ancient Economy*, eds. P. Garnsey, K. Hopkins, and C. R. Whittaker (Berkeley, 1983), 114–117; contra A. Jones, "The Urbanization of Palestine," *JRS* 21 (1931), 78–85.

The Roman empire may have been "borne on the backs of its peasants" but peasants received in turn:

> law, protection, peace, rituals, ceremonies and medical advice, even surgery. Towns gave independent peasants and free tenants opportunity to buy extra food and services, necessities and luxuries (tools, pots, clothes, seeds, pastries). Moreover, the towns themselves generated economic activity. Urban artisans had to be serviced, housed; they bought goods.[49]

In short, villages in the Lower Galilee, like villages in many areas of the Roman empire, had the advantage of urban markets for their produce as well as the ability to buy goods not readily available in their own villages.

Economic models for the Lower Galilee in the first century that propose an innate or structural hostility between urban and rural areas fail to recognize the degree of economic reciprocity that often existed between these two areas; the bond was often beneficial to both.[50] Moreover, any suggestion that the Galilee was isolated from its gentile neighbors either locally or internationally, especially prior to the mid-first century C.E., is not borne out by the ceramic or numismatic evidence. On a very basic level, common cooking wares (and one supposes other sorts of goods and services) were traded.[51]

Economics and Crisis in the Galilee

Economic systems do not *per se* cause or prevent friction. Rather, as G. Theissen argues, it is the perception that one's economic status will change rather than the extent of one's poverty that may contribute to disaffection and possible revolt.[52] Circumstantial evidence suggests that just such a condition appeared in first-century Galilee. In the early years of Herod Antipas' rule conditions were favorable for growth in the economy, an unusual situation since, generally, economic growth was sporadic in the static Roman economic system.[53] Several events, however, combined to cause the economy to "heat up" in the Lower Galilee.

First were Herod Antipas' building projects. Like his father, Antipas built (or rebuilt in the case of Sepphoris) two cities in the Lower Galilee.

---

[49] K. Hopkins, "Economic Growth," 75.
[50] Cf. Strabo, *Geog.* 2, 5, 26.
[51] Cf. Adan-Bayewitz, "Manufacture and Local Trade," 264–266.
[52] Theissen, *Sociology of Early Palestinian Christianity*, 39–40.
[53] Garnsey and Saller, *The Roman Empire*, 47–51.

Such building projects provided long-term employment for a significant number of people, skilled and unskilled. Josephus illustrates the importance of such employment for economic and social stability when describing the scramble by Jerusalem authorities to find employment for 18,000 workers (probably an exaggerated figure) who were laid off when construction of the Temple was completed in the mid-sixties C.E.[54] Workers on Herod Antipas' building projects (no doubt from the surrounding villages) needed shelter, food, and other support services, which certainly would have boosted the local economy. In addition, support personnel were needed upon completion of public structures, including persons to maintain and repair buildings, the water system, the marketplaces, and so forth. The building projects, therefore, which lasted until at least the early to mid-twenties, contributed to a growth economy in the region.

Increases in population also spur growth.[55] More people create a demand for increased food production and other support services, at least in the short run. Increased food production provides larger tax revenues which, in turn, allow more building or the continued maintenance of institutions. As noted earlier, a significant population increase occurred during the late Hellenistic and early Roman period. Indeed, the gospel accounts and Josephus also depict the Galilean region as teeming with people.[56] Thus, we have a second stimulus to the economy, occurring near the time of Herod Antipas' building program.

The third and perhaps most important condition for economic growth was the *pax Romana* and Herod Antipas' willing acceptance of his role within the Roman order.[57] The civic peace that followed the internal fighting for primacy in the Roman government prior to the Augustan period favored economic recovery and a degree of expansion. Combined with the building program, the increase in population, and the general stability of his own rule, the *pax Romana* permitted Herod Antipas to control a strong economy.

Several factors suggest that it did not last. R. Jones notes that in the Roman period "continuing economic prosperity of the towns depended on prevailing economic systems and was not susceptible to much change

---

54 *Ant.* XX, 9, 7, 219–220.
55 Garnsey and Saller, *The Roman Empire*, 51.
56 *War* III, 3, 2, 42–43; Mark 3:7 (= Matt. 4:25; Luke 6:17).
57 Garnsey and Saller, *The Roman Empire*, 51.

through acts of political will."[58] By the mid-twenties, Tiberias and Sepphoris had, for the most part, been completed.[59] Administrative structures and buildings were in place, the political apparatus was functioning, and a continual supply of funds was needed to keep it going. Furthermore, Herod Antipas entered a period of political instability epitomized by the dissolution of his marriage to his Nabatean wife, thus changing his relationship with the Nabatean ruler, Aretas IV.[60] It is difficult to know the reasons for Herod Antipas' move at this point; trade patterns were changing and Nabatean participation in this lucrative trade was on the wane,[61] perhaps further increasing tensions between the two kings. It is possible that Herod Antipas derived income from customs duties on the north-south route followed by the Nabateans, which was then threatened by the decline in trade.[62] In any case, Herod Antipas entered an unstable political period. Not only did he lose in a brief skirmish to Aretas, but shortly thereafter he lost his power and was displaced by Agrippa I, whose reign lasted only until 44 C.E.

Several consequences were possible according to the above scenarios. First, the rural areas would have experienced a changed economic situation; no longer would they have been part of an economy where jobs and extra money would be available from urban building programs. Furthermore, in order to maintain the added bureaucracy as well as the buildings, additional taxation (perhaps from the elite classes or on produce) would have been required. This would have created an atmosphere of perceived if not real decline in the standard of living of both the elite and peasant classes. Such conditions would have encouraged a volatile environment that could have led to the type of increased hostility posited by Theissen. Indeed, this may help explain sayings traditions in the gospels that berate the rich.[63] This is not, however, simply an urban vs. rural or city vs. village situation. The urban poor, the "artisan," and

58 R. Jones, "A False Start? The Roman Urbanization of Western Europe," *World Archaeology* 19 (1987), 50.

59 Considerable building again occurred at Sepphoris toward the latter part of the first century and into the second; however, this has no bearing on the point being made here. See E. M. Meyers, E. Netzer, and C. L. Meyers, "Artistry in Stone: The Mosaics of Ancient Sepphoris," *BA* 50 (1987), 230–231.

60 *Ant.* XVIII, 5, 1, 109–115.

61 G.W. Bowersock, *Roman Arabia* (Cambridge, MA, 1983), 64–65.

62 Galen, for example (11, 821; 12, 216), notes that imports from India came by way of Palestine to Phoenicia. See E. H. Warmington, *The Commerce between the Roman Empire and India* (Cambridge, 1928), 356, n. 124.

63 E.g., Luke 6:24–26; Matt. 19:23 (= Mark 10:23 = Luke 18:24); Luke 16:19–31.

the trades would also have been affected. One must, of course, be wary of economic determinism. Increased hostility toward those in power would have involved other factors including famine,[64] ideological considerations, status struggle, and political events on both a local and international level.[65]

Political and Administrative Interaction

Agriculture and Urbanization as Roman Policy

Reciprocal trade relations between village and urban area in the Galilee fit the political and economic aims of the Roman empire. Galilean society, like Roman society in general, was essentially pre-industrial. Agriculture, although not the sole economic base for the Lower Galilee or the Roman empire, was, nevertheless, a major source of income and investment possibility for those with some means; in addition, it served as a means of livelihood (and identity) for a large proportion of the populace.[66] Yet, both rural development and urban-rural cooperation became essential ingredients for peace and prosperity in the Roman empire.

For Palestine, one can discern the presence of this attitude in the Jewish text, *The Letter of Aristeas,* probably written in the late Hellenistic or early Roman period.[67] The leadership, the writer contends, must pay "continuous attention to husbandry and the care of the land" in order "to

---

[64] M. Goodman, *The Ruling Class of Judaea: The Origins of the Jewish Revolt against Rome A.D. 66–70* (Cambridge, 1987), 54.

[65] Goodman, *State and Society*, 88–89; Theissen, *Sociology of Early Palestinian Christianity*. The economic sphere probably played a role in the revolt of 66 C.E. Yet, economic hardships were not confined to peasants in the hinterland. See J. Klausner, "The Economy of Judea in the Period of the Second Temple," in: *The Herodian Period*, 191. As Applebaum, "Economic Life," 663, notes, antagonisms "cut across the urban and rural population alike, and the non-agricultural urban craftsmen and petty traders were also a politically radical factor." Cf. T. Donaldson, "Rural Bandits, City Mobs and the Zealots," *JSJ* 21 (1990), 19–40. Ideological factors and status questions include tensions between Roman, Jew, and Greek, between aristocrat and techne, priest and Pharisee, wealthy and poor, and over nationalism and messianism—however, this lies beyond the scope of this paper.

[66] Garnsey and Saller, *The Roman Empire*, 43f.; cf. D. Urman's similar observation on the Golan area in his *The Golan: A Profile of a Region during the Roman and Byzantine Periods* (*BAR* 269; London, 1985), 141ff.; for the Galilee, see Goodman, *State and Society*, 22ff.

[67] The dates for this letter range from 250 B.C.E. to the first century C.E.; see discussion by R. J. H. Shutt, "Letter of Aristeas," in: *The Old Testament Pseudepigrapha*, ed. J. H. Charlesworth (2 vols.; Garden City, 1983–85), II, 8–9. Quotations are taken from Shutt's translation.

ensure good yield as a result for the inhabitants."[68] Furthermore, in order to increase one's profits one must prohibit farmers and the leadership of the city from "engaging in business, thus diminishing the treasury, that is to say the profits of farming."[69] Cities and villages in Palestine, the author relates, are "well populated" and designed to give ample produce (including olive trees, corn, vines [wine], honey, fruit trees, dates, and numerous flocks and herds).[70] Urban centers with strong, productive agricultural areas were crucial to the organized well-functioning political system. In Roman Palmyra, for example, the tax codes indicate that villages were granted tax breaks, at least those villages within the influence of the city.[71]

Administration and the Lower Galilee

One approach used in the Roman empire to develop and maintain political, social, and economic stability was the establishment of *poleis* by local elites with attendant villages and rural areas.[72] The character of *poleis* in antiquity has been difficult to establish. As is clear from ancient sources, no clear-cut definition for *polis* or *kome* existed. Pausanias, for example, derides Panopeus for claiming status as a *polis* when the city had no government buildings, gymnasium, theater, marketplace or water descending to a fountain. What is more, he argues, its inhabitants lived in hovels on the edge of a ravine. He does grant that they shared boundaries with their neighbors, indicating that at least they had land under their control.[73] Strabo was less kind; the city of Thebes, in his opinion, did not even merit recognition as a respectable village.[74] One assumes that the residents of Thebes did not agree. Clearly, legalistic definitions had limited use in antiquity. Yet, for comparative purposes, some rubric is necessary; urban centers such as Sepphoris had a different character than nearby villages like Nazareth.

In the Greek East, the administrative and cultural apparatus reflect the distinctive character of a city or village. A city generally had a civic

68 Letter of Aristeas, 108–109.

69 Ibid., 111.

70 Ibid., 112–113.

71 J. F. Matthews, "The Tax Law of Palmyra: Evidence for Economic History in a City of the Roman East," *JRS* 74 (1984), 179.

72 Finley, *The Ancient Economy*, 124; idem, "The Ancient City: From Fustel de Coulanges to Max Weber and Beyond," in: *Economy and Society in Ancient Greece*, eds. B. D. Shaw and R. P. Saller (Harmondsworth, 1983), 2.

73 Pausanias, 10, 4, 1.

74 Strabo, *Geog.*, 9, 2, 5.

organization that often included a constitution, council, magistrates, a rural area under its control, an organized street plan and market complexes (with associated government services).[75] The cultural apparatus is reflected architecturally in the types of structures mentioned by Pausanias: theaters, hippodromes, bath complexes and "water descending to fountains." Builders in Palestine, however, did not accept the cultural legacies of Greece and Rome wholesale. In a persuasive study of first-century bath complexes, D. Small argues that late Hellenistic baths in Palestine were altered, most particularly to allow for small stepped pools, perhaps *miqva'ot*.[76] The baths reflect eastern as much as western traditions in their designs. Participation in Roman society no doubt dictated that local elites build theaters, hippodromes or bath complexes. Alterations in such institutions, however, allowed local elites to define Roman power within the context of their own symbolic world, thus giving them a modicum of control.[77]

Less is known about villages. Apparently, the Upper and Lower Galilee had villages that elected village councils and assemblies. Local magistrates probably erected public buildings and provided a modicum of civic organization (e.g., tax collection, market days).[78] The primary political relationship between village and city organizations appears to have been administrative;[79] Sepphoris and Tiberias lobbied for the right

75 Garnsey and Saller, *The Roman Empire*, 28–34.

76 D. B. Small, "Late Hellenistic Baths in Palestine," *BASOR* 266 (1987), 59–74.

77 For the Greek East's reinterpretation of Roman power in light of their symbol systems, see S. Price, *Rituals and Power: The Roman Imperial Cult in Asia Minor* (Cambridge, 1984); cf. A. N. Barghouti, "Urbanization of Palestine and Jordan in Hellenistic and Roman Times," in: *Studies in the History and Archaeology of Jordan*, ed. A. Hadidi (3 vols.; London/New York, 1982–85), I, 209–227, who argues that Gerasa employed typical Hellenistic and Roman building features but with unique additions.

78 Data for the operation of first-century villages in the Greek East are sparse. For later periods, see the excellent discussion by Goodman, *State and Society*, esp. 120ff.; cf. the analysis by G. Harper, "Village Administration in Syria," *YCS* 1 (1928), 105–168. Harper draws much of his evidence from the second through fourth centuries and must be used with caution.

79 Goodman, *State and Society*, 131–132, argues that there was little need on the part of villages to draw on urban areas for security, market facilities or coinage. This may be true for the second century but several villages and urban areas had walls or were built strategically on hills or mountainsides (e.g., Jotapata and Gamla in the Golan), suggesting that security remained a concern.

to maintain legal records,[80] collect taxes,[81] and provide a judicial system.[82] The exact nature of the village's participation remains clouded; it
also remains unclear to what extent the *poleis* Tiberias and Sepphoris
controlled the areas around them in the first century.[83] Nevertheless, as
Garnsey and Saller argue, the fact that village and urban organizations
existed reflects the empire's goal "to build up a structure of centres of local government that could render practical services to the imperial
power."[84] Both village and city helped sustain a peaceful, civilized environment.[85]

Cultural Interaction

Economic and administrative structures do not convey fully the values, aspirations, and beliefs of a people, although they do imply a good
deal about the economic, political, and social networks in which village
and urban dwellers in the Galilee were willing to participate. The cultural framework, however, is potentially the most valuable aspect of
urban-rural relations. How much did the villages participate in the elite-
laden culture of urban areas operative in the Lower Galilee and its envi-
rons during the early empire? Clearly, the Galilee in the first two centuries of this era was no "Semitic enclave surrounded by Hellenism," as
M. Goodman has phrased it. He rightly argues that one must determine
the correct "cultural mixture" when discussing the interaction of Greek
and Semitic influences.[86]

---

[80] See discussion by S. S. Miller, *Studies in the History and Traditions of Sepphoris* (Leiden, 1984), 14–45; Goodman, *State and Society*, 119–154.

[81] Tax collection was a major function of cities (Garnsey and Saller, *The Roman Empire*, 57; Goodman, *State and Society*, 131). Goodman overstates the case when he argues that the villages and rural areas did not look to the urban areas to market their goods. As we have shown, ceramic evidence indicates vital economic connections be-tween urban and rural areas. Cf. the discussion by Freyne, *Galilee from Alexander the Great to Hadrian*, 183ff.

[82] Goodman, *State and Society*, 119ff.

[83] Ibid., 130. Goodman suggests that the *poleis* had no major influence in the Lower Galilee and that no culture gap existed between the cities and the countryside.

[84] Garnsey and Saller, *The Roman Empire*, 32.

[85] Strabo, for one, did not view city and rural areas as separate and unequal enter-prises. Europe, for example, "is diversified with plains and mountains, so that throughout its entire extent the agricultural and civilized elements dwell side by side with the war-like element" (*Geog.* 2, 5, 26 in: *LCL*, ed. H. Jones [Cambridge, MA, 1949]).

[86] Goodman, *State and Society*, 65–66.

As many have shown, Greek language and Hellenistic architecture occur throughout first-century Palestine.[87] Even at geographically isolated villages of the Upper Galilee one finds Greek ostraca (Gush Ḥalav and Meiron), as well as a public announcement in Greek (Qatzion).[88] Up to now, however, the linguistic and architectural evidence in the Upper Galilee seems to lean away from a strongly Hellenized environment although the lack of clear first-century horizons precludes any certainty in the matter. It is interesting, though, that the early Roman site in the north, Tel Anafa, shows strong Hellenistic influence into the first century C.E.[89]

Areas surrounding the Galilee proper provide clues to the degree and nature of Hellenization in the region. The territory of Scythopolis-Beth Shean, for example, a city of the Decapolis that borders the Lower

[87] For example, ossuaries of the so-called "Goliath" family, a clan buried in Jericho between the mid-first century B.C.E. and 68 C.E., contain a number of Greek (and Aramaic) inscriptions; R. Hachlili, "A Jerusalem Family in Jericho," *BASOR* 230 (1978), 45–56; idem, "The Goliath Family in Jericho: Funerary Inscriptions from a First Century A.D. Jewish Monumental Tomb," *BASOR* 235 (1979), 31–66. The excavator concludes that the inscriptions indicate the prevalence of Greek in the Second Temple period, although she may overstate her evidence in claiming that "Greek was more common than Aramaic at this time" (ibid., 62). Hachlili is certainly correct that the large number of inscriptions indicates a family that was "literate, bilingual and prominent" (ibid.). This may say more about the education of a certain class (in this case, a family that may have been connected with the priesthood and with the royal family) and may, as argued by L. Rahmani, "Some Remarks on R. Hachlili's and A. Killebrew's 'Jewish Funerary Customs'," *PEQ* 118 (1986), 98, present a unique circumstance that does not warrant such general conclusions. Nevertheless, the evidence clearly shows the inroads that Greek culture made among the more prominent members of Jewish society. Furthermore, the presence of a Greek abecedary possibly used for magical purposes, leather sandals placed with the dead, and coins found in two skulls suggests to Hachlili and Killebrew that surrounding cultures (in particular, Greek culture) may have influenced Jewish burial practices in the Second Temple period; see R. Hachlili and A. Killebrew, "Jewish Funerary Customs during the Second Temple Period in the Light of the Excavation at the Jericho Necropolis," *PEQ* 115 (1983), 109–132, and R. Hachlili, "A Jewish Funerary Wall-Painting of the First Century A.D.," *PEQ* 117 (1985), 112–127; cf. a similar but later example of an abecedary found at Beth She'arim and published in: M. Schwabe and B. Lifshitz, *Beth She'arim, II: The Greek Inscriptions* (Jerusalem, 1974), 46–47. The first-century Greek and Aramaic inscriptions found at Masada are witness to the multilingual character of the populace in this period. See H. Cotton and J. Geiger, *Masada, II: The Latin and Greek Documents* (Jerusalem, 1989).

[88] See discussion by Meyers, "Galilean Regionalism: A Reappraisal," 115–131.

[89] A. Berlin, "The Hellenistic and Early Roman Common-Ware Pottery from Tel Anafa" (doctoral dissertation, University of Michigan; Ann Arbor, 1988), 21–24.

Galilee to the south, had a Jewish population significantly influenced by the Greek language. At least four first-century Jewish ossuaries from Scythopolis containing bilingual inscriptions in Hebrew and Greek have been discovered near Jerusalem. Yet, thirty ossuaries of Scythopolitan Jews found in a cemetery north of Scythopolis[90] contain only Greek inscriptions. The evidence at hand suggests that the Hebrew inscriptions in Jerusalem were religiously motivated.[91] M. Avi-Yonah has argued that most Jews in Scythopolis were peasants living in the *chora* of the city;[92] G. Fuks disagrees and contends that most lived in the cities with the legal status of "co-dwellers."[93] In either case, the ossuaries are an indication of Jews near the Galilee who lived in a world of various allegiances; they identified themselves as Jews, as Greek speakers, and as connected to the city proper. The latter bond must have been strong, as indicated by Josephus' description of the Jews of Scythopolis battling Galilean Jews during the First Revolt.[94]

Linguistically, Greco-Roman culture made inroads into the lower strata of society in first-century Palestine,[95] and it seems clear that some Jewish families "were literate and bilingual in Aramaic or Hebrew, and Greek."[96] E. M. Meyers and J. F. Strange argue that Greek was pervasive in the Lower Galilee, especially around the Sea of Galilee.[97] A recent ex-

[90] G. Fuks, "The Jews of Hellenistic and Roman Scythopolis," *JJS* 33 (1982) (*Essays in Honour of Yigael Yadin*, eds. G. Vermes and J. Neusner), 409 and n. 14.

[91] Ibid., 409–410; cf. the use of Hebrew for religious purposes at Masada, in: Y. Yadin and J. Naveh, *Masada*, I: *The Aramaic and Hebrew Ostraca and Jar Inscriptions* (Jerusalem, 1989), 8–9.

[92] M. Avi-Yonah, "Scythopolis," *IEJ* 12 (1962), 131.

[93] Fuks, "The Jews of Scythopolis," 410, n. 18.

[94] *War* II, 18, 3, 466–468.

[95] N. Avigad discusses unadorned ossuaries found in a small cave which show signs of extensive use; nine of the eleven ossuaries were inscribed, eight in Greek, one bilingual, and one in Hebrew; N. Avigad, "A Depository of Inscribed Ossuaries in the Kidron Valley," *IEJ* 12 (1962), 1–12; for a discussion of ossuaries around Jerusalem, see J. F. Strange, "Late Hellenistic and Herodian Ossuary Tombs at French Hill, Jerusalem," *BASOR* 219 (1975), 39–70. Note also the personal letter written in Greek which was found among those who participated in the revolt at Masada; see G. Mussies, "Greek in Palestine and the Diaspora," in: *The Jewish People in the First Century*, II, 1045, 1058. The letter was written to one of the last survivors of the revolt against the Romans and concerned such "an ordinary affair as the supply of vegetables"; see also Y. Yadin, "The Excavation of Masada—1963/64, Preliminary Report," *IEJ* 15 (1965), 110.

[96] R. Hachlili, *Ancient Jewish Art and Archaeology in the Land of Israel* (Leiden, 1988), 99.

[97] Meyers, "Galilean Regionalism as a Factor in Historical Reconstruction," 97.

ample is the lead weight from the reign of Herod Antipas bearing the Greek inscription, "Gaius Julius, *agoranomos* from Tiberias."[98] Additional evidence, though late, comes from the plethora of Greek inscriptions found at Beth Sheʿarim in the Lower Galilee, most of which date from the second through the fourth centuries. The persons who had the inscriptions written included "rabbis, public officers, merchants, craftsmen, and scribes."[99] The inscriptions have led at least one commentator to conclude that the Greek language was as common among Jewish communities in the Galilee and in Beth Sheʿarim as it was among Diaspora Jewry of that period. Indeed, a wide range of people, not just the upper class and not just those in the coastal areas, was influenced by Greek language and culture.[100]

It appears that the Lower Galilee displayed a "Hellenized linguistic and artistic vocabulary."[101] However, was there significant cultural antagonism in the Lower Galilee between largely conservative, Aramaic-speaking rural areas and Hellenistically-oriented urban areas? The evidence suggests that the answer is "no." Goodman challenges Applebaum's unsupported conclusion that such cultural antagonism existed.[102] Hostility directed at Tiberias and Sepphoris during the Jewish Revolt, for example, resulted from political disputes, not a "cultural split." Indeed, there exists "a cultural continuum from city to country."[103]

Did the Galilean urban environment accept Greco-Roman culture wholesale? The answer again must be "no." Roman control permeated the Lower Galilee, as it did much of the rest of the Greek East. But the Galilee, like the Greek East, did not accept Roman control unaltered; the people interpreted it through their own particular traditions, thus allowing themselves a modicum of control. As Goodman persuasively argues, local elite classes in Palestine (and one assumes the Galilee as well) had much to gain by maintaining close cultural, economic, and political ties

---

98 S. Qedar, "Two Lead Weights," 29–35.

99 Hachlili, *Ancient Jewish Art*, 103.

100 Schwabe and Lifshitz, *Beth Sheʿarim*, II, 217–222. Such material, of course, must be used judiciously since the bulk of it dates later than the first century. Nevertheless, it indicates the inroads Greek culture had made in an area that gave rise to the Mishnah.

101 Meyers, Strange, and Groh, "Meiron Excavation Project, 1976," 20; cf. Goodman, *State and Society*, 88.

102 S. Applebaum, "Judaea as a Roman Province: The Countryside as a Political and Economic Factor," *ANRW* II.8, eds. W. Haase and H. Temporini (Berlin/New York, 1977), 371; Goodman, *State and Society*, 89, 231, n. 406.

103 Ibid., 88.

with Rome. Nevertheless, as he shows, even members of this class were willing to alter or redefine that relationship when political, economic or religious reasons made it expedient.[104]

Conclusion

For the most part, the canonical gospels place the Jesus movement in village contexts. This paper has indicated, however, that it would be a mistake to assume that the movement operated in cultural, political or economic isolation from major urban areas. Villages mentioned in the tradition were near (Capernaum, Bethsaida) or connected to (Nazareth, Caesarea Philippi, region of Tyre and Sidon) urban areas and linked to a vibrant regional market network. Nor does an innate rural hostility toward urban areas appear to have existed in the movement. Indeed, the audience could have been and probably was urban- as well as village-centered. As an agrarian economy dominated Roman society, agricultural images neither prove nor disprove a rural audience. This need not imply that members of the movement adopted or reflected values of the urban elite or that antagonism toward gentiles did not exist. Communities or groups that are culturally distinct may nevertheless buy pottery from the same potters.[105] Indeed, Jesus' abrupt remark to the Syro-Phoenician woman comparing gentiles with dogs[106] expresses vividly the tension that could exist among differing ideological frameworks. Nevertheless, marketplace images in Mark and Q suggest that the Jesus movement was part of an itinerant stream which took advantage of a market network linking village and city as well as Jewish and gentile settlements. The economic network provided a vehicle for expansion of the Jesus movement and contact with a non-Jewish population.

Furthermore, judicial imagery, financial analogies that envision interest-bearing accounts,[107] and the portrait of an absentee landlord (city-dweller or connected to an urban environment) who figures in the parable as representing God[108] reflect an awareness of the economic and administrative structure that governed rural and urban areas alike. The movement was not separate from but part of an economic, political, and cultural network that organized the lives of those in the Roman empire.

104 Goodman, *The Ruling Class of Judaea*.
105 G. Gibbon, *Anthropological Archaeology* (New York, 1984), 223.
106 Mark 7:26–30.
107 Matt. 25:27; Luke 19:23.
108 Mark 12:1–12.

Yet, why does the movement in its early stages appear to have avoided urban centers? This may reflect the movement's awareness that political authorities centered in the cities desired to maintain the status quo and would not favor a renewal movement that talked about new kingdoms and the immoral rich; indeed, John the Baptist, according to Josephus, died because of his threat to the public order.[109] Although conflict did take place between the Jesus movement and the next rank of authorities, retainers of the local elites and Herod Antipas,[110] the movement no doubt by-passed major urban areas such as Sepphoris and Tiberias to avoid direct confrontation with Herodian power.[111] Nevertheless, the movement took full advantage of the socio-economic and cultural networks operative in the Galilee to spread its message of renewal. It should come as no surprise, then, that Peter, once described by E. Renan as part of a happy band of Jesus followers, free from the "busy civilization"[112] of the Greco-Roman world, had few qualms about sitting with gentiles in Antioch, one of the largest cities of the Roman empire, a few years after the death of Jesus.[113] He was not in unfamiliar territory.

[109] *Ant.* XVIII, 5, 2, 116–119.
[110] J. Overman, "Who Were the First Urban Christians? Urbanization in Galilee in the First Century," in: *SBL Seminar Papers*, ed. D. J. Lull (Atlanta, 1988), 167–168.
[111] Freyne, *Galilee, Jesus and the Gospels*, 140.
[112] E. Renan, *A Life of Jesus* (New York, 1927), 184–193.
[113] Gal. 2:12.

Urban-Rural Relations in First-Century Galilee: Some Suggestions from the Literary Sources

SEAN FREYNE

Our efforts to understand the culture of the Galilee in late antiquity are considerably enhanced by the fact that two major world religions originated in this region. The literature that these religions generated in their formative periods reflects *in some way* the world of their origins, and thus the history and culture of the Galilee are, relatively speaking, much more open to recovery than those of almost any other region in antiquity. I say that the Galilee is reflected *in some way* in the literature of early Christianity and formative Judaism since the ways in which these corpora of literature can be used as documentary evidence for life in the Galilee of late antiquity is one of the most hotly debated issues in modern critical studies of both the gospels and rabbinic writings. The fact that so many methodological questions arise in regard to the literary sources should not, however, blind us to the fact that it is not just these sources but also the material remains that require critical interpretation and evaluation. The contrast between hard archeological facts and biased literary sources is as hermeneutically naive as is the opposite point of view, which uses material remains to validate the Bible or Talmud. Each of us begins from the point at which we are most comfortable in terms of our particular expertise, but we should also include a hermeneutic of suspicion regarding the so-called objective character of the literary and material sources, coupled with a critical awareness of our cultural, academic, and social presuppositions through which the understanding of the past is filtered.

These reflections may help to explain why I propose to draw on an "outside" discipline to provide both a heuristic model and a set of critical criteria for evaluating the evidence for the impact of the Hellenistic urban environment on Galilean life in the first century C.E. A modern discipline, if sensitively employed, can provide us with the right framework and the proper set of questions for defining our tasks and articulating the problems to which we seek solutions. The proposed model embraces two different views of society, representative, broadly speaking, of functionalist and conflictual approaches. Thus, since no society is totally homogeneous, and the Galilee in the first century was not, we may hope to uncover rather different aspects of that world, representing the top and bottom levels of the social stratum.

Of the many different topics that suggest themselves as possible probe areas for examining Galilean life in the first century, I have chosen to address the cultural role of the cities, both because cities were the main agents for change in the Hellenization process and because in certain circles, in the Galilee in particular, the name *Gĕlîl ha-gôyîm* took on a new focus, because of what was perceived by the Jews as a Hellenistic threat.[1] The accuracy of this perception was borne out almost 200 years later with the anti-Jewish attitudes that surfaced in all the surrounding city territories prior to the First Revolt, most notably in the north of the country, even in such centers of long established Jewish-gentile relations as Scythopolis.

Instead of approaching the problem by attempting to define city (*polis*) and village (*kōmē*), I shall first summarize the theoretical considerations concerning the cultural role of cities. Several important distinctions are called for in this regard. Primary is that made by Redfield and Singer[2] between "the carrying forward into systematic and reflective dimensions of an old culture" (described as the "orthogenetic" role of the city) and "the creating of original modes of thought that have authority beyond or in conflict with old cultures and civilizations" (the "heterogenetic" role of the city). Each gives rise to a different ethos, characteristic type, and relation to the surrounding folk-culture. A further refinement calls for a distinction between primary and secondary urbanization. The former relates to the development of the surrounding folk-culture into a Great Tradition by the *literati*, to the virtual exclusion of

---

1　I Macc. 5:15.
2　R. Redfield and M. Singer, "The Cultural Role of Cities,"*Economic Development and Social Change* 3 (1954), 57–73.

other elements considered alien or hostile influences; in contrast, the latter occurs when an already existing culture—folk, peasant, or partly urbanized—is perforce brought into contact with wider and divergent cultures either through expansion or by invasion and/or conquest.

The following table delineates some of the more important aspects of these two types of cities and the corresponding stages of social urbanization to which they give rise. Although by no means exhaustive, it serves as a helpful framework for interpreting the scattered pieces of literary and material evidence for pre-70 Galilean life.

	Orthogenetic Cities	*Heterogenetic Cities*
1. Dominant Social Types	*Literati* who fashion the Great Tradition; scribes who create a common legal system; priests; kings; chiefs and local "Big Men"	Businessmen, bureaucrats (mostly foreigners or natives who have been deeply influenced by outside cultural forces); officials; military men; tax collectors
2. Basis for Relationship with Countryside	Common loyalty to a shared worldview; acceptance of the past and its myths, especially as recreated by the *literati*	Pragmatic, based on mutuality of interests, despite mistrust at the cultural level; attempted myth-making for the future, to cloak cultural differences
3. Economic Patterns	Inequality, cloaked as social necessity or divine arrangement	Openly exploitative, giving rise to resentment
4. Social Unity	Achieved by consensus; dissent perceived as disloyalty	Achieved by coercion; dissent perceived as rebellion

The tendentiousness of two basic sources for this investigation, Josephus' *Life* and the gospels (especially the synoptics), presents difficulties for the scholar. One must consider to what extent the apologetic purposes of Josephus in *Life,* so ably exposed by S. J. D. Cohen,[3] distort this account of internal social relations, especially since his own relations with the Herodian cities were anything but cordial. Similarly, one must monitor the degree to which later gospel writers may have introduced urban categories on what was the original rural coloring of the Jesus narrative. These considerations should be kept in mind when addressing the question of urban-rural relations in first-century Galilee as portrayed in the sources.

Dominant Social Types

At first reading, both Josephus and the gospels appear to deal in generalities. "The Galileans" is the former's constant appellation for those who rally around the main character, Josephus, whereas "the crowd" or "many" are the evangelist's usual description of those who are attracted to the wandering teacher-healer, Jesus of Nazareth. The designation "the Galileans" in Josephus' narrative offers some possibilities for social description, as we shall see, but the latter is much too general to be of any real assistance. Nevertheless, both narratives offer further insights into the character of the province on the basis of their dominant social types.

Apart from Josephus, the two main characters in *Life* are John of Gischala and Justus of Tiberias, though their prominence may be more a reflection of the apologetic nature of the work than of the actual situation. Both may be classed as products of the heterogenetic environment of the Greek cities as far as a Jewish ethos is concerned, but each for different reasons. Both were obviously Jewish in their basic upbringing. Josephus presumes that they should accept his authority in the Galilee because of his appointment by the Jerusalem Council.

John was ambitious, unscrupulous, capable of moving with the political tides, and resentful of those whom he perceived to have bested him, such as Josephus. He may have had some official status in the Roman administration of the Upper Galilee, but his power-base was his entrepreneurial skill that made it possible for him to exploit his native village of Gischala as a hinterland supply center (of oil and grain) for such Hellenistic-Roman cities as Tyre, Sidon, and Caesarea Philippi, despite current Jewish-gentile hostilities.[4] However, the countrypeople of Gis-

---

3 S. J. D. Cohen, *Josephus in Galilee and Rome* (Leiden, 1979), 101–170.

4 *Life* 10, 44; cf. *War* II, 18, 1, 457f. See the studies of U. Rappaport, "John of Gischala: From Galilee to Jerusalem," *JJS* 33 (1982), 479–490, and "John of Gischala in

chala were less than enthusiastic about his show of zealotry and more interested in agricultural matters.[5] His contacts with the powerful Simeon b. Gamaliel in Jerusalem proved in the end to have been his undoing, since he was bitterly disappointed at having been passed over as governor of the Galilee by the Jerusalem Council.

Justus, on the other hand, had a thorough Greek education and had come up through the Herodian bureaucracy.[6] He, too, was an urban type who found a common link with John;[7] like his counterpart in the Upper Galilee, he led attacks on the Greek cities of the Decapolis although not openly advocating war with Rome.[8] His history of Jewish kings from Moses to Agrippa II was clearly an attempt, like that of Josephus, to produce an apologetic account of his people's history in the medium and genre of the Hellenized world in which he had been educated. Like John, he, too, was from the wealthy upper class; Josephus tried to dissociate him from the other Tiberians who owned estates in the countryside.[9] The countrypeople designated as "the Galileans" were no more trusting of Justus than they were of John.[10]

Both of these characters represented the type of Jew who was a product of the Hellenistic environment and who was used by Rome to help control this fractious people; both came from the fringes of Galilean life, Gischala being close to the borders of the Phoenician cities, and Tiberias, Herod's new city, with its mixed population.

Josephus' account mentions a number of other social types—Philip son of Jacimus, Ptolemy, Aebutius, Neapolitanus, and Modius[11]—all of whom were Agrippa's officers operating either in the king's territory or on the borders, such as on the Great Plain. The attack by villagers of Dabaritta on Ptolemy's wife, as she travelled with pomp across the Great Plain protected by an escort of cavalry, may be understood as symptomatic of local resentment of these types. Their ostentatious wealth and other trappings of power made them constant targets of brigandage, which seems to have been a common occurrence. The brigands were not

---

Galilee," in: *The Jerusalem Cathedra*, ed. L. I. Levine (3 vols.; Jerusalem, 1981-83), III, 46–57.

5 *War* IV, 2, 1, 84.

6 *Life* 9, 40; for a recent study, see A. Barzano, "Giusto di Tiberiade," in: *ANRW*, II, 20.1, eds. W. Haase and H. Temporini (Berlin/New York, 1986), 337–358.

7 *Life* 17, 88.

8 *Life* 9, 42; 10, 45.

9 *Life* 9, 32–37; cf. 12, 65.

10 *Life* 35, 176; cf. 70, 390–392.

11 *Life* 11, 46; 26, 126; 24, 115, 120; 11, 61, respectively.

a unified social movement; they were partly the result of the emergence of soldiering as a profession in the Hellenistic period and partly the outcome of the particular socio-political circumstances. In the former category we can include leaders of organized armies such as Jesus of Galilee, who operated on the borders of Ptolemais and was hired by the Sepphorians to protect them from Josephus.[12] Later we find him in Jerusalem employed by the authorities to accompany the delegation they were sending to oust Josephus.[13] Josephus, for his part, had also availed himself of the services of other brigands in his efforts to assemble an army and employed them as mercenaries.[14]

From these differing profiles we can capture something of the Hellenistic ethos of the Galilee under Roman and Herodian rule. The first two represent the second phase of the urbanization process—native Jews who, at one level, shared the folk-culture but who, for one reason or another, had availed themselves of the commercial, educational, and professional opportunities of the times. This stance left them in an ambivalent position at a period of internal crisis such as that covered by *Life*: they were to some extent aliens in their own culture, as is evident in the attitude which the Galileans "from the country" adopted towards them.[15] The brigands-mercenaries were no befrienders of the powerless in view of their undiscriminating tactics;[16] neither John nor Justus was able to muster sufficient support to oust their arch-rival Josephus, who seems to have intentionally cultivated the countrypeople on the basis of his Jerusalem and priestly connections. It is in the villages, not in the cities, that we find him constantly billeted: in Bethmaus, Cana, Simonias, Chabulon, Japhia, Asochis, Gabaroth, and Garis.[17] Only Tarichaeae seems to have broken that pattern, but this city had a much more clearly defined Jewish ethos than Tiberias, as it also served as a refugee center for the countrypeople. The unpopularity of Justus must have been directly related to the hostility of Galileans towards his native place, which was regarded as alien and unfriendly to deep-seated Jewish sensibilities from the outset,[18] and it is no surprise to find Galileans, i.e., "countrypeople"

---

12 *Life* 22, 104–111.

13 *Life* 40, 200.

14 *Life* 14, 77f.; cf. 35, 175; 41, 206.

15 For details, see S. Freyne, "The Galileans in the Light of Josephus' *Vita*," *NTS* 26 (1980), 397–413.

16 *Life* 14, 77; 41, 206.

17 *Life* 12, 64; 16, 86; 24, 115; 43, 213; 45, 230, 233; 47, 242; 71, 395, respectively.

18 *Ant.* XVIII, 2, 3, 38.

in Josephus' terminology, involved in the destruction of Herod's palace there.[19] Gischala never generated quite the same opposition, since it was isolated from the more densely populated areas of the Lower Galilee. John was clearly not trusted even by the inhabitants of his own town; Gabara, one of the three major cities that had sided with him, according to Josephus, was extremely cautious because of the animosity of the Galilean countrypeople.[20]

On the basis of this particular criterion from our model of dominant social types, urbanization of the heterogenetic type had by no means "taken over" in terms of the cultural affiliations of the people of the Galilee. Josephus and his colleagues were Jerusalemites who apparently claimed the tithes on the basis of their priestly status.[21] Likewise, the composition of the delegation sent to oust Josephus had a decidedly religious status, implying that only those who publicly adhered to the Jewish way of life could have been expected to have had any influence among the countrypeople.[22] Nor are "the Galileans" to be regarded as unskilled or unlettered "down and outs." Repeatedly we hear of the Galileans assembling with their women and children, expressing ties of kinship with a strongly Jewish and rural value system; they provisioned themselves and served as temporary militia to support Josephus. They may be compared to the hoplites, landed peasantry of Greek society on whom the city depended and around whom landowning policy developed, who could afford the arms necessary for infantry engagements.[23] The Babylonian Jews from Batanea mentioned in *Life* give us insight into earlier Herodian policy in this regard: they had well-stocked villages and could be relied upon to support central authority while maintaining their deep religious convictions.[24]

Thus, insofar as any urban center dominated the cultural life of the Galilee, it would seem that it was Jerusalem, not the Hellenistic cities, that had the controlling influence over the majority of the population. The gospels confirm this picture. On the one hand, "tax-collectors" are identified as "sinners," i.e., unacceptable outsiders, but in socio-economic terms they represent the heterogenetic influence on the city. On the other

[19] *Life* 12, 66.
[20] *Life* 25, 123 and 125.
[21] *Life* 14, 77.
[22] *Life* 39, 197.
[23] T. F. Carney, *The Shape of the Past, Models and Antiquity* (Lawrence, Kansas, 1975), 236–242.
[24] *Life* 11, 58; cf. *Ant.* XVII, 1, 2, 26–31.

hand, the *literati* (scribes) of the Great Tradition came from Jerusalem in order to ensure that no deviant trends predominate.[25] The concern for orthodoxy among the scribes was not always appreciated in its finer points by the peasants, the primary bearers of the folk-tradition who could combine such deviance as sorcery and magic with a more "enlightened" religious belief[26] without necessarily seeing any contradiction between the two. With the exception of Luke,[27] the Herodian court and its ethos imposed itself only minimally on the gospel narratives; the Herodians were opponents of the Jesus movement in all the accounts.[28] While the precise identity of the Herodians is debatable, the part they played points to genuine social divisions in the Galilee between centers of power and affluence on the one hand and a populist religious movement on the other.[29] Both Mark and Josephus mention the *hoi prōtoi tēs Galilaias*, but Mark locates them at the Herodian court on the occasion of Herod's birthday, together with the military men (*chiliarchoi*), government officials (*spekulatōr*), and "the great ones" (*megistanes*).[30] The precise distinction between the *hoi prōtoi* and the *megistanes* is unclear, but the evangelist differentiates between them by his use of the definite article before each. In *Life* the latter term refers to the non-Jewish noblemen closely associated with the king who came from Trachonitis as refugees,[31] whereas the former were Jewish leaders, "aristocratie du pays." This would seem to fit Mark's usage. Given Herodian pressure on the native Galileans to inhabit Tiberias,[32] the presence of "the leading men of Galilee" at the king's birthday need not conflict with their social role in *Life*, where they appear supportive of Josephus' position in the region.

---

25 Mark 3:22; 7:1. The episode concerning Yoḥanan b. Zakkai's stay at Arav (J Shabbat 16, 8, 15d) may be legendary, as J. Neusner, *A Life of Rabban Yohanan ben Zakkai, ca. 1–80 C.E.* (Leiden, 1962), 27–28, has ably argued, yet it should be seen as typical of the concern of Jerusalem scribes for the Galilee generally.

26 *Life* 31, 149.

27 Luke 8:1–3; 13:33.

28 Mark 3:6; 12:13.

29 H. Hoehner, *Herod Antipas, A Contemporary of Jesus Christ* (*SNTS Monographs* 7; Cambridge, 1972), 331–342.

30 Mark 6:21, 27.

31 *Life* 23, 112; 31, 149.

32 *Ant.* XVIII, 2, 3, 35–38.

Basis for Relationships between City and Countryside

We shall attempt first to sketch briefly the overall picture. Both Josephus and Mark clearly distinguish between city and country and describe the links between the two. The evangelist describes Jesus' visits to the borders of Tyre, the villages of Caesarea Philippi, and the territory of Gadara,[33] but not to any of the actual cities. One suspects a hint at two very different environments, at least as far as the rural-based prophet and his followers were concerned (but who, incidentally, like others of his ilk such as Jesus ben Hananiah, did not hesitate to go to Jerusalem and proclaim his message there).[34] Josephus helps us to fill out this picture. All ancient cities had their own territories, which were comprised of a network of villages where those who worked the land, either as crop sharers, free landowners or tenants of absentee landlords lived, while the landowning aristocracy, like Crispus of Tiberias,[35] were often city dwellers.

It is certain that such a situation existed in the Galilee. Sepphoris, according to Josephus, could have withstood a Roman siege because it was "surrounded by numerous villages."[36] Similarly, Tiberias and Tarichaeae had their own *chōra* or territory,[37] and the same was true for such surrounding cities as Scythopolis, Hippos, Gadara, and Gamla.[38]

To suggest that the relationship between the Galilean *ek tēs chōras*[39] and these cities was uniformly hostile is a generalization and ignores particular circumstances operative in individual instances. The hostility toward Sepphoris, for example, was based on its alleged pro-Roman stance, whereas the attitude toward Tiberias may have been partly due to the social division resulting from the comparative opulence of the Herodian court[40] and partly the result of the constraints on Galileans to join this new city against their will.[41] Yet, when all this is taken into account, there can be no doubt that the rural animosities toward the cities were deep-seated and permanent. Galilean hatred of Sepphoris, Tiberias, and

---

33 Mark 7:24, 31; 8:27; 5:1.

34 *War* VI, 5, 3, 300–309. For a discussion of this and other aspects of Jesus' career in the Galilee, see my recent study, *Galilee, Jesus and the Gospels* (Philadelphia, 1988).

35 *Life* 9, 33.

36 *Life* 65, 346; cf. *War* I, 16, 1, 304.

37 *War* II, 13, 2, 252f.; *Life* 32, 155.

38 *War* III, 3, 1, 37; *Life* 9, 42; 11, 58, respectively.

39 E.g., *Life* 21, 102; 47, 242–244.

40 E.g., *Life* 12, 66.

41 *Ant.* XVIII, 2, 1, 27.

Gabara, the three cities of the Galilee, according to Josephus, is a distinct theme in *Life*.

It may be argued that this is simply part of the apologetic rhetoric of the document or that the immediate pre-war period was exceptional. Yet a perusal of the Jesus tradition, with its strongly rural coloring, especially in the parables, points to a similar pattern of relationships. In Jesus' praise of the rustic John the Baptist we can imagine the chasm that existed in social and cultural terms between the two environments: "What did you go out into the desert to see? . . . A man clothed in fine linen? Behold, those who are dressed in fine linen are in the houses of kings."[42] In a saying such as this we capture something of the social and cultural differences between city and country as perceived from a rural perspective.

There is little in this emerging picture that is surprising in the light of urban-rural relations generally in antiquity. What specifically concerns us, however, is whether and to what extent heterogenetic factors as suggested by our model could explain the tensions in the Galilee. Aside from the Greek cities, whose ethos was deemed hostile despite the presence of Jewish minorities in Scythopolis, Caesarea, and other places, the Herodian centers boasted many of the trappings of the Greek way of life, such as the stadium at Tiberias, the hippodrome at Tarichaeae, and the theater at Sepphoris, that were unacceptable in theory in conservative Jewish circles. Yet, this statement calls for qualification since these places were by no means monochromic in their cultural affiliations. Tarichaeae was the place where xenophobic tendencies surfaced, yet it had a hippodrome; the Jewish fire-brand, Jesus son of Sapphias, became the leader of the city council of Tiberias for a while, despite its Herodian ethos; in Sepphoris animosity was caused by the city's failure to support the national struggle, when the opposite should have been the case here.

We cannot simply assume, therefore, that Galilean hostility to these places was due to the fact that they were centers of Greek culture. Jews had learned to accommodate themselves to such an environment while retaining their distinct identity, even in the Galilee, as the examples of Scythopolis and Caesarea indicate. The opposition, even hostility, must have had another basis and motivation; the evidence of the texts we are examining suggests that it was due to a considerable extent to the orthogenetic role of Jerusalem vis-à-vis Jewish culture in the Galilee. The prophetic lament for Jerusalem by the Jesus movement, stemming from

---

[42] Matt. 11:8; cf. Mark 1:6.

the Q source and therefore dating to pre-70, suggests an emotional attachment to the holy city.[43] According to all accounts of the trial, a charge made before the high priests that Jesus was about to destroy the Jerusalem Temple was instrumental in the rejection of Jesus by the pilgrimage crowd.[44] Equally, Josephus could chide Sepphoris for not supporting "the Temple that is common to us all,"[45] and the suggestion that using the booty which the highwaymen of Dabaritta had confiscated to repair the walls of Jerusalem could exonerate him of the charge of treachery.[46] The Galileans honored the priestly status of Josephus and his colleagues with the tithes that they claimed,[47] and the delegation sent to unseat Josephus was unsuccessful in the villages of the Galilee despite its priestly and Pharisaic composition.[48]

While Galilean peasant loyalties appear to have been firmly anchored in Jerusalem, the *literati*, or scribes, attempted to mould that loyalty along particular lines. They attributed the healing powers of the rural prophet, Jesus, to Beelzebub, the prince of demons, in an obvious attempt to denigrate any alternative myth among the ordinary populace. While this attempt appears to have had little impact in the Galilee, the charge about destroying the Temple had much more serious consequences and succeeded in removing the crowd's support in Jerusalem.

Our evidence shows that two rather different forces were exerted on the village people of the Galilee throughout the first century. The fact that many of the villages were economically controlled by the Herodian cities of the Lower Galilee did not in any way destroy the much older and deeper loyalties to Jerusalem and its cult center. Regardless of the amount of shared material culture that archeology has uncovered, there is little evidence of any alternative myth emanating from the Greek cities that might have successfully competed for the loyalties of the villagers. Architectural styles, artifacts, and even language patterns are not the ultimate indicators of cultural affinity, as attested by Cestius Gallus' burning of the Jewish village of Chabulon—despite his admiration for its houses built in the Phoenician style.[49]

---

43 Luke 13:34f.; Matt. 23:37.
44 Mark 14:58.
45 *Life* 65, 348f.
46 *Life* 26, 128.
47 *Life* 12, 63; 15, 81.
48 *Life* 45, 232. See S. Freyne, "Galilee-Jerusalem Relations according to Josephus' *Life*," *NTS* 33 (1987), 600–609.
49 *War* II, 18, 9, 502.

Economic Patterns

Cities were obviously the centers of wealth in the ancient world, in terms of both wealth-generating and wealth-amassing activities. According to Josephus, the dispute between Sepphoris and Tiberias was over the fact that the former city contained the royal bank (*trapeza*) and archives (*archeia*). Both institutions were part of the redistributive exchange system which indicated a thriving market situation, with moneylending and the storing of coinage at the discretion of the wealthy. Little wonder that Sepphoris was reluctant to break with Rome![50]

It is interesting to note that in several instances reported by Josephus where rural opposition to the cities erupted, wealth, in one form or another, was directly involved. The Galileans decided to pillage Sepphoris, allegedly because of its pro-Roman stance, but in fact because of its wealth.[51] The destruction of Herod's palace at Tiberias by some Galileans, together with the city's destitute classes, raised expectations of gaining considerable booty. Among the items that Josephus claims to have recovered were a large supply of coin blanks and some palace furnishings.[52] Similarly, the affair of the highwaymen of Dabaritta revealed rural resentment of ruling class opulence: four mules laden with apparel and other goods as well as a large supply of silver and 500 pieces of gold.[53] In addition to these references to the wealth of the Herodian cities, we hear of the imperial granaries of the Upper Galilee coveted by John which served to increase his wealth. Heretofore he had amassed a fortune by the inflation of oil prices in the region. This, too, led to resentment of Gischala by the countrypeople.[54] Also Josephus sequestered for himself corn from the royal estates of the Lower Galilee.[55]

On the basis of this evidence, wealth was in the hands of the urban-based elites and gave rise to resentment, despite the fact that the Galileans who supported Josephus were apparently not poor, as attested by the fact that they armed themselves and provided for the army's needs.[56] We hear of a destitute class only in Tiberias.[57] However, in sharp contrast with this resentment of Herodian wealth among the Galileans is

---

[50] Carney, *The Shape of the Past*, 147–149.
[51] *Life* 8, 30.
[52] *Life* 13, 66–68.
[53] *Life* 26, 128.
[54] *Life* 13, 71; 13, 75; 21, 103f.
[55] *Life* 24, 118f.
[56] *Life* 43, 210; 47, 242–244.
[57] *Life* 13, 76.

their apparent willingness to pay the tithes to Josephus and his colleagues. While we are undoubtedly dealing with one of Josephus' apologetic motifs in *Life*, wherein he refuses to accept the tithes even though due him, the fact that the tithes are mentioned and assumed to be owed indicates that in his relationship with the Galilee he regarded himself as a Jerusalem priest.[58] Thus, we encounter rather different attitudes towards social inequality arising from the distribution of wealth. On the one hand there is a genuine resentment of the inequality represented by Herodian opulence, whereas there is no hostility concerning the payment of religious dues connected with the Jerusalem Temple. Once again, the orthogenetic and heterogenetic dimensions of the different cities stand out clearly.

The Jesus movement adopted a rather different strategy regarding social inequality. The situation presumed by many of the sayings is not one of penury, but rather of possessions and greed. Advice such as "Lay not up for yourselves treasures on earth where moths and worms destroy and thieves break through and steal"[59] presupposes a situation that is not dissimilar to that which befell the Herodian lady at the hands of the brigands of Dabaritta. Injunctions to the disciples not to be concerned about money or possessions as they travel from town to town[60] proposes a totally different value system with regard to wealth than that discussed above. It is not a question of giving up a tithe for religious dues, but rather forfeiting all that one has. True, the question of debt looms very large on the horizon, and sayings about violence, reconciliation with neighbors, etc. reflect a world in which the harsh realities of life cause much injustice at a local level. Jesus calls for a transformation of human relations not on a global or even national scale at first, but within the village life of the Galilee.[61]

The gospel evidence confirms the picture drawn by *Life* and offers a more radical solution to the problem. The wealth-distributing mechanisms of Jewish law, such as the poor man's tithe, did not ultimately challenge the inequalities that Herodian-Roman rule perpetuated through lifestyle, apparel or buildings; the value system of the Jesus movement, had it been adopted, would have proposed an ideal in the name of the God of Israel that was the antithesis of prevailing norms, in

---

58   *Life* 12, 63; 15, 81.
59   Matt. 6:19.
60   Mark 6:8–10 and parallels.
61   See R. Horsley, "Ethics and Exegesis: 'Love Your Enemies' and the Doctrine of Non-Violence," *JAAR* 54 (1985), 3–31.

religious as well as social terms. From this perspective, both Herodian and Jerusalem values were under attack and both were regarded as distorting and alienating.

Recently it has been suggested that this worldview was Cynic-inspired and that it reflected the "urbanized" situation of all the Lower Galilee.[62] In terms of our model, heterogenetic cities supposedly provided new mythic patterns that were forward-looking and alternative; undoubtedly the Cynic movement was an urban phenomenon that is attested for nearby Gadara and Tyre. On closer examination, however, there are distinct differences between the Jesus sayings and typical Cynic instructions, particularly in the matter of purse, staff, and begging. Indeed, as Horsley points out, the Pauline letters reflect Cynic attitudes much more obviously than does the Jesus tradition.[63] It would be a mistake, though, both methodologically and factually, to transpose later Pauline, urban Christianity back onto the Palestinian Jesus movement and thereby infer an urbanized Galilee, despite similarities in external form with other counter-cultural movements. The inspiration of the Jesus movement was scriptural and rooted in the Israelite tradition, as indicated by the selection of the core group of the Twelve, symbolizing the league of the twelve tribes. It therefore cannot be considered a product of the urban environment, even when its universalist outlook seems to correspond to the *Zeitgeist* of the Hellenistic age.

Social Unity and Dissent

The final element of the model deals with the different ways in which our two contrasting city-types view the issue of social unity and dissent.

As the representative of the Jerusalem hierocracy, and therefore acting as an agent of the orthogenetic city, Josephus emphasizes loyalty in his dealings in the Galilee. While serving the Josephan rhetoric of self-defense and self-exoneration, it nonetheless indicates that this was indeed the strategy which he and others employed. *Homophulia* is a key term denoting the shared worldview and lineage of all Jews,[64] and the

---

[62] G. Downing, *Jesus and the Threat to Freedom* (London, 1987); J. Overman, "Who Were the First Urban Christians? Urbanization in Galilee in the First Century" in: *SBL Seminar Papers* (Atlanta, 1988), 160–168; D. A. Edwards, "First Century Urban/Rural Relations in Lower Galilee: Exploring the Archaeological and Literary Evidence," ibid., 169–182.

[63] R. Horsley, *Sociology and the Jesus Movement* (New York, 1989), 116–121.

[64] *Life* 11, 55; 19, 100; 33, 171.

absence of this basic quality was the greatest indictment of his oppo-nents. An assembly (*synodos*) of Galileans was called on one occasion,[65] and Josephus also set up a legal institution of seventy Galilean elders to try cases based on the Mosaic model.[66] The term "traitor" is repeatedly applied to Josephus, to Sepphoris, to Justus, and to all those who, for one reason or another, were deemed not to share in the common point of view. The action of Jesus, the revolutionary leader in Tiberias who bran-dished the law of Moses and called on the populace of Tarichaeae to reject Josephus, is a strident example of this theme of loyalty and dissent, a typical feature of the Jewish ethos of the period when faced with politi-cal and cultural threat.

I have repeatedly contended that the Jesus movement was rurally based. Even when we allow for the evangelists' later interests, it seems to have achieved, initially at least, a widespread popularity among the countrypeople. However, the reasons for this enthusiasm and subse-quent rejection should be examined carefully before concluding that his movement does not fit into our model. As already noted, the *literati* of the Great Tradition sought to discredit Jesus by claiming that his mighty deeds were evilly inspired. This charge points to the very source of his popularity—that he was a charismatic healer who fulfilled a social need for the countrypeople. Charges of magic by the enlightened are not al-ways appreciated within a folk culture; instead, it was the charge made in Jerusalem of destroying the Temple that eventually turned the crowds, including presumably his fellow-Galilean pilgrims, against Jesus. The common Great Tradition could tolerate a certain deviance, especially at the periphery, provided it did not strike at the very core of the religious establishment, and, in the case of first-century Judaism, this was Jerusalem and the Temple.

On the other hand, the Herodian and Greek cities were, from the per-spective of the countrypeople, the base of military power from whence destruction could come at any moment. Hence, mistrust and hostility were always part of the relationship. A Roman army advancing from Ptolemais pillaged Galilean villages as a matter of course.[67] On the other hand, an Herodian stronghold like Tiberias could be the source of danger for the villages belonging to other city territories.[68] A precarious relation-ship such as this, based solely on power and control and without any

---

65 *Life* 60, 310f.
66 *War* II, 20, 5, 570f.; cf. *Ant.* IV, 7, 14, 214; 7, 38, 287; *Life* 14, 79.
67 *Life* 43, 213.
68 *Life* 9, 42.

built-in corrective in terms of shared worldview, was hardly likely to generate trust or transform cities, even Herodian ones, into orthogenetic centers for the Galileans. Both Josephus' portrayal of the Galileans and Jesus' avoidance of all cities, especially the Herodian ones of the Lower Galilee, are strong indications that these centers were less than fully integrated into their rural hinterland.

Conclusion

On all four points of our model—dominant social types, basis for relationships between city and countryside, economic patterns, and social unity—we have found considerable evidence that both the Greek and Herodian cities of first-century Galilee were heterogenetic in terms of cultural interchange. This was due to the older and more pervasive relationship with Jerusalem, the orthogenetic city-type, that had been shared by many of the inhabitants of the region—"the Galileans" of our literary sources.

In formulating such a conclusion we must remember that sociological models always operate according to ideal types; however, when dealing with the real world historical occurrences can blur our academic distinctions. In our discussion we have often pointed to Josephus as a representative of the orthogenetic city of Jerusalem, yet he was also a product of the Hellenistic world in his style, position, and outlook. It was his role as a Jerusalemite priest that he seems to have exploited to the fullest in his dealings with the countrypeople. Similarly, the fact that Sepphoris emerges as heterogenetic on the basis of our model may appear surprising in view of its earlier Jewish character.[69] This merely points to the gradual process of secondary urbanization, in which accommodation to the dominant cultural pattern may have begun already with its refurbishment by Antipas. Material remains attesting to the later period have uncovered ritual baths and Dionysiac mosaics in very close proximity to one another, indicating that the process was considerably accentuated in later centuries.

However, when all due allowances are made for the various shades of Hellenistic influences operating within all branches of Judaism, including Palestinian Judaism, the fact remains that two quite distinctive environments in close proximity to each other can be discerned in the Galilee. Each had its own identity, values, and norms, despite a degree of influ-

---

[69] M 'Arakhin 9:6.

ence that each had on the other. The task of the historian of antiquity is to find appropriate tools to evaluate those differences and to be sensitive to the compromises and choices made by people struggling to maintain their social identity in the Galilee so long ago.

III. ROMAN RULE IN THE GALILEE

How Anti-Roman Was the Galilee?

URIEL RAPPAPORT

The Galilee plays a major role in various historical surveys of the Great Revolt against Rome in 66–70 C.E. It has been described by many historians, among them H. Graetz, E. Schürer, J. Klausner, and most recently M. Stern,[1] as a seat of "Zealot" activity, where the general population sided with the rebels and the Romans invested considerable effort to overcome the heroic opposition of the Galileans.

These views are untenable on a number of grounds. They seem to be based partly on Josephus' description of events in the Galilee in his *War* and partly on the ideology of those historians who saw this episode as one of the nation's cherished heroic memories which would strengthen national spirit. However, the position of the Galilee in the revolt, and the attitude of the Galileans to it, must be ascertained by critical evaluation of the sources, i.e., *War* and *Life*, and by analysis of those facts which can be safely extracted from the source material.

---

[1] H. Graetz, *History of the Jews* (6 vols.; Philadelphia, 1891–98), II, 272–290; J. Klausner, *History of the Second Temple* (5 vols.; Jerusalem, 1949–52), V, 173ff. (Hebrew), is based on Josephus' account, with his own embellishments. He even believes that Josephus assembled about 65,000 Galileans for his army (p. 174); E. Schürer, *The History of the Jewish People in the Age of Jesus Christ*, revised and ed. G. Vermes, F. Millar and M. Goodman (3 vols.; Edinburgh, 1973–87), I, 489ff., generally follows Josephus' narrative (cf. to the similar account in E. Schürer's 1901 ed., 607ff.); M. Stern, in: *History of the Jewish People*, eds. H. H. Ben-Sasson and S. Ettinger (Tel-Aviv, 1969), 266 (Hebrew), discusses Galilean circles and Galilean Sicarii in the period before the revolt; E. M. Smallwood, *The Jews under Roman Rule* (Leiden, 1976), 302, writes: "Feeling throughout much of Galilee, a hotbed of guerillas for over a century, was strongly anti-Roman." This is in contrast to statements made elsewhere in her book, cf. 296.

Let us begin with a comparison of the anti-Roman activity among the Jews of the Galilee and Judea. We will focus on the political dimension, since those studies which have attempted to compare different types of "Judaism" in the Galilee and Judea are both unconvincing[2] and largely irrelevant to the anti-Roman movement in Palestine.

Many of the events which can be described as rebellious and anti-Roman occurred in the period between Pompey's conquest and the establishment of Herod's rule (63–37 B.C.E.); they are all expressions of the widespread resistance of Galileans and other Jews to the new order of Roman rule. Scholars have hypothesized[3] that many of the residents of the Galilee were settled there by the Hasmoneans to strengthen the northern border of the Hasmonean state and to support its military activity, which continued until the advent of the Romans.[4] Moreover, peasants and other civilians may have migrated there to alleviate the demographic pressure in Judea and to bolster the Judaization process of the Galilee. These settlers deeply resented the new Roman rule for a number of reasons. For one, it aborted the expansionist policy of Alexander Jannaeus that was continued after his death by his son, Aristobulus II, who was supported by the military command of the Hasmonean army. Secondly, the Romans put the reins of government in the hands of Hyrcanus II, who was the complete antithesis of his brother, Aristobulus II, and granted him limited authority over a curtailed state; they not only stopped any Jewish expansionist expectations, but apparently pushed them back into a narrower territory than that held up to 63 B.C.E.[5] Both loss of territory and frustrated expectations aroused Jewish opposition to Roman rule, particularly in the Galilee.

---

[2] See A. Oppenheimer, "The Jewish Community in Galilee during the Period of Yavneh and the Bar-Kokhba Revolt," *Cathedra* 4 (1977), 53–54 (Hebrew) and further bibliography there.

[3] A. Schalit, *The Hellenistic Age* (*The World History of the Jewish People*, VI; Jerusalem, 1972), 224–225; U. Rappaport, "The Hasmonean State (160–37 B.C.E.)," in: *The History of Eretz Israel*, ed. Y. Shavit (10 vols.; Jerusalem, 1981–85), III, 250–251 (Hebrew).

[4] See *Ant.* XIV, 3, 2, 39–40 (and further references in Loeb ed., ad loc.) regarding Silas the Jew, who ruled the fortress of Lysias, and Dionysius, rightly or wrongly identified as Bacchius Judaeus, whose name is inscribed on the famous Roman coin of 54 B.C.E.

[5] The territorial dispute between the Jews of the Galilee and the Tyrians possibly began in this period (*Ant.* XIV, 12, 2, 304; 12, 3, 313; 12, 4, 314). This territory was occupied by the Tyrians when Cassius was in Syria (*Ant.* XIV, 12, 1, 298; 12, 2, 304), but the origin of the dispute might have been earlier, when Jannaeus attacked Tyre. Though he failed to take the city (Syncellus, ed. Dindorff, 559), he may have annexed

Unrest in the Galilee persisted for about a quarter of a century. It is unnecessary to discuss the details of the various incidents which occurred in the Galilee, exemplified by Ezekias,[6] the people at the caves of Arbela,[7] and Aristobulus' and his sons' supporters. The iron fist of Herod and the passing away of the generation which remembered the Hasmoneans terminated this phenomenon. In the period between 37 B.C.E. and 66 C.E., more than one hundred years, only one incident of explicit anti-Roman activity is recorded—the assault on the royal palace at Sepphoris in 4 B.C.E. and the seizure of arms there by Judas, son of Ezekias[8]—the reason for this perhaps being little direct Roman rule over the inhabitants of the area and the lack of military presence there.[9] The Galileans were under almost continuous Herodian rule:

39/38–4 B.C.E. - Herod's reign;

4 B.C.E.–39 C.E. - Antipas' reign;

39–44 C.E. - Agrippa I's reign;

44–61 C.E. - transitory period between Agrippa I and II;

61–66 C.E. - division of the Galilee: eastern Galilee ruled by Agrippa II, western Galilee part of the province of Judea.

From the above chronology, it seems that the Herodian dynasty had a significant hold on Galilean society. Herod the Great even managed to gain a certain amount of support from the Galileans at the beginning of his war against Antigonus.[10]

However, this description of the Galilee as a relatively peaceful region in Jewish Palestine may be challenged. The flare-up resulting from the Samaritan disruption of a convoy of Galileans en route to Jerusalem during a festival,[11] for instance, may be seen as an indication of the belligerent spirit of the Galileans. This incident, however, including the involvement of Eleazar son of Deinaeus, does not point to an anti-Roman

---

some of its territory. The removal of petty Jewish tyrants from the Lebanese mountain regions was part of the same policy of pushing the Jews back into their own borders. See *Ant.* XIV, 3, 2, 39–40, and Schürer, *History*, I, 237, n. 14.

[6] *Ant.* XIV, 9, 2, 159–160.

[7] *Ant.* XIV, 15, 4–5, 415–430.

[8] *Ant.* XVII, 10, 5, 271–272.

[9] We may assume that, with the exception of Varus who destroyed Sepphoris in 4 B.C.E., Herodian troops, mainly Jewish, took care of security problems. The western Galilee as well was probably under Sepphoris' jurisdiction for a considerable time. See the correct observation of S. Freyne, *Galilee from Alexander the Great to Hadrian* (Wilmington, 1980), 76–78.

[10] *Ant.* XIV, 15, 1, 395; 15, 10, 450.

[11] *Ant.* XX, 6, 1, 118–121; *War* II, 12, 3, 232–235.

movement in the Galilee; rather, it should be viewed as one aspect of Jewish-Samaritan relations and of the sensitivity over pilgrimage to the Temple. Moreover, most of Eleazar son of Deinaeus' activity did not take place in the Galilee.[12]

Another argument for Galilean "zealotism" is the Galilean origin of the Fourth Philosophy, later the Sicarii movement. We support the assumption that the leadership of this movement was Galilean and that it may even have originated with Ezekias, who was executed by Herod in 45 B.C.E. It was then continued under the leadership of his son Judas, one of its two founders, in 6 C.E., and culminated under the command of Eleazar son of Yair at Masada.

But these later events have nothing to do with the Galilee in the first century C.E. The roots of Judas' family were Galilean, as his father, Ezekias, was active in the Galilee at the first stage of Roman rule in Palestine, from 63–37 B.C.E. After his son's attack on Sepphoris in 4 B.C.E, all their activity took place in Judea. There is nothing to hint at any link with the Galilee, neither the imprisonment and execution of James and Simon by Tiberius Julius Alexander[13] nor the Sicarii terrorism in Jerusalem under the rule of the last governors, nor during the revolt itself, in Jerusalem or at Masada.

Thus, it is evident that the Galilee was relatively quiet; it seems that any existent tension or conflict was successfully quelled by the local leadership, Herodian or other. These tensions were generally less anti-Roman and more local—ethnic and social—in nature. As we draw nearer to the Great Revolt and to Josephus' report, the overall picture changes somewhat, but not too much: there was not much warfare against the Romans in the Galilee and some of the activity was a product of local circumstances and the dynamics of the situation.

The only places in the Galilee which resisted the Romans in 67 C.E. were Jotapata and Gamla; a number of sporadic battles took place, such as that on Mt. Tabor, a punitive expedition to Gabara, and the battle and slaughter of fugitives at Tarichaeae.[14] In the final analysis, there was very little real activity. The two "capitals" of the Galilee, Sepphoris and Tiberias, opened their gates to the Romans, as did Gischala. No Jewish

12 After the first upheaval in the Galilee, the stage of events moved to Judea (*War* II, 15, 5, 325) and to Jerusalem (*Ant.* XX, 6, 1, 124; 6, 2, 133), and the Galileans are not mentioned again.

13 *Ant.* XX, 5, 2, 102.

14 Mt. Tabor – *War* IV, 1, 8, 54–61; Gabara – *War* III, 7, 1, 132–134; Tarichaeae – *War* III, 10, 4, 492ff., esp. 10, 10, 532–542.

army took the field. The relatively minor damage to the Galilee indicates as well that no fierce fighting took place there. Even the Roman attack on Chabulon at the very beginning of Cestius Gallus' expedition should be explained as a consequence of Jewish-Syrian enmity.[15] A minor confrontation under the direction of a sub-commander, Caesennius Gallus, took place on Mt. Asamon, after which the Galilee was considered clean of rebels.[16]

We do not maintain that anti-Roman feelings did not run high in the Galilee in the years 66–68 C.E. Jesus son of Sapphias[17] was probably a persistently anti-Roman leader, as was Joseph son of the midwife.[18] However, the Galilee was not receptive to their influence: Jesus was forced out of Tiberias, and his supporters (probably partly Galileans, partly fugitives) found their way to Jerusalem.[19] The story of Gamla is interesting, but exceptional, and may reflect the situation in the Golan at that time.[20] As for Jotapata, we lack the background to this incident. Regarding John of Gischala,[21] I would stress that his town did not take a stand against the Romans and that his supporters were composed not only of Galileans but also of fugitives.

Let us turn now to Josephus' testimony. It is impossible to discuss here the broader questions of the revolt raised by the various scholars, or Josephus' position in it. My inclination is to treat his testimony with the

15 *War* II, 18, 9, 503. From the narrative there it seems that the recruits from Syrian towns played a major role in this affair (See also *War* II, 18, 9, 502, 506).

16 *War* II, 18, 11, 510–512; II, 19, 1, 513.

17 Regarding Jesus son of Sapphias, see *War* II, 21, 3, 599; III, 9, 7, 450, 452; 9, 8, 457; 10, 1, 467; 10, 5, 498; *Life*, index, s.v.

18 On Joseph, see *Life* 37, 185–186; he is to be identified with the Joseph mentioned in *War* IV, 1, 4, 18; 1, 9, 66.

19 *War* III, 9, 8, 457. From *War* III, 10, 5, 497 it may be assumed that Jesus fell in battle or died and that his surviving supporters may be identified with the two thousand Tiberians who were in Jerusalem in 70 C.E. (*Life* 65, 354).

20 It is tempting to link the anti-Roman position of Gamla, which was consolidated only after internal conflict, with the specific conditions of this part of Agrippa II's princedom. The Golan was almost continuously under Herodian, not Roman, rule. The majority of its population was gentile, yet the Jews were a considerable minority and were dominant among the circles of the ruling dynasty, the army, the court, etc. On the mixed population there, see *War* II, 4, 2, 57. Cf. also *Life* 11, 46–61.

21 See my articles, "John of Gischala: From Galilee to Jerusalem," *JJS* 33 (1982), 479–493; "John of Gischala in Galilee," in: *Jerusalem Cathedra*, ed. L. I. Levine (3 vols.; Jerusalem, 1981–83), III, 46–57; "John of Gischala in Jerusalem," in: *Nation and History*, ed. M. Stern (Jerusalem, 1983), 97–115 (Hebrew); "John of Gischala – The Changing Fortunes of a Galilean Leader," in: *Proceedings of the Eighth World Congress of Jewish Studies* (Jerusalem, 1982), 1–4 (Hebrew).

greatest reservation; so many factors—social, political, national, psychological, and personal—have a bearing upon it that no single key can decipher it. The only pragmatic approach is to assess each paragraph and topic separately with as few general assumptions and preconceptions as possible.

We reject the picture drawn by Josephus in *War* concerning his aims and tasks in the Galilee, and prefer the one in his *Life*. Josephus was sent to the Galilee to prevent its involvement in an uprising against Rome, and he achieved this easily and successfully. His opponents in the Galilee held similar politics and opposed him only for personal, local, and perhaps tactical reasons. The only real opposition to him was demonstrated by Sepphoris, which did not agree even to a sham revolt,[22] and Jesus, who opposed Josephus' pretended support of the revolt.[23]

Josephus' detailed account of his relations with John of Gischala and Justus of Tiberias reflects a quarrel within the moderate camp in the Galilee. Since Josephus pretended in *War* to belong to the leadership of the revolt, which he claimed was ready for armed resistance against Rome, he attempted to give the impression that he was the general who prepared the Galilee for war. He also gave the same impression to the Jerusalem government under Ḥanan son of Ḥanan.

Josephus claimed to have undertaken the fortification of about a dozen places in the Galilee against the expected Roman attack. Were this true, it would prove that most of the Galilee had prepared itself for Roman attack under Josephus' leadership. However, this story, surprisingly accepted at face value by many historians, is completely false.[24] The list of fortresses is fabricated and at most includes various fortifications in the Galilee which had little in common and certainly no connection to Josephus. If Sepphoris fortified itself, it was against Josephus or unruly Galileans, not against Rome. Gischala under John did not recognize Josephus' authority and, being on the Tyrian border, had more pressing

---

[22] Sepphoris' coins are the most telling evidence for its firm support of Rome. S. J. D. Cohen's opinion concerning Sepphoris' pro-Roman position should be accepted. For complete references to the relevant literature, see S. S. Miller, *Studies in the History and Traditions of Sepphoris* (Leiden, 1984), 2–3 and notes. No doubt antagonism existed between Sepphoris and the "Galileans," i.e., the agricultural population of Sepphoris' *chora* (= territory). Yet this antagonism was only partially responsible for mass opposition to Rome. The extent of Sepphoris' territory is not known, but its connection to Jotapata may provide some explanation of the latter's strong opposition to Rome.

[23] See n. 17 above.

[24] See U. Rappaport, "The Great Revolt," in: *Judea and Rome – The Jewish Revolts*, ed. U. Rappaport (Jerusalem, 1983), 39 (Hebrew).

reasons to build its wall than a Roman attack.[25] Gamla was too distant to be under Josephus' command. It is therefore a pity that so much effort has been made to analyze the strategical and geopolitical scheme of Josephus' fortresses, as they are sometimes called, since his account is a complete fabrication. The Galilee did not take serious steps towards armed resistance or revolt against Rome. All that existed in 67–68 were a few pockets of resistance by some groups of rebels.

Josephus is consistently misleading in his narratives about the Galilee; in *War* he pretends to be the leader of a full-scale revolt there and in *Life* he pretends to oppose it. In reality he did neither. He came to the Galilee to squash any nascent rebellion (*Life*) and to prepare the way for the Romans and Agrippa II to regain control. He failed in both tasks, primarily because of his inability to gain the confidence of any social class among the Galileans and because of the general upheaval throughout the Galilee;[26] however, he caused a chain of events which bore its own dynamics. The Galilee had at most a secondary position in the outbreak and course of the Great Revolt.

The focus of Jewish anti-Roman activity was in Judea, around and in Jerusalem, in which the Temple, the most sensitive organ of the Jewish national body, was central. The Sicarii terrorists concentrated their activity in Jerusalem,[27] and it was there that anti-Roman propaganda, as well as prophetic and Messianic ferment, spread. Even pilgrims from other regions who entered this environment turned into fervent believers.[28] This atmosphere did not prevail in the Galilee, and the local leadership generally was able to restrain public resentment. Any tension created by Herod Antipas' construction of Tiberias was contained, and resentment of his behavior could not be easily turned against Rome.

The Galilean contribution to the revolt consisted mainly of the heroic resistance of Jotapata and Gamla, and of the Galilean troop(s) participating in the defense of Jerusalem. Thus, after the initial stage of fierce opposition to Rome in 63–37 B.C.E., the Galilee became a relatively

[25] *Life* 10, 44–45; *War* IV, 2, 3, 105.

[26] Violent disturbances took place in many parts of the Galilee, like Gischala, Tiberias, Beth Shean and Chabulon. Roman forces were involved only in Chabulon, and even there they served local interests (see n. 15 above).

[27] On the Sicarii as urban terrorists, see esp. R. A. Horsley, "The Sicarii, Ancient Jewish Terrorists," *JR* 52 (1979), 434–458, and R.A. Horsley and J. S. Hanson, *Bandits, Prophets, and Messiahs* (Minneapolis, 1985), 200–207.

[28] The Galileans involved in violent clashes were either in Jerusalem at the time of the occurrences or somehow connected to the holy city; e.g., Luke 13:1, and n. 12 above.

peaceful region. It was generally under Herodian rule, which had some support among the local gentry. Sepphoris' pro-Roman position is no less typical of the Galilee than Gamla's or Jotapata's anti-Roman one. The history of the ensuing period—the revolt of Bar-Kokhba and its aftermath—points to strong stabilizing forces in Jewish Galilean society. Such forces were not created overnight, but had taken root already at an earlier time.

The Roman Army in the Galilee

ZEEV SAFRAI

It is generally accepted among historians that every province of the Roman empire was responsible for financing and supporting military forces stationed within its borders, both in peacetime and at times of war. This means that the larger the army in a particular province the greater the burden on its inhabitants—a view originally challenged by E. Gren and subsequently by a number of other scholars.[1] However, while residents of the provinces were theoretically responsible for maintaining the army, in practice the troops were supported by the central government or treasury. Thus, there was a dual cash flow in the Roman empire; on the one hand, monies were sent from all provinces to the central government while, on the other, the wealthy provinces (Gaul, Egypt, Syria, etc.) sent funds to the border provinces to support the large forces concentrated there.

The German provinces and Britain are generally portrayed as having been relatively poor provinces accommodating a large concentration of soldiers and thus receiving a significant amount of funding. Much has

---

1 E. Gren, *Kleinasien und die Ostbalkan in der wirtschaftlichen Entwicklung der römischen Keiserzeit* (Upsala, 1941); A. H. M. Jones, *The Roman Economy* (Oxford, 1974), 274ff.; A. R. Birley, "The Economic Effects of Roman Frontier Policy," in: *The Roman West in the Third Century – Part I*, eds. A. King and M. Hoenig (*BAR* 109; Oxford, 1981), 39–53; D. C. Burnham and H. B. Johnson, eds., *Invasion and Responses: The Case of Roman Britain* (*BAR* 73; Oxford, 1979); R. MacMullen, "Rural Romanization," *Phoenix* 22 (1968), 337–341; A. L. F. Rivet, "Social and Economic Aspects," in: *The Roman Villa in Britain*, ed. A. L. F. Rivet (New York, 1969), 173–216; T. F. C. Blagg and A. C. King, eds., *Military and Civilian in Roman Britain* (*BAR* 136; Oxford, 1985), and dozens of other articles.

been written about the influence of this flow of capital on the economies of these provinces, and attempts have been made to analyze the various parts of this process and its economic consequences. In what follows, we shall examine the impact of the Roman army on the small province of Judea.

The Roman army in Judea underwent many far-reaching changes. For our purposes, we shall single out four stages:

1) Until 66 C.E. the Roman army in Judea was rather small. The three–six auxiliary units stationed there were composed, in part, of local militia from Sebaste and Caesarea.[2]

2) During the period from 70–120 C.E. (or perhaps a bit later) the Tenth Legion was stationed in Judea together with a number of auxiliary units. Six–twelve auxiliary units were usually attached to a legion, thereby adding about as many soldiers as in the legion itself. We do not have a complete list of all the forces in Judea at the time; it is possible that there were fewer forces than usual, numbering perhaps 10,000 soldiers.

3) From 120 C.E. to the beginning of the fourth century C.E. there were two legions in Palestine—Legio X Fretensis and Legio VI Ferrata—to which were attached auxiliary units composed of about 25,000 soldiers.[3] Legio X Fretensis was based in Judea proper and had military camps in Jerusalem and Caesarea. Legio VI Ferrata was based in the Galilee, with its headquarters in Legio (= Kefar 'Otnai). Numerous auxiliary forces were sent to Palestine during the Bar-Kokhba revolt, but they were there for only a short period.

4) During the fourth century, Legio VI Ferrata was removed from Palestine and Legio X Fretensis was transferred to the south of Palestine, along the *limes*, with its headquarters in Aila.[4] There was a relatively small number of soldiers in Palestine at this time, probably no more than 7,000–8,000. The shift of units to the *limes* region was of great economic significance. It was necessary, for instance, to extend supply

---

[2] M. Mor, "The Roman Army in Eretz-Israel in the Years A.D. 70–132," in: *The Defence of the Roman and Byzantine East*, eds. P. Freeman and D. Kennedy (*BAR* 297; Oxford, 1986), 575–602.

[3] B. Lifshitz, "Sur la date du transfert de la Legio VI Ferrata en Palestine," *Latomus* 19 (1960), 109–111; B. Isaac and I. Roll, "Judea in the Early Years of Hadrian's Reign," *Latomus* 38 (1979), 54–66; idem, "Legio II Traiana in Judaea," *ZPE* 33 (1979), 149–156; idem, "Legio II Traiana – A Reply," *ZPE* 47 (1982), 131–132; D. L. Kennedy, "Legio VI Ferrata: The Annexation and Early Garrison of Arabia," *HSCP* 84 (1980), 283–309.

[4] M. Gichon, "The Origin of the Limes Palestinae and the Major Phases in Its Development," in: *Studien zu den Militärgrenzen Roms* (Köln, 1967), 175–193.

lines to this desert region from the central areas of the province. The specific problems created by this change, however, are evident in the Byzantine period and are beyond the realm of our present discussion.

The above information shows that during the Roman period (approximately 120–300 C.E.) Judea contained the greatest number of Roman troops of any province of its size (approximately 20,000 sq. km.); half of this army was stationed in the Galilee, the area of which was only 25% that of Judea. It is therefore important to examine the impact of the Roman army on the residents of the Galilee. However, due to the dearth of data in this regard we must supplement what we know with inferences from similar conditions in other provinces.

What do we know about the Roman army in the Galilee? The headquarters of the legion which arrived in the Galilee about the year 120 C.E. was, as noted, near Kefar ʿOtnai (Legio). The site was surveyed by G. Schumacher, who claimed to have discovered a small 2–3 dunam enclosure surrounded by a larger one.[5] He suggested that the smaller enclosure was the legionary camp, although hundreds of soldiers could hardly have been quartered within such a small area. At most, this smaller area was the *principia* of the legionary camp. If the larger enclosure (two sides of which clearly existed) were closed on all four sides it would have measured about 20 dunams, which is the usual size of a camp designated for a cohort (or about 1,000 soldiers).

A Roman army unit was stationed at Sepphoris,[6] but this was during the time of R. Eliezer b. Hyrcanus, i.e., before 120 C.E. and the "official" arrival of the Roman army in the Galilee. A Roman military fortress (*castrum, qatzrin*) was located on the hill above Tiberias, and, based on a reconstruction of the city, would have measured about 20 dunams or the size of a camp designated for a cohort.[7] A small fortified enclosure was discovered on Mt. Ḥazon,[8] and a Roman camp measuring about 20 dunams was located at Tel Shalem, about 12 kms. south of Beth Shean. The southern gate of Beth Shean was referred to as the "gate of the camp" (*pilei de-qampon*) since it led to the Roman camp at Tel Shalem. A

---

5 G. Schumacher, *Tell el-Mutesellin* (Leipzig, 1908), 188–190.

6 T Shabbat 13 (14):9; J Shabbat 16, 15d and parallels.

7 J ʿEruvin 5, 22b. See also M. Avi-Yonah, *Carta's Atlas of the Period of the Second Temple, the Mishnah and the Talmud* (Jerusalem, 1966), 92, map 42 (Hebrew); idem, "Newly Discovered Latin and Greek Inscriptions," *QDAP* 12 (1946), 88; S. S. Miller, *Studies in the History and Traditions of Sepphoris* (Leiden, 1984), 15–46.

8 D. Bahat, "A Roof Tile of the Legio VI Ferrata and Pottery Vessels from Horvat Ḥazon," *IEJ* 24 (1974), 160–169.

number of structures have been discovered at this camp, as well as an inscription mentioning expeditionary troops (*vexilla*) from the Legio VI and an impressive statue of Hadrian.[9]

We thus have evidence of three camps for cohorts. The rest of the army was probably stationed at rural outposts. This situation would explain the repeated reports of confrontation between the Roman army and Galilean Jews attested by numerous rabbinic traditions.[10] An encounter with the Roman government at this time probably meant running into a local military unit or troops passing through the region.

As indicated above, the commanders of the Roman army had recourse to the resources available in a specific province as well as to external funds for maintaining their armies. The tax rate was not affected by the presence of military forces in a province, since the tax base in the various provinces was more or less the same. It is known that taxes were particularly high in Judea[11] and that a special tax was levied on the Jews after 70 C.E. If this small province also had to support the military forces stationed there, it would have been an unbearable and indeed unique burden. We have no indication that this was the case. Based on the above and on the somewhat gratuitous assumption that the tax base levied on the provinces was the same, it is possible to estimate the inflow of capital needed to support the army in Judea.

K. Hopkins has suggested a method of arriving at cost quantification of the Roman army, whereby the government levied a tax of 10% of the empire's gross national product (GNP).[12] Moreover, about half of Rome's expenses went towards support of the army.[13] Hopkins does not include unique or unusual income, such as that due from estates, since this is

---

[9] G. Foerster, *A Cuirassed Bronze Statue of Hadrian* (ʿ*Atiqot* 17 [English Series]; Jerusalem, 1985), 139–157. Eusebius (early fourth century C.E.), in his Onomasticon (ed. Klostermann, 152; ed. Melamed, no. 813), mentions Shalem but not the military camp there, even though he was wont to do so in his description of other sites having military camps. Eusebius still refers to the Jezreel Valley as the "Campus Legionis"; perhaps the camp at Shalem was only a temporary one and was abandoned before the end of the third century. This matter relates to the larger issue of the sources of the Onomasticon and will not be dealt with here.

[10] S. Krauss, *Persia and Rome in the Talmud and Midrashim* (Jerusalem, 1948) (Hebrew).

[11] Appian, *Syr.* 50.

[12] K. Hopkins, "Taxes and Trade in the Roman Empire (200 B.C.–A.D. 400)," *JRS* 70 (1980), 101ff.

[13] M. H. Crawford, "Money and Exchange in the Roman World," *JRS* 60 (1970), 40–48.

impossible to calculate. He does, however, take into account the role of the residents of the empire in supporting the corrupt system of tax collection. In economic terms, it made little difference whether the monies went directly to the Roman fiscus or to the corrupt freedmen collecting the taxes.

Hopkins' calculations of the cost of the army, which is based on the rate of salary paid to its soldiers, are too low. It is known that the Roman soldier had to pay for his food and that of his horses out of his salary. There is no certainty, however, that they were charged realistic prices; there are indications that the prices were lower than market value. If Hopkins' cost estimates are to be raised, then the taxation rates must be changed as well. The figure of 10% of the GNP seems to be too low, as the accepted rate of payment in estates was 33.3% in grain fields and up to 50% in orchards and the like.[14] Even in Judea, payment of up to 50% of the produce was customary. This would seem to indicate that the average family had to sustain itself, albeit with difficulty, on half the produce it succeeded in cultivating. Had the rate of taxation been only 10%, the farmer would have had about 40% more than his subsistence needs, which could have been marketed at a profit, placing him in a better economic position than we know him to have had. It is possible that the tenant farmer had larger tracts of land at his disposal than the average independent farmer, but the question still pertains. Under the rule of John Hyrcanus II, the Roman empire levied a tax of 12.5% from wheat fields in Judea. Another 10% was the customary percentage handed over to the semi-autonomous rulers and the Temple.[15] Is it possible that when autonomous rule was later abolished the tax rate was lowered?

Although Hopkins' estimations appear low, it is still impossible to determine the exact tax rate in Judea or the Roman empire in general. We shall, however, use his low estimates in the course of our discussion, bearing in mind that when the tax burden becomes greater, the support of the army by the residents becomes greater; this, in turn, leads to a larger influx of capital into the province for maintenance of the army.

Judea comprised less than 1% of the entire Roman empire. It would thus seem likely that the tax revenues from that province did not exceed 1%. For the sake of caution, however, we shall assume that the tax income from Judea comprised 1.5% of the empire's total revenue. Approximately 8% of the Roman forces of the empire (25,000 soldiers) were

---

14 A. C. Johnson, et al., eds., *Ancient Roman Statutes* (Austin, 1961), 173–175.
15 *Ant.* XIV, 10, 5, 203.

encamped in Judea; the empire would have had to allot 4% of its revenue for the support of these units (assuming that support of the army constituted 50% of Roman expenses). Thus, for every 1.5 dinars which reached the Roman treasury from Judea, it was necessary to allocate an additional 2.5 dinars to support the army there, and an additional amount to maintain the army stationed in the Galilee. If taxes constituted 10% of the GNP of every province in the Roman empire, the Roman government had to allocate to Palestine 16.6% of its GNP for this province's military expenses. The tax burden undoubtedly was greater, as well as the expenses for support of the army. The flow of capital to the provinces would have had to have been even higher. Not all this money actually reached the provinces, since some of it was saved for the soldiers' salaries when they left the province. Even if these numbers are somewhat inflated, it is clear that the contribution of the Roman army to the province, especially to the Galilee, was of great importance to the economy of the province and the region.

The land was devastated after the Bar-Kokhba revolt; income from taxes was especially low. During this time, and at least until 139 C.E.,[16] additional legions were stationed in Palestine, thus necessitating a large inflow of capital to support them. In this manner the Roman army unwittingly helped to restore somewhat the economy of the province. There is evidence that commodities were transferred from Egypt at this time;[17] during the period of anarchy, when governmental or Imperial support was often delayed, the legions took care of themselves—at the expense of the local residents—thereby adding yet another economic burden to the already existing economic catastrophe.

It is likely that the army based in Judea had at its disposal large sums of money to buy food supplies, clothing, and weapons on a regular basis. Cassius Dio, for example, cites a specific instance when Roman forces bought weapons from local manufacturers in Judea.[18] This was probably

16 S. Applebaum, *Prolegomena to the Study of the Second Jewish Revolt (A.D. 132–135)* (Oxford, 1976), 25–27; L. J. F. Keppie, "The Legionary Garrison of Judaea under Hadrian," *Latomus* 32 (1973), 859–864.

17 A. S. Hunt et al., *Catalogue of Greek Papyri in the John Rylands Library* (Manchester, 1911–52), II, 237, n. 189.

18 Cassius Dio 69, 12, 2; R. MacMullen, "Inscription on Armor and the Supply of Arms in the Roman Empire," *AJA* 64 (1960), 23–40; idem, "Rural Romanization,"; R. W. Davies, "The Supply of Animals to the Roman Army and the Remount System," *Latomus* 28 (1969), 429–459; M. Speidel, "The Prefect's Horse Guard and the Supply of Weapons to the Roman Army," in: *Roman Army Studies*, I (Amsterdam, 1984), 329–331.

the case regarding other army supplies as well. Although there has been much scholarly debate regarding the provision of supplies to the Roman forces,[19] we have no information on this matter for Judea. Since the army was relatively large there, it presumably had relatively greater buying power than in most other provinces.

This seems to have been the case regarding the supply of linen. The army probably received supplies from the Imperial weaveries in Scythopolis, although some linen, at least, was undoubtedly bought on the open market from other countries that produced flax (e.g., Egypt).[20] The food supplies of the Roman army were naturally dependent upon the customs storehouses, and it is clear that taxes in kind or commodities were usually earmarked for the forces regularly garrisoned in the province. It seems likely, therefore, that a good deal of the tax debt in Judea was paid in kind. Talmudic literature contains many halakhic statements concerning payment of taxes in cash and in kind. The relation between the amount of taxes paid in cash and that paid in kind is difficult to determine, however, and the situation in the provinces, perhaps apart from Egypt, is not very clear.

Every province apparently had its own policy. In Judea, it seems likely that the Romans would have been more interested in being paid in kind so that the goods collected could be directly transferred to the units as part of their food supplies. This, however, was not always the case; a number of talmudic references indicate that commodities which reached these storehouses were sold to the general public. Two independent traditions specifically mention merchants (from the Galilee) who bought commodities (wheat?) from a storehouse in Jamnia (= Yavneh), which was specifically referred to as government property. One of these traditions dates to the Ushan period (140–180 C.E.);[21] the second involves two sages, R. Judah the Prince and R. Yose b. Judah (180–225 C.E.).[22] A number of laws deal specifically with produce bought from such storehouses,[23] and the purchase of produce there seems to have been a common occurrence. It seems that even in a small province the govern-

---

[19] P. S. Middleton, "Army Supply in Roman Gaul: An Hypothesis for Roman Britain," in: *Invasion and Responses*; J. Lesquier, *L'armée romaine d'Egypte d'Auguste à Dioclétien* (Cairo, 1918).

[20] E. Wipszycka, "Das Textilhandwerk und der Staat im römischen Agypten," *Archiv für Papyrus Forschung* 18 (1966), 1ff.; J. P. Wild, "Romans and Natives in Textile Technology," in: *Invasion and Responses*, 123–131.

[21] T Demai 1:12–13.

[22] Genesis Rabbah 76:8, Theodor-Albeck, p. 960.

[23] T Demai 1:11–14.

ment preferred to sell commodities collected as taxes and to transfer the
money to the military units.

Perhaps the structure of the local economy dictated this situation.
Units stationed in the plains, such as those at Jamnia, had an abundance
of grain at their disposal while others stationed in the Galilee suffered
from more limited grain supplies. The surplus of tax revenues in kind,
from olive oil or flax, could not compensate for the lack of grain. This
was, of course, the result of the trend at the time to cultivate less grain in
the Galilee in order to free lands for the cultivation of other crops. Moreover, the Roman soldiers stationed in the provinces usually enjoyed a
diet which was much richer in meat than that of the local residents.[24]
There was not much meat production in Palestine, nor was pig-meat, a
staple of the Roman troops, readily available there. This imbalance between the agricultural system and the commodities paid as taxes on the
one hand, and the needs of the Roman army on the other, probably resulted in the sale of local tax commodity surplus in order to purchase
other supplies. A Roman law from the end of the fourth century C.E.
provides additional testimony for this economic interaction in Palestine
and particularly in the region of the *limes*.[25] We shall return later to the
modes of tax collection and their implications.

Based on our above analysis, it appears that the Roman army had an
extremely positive influence on the economy of Palestine. Since the support of the standing army there required an inflow of 16.6% of Palestine's
GNP, this money was used to buy various supplies from the residents of
the province. Moreover, providing supplies for the army encouraged
further business activity.

*   *   *

The presence of such a large army in a small province undoubtedly
had many effects on the country's socio-economic framework. We shall
examine the extent to which R. MacMullen's short summary of this

---

[24] J. H. Davies, "The Roman Military Diet," *Britannia* 2 (1971), 122–142; idem, "The
Daily Life of the Roman Soldier under the Principat," in: *ANRW*, II, 1, eds. H. Temporini and W. Haase (Berlin/New York, 1974), 299–338; A. King, "Animal Bones and
the Dietary Identity of Military," in: *Military and Civilian*, 187–192.

[25] *Codex Theodosianus* 7, 4, 30.

matter,[26] as well as those studies mentioned at the beginning of this article,[27] pertain to Palestine.

1) The Roman soldier received a rather good salary. From the period of Diocletian wages were about 300 dinars; auxiliary forces received 75% of this amount.[28] The soldier set aside a fixed sum to pay the army for his food supplies. He could save some of his money in the camp treasury and withdraw it only upon his release. Another part of his salary, which is impossible to estimate, was used for personal expenses or towards purchasing communal sacrifices. The amount set aside for savings determined the sum which the soldier could spend in the province. Undoubtedly, there was no set rule and each soldier made his own decision in this regard.

   We do not know how much money a soldier spent in his camp. We do know, however, that large civilian settlements (*canaba*) and small ones (*pagi*) that sprang up around the camps usually housed people who provided services for the military. Soldiers' families lived there as well, even though they were not recognized by Roman law.[29] It is likely that the situation was similar in the Galilee; it might explain why the village of Legio, the civilian settlement next to the Legio VI Ferrata headquarters, contained a theater,[30] since no other village in Judea or the Galilee had one. In the third century C.E. this same village became the *polis* Maximianopolis. It would appear, from the large number of Byzantine inscriptions found at Beer Sheva and from the relatively large size of the town, that this civilian settlement also developed out of a *canaba* of the military headquarters of the *limes*. There were undoubtedly other such settlements throughout Palestine.

2) Since the army camp served as a consumer of services and supplies, it perforce became a merchandising center surrounded by markets. We have no information about this phenomenon in the Galilee, but it seems to have been fairly common in other provinces at the time. An

26 MacMullen, "Rural Romanization."

27 See literature above, n. 1.

28 Speidel, "The Prefect's Horse Guard," 83–90; R. Davelin, "The Army Pay Rises under Severus and Caracalla," *Latomus* 30 (1971), 687–695; G. R. Watson, "The Pay of the Roman Army," *Historia* 5 (1956), 332–340; idem, "The Pay of the Urban Forces," in: *Acta of the Fifth Epigraphic Congress* (Cambridge, 1971), 413–416; H. C. Boren, "Studies Relating to the Stipendium Militum," *Historia* 32 (1983), 427–460; P. A. Brunt, "Pay and Superannuation in the Roman Army," *PBSR* 18 (1950), 50–71.

29 R. O. Fink, *Roman Military Records on Papyrus* (London, 1975), nos. 68–70, 83, 77.

30 See above, n. 5.

indication of this may be a weight measure of the Fifteenth Legion found in Palestine.[31]

3) The army was a consumer of technology and Roman lifestyle. The soldiers and officers of the legion consumed large quantities of high quality wine and used Roman pottery[32] and other such implements.[33] This encouraged local manufacturers to raise the quality of their goods and local residents to buy them. Tiles stamped with the imprint of Legio VI Ferrata have been discovered at Horvat Hazon, Kefar Hananyah, and Legio;[34] however, it is not known whether these finds are indicative of a local factory which produced for the Roman army or for the villagers (see below). Another factory for the manufacture of such tiles for the Tenth Legion was found near Jerusalem, although here, too, it is not clear whether this was a civilian or military establishment.[35] Bricks from this factory have been found in Joppa (60 kms. from Jerusalem) and at Ramat Rachel south of Jerusalem, the latter site clearly having been civilian.[36]

4) The army manufactured utensils and sold them in civilian markets (see above).

5) The army provided services (such as bath houses) in order to demonstrate to the local population the quality of a Roman lifestyle.

6) The army provided and built services for its own use which also benefited the province itself. It constructed many roads in Judea and the Galilee, such as the road network between Scythopolis and Caesarea, Diocaesarea (i.e., Sepphoris), and Legio.[37] Many sources indicate, however, that the local population often paved these roads or provided for their upkeep through the various *liturgiae* imposed by the

---

[31] S. Qedar, *Münz Zentrum Auktion*, XLV (Köln, 1981), 45.

[32] P. S. Middleton, "The Roman Army and Long Distance Trade," in: *Trade and Famine in Classical Antiquity*, eds. P. Garnsey and C. R. Whittaker (Cambridge, 1983), 75–83; cf. C. R. Tchernia, "Italian Wine Trade in Gaul and in the Republic," in: *Trade in an Ancient Economy*, eds. P. Garnsey, K. Hopkins and C. R. Whittaker (Berkeley, 1983), 87–104; P. Green, "Pottery and the Roman Army," in: *Invasion and Responses*.

[33] For example, see King, "Animal Bones," 187–192.

[34] Bahat, "A Roof Tile"; D. Adan-Bayewitz, "Kefar Hananya 1986," *IEJ* 37 (1987), 178.

[35] D. Barag, "Brick Stamp-Impressions of the *Legio X Fretensis*," *Eretz-Israel* 8 (1967), 168–182 (Hebrew).

[36] Contra Y. Aharoni, *Excavations at Ramat Rachel* (Rome, 1962, 1964).

[37] B. Isaac and I. Roll, "Judea"; idem, *Roman Roads in Judea, I: The Legio-Scythopolis Road* (*BAR* 141; Oxford, 1982).

Romans.[38] M. Avi-Yonah published an inscription testifying to the contribution of two villages near Ptolemais to the construction of the road from Ptolemais to Tyre.[39] Also sections of local aqueducts, such as those at Caesarea, were occasionally built by Roman troops.

7) The army served as a roving ambassador of Roman culture, religion, and economics. At times, however, the presence of large Roman troops created difficulties for local residents because of the numerous *angariae* imposed on them. During certain seasons of the year, a large military presence could result in shortages of various commodities and rising prices, as was once the case in Antioch.[40] On the whole, however, the presence of the military was beneficial to the economy of the province. This might explain why rabbinic literature generally evinces a positive attitude to the Roman army in spite of the marked hostility towards Roman rule expressed by this same literature.[41]

Rabbinic traditions attest to cooperation and reciprocity between the army and local populations of Palestine in matters of everyday life. Thus, for example, soldiers stationed in Sepphoris sought to aid in extinguishing a fire at the house of a senior Jewish official.[42] In spite of the general hostility to Roman rule, good relations with local troops might have developed, at least on the personal level. Undoubtedly, such positive relations had great economic potential.

Another means of providing supplies for the army was through the *territorium legiones*. A legion was given a territory from which it could demand the provision of its supplies, in a manner similar to that of the Roman century or any other sub-unit which received an area that was to provide for its needs. The details of this system are not entirely clear, such as whether the legion received a government estate or whether the

---

38 W. H. C. Frend, "A Third Century Inscription Relating to *Angareia* in Phrygia," *JRS* 46 (1956), 46–56.

39 Avi-Yonah, "Newly Discovered Latin and Greek Inscriptions," 85–86.

40 G. Downey, "The Economic Crisis at Antioch," in: *Studies in Roman Economic and Social History in Honor of A. C. Johnson*, eds. P. R. Coleman-Norton, et al. (Princeton, 1951); B. Isaac, *The Limits of Empire* (Oxford, 1990), 269–310.

41 S. Safrai, "The Relations between the Roman Army and the Jews of Eretz Israel after the Destruction of the Second Temple," *Roman Frontier Studies, 1967*, ed. S. Applebaum (Tel Aviv, 1971), 224–230; see also D. Sperber, "Angaria in Rabbinic Literature," *L'antiquité Classique* 38 (1969), 164–168.

42 T Shabbat 13:9, Lieberman, p. 60; cf. J Shabbat 16, 7, 15d; J Yoma 8, 5, 45b; J Nedarim 4, 9, 38d; B Shabbat 121a.

army or the soldiers collected the usual taxes from the *territorium*.[43] Interestingly, rabbinic literature contains references to officers functioning as tax collectors.[44] Such a *territorium* might have existed in the Jezreel Valley, near the camp of Legio VI Ferrata at Legio,[45] since the Jezreel Valley contained government estates; its exact location, however, is unknown. The system, therefore, apparently existed in the Galilee, but, due to insufficient data, it is impossible to determine its economic implications.

[43] M. Kandler, "Zur Territorium Legiones von Carnuntum," *Limes Frontier Studies* 9 (1975), 145ff.; A. Schulten, "Das Territorium Legiones," *Hermes* 29 (1984), 481–516.

[44] D. Sperber, "The Centurion as a Tax Collector," *Latomus* 28 (1969), 186–188.

[45] Contra Isaac and Roll, *Roman Roads*, 105–106.

Roman Rule and the Cities of the Galilee in Talmudic Literature*

AHARON OPPENHEIMER

A. City Organization and Colonial Status

A well-known talmudic source relates a case from the time of R. Judah ha-Nasi:

> When R. Isaac b. Joseph came, he said: There was that *kelila* [*aurum coronarium*] which the Imperial government imposed on the *boule* and the *strategoi*. Rabbi said: *boule* shall give half and *strategoi* shall give half.[1]

A parallel passage in the Jerusalem Talmud describing a discussion on this subject between members of the *boule* and the *strategoi*, and which was brought before R. Judah ha-Nasi, offers some background information on this case:

> Like this. The *boule* and the *strategoi* had a lawsuit. The case came before Rabbi, and he said: Is *boule* not included in *strategoi*? For what matter did it state: *boule* and *strategoi*? So he said: These shall give half and those shall give half.[2]

In these two parallel sources Rabbi divides the burden of crown gold (*aurum coronarium*) equally between both institutions, irrespective of the

---

* I want to thank Professor B. Isaac who read the manuscript, referred me to the relevant Greek and Roman literature, and made stimulating remarks.

1 B Bava Batra 143a, according to the Munich ms. in: G. Alon, *Jews, Judaism and the Classical World*, trans. I. Abrahams (Jerusalem, 1977), 458–475.

2 J Yoma 1, 2, 39a (trans. I. Abrahams, ibid.).

number of members in each. The crown gold itself is a well-known Roman tax; it originated as a military tax and later developed into a surtax, initially paid in gold crowns but in the course of time in local currency.[3] In the above cases, the burden of this tax fell on the *boule* and the *strategoi*. This information sheds light on the nature of these institutions and their function and also explains why someone would avoid nomination to these bodies in the third century, at a time when the empire was in a period of crisis. This is apparent from the words of R. Yoḥanan, "If your name is mentioned for [service in] the *boule*, let the Jordan [River] be your border."[4]

We have yet another reference to the imposition of the crown tax in the Babylonian Talmud, where an appeal was made to R. Judah ha-Nasi: "As in the case of the crown tax which was levied on Tiberias. They came before Rabbi and said to him, 'Let the Rabbis give their share with us.'"[5] One can surmise that the incident mentioned here is the same as those quoted earlier.

Various conjectures have been advanced as to the identity of the institution of the *strategoi*.[6] There can, in fact, be no doubt that this is the Greek translation of the Latin *duoviri*, denoting the two senior officials in a city.[7] The existence of this institution is attested in several cities of the eastern provinces: an inscription from Gerasa mentions a centurion whose son was an *eques*, a member of the *boule*, and one of the *strategoi* who had once served as a priest of the city.[8] In Sebaste, *strategoi* are mentioned in an inscription found in the basilica, which dates possibly to the

---

[3] See F. Millar, *The Emperor in the Roman World, 31 B.C.–A.D. 337* (London, 1977), 140–142.

[4] J Moʿed Qatan 2, 3, 81b. Cf. also the text of the midrash, "this alludes to the wicked Kingdom which casts an envious eye upon man's wealth, [saying] so-and-so is wealthy, let us make him an *archon*; so-and-so is wealthy, let us make him a *bouleutes*" (Genesis Rabbah 76:6, Theodor-Albeck, p. 904).

[5] B Bava Batra 8a. For different viewpoints concerning this source, see L. I. Levine, *The Rabbinic Class of Roman Palestine in Late Antiquity* (Jerusalem, 1989), 148–149, and bibliography cited therein.

[6] See, for instance, A. Büchler, *The Political and Social Leaders of the Jewish Community of Sepphoris in the Second and Third Centuries* (London, 1909), 39–43; A. Gulak, "Boule and Strategoi," *Tarbiz* 11 (1940), 119-122 (Hebrew); Alon, *Jews, Judaism*, 458–475.

[7] As to the nature of this institution, see *Der kleine Pauly Lexikon der Antike*, eds. K. Ziegler, W. Sontheimer, and H. Gärtner (5 vols.; Stuttgart, 1969; reprint Munich, 1975), II, 176–178, s.v. "duoviri."

[8] C. H. Kraeling, *Gerasa: City of the Decapolis* (New Haven, 1938), 404, no. 62.

Severan period.[9] It is apparent that an important change in the status of Palmyra occurred when it was made a colony, for between the years 224 and 262 the standard practice of calling city officials *strategoi* was introduced. The Syriac version of one of the documents mentions Julius Aurelius who "satisfied the people of the town in his *istratequtah*."[10] The institution of *strategoi* is mentioned on a bill of sale that was written in Edessa and found in the excavations at Dura Europos, as well as in Syriac sources which deal with acts of martyrdom alluding to Edessa. In these acts, which relate events that apparently occurred in the year 309 C.E., the date is established according to the *istratequtah* of Avgar and Abba. Another act, wherein events that possibly occurred in 314 C.E. were treated, similarly gives a local date according to the *istratequtah* of Julius and Baraq.[11] *Strategoi* are also mentioned in connection with Petra and Gaza.[12]

Two *strategoi* are mentioned in several places in talmudic literature:

> R. Levi said: To what can this be compared, to the friend of a king who had deposited some article with him. His son came and claimed the article. The king said to him: Go, bring me two *strategoi* and twelve *bouleutai*, and through them I will give you the article.[13]

9 G. A. Reisner, et al., *Harvard Excavations at Samaria 1908–1910* (Cambridge, MA, 1924), I, 250, no. 7; II, Pl. 59c; for the dating, ibid., I, 20, no. 30; II, Pl. 59d.

10 J. Cantineau, *Inventaire des inscriptions de Palmyre*, III (Beirut, 1930), nos. 10, 14 (= P. Le Bas and W. H. Waddington, *Inscriptions grecques et latines recueillies en Grèce et en Asie Mineure*, III: *Syrie* (Paris, 1870), no. 2601.

11 For the bill of sale, see C. C. Torrey, "A Syriac Parchment from Edessa of the Year 243 AD," *Zeitschrift für Semitistik und verwandte Gebiete* 10 (1935), 33–45; A. R. Bellinger and C. B. Welles, "A Third-Century Contract of Sale from Edessa in Osrhoene," *YCS* 5 (1935), 93–154; J. A. Goldstein, "The Syriac Bill of Sale from Dura-Europos," *JNES* 25 (1966), 1–16. For the acts of martyrdom, see F. C. Burkitt, *Euphemia and the Goth* (London, 1913), 90, 112 and the Syriac text; F. Millar, "The Roman Coloniae of the Near East: A Study of Cultural Interactions" (forthcoming).

12 For Petra, see J. Starcky and C.-M. Bennett, "Découvertes récentes au sanctuaire du Qasr à Pétra: III - Les inscriptions du téménos," *Syria* 45 (1968), no. xiii, 60–62 (= idem, *ADAJ* 12/13 [1967/68], no. xiii, 45ff.). For Gaza, see Hieronymus, *Vita S. Hilarionis*, 20, *PL* 23, 36; Sozomenus, *Hist. Eccles.* 5, 3. Cf. C. Glucker, *The City of Gaza in the Roman and Byzantine Periods* (*BAR* 327; Oxford, 1987), 45, 77.

13 Deuteronomy Rabbah, Lieberman, p. 84 (according to the Oxford ms.); Deuteronomy Rabbah 3:3. The significant fact in this case is that the *strategoi* numbered two and the members of the *boule* twelve, linking them with, respectively, Moses and Aaron and the heads of the twelve tribes (see also Alon, *Jews, Judaism*, 467, n. 16, who also mentions the *duoviri* when noting the number of *strategoi*).

or: "They made a comparison: To what is this to be compared? It is like a king who has two *strategoi* . . . ."[14] The fact that the sages state that the *strategoi* were two in number corroborates the identification of the *strategoi* with the institution of the *duovirate*.

Alon was probably right when he proposed that the discussion between the members of the *boule* and the *strategoi* concerned the division of the tax burden between the two institutions whose members were not equal in number. But he did not understand correctly the function of the *strategoi*, since he gave examples at one and the same time of *strategoi* in cities and in villages, which were definitely two different institutions.[15]

It is important to note that the institution of the *duovirate* existed only in cities with the status of a Roman colony, as it reflected the two consuls in the city of Rome. The Babylonian Talmud relates a conversation between Antoninus and Rabbi, in which the former mentions the possibility of granting colonial status to Tiberias:

> . . . and as to your question about their not appointing a king's son as king, such appointment *would* be made at the [king's] request, as was the case with Asverus the son of Antoninus who reigned [in his father's place]. Antoninus once said to Rabbi: It is my desire that my son Asverus should reign instead of me and Tiberias should be declared a Colony. Were I to ask one of these things it would be granted while both would not be granted. Rabbi thereupon brought a man, and having made him ride on the shoulders of another, handed him a dove bidding the one who carried him to order the one on his shoulders to liberate it. The Emperor perceived this to mean that he was advised to ask [of the Senate] to appoint his son Asverus to reign in his stead, and that subsequently he might get Asverus to make Tiberias a free Colony.[16]

Essentially, this evidence fits what is known about the granting of colonial status by the Severans to a number of cities in the East. The Severans actively dealt with urbanization in general, and with the status of settlements in particular. Septimius Severus used the granting of this status as a function of reward or punishment for the attitude of settlements during his struggle with Pescennius Niger over the imperial throne. In the province of Syria-Palaestina, Severus granted city status to Lydda and Beth Guvrin, which then became Diospolis and Eleutheropolis,

[14] J Berakhot 8, 6, 12c.

[15] Alon, *Jews, Judaism*, 464–465. For *strategoi* in villages, see H. I. MacAdam, *Studies in the History of the Roman Province of Arabia* (*BAR* 295; Oxford, 1986), passim.

[16] B 'Avodah Zarah 10a (trans. Soncino). See S. Krauss, *Antoninus und Rabbi* (Vienna, 1910), 52–55.

respectively.[17] Sebaste was granted colonial status,[18] whereas Neapolis was temporarily deprived of its city status because it had supported Niger in the year 194.[19] It seems probable that there is a connection between the punishment of Neapolis and the elevation of neighboring Sebaste. Severus also occupied himself with the organization of the new province of Mesopotamia; he or his successors granted colonial status to Rhesaina, Nisibis, and Carrhae.[20] Caracalla and Elagabalus continued this practice by granting colonial status to Edessa in Osrhoene. Emesa and Antioch in Syria received the same status.[21] Palmyra also became a colony, either during Severus' reign or under Caracalla.[22] Elagabalus gave city status to Emmaus and Antipatris in Syria-Palaestina,[23] while

17 For Lydda, see G. F. Hill, *BMC – Palestine* (London, 1914), 141, nos. 1–2; M. Rosenberger, *City Coins of Palestine* (4 vols.; Jerusalem, 1972–78), II, 28–31; III, 80; A. Kindler and A. Stein, *A Bibliography of the City Coinage of Palestine* (*BAR* 374; Oxford, 1987), 96–99. For Eleutheropolis, see A. Spijkerman, "The Coins of Eleutheropolis Iudaeae," *LA* 22 (1972), 369–384, Pls. 1–4; Kindler and Stein, *Bibliography of City Coinage*, 112–116.

18 *Digesta* L 15, 1, 7. This occurred between the years 201 and 211, but numismatic evidence shows that it apparently took place in 201/202. See also Hill, *BMC – Palestine*, xxxix, 80, nos. 12–13; Kindler and Stein, *Bibliography of City Coinage*, 222–229.

19 *SHA, Severus* 9, 5.

20 A. H. M. Jones, *The Cities of the Eastern Roman Provinces*[2] (Oxford, 1971), 220–221; A. Kindler, "The Status of Cities in the Syro-Palestinian Area As Reflected by Their Coins," *INJ* 6–7 (1982–83), 79–87; on Nisibis, see A. Oppenheimer (in collaboration with B. Isaac and M. Lecker), *Babylonia Judaica in the Talmudic Period* (Wiesbaden, 1983), 319–334.

21 For Edessa, see Bellinger and Welles, "A Third-Century Contract"; Goldstein, "Syriac Bill of Sale." For Emesa, see *Digesta* L 15, 1, 4; cf. L 15, 8, 6; W. Wroth, *BMC – Syria* (London, 1899), 237–241. For Antioch in Syria, see *Digesta* L 15, 8, 5; *BMC – Syria*, lviii–lxiii, 151–232.

22 J. C. Mann, *Legionary Recruitment and Veteran Settlement during the Principate* (London, 1983), 219. Colonial status is mentioned in *Digesta* L 15, 1. Also D. Schlumberger, "Les gentilices romains des Palmyréniens," *Bulletin des Etudes Orientales* 9 (1942/43), 54-82.

23 For Emmaus, see Jones, *Cities of the Eastern Provinces*, 279 and n. 72. E. Schürer, *The History of the Jewish People in the Age of Jesus Christ*, rev. and ed. G. Vermes, F. Millar, and M. Goodman (3 vols.; Edinburgh, 1973–87), I, 512–513, n. 142; Kindler and Stein, *Bibliography of City Coinage*, 177–179. Seven types of coins are known from Antipatris, all dating from the reign of Elagabalus; see Hill, *BMC – Palestine*, xv-xvi, 11; N. van der Vliet, "Monnaies inédites ou très rares du médaillier de Sainte Anne de Jérusalem," *RB* 57 (1950), 116–117, nos. 11–12; Y. Meshorer, *City Coins of Eretz-Israel and the Decapolis in the Roman Period* (Jerusalem, 1985), nos. 149–152; Kindler and Stein, *Bibliography of City Coinage*, 41–42; Schürer, *History*, II, 167–168. See also *IGR* I, no. 631; republished by L. Robert, *Les gladiateurs dans l'Orient grec* (Limoges, 1940;

Petra in Arabia,[24] Tyre in Syria,[25] and Arca or Caesarea ad Libanum[26] were made colonies. Under Severus Alexander, Bostra was also granted the status of colony.[27]

Returning to the above-mentioned talmudic passage, however, it should be noted that Antoninus is generally identified with Caracalla. The source in question raises the possibility that "the son" of Antoninus would make Tiberias a colony. This fits well with what we know of Elagabalus, that he indeed acted formally as if he were the son of Caracalla. This also matches the chronology of Rabbi's patriarchate, as, according to the testimony of Rav Sherira Ga'on, Rabbi was still alive in the year 219, the year in which Rav journeyed to Babylonia after he had been ordained by Rabbi.[28] These circumstances also shed light on the fact that the leadership institutions moved from Sepphoris to Tiberias during the first half of the third century, thus reflecting the enhanced status of Tiberias as the major city in the Galilee as well as the tendency of the leadership institutions to gain strength from frequent changes of residence. This was the culmination of the process that had begun one hundred years earlier, with the re-establishment of the leadership institutions in Usha; gradually acquiring power as they moved to Shefarʿam, Beth Sheʿarim, and Sepphoris, they finally established themselves permanently in Tiberias.[29] Moving the leadership institutions from one city in the Galilee to another, first to Sepphoris and later to Tiberias, entailed the submission of the Jews in the city councils—who maintained contact with the Roman rulers—to the authority of the Patriarch.[30] The abovementioned fact, that the *boule* and the *strategoi* turned to R. Judah ha-

---

reprint Amsterdam, 1971), 103–104, no. 43. Here a member of the *boule* who served for Antipatris as well as for Neapolis is mentioned (ibid., 101–103, nos. 41–42).

[24] S. Ben-Dor, "Petra Colonia," *Berytus* 9 (1948/49), 41–43; A. Spijkerman, *The Coins of the Decapolis and Provincia Arabia*, ed. M. Piccirillo (Jerusalem, 1978), 218–219, 236.

[25] G. F. Hill, *BMC – Phoenicia* (London, 1910), lxxxvii–cxvi, 139–199; N. Jidejian, *Tyre Through the Ages* (Beirut, 1969), 99.

[26] Hill, *BMC – Phoenicia*, lxxi–lxxiii, 108–110; H. Seyrig, "Une monnaie de Césarée du Liban," *Syria* 36 (1959), 38–43.

[27] A. Kindler, *The Coinage of Bostra* (Warminster, 1983), 64; *IGLS* XIII, no. 9057.

[28] B Sanhedrin 5a; Iggeret Rav Sherira Ga'on, Levin, p. 78.

[29] Genesis Rabbah 97, Theodor-Albeck, pp. 1220–1221; B Rosh Ha-shanah 31a–b (see as well *Diqduqei Soferim*). There is no concrete evidence concerning the activities of the leadership institutions in Shefarʿam.

[30] See for instance G. Alon, *The Jews in Their Land in the Talmudic Age*, trans. G. Levi (2 vols.; Jerusalem, 1980–84), II, 716–717; A. Oppenheimer, "The History of the Sanhedrin in the Galilee," in: *The Lands of the Galilee*, eds. A. Shmueli, et al. (2 vols.; Haifa, 1983), I, 257–268 (Hebrew).

Nasi, asking him to divide the tax burden between them, clearly illustrates this point.

In general, and as has already been pointed out by others in several studies, one can discern a fair measure of coordination between the Severan policy of urbanization and the activities of R. Judah ha-Nasi. Apart from what we have said above, the decree of Septimius Severus and Caracalla stated that Jews may serve as city functionaries and must perform liturgies as long as these are not irreconcilable with their religious precepts.[31] One issue which surfaced involving R. Judah ha-Nasi was exemption from the observance of commandments related to the produce of cities in Palestine having a considerable gentile population, such as Ashkelon, Caesarea, Beth Guvrin, and Beth Shean.[32] His intention was not to separate these and other places from the territory of the Land of Israel, nor to declare them unclean, as if they were in gentile lands.[33] Rather, Rabbi wished to encourage Jews to settle in these cities by supporting them in their economic competition with the gentile population.[34] As a result of the activities of the Severans, and in contrast to Hadrian's policy of encouraging the Hellenization of cities (including Tiberias and Sepphoris) and transferring local government to pagan elements of the city population, an essential change in the status of the cities of Palestine in the time of R. Judah ha-Nasi can be observed.[35]

B. The Roman Army

The Roman authorities used their army units in order to become directly involved in the daily life of the towns of the Galilee. Various legal discussions relating to events unconnected with a period of revolt mention the entry of army units into settlements, usually implying a disturbance of sorts in the life of the community. These forms of interference

31 See A. Linder, *The Jews in Roman Imperial Legislation* (Detroit, 1987), 103–107.

32 J Demai 2, 1, 22c; J Shevi'it 6, 1, 36c; J Yevamot 7, 2, 8a; T Oholot 18:18, Zuckermandel, p. 617; B Ḥullin 6b. See A. Büchler, *Studies in Jewish History* (London, 1954), 179–198. For different viewpoints concerning these sources, see M. Goodman, *State and Society in Roman Galilee A.D. 132–212* (Totowa, N.J., 1983), 178–180.

33 T Oholot 18:4, Zuckermandel, p. 616.

34 See S. Safrai, "The Practical Implementation of the Sabbatical Year after the Destruction of the Second Temple," *Tarbiẓ* 36 (1966), 1–12 (Hebrew); A. Oppenheimer, "Separating First Tithes Following the Destruction of the Second Temple," *Sinai* 83 (1978), 277–282 (Hebrew).

35 Jones, *Cities of the Eastern Provinces*, 278; B. Isaac and I. Roll, "Judaea in the Early Years of Hadrian's Reign," *Latomus* 38 (1979), 63–64.

are encountered especially in the period of crisis of the empire in the third century. Sages of this period stressed that Roman army units and officials never failed to enter Tiberias or Sepphoris on holidays:

> R. Isaac said: There is no festival without a patrol coming to Sepphoris. And R. Ḥanina said: There is no festival without the *hegemon* [the governor] or the *comes* or the holder of the *zemora* [an official who cannot be identified with certainty] coming to Tiberias.[36]

The major problem of the Jewish population in Roman Palestine during the period of crisis of the empire was the heavy tax burden,[37] so one may assume that the aim of the Roman soldiers' and officials' entry into Tiberias and Sepphoris in the situations cited above was to impose taxes and demand various services from the inhabitants. There are a number of traditions in talmudic literature that refer to soldiers engaged in collecting taxes in town, as, for example: "Once, a legion was passing and wanted to collect the *demosia* [taxes] of a certain town."[38]

The entry of Roman patrols into a settlement is also mentioned in the Mishnah, and that by itself may be seen as evidence of the scale of the intrusions of the Roman army into cities, even before the period of crisis of the empire in the third century:

> [When] a patrol of gentiles enters a city in times of peace open wine-jars are forbidden, closed ones are allowed. [When it happens] in times of war both are allowed because there is no time for libation.[39]

This source is important not so much because it makes a distinction between times of peace and times of war—a point of academic interest—but because it deals with actual incidents when "a patrol of gentiles enters a city." It appears that such incursions were common and inflicted a certain amount of harm on the population. This becomes clear from references in the Babylonian Talmud to army units opening wine barrels when passing through Neharde'a.[40] Obviously, the Roman army is not meant in this case, but it may well reflect the situation whenever there is military presence in towns. Evidence from the Yavneh period includes

---

36 B Shabbat 145b.

37 See for instance G. Alon, *The History of Jews in Eretz-Israel in the Period of the Mishna and Talmud (Toldot)* (2 vols.; Tel-Aviv, 1953–56), II, 182–193 (Hebrew); B. Isaac, *The Limits of Empire: The Roman Army in the East* (Oxford, 1990), Chapters III, VI.

38 PRK 27:6, Mandelbaum, p. 411.

39 M ʿAvodah Zarah 5:6.

40 B ʿAvodah Zarah 70b. See Oppenheimer, *Babylonia Judaica*, 289–290.

the case of Simeon the Yemenite, who did not arrive at the study house on the eve of a holiday and explained this the next day as follows:

> A patrol of gentile [soldiers] came into town and [the townspeople] were afraid that they [the soldiers] might harm the townspeople. [Therefore] we slaughtered a calf and we fed them [the soldiers]. . . .[41]

We can also deduce the frequency of entries of Roman army units into towns from the ruling on the question whether one may place two *ʿeruvim* (of town limits) on Sabbath eve. The case concerns someone who fears that gentiles—apparently soldiers—will arrive in town and, as he does not know from which direction they will come, he wants to keep open the possibility of fleeing in either direction.[42]

A ruling in the Mishnah states that "if a city was overcome by a besieging troop, all women therein permitted to marry priests become ineligible [for marriage with them]."[43] This is an indication of yet another negative consequence of the army's presence in towns. This particular ruling indeed applies to times of military conflict, but other sources show that sexual violence against women by soldiers was not restricted to times of tension. See, for example:

> Soldiers came into a city, and a woman came and said: A soldier embraced me and ejaculated between my knees. [Nonetheless], he permitted her to eat

---

[41] T Yom Tov 2:6, Lieberman, p. 287; cf. Mekhilta de-Rabbi Simeon bar Yoḥai, Bo, 12:16, Epstein-Melamed, p. 21; B Betza 21a.

[42] "A man may make conditions about his *ʿeruv* and say, 'If gentiles come from the east let my *ʿeruv* be to the west; if from the west let my *ʿeruv* be to the east; if from both sides let me go to which side I will'" (M ʿEruvin 3:5, trans. Danby, p. 124). A *baraita* in the Jerusalem Talmud states that the purpose of the one who places the *ʿeruv* is to be able to approach newcomers and not avoid them: "There is a *tanna* who says in the east" [i.e., when the gentiles came from the east my *ʿeruv* was in the east]. This is explained by the posing of the following problem: "Who says in the east means *taxiotai*, who says in the west means Romans" (J ʿEruvin 3, 5, 21b; cf. B ʿEruvin 36b). The text of the Jerusalem Talmud, "those Romans," supports the interpretation of the Mishnah that Roman units are meant. Also of interest is the explanation of the *baraita*, which raises the possibility of approaching soldiers, even though the aim of the reception—whether to honor them or to make requests of them, etc.—is not specifically stated; see S. Lieberman, *Hayerushalmi Kiphshuto* (Jerusalem, 1935), 272 (Hebrew); J. N. Epstein, *Introduction to the Mishnaic Text*[2] (2 vols.; Jerusalem, 1964), I, 107–108 (Hebrew).

[43] M Ketubot 2:9.

food in the status of the heave-offering [even though she said she had been sexually abused].[44]

A list of sorts accusing the Roman authorities of persecution, extortion, and interference in Jewish daily life in the settlements of Palestine can be found in Sifre to Deuteronomy 32:13–14:

> "And he made him suck honey out of the rock and oil out of the flinty rock," these are the oppressors who have taken hold of the Land of Israel, and it is as hard to receive a farthing from them as from a rock, but tomorrow Israel inherits their property and they will enjoy it as oil and honey. "Curds from the herd," these are their consulars and governors; "fat of lambs," these are their tribunes; "and rams," these are their centurions; "herds of Bashan," these are *beneficiarii* who take away [food] from between the teeth [of those who eat]; "and goats," these are their senators; "with the finest of the wheat," these are their *matronae*.[45]

Exceptional in its positive attitude towards an appearance of the Roman army in a Jewish settlement is a tradition regarding soldiers from the "castra of Sepphoris" who were prepared to extinguish a fire on the Sabbath in the yard of a Jew of Shiḥin near Sepphoris:

> It happened that there was a fire in the courtyard of Joseph b. Simai from Shiḥin. And the men from the "castra in Sepphoris" came to extinguish [it], but he would not let them, and a cloud descended from heaven and extinguished [it]. The sages said: He did not have to [prevent them from extinguishing the fire]. Nevertheless, after the Sabbath he sent a *selaᶜ* to each of the men and fifty dinarii to the *hipparchos*.[46]

Nevertheless, this is not clear evidence for the better face of the Roman army in its relations with the local population, for a parallel source in the Babylonian Talmud adds that Joseph b. Simai was "a steward of the king,"[47] i.e., a procurator, trustee of an estate of the king, presumably Agrippa II.

[44] J Nedarim 12, 13, 42d.

[45] Sifre–Deuteronomy, 317, Finkelstein, pp. 359–360.

[46] T Shabbat 13:9, Lieberman, p. 60; cf. J Shabbat 16, 7, 15d; J Yoma 8, 5, 45b; J Nedarim 4, 9, 38d; B Shabbat 121a. For the entire passage and on the problem regarding the identity of Joseph b. Simai, see S. S. Miller, *Studies in the History and Traditions of Sepphoris* (Leiden, 1984), 31–45.

[47] B Shabbat 121a; cf. B Sukkah 27a; the same person is mentioned there and, among other things, it is said that he had two wives, one in Tiberias and one in Sepphoris.

The above evidence gives us an indication of the consequences brought about by Roman military presence in the cities of the Galilee, as well as elsewhere. It clarifies and corroborates the Greek and Latin sources and epigraphical testimonies, from which it can also be deduced that it was standard practice in the eastern Roman provinces for the military to present themselves regularly in the towns.[48]

To conclude, it can be said that Roman rule left its mark on daily life in the cities of the Galilee. The discussion has centered upon two facets of that involvement—first, the organization of the cities, including the granting of status, instituting the urban leadership, and imposing various duties on these institutions; and second, the Roman military presence in towns. While Jewish sources generally are positive in their appreciation of Roman urban organization, especially in the period of R. Judah ha-Nasi, their attitude regarding the military presence is on the whole negative, particularly in the period of crisis of the empire in the third century.

[48] See Isaac, *The Limits of Empire*, Chapter III. For the Galilee, see Goodman, *State and Society*, 140–145, 175.

The Roman State and the Jewish Patriarch in the Third Century

MARTIN GOODMAN

In the second and third centuries C.E. the Near East suffered or profited from increasing intervention by the Roman state.[1] Whereas in the first century provincials were left much of the time to their own devices, with only occasional forays by Roman magistrates or military units to demonstrate the might of the suzerain power, by the time of Diocletian the apparatus of the state was much more widely and frequently in evidence. Thus, on the one hand many more troops were permanently stationed in the region and a network of roads was constructed to facilitate their rapid deployment, while on the other hand many areas previously controlled on behalf of Rome by native dynasties were subjected to direct Roman rule, a process which culminated in the creation of Provincia Arabia out of the old Nabatean kingdom in 106 C.E.[2]

It would be wrong to see increased Roman intervention as evidence of increased oppression, for this same period witnessed a gradual shift in perceptions of the state by many provincials. The emperor's subjects were encouraged to identify their interests with those of the state via the entrenched system of government, i.e., through local elites, whose loyalty to Rome was stimulated in this period by frequent grants of *polis* status to villages and of *colonia* status to favored cities. Provincials with Roman citizenship, if so inclined, could come to regard themselves as Roman; after 212 C.E., when citizenship was granted to all inhabitants of the

---

[1] For a general survey, see F. Millar, "Empire, Community and Culture in the Roman Near East: Greeks, Syrians, Jews and Arabs," *JJS* 38 (1987), 143–164.

[2] See G. W. Bowersock, *Roman Arabia* (Cambridge, MA/London, 1983), 76–89.

empire, it was possible in theory for a Syrian peasant to consider himself a full-fledged member of a unified society rather than a powerless minion oppressed by a foreign conqueror. Nor was such a view wholly imaginary: after all, the Roman emperor in 218–222 C.E. was Elagabalus, a priest from Emesa, and Philip the Arab, who reached the pinnacle of power in the Roman world and celebrated the secular games in honor of Rome's thousandth birthday in 248 C.E., came from Shahbá, at the edge of the Leja' near the western slopes of Jebel Druz.

Against such a background of increasing Roman intervention and provincial cooperation, Origen's description of the Jewish *nasi* in the Galilee in the mid-third century should come as a considerable surprise.[3] The relevant evidence is familiar and often quoted, but worth repeating since it comprises the only clear indication from a gentile source of the role of the *nasi* before Constantine.

In a letter to Africanus,[4] Origen wrote about the historicity of the story of Susanna:

> Now that the Romans rule and the Jews pay the two drachmas to them, we, who have had experience of it, know how much power the ethnarch has among them and that he differs in little from a king of the nation. Trials are held according to the law, and some are condemned to death. And though there is not full permission for this, still it is not done without the knowledge of the ruler.

Origen's testimony is to be believed, not least because his argument about the story of Susanna would be ruined if this appeal to current political conditions could be disputed.

Only one other passage can be confidently added to this remarkable piece of evidence.[5] In a discussion of the exegesis of Gen. 49:10, Origen

---

3 On this whole topic, see J. Juster, *Les juifs dans l'empire romain: leur condition juridique, économique et sociale* (2 vols.; New York, 1914), I, 391–402; H. Mantel, *Studies in the History of the Sanhedrin* (Cambridge, MA, 1961), 175–253; and esp. L. I. Levine, "The Jewish Patriarch (*Nasi*) in Third Century Palestine," in: *ANRW*, II, 19.2, eds. H. Temporini and W. Haase (Berlin/New York, 1979), 649–688. I do not intend here to contribute to the ongoing debate about the extent and causes of the *nasi's* influence among Jews. All scholars agree that the patriarch had achieved considerable influence by the mid-third century. I will attempt only to explain the Roman government's attitude to this state of affairs.

4 *Ep. ad Afric.* 20, 14, PG 11, 81–83.

5 I do not think any arguments about the *nasi* should be based on *Cod. Just.* 3.13.3, which preserves a rescript of Diocletian to a certain Judah in 293 C.E. The reasons for

stated the Jewish claim that a ruler descended from Judah still exists: "They say that the ethnarch, being from the family of Judah, rules the people."[6] This passage reinforces the view universally held by scholars that the ethnarch mentioned by Origen was the *nasi* of the rabbinic texts, whose descent from Judah was implicitly asserted in the third-century claim that Hillel, ancestor of R. Judah I, was of Davidic lineage.[7] Rabbinic texts, like Origen, describe the status of the *nasi* as hardly inferior to that of a king.[8]

The problem I wish to address here is simply: why did the Romans allow the ethnarch in the Galilee to wield such power? Various possibilities may be considered. One might argue that the state felt unable to oppose an anti-Roman national leader too powerful to be suppressed. Or one might suggest that the Romans did not like the influence of the *nasi*, but felt that the Galilee was too insignificant a region for its semi-independence to be seen as a threat. Or one might claim that Rome viewed the *nasi* positively, as a compliant local ruler through whom troublesome Jews could best be controlled. Or one might espouse a fourth possibility, which is the one that I shall eventually adopt here, that the Roman authorities may have permitted the *nasi* to exercise a jurisdiction voluntarily accepted by Jews, precisely because they did not see him as a local ruler at all, but simply as a religious leader. I shall examine each possibility in turn.

The first view posits that the *nasi* was leader of an independent Galilee whose power could not be suppressed by Rome. Such political independence was not unknown in the region in this period. Most famous are the rulers of Palmyra who took advantage of Roman military failure on the eastern frontier in the 260s and 270s to concentrate power in their own hands. In 253 C.E. a priest of Aphrodite from Emesa, named Sampsigeramus, was sufficiently powerful to defeat a Persian invasion without Roman aid.[9] However, it is debatable in the one case whether the Roman senator Odenathus of Palmyra sought local independence for its own sake or only as a stage towards hegemony in the wider Roman sphere; in the other case the coins issued at Emesa in the 250s, which

---

identifying this Judah with the *nasi*, Judah III, are not convincing. See the commentary in A. Linder, *The Jews in Roman Imperial Legislation* (Detroit, 1987), 114–117.

6 *De princip.* 4.3, PG 11, 348.

7 J Ta῾anit 4, 2, 68a. Cf. I. Lévi, "De l'origine davidique de Hillel," *REJ* 31 (1895), 202–211; 33 (1896), 143–144.

8 For example, J Sanhedrin 2, 6, 20d.

9 Malalas, *Chronographia*, ed. Niebuhr (Bonn, 1931), pp. 296–297.

celebrate an emperor—probably Sampsigeramus himself—with the Roman title, "Imperator Iulius Aurelius (Sulpicius) (Uranius) Antoninus," suggest that he, too, had grander ambitions.[10] In any case, both were figures rather different from the *nasi* described by the rabbis, for they commanded troops, issued coins, and held high Roman rank, none of which attributes can be plausibly applied to the third-century *nasi*; only from the mid-fourth century and later do we have evidence of a *nasi* achieving the Roman status of a *clarissimus*.[11] It is striking that, in contrast to that earlier *nasi* of Israel, the rebel Bar Kosiba, the later *nasi* is consistently described in rabbinic sources as conciliatory rather than antagonistic to Rome.[12]

The second suggestion, that the Romans ignored the power of the *nasi* without sanctioning it, simply because the Galilee was too unimportant in their eyes to be worth intervention, seems to me more attractive. The Galilean hills were of little significance in the strategic defense of the eastern frontier against Sassanian attack, since the brunt of aggression from Mesopotamia was taken by northern Syria, and the coast road or the road built by Trajan east of the Jordan provided a better route for invasions into Egypt from the north than a march through the Galilee. If the Jews wanted to have their own ruler, what cause did the Romans have to intervene in their lives, provided that taxes were paid? This explanation of the evidence, which is essentially the one I offered in 1983,[13] does not seem to me disprovable. Such a policy, however, does not fit very well into the general picture of increased Roman intervention outlined above.

[10] On Palmyra and Emesa in this period, see in general Millar, "Empire, Community and Culture," 155–159. On the coins of Emesa in the 250s, see H. R. Baldus, *Uranius Antoninus: Münzprägung und Geschichte* (Bonn, 1971).

[11] See the texts cited in Juster, *Juifs*, I, 397. M. Dothan, *Hammath Tiberias: Early Synagogues and the Hellenistic and Roman Remains* (Jerusalem, 1983), 33–70, argues that the mosaic inscription from the Hammath Tiberias synagogue, which refers to a certain Severos as *threptos tōn lamprotatōn patriarchōn*, should be dated to the late third or early fourth century C.E. on the basis of parallels in the design of the mosaic floor to mosaics found in Antioch in that period. Although I accept that such parallels provide a *terminus post quem*, I am not convinced that Jewish artists living in the cultural backwater of the Galilee (in contrast to the pioneering artists of Antioch) might not have adopted such motifs much later in the fourth century.

[12] On Bar Kosiba's use of the title, see P. Schäfer, *Der Bar Kokhba – Aufstand: Studien zum zweiten jüdischen Krieg gegen Rom* (Tübingen, 1981), 67–73.

[13] M. Goodman, *State and Society in Roman Galilee, A.D. 132–212* (Totowa, N.J., 1983), 135–154.

The third possibility will require lengthier consideration. Was the *nasi* in effect a governor of the Galilee on behalf of Rome? I am inclined to think that he was not, but since this hypothesis has been put forward in one form or another by many eminent scholars up to the present day,[14] the reasons for my caution must be expounded in some detail.

At a first glance at the relevant rabbinic texts, the grounds for believing that the *nasi* was appointed by Rome to a post as ruler of the Galilee, or was recognized in such a post by the Roman state, appear quite strong, for some aspects of his social position and political functions as described by the rabbis seem quite well suited to such a role. Judah ha-Nasi and his descendants were all reputed to be exceedingly rich (in comparison, presumably, with other Galileans). There are hints that the *nasi* was expected to speak competent Greek, and, if the stories about Rabbi's dialogues with Antoninus have any factual basis, it would seem that he was able to converse easily with Roman officials.[15]

However, although such attributes would assuredly distinguish the *nasi* as an important local aristocrat among others worthy of Roman attention, they would not require the Roman state to appoint him to quasi-monarchical power; there is no explicit evidence in rabbinic texts that the *nasi* owed his position to Rome in any such way. The lack of rabbinic references to the nasi's reliance on Rome is suggestive, for if the *nasi* were dependent on imperial favor, one might expect this reliance on the wicked king of Edom to be brought up against him during the not infrequent power struggles between him and the sages.

But the main reasons for doubting the accuracy of this picture of the *nasi* as a creature of the Roman state may be found in the testimony of Origen discussed above. Origen's explicit evidence regarding the attitude of the Romans to the ethnarch is not very helpful here: his assertion in the *Epistle to Africanus* that the state turned a blind eye when the ethnarch executed condemned criminals, despite the semi-illegality of such a procedure,[16] is compatible with any view about the original source of the ethnarch's power. However, closer examination of the implications of Origen's brief description of the ethnarch may suggest quite good indirect arguments against believing that the Jewish leader was appointed by Rome.

---

14 Cf. Juster, *Juifs*, I, 393; Levine, "Jewish Patriarch," 683.

15 See S. Krauss, *Antoninus und Rabbi* (Vienna, 1910).

16 Elsewhere, in *Ad Rom.* 6.7, *PG* 14, 1073, he states outright that the Jews were not permitted to put people to death.

First, let us examine the title by which Origen referred to this Jewish ruler. In both the extant passages Origen described the *nasi* as the "ethnarch." The office in question is clearly to be identified with that of the patriarch of the Jews, to whom reference was made in many Greek and Latin texts of the following century; the equation was sufficiently obvious to the Christian author, Rufinus, who rendered Origen's Greek writings into Latin in the late fourth century, for him to translate *ethnarches* in Origen's text as *patriarcha*.[17] Why, then, did Origen not use the term "patriarch"? Most likely he simply was unaware of the title "patriarch" in connection with the *nasi*. Thus he described as a "patriarch" an apparently local Jewish sage in Caesarea—a man named Iullos from whom Origen learned a midrash on Psalms[18]—without attempting to distinguish this local patriarch from the grander ruler based in the Galilee.[19] "Patriarch" seems to have been the Greek title given to the *nasi* not by the Romans but by the Jews: Eusebius, in an attack on the foolishness of the patriarchs, called them "those named 'patriarch' among Jews,"[20] and later in the fourth century Rufinus, in his translation of Origen's *De Princip.* 4.3, described the *nasi* as "that man, namely, he who is of their people the leader, whom they call 'patriarch'." Apparently Origen either did not know or did not care to use the name used by the Jews for their leader.

In theory, one could posit that by ignoring the Jews' title Origen preferred the name given to the *nasi* by the Romans, and that "ethnarch" was therefore a formal Roman designation. This is not impossible: the title "ethnarch" used by Archelaus, son of Herod the Great, had been assigned to him in 6 C.E. by the decision of the Roman emperor, Augustus,[21] and it could be argued that a later emperor might have revived the title for the new Jewish leader. Such a solution, however, is not very plausible, for the term for the *nasi* used consistently by official Roman sources throughout the fourth century was not "ethnarch" but "patriarch"[22] and the Roman state was usually very precise about the designa-

---

17 *PG* 11, 347.

18 *Comm. in Ps., PG* 12, 1055.

19 See N. R. M. de Lange, *Origen and the Jews: Studies in Jewish-Christian Relations in Third-Century Palestine* (Cambridge, 1976), 23–24. "Iullos" may well be equivalent to "Hillel," which was a traditional name in the *nasi*'s family, but no *nasi* of this name is attested in the rabbinic sources referring to the third century.

20 *In Isa.* 3.3–4, *PG* 24, 109.

21 Josephus, *War* II, 6, 3, 93–100.

22 Cf., for instance, *Cod. Theod.* 16. 8. 8, 22, 29.

tions given to client rulers—as the carefully graduated titles given to Herodian princes in the first century testify.[23] To uphold the view that Origen was using the Roman name for the *nasi* in his day, it would be necessary to assert, rather implausibly and without evidence, that the Romans in the late third or fourth century abandoned (for unknown reasons) the title for the *nasi* to which they were accustomed and adopted the Jews' own terminology—despite the fact that the word "patriarch" was not in common Roman use; it was only in the later fourth century that the Romans began gradually to apply the title to some Christian leaders.[24]

I prefer to explain Origen's ignorance of the title "patriarch" by suggesting that the *nasi* was not assigned any formal designation by the Roman state in the third century, in which case Origen used the title "ethnarch" as a description rather than as a formal title. A similarly loose use of the title was found in first-century Alexandria, where the leader of the Jewish community was described by the emperor Claudius (as quoted by Josephus) as "ethnarch," but by Claudius' contemporary, Philo, as "genarch."[25] Since the two names describe the same position ("ruler of the people"), it seems likely that neither was a formal designation by the Roman state.

A second argument against any formal recognition of the ethnarch as local ruler may be found in the functions of the *nasi* as described in rabbinic texts. As L. I. Levine has carefully established, the third-century *nasi* declared fast days, instituted and annulled bans, sent judges to serve communities (perhaps only if requested to do so), controlled the calendar, and, with his court, issued decrees about religious obligations such as the laws of Sabbath, purity, tithing, and the sabbatical year.[26] But what the *nasi* did not do, as far as I can tell, was the standard task of a local authority delegated power by the Roman government, namely, the collection of taxes on behalf of Rome.[27] It is true that the *nasi* became involved

---

[23] See the long discussion in E. Schürer, *The History of the Jewish People in the Age of Jesus Christ*, rev. and ed. G. Vermes, F. Millar, M. Black and M. Goodman (3 vols.; Edinburgh, 1973–87), I, 333–334.

[24] J. D. Mansi, *Sacrorum Conciliorum Nova et Amplissima Collectio* (reprint; Graz, 1960), II, 992 (Council of Nicaea in 381 C.E.), cited by Juster, *Juifs*, I, 396, n. 1.

[25] *Ant.* XIX, 5, 2, 283; Philo, *In Flaccum* 10, 74.

[26] Levine, "Jewish Patriarch," 663–676.

[27] I am compelled here to disagree with Levine, "Jewish Patriarch," 673. Note the comments on these passages by Mantel, *Studies*, 203. Reuven Kimelman points out that the most plausible deduction from rabbinic stories about the *nasi* 's need to use

in matters dealing with tax collection, but, it seems, not necessarily as the individual responsible for the collection. Thus, in B Bava Batra 7b R. Judah Nesiah is described as having required the rabbis to pay something towards building a wall for the city, and in B Bava Batra 8a R. Judah ha-Nasi is portrayed as having taken the side of the sages in their wish to evade contributing to the *aurum coronarium* tax. But both these passages may demonstrate only R. Judah's presumed moral influence over the sages who were unwilling to pay. Another talmudic passage has been interpreted as evidence that R. Judah Nesiah was accused of extorting money from the people,[28] but even if "the king who takes all" indeed refers to the patriarch rather than Rome (which is probable but not certain), there is no hint in the passage that any such extortion by the patriarch was for payment to Rome. On the contrary, tax collection was presumably supervised by the city councillors (*bouleutai*) who crop up in rabbinic texts[29] and who must also have supervised the civic coinages of Tiberias and Sepphoris; there is no evidence that the *nasi* was a member of any city's *boule*.

A third, brief, argument against Roman recognition of the ethnarch as a local ruler is bound to the implications of R. Judah ha-Nasi's reported request to the emperor that Tiberias be granted the status of a *colonia*.[30] Whether or not the appeal was successful, as A. Oppenheimer has argued it was,[31] the fact that the appeal was made at all puts in doubt any view of the *nasi* as a recognized monarch. Roman colonies were ruled by boards of magistrates who expected to have considerable influence with the Roman governor. If R. Judah was already in control of the Galilee on behalf of Rome, the request that Tiberias be given an elevated Roman status would have diminished his own power.

If the Romans did not view the ethnarch as a local ruler, what other reason could they have had for turning a blind eye when his court put people to death? There is, I think, a possible clue in Rome's treatment of the Christian church and, in particular, in the affair of Paul of Samosata, bishop of Antioch in the 270s C.E.[32] The Christian congregation of Antioch, which objected to Paul as bishop and convened an episcopal council

---

his Gothic bodyguards on occasion is that he lacked the backing of the Roman state. Roman support would have made physical force otiose.

28 J Sanhedrin 2, 6, 20d.

29 For example, Sifre Deuteronomy 309, Finkelstein, p. 348.

30 B ʿAvodah Zarah 10a.

31 See the contribution by A. Oppenheimer to this volume, pp. 118–120.

32 Eusebius, *Hist. Ecc.* 7.27–30.

to deprive him of his office, appealed successfully to the pagan Roman emperor Aurelian to remove Paul from the Church's house in the city when he refused to vacate it. Aurelian's agreement to intervene and uphold the decision made by the bishops of Italy and Rome presupposed his recognition of the Christian community as an institution with the right to choose its own leader and to have that choice enforced, when necessary, by the Roman state.[33] In the eyes of Rome, the bishop's function (as indeed that of the whole Christian congregation of Antioch) was presumably entirely religious. In practice, however, bishops often had a much wider secular role in governing their flock. Thus, among Constantine's earliest acts after the edict of toleration was the promulgation of laws granting formal status to the secular jurisdiction of Church courts in the manumission of slaves and other such matters.[34]

The position of the Jewish ethnarch appears in some ways remarkably similar. Like that of the bishop, his religious authority sometimes gave him secular power over his flock, and, like that of the bishop, his role was permitted but neither officially sanctioned nor encouraged by the Roman state.

But why should the Romans have permitted a Jewish religious leader to wield secular power in the Galilee when the ordinary civic authorities might have been expected to fulfill the necessary civic functions quite adequately? A partial explanation may be found in the fact that the Jews, unlike other peoples, had themselves traditionally ascribed power to a religious leader, the High Priest, at the time Rome first came into contact with Jews in the Land of Israel. Thus, the high-priestly families were natural candidates as local administrators in Jerusalem when Judea was eventually brought under direct Roman rule by a procurator in 6 C.E.[35] But the rabbinic ethnarch had a function rather different from that of a Judean high priest. The extraordinary influence of the Temple over the economic and political stability of Jerusalem provided much of the justi-

---

33 On the whole episode, see F. Millar, "Paul of Samosata, Zenobia and Aurelian: The Church, Local Culture and Political Allegiance in Third-Century Syria," *JRS* 61 (1971), 1–17. On the developing relationship between the Church and emperors before Constantine, see F. Millar, *The Emperor in the Roman World, 31 B.C.–A.D. 337* (London, 1977), 571–577.

34 See the laws cited in P. R. Coleman-Norton, *Roman State and Christian Church* (London, 1966), and esp. *Cod. Just.* 1.13.1 (316 C.E.); *Cod. Theod.* 1.27.1 (318 C.E.). On the monarchical role of bishops, see R. Lane Fox, *Pagans and Christians* (Harmondsworth, 1986), 493–545.

35 See M. Goodman, *The Ruling Class of Judaea: The Origins of the Jewish Revolt against Rome, A.D. 66–70* (Cambridge, 1987), 42–43.

fication for the power delegated to the high priest: the Romans needed all the help they could get in controlling volatile pilgrim crowds. So far as is known, no such considerations applied to the position of the *nasi* in third-century Galilee.

A more important reason for Roman acceptance of a religious leader's great influence among the Jews may be found in a general Roman perception in this period that the Jews were to be regarded more as a religious group than as a nation. I have discussed the arguments in favor of this in detail elsewhere, and I shall review them here only briefly.[36]

The crucial change in Roman perceptions of Jewish identity occurred with the reform of the *fiscus Judaicus* by Nerva in 96 C.E. An annual poll tax of two denarii had been imposed on all Jews by Vespasian after the failure of the first revolt in 70 C.E. This tax, assiduously collected from the start, as papyri from Egypt testify,[37] aroused resentment in Rome under Domitian, when apostate Jews and those who carried on their religious practices in secret were compelled to contribute.[38] It was probably awareness of this feeling of resentment which prompted the reform loudly proclaimed on the coins of Domitian's successor, Nerva: FISCI IUDAICI CALUMNIA SUBLATA. If Nerva's policy was indeed aimed against the abuses under Domitian, it seems probable that from 96 C.E. apostate Jews were freed from the tax. The consequences were considerable, for only those Jews who still practiced their religion were now defined as Jews for the purpose of the *fiscus*; in the early third century C.E. Cassius Dio took this for granted.[39]

The immediate effect of making religious practice an essential element in the Roman state's definition of Jewishness was a greater consciousness among non-Jews of the Jewish custom of accepting proselytes as full Jews on the sole condition that they conform to the Jewish religion. This custom was considered extremely odd by the Greeks and Romans, hence the significance of the near-total silence about it in gentile sources composed before 96 C.E. and the contrasting rash of references to

---

[36] See M. Goodman, "Nerva, the *Fiscus Judaicus* and Jewish Identity," *JRS* 79 (1989), 40–44.

[37] See V. A. Tcherikover, A. Fuks and M. Stern, *Corpus Papyrorum Judaicarum* (2 vols.; Cambridge, MA, 1957–64), I, 80–82; II, 111–116.

[38] Suetonius, *Dom.* 12.2. See L. A. Thompson, "Domitian and the Jewish Tax," *Historia* 31 (1982), 329–342.

[39] Cassius Dio, *Hist. Rom.* 66.7.2.

it in Greek and Latin literature of the early second century, after Nerva's reform.[40]

Such references are frequently hostile—not surprisingly, for the proselyte abandoned the gods of his ancestors and his native society to enter Judaism. It was no accident that when Antoninus Pius relaxed the prohibition of circumcision, which Hadrian had imposed on all his subjects for humanitarian reasons, he permitted only the circumcision of the sons of existing Jews,[41] thereby in theory (though not, it seems, very effectively in practice) preventing the accretion of male proselytes to Judaism. In other words, from the time of Antoninus Pius Jews were defined by the Roman state as the practitioners of a religion which was in theory, though not always in practice, confined to the *ethnos* among whom it had originated.[42]

What was the significance of this new Roman definition of Jewishness for the inhabitants of Palestine? On the one hand, implementation of the policy described in Justin Martyr's famous assertion, that any Jew found within the area of Jerusalem was punished by death,[43] would have been feasible only if Jews were defined as those who still practiced Judaism: exclusion of all those of Jewish ethnic origin was hardly practicable, owing to the difficulty of establishing the parentage of individuals who were not Roman citizens, the problem of children of mixed marriages, and presumably the need for the presence of some peasants in the fields around Aelia Capitolina in order to produce commodities for local consumption. The rabbinic traditions regarding a general attempt by Hadrian to suppress Jewish religious practices after the Bar Kokhba war may reflect this same ban on Jews settling around Aelia rather than a more widespread persecution; after all, Justin Martyr himself bore witness to the lack of persecution of Jews in Asia Minor in this period, and there is no evidence that any diaspora Jewish community was molested.[44]

On the other hand, if Jews were to be defined by Romans primarily by their religion, it was natural for Romans to assume that Jewish institutions belonged essentially to a religious group, like other religious

40 Epictetus, ap. Arrian, *Diss.* 2.9.20; Juvenal, *Sat.* 14.96–104; Tacitus, *Hist.* 5.5.2.

41 Modestinus, ap. *Digest* 48.8.11.

42 See Linder, *Jews in Roman Legislation*, 55–59, for interesting remarks about Roman jurists' terminology when referring to Jews.

43 *I Apol.* 47.6.

44 See M. Avi-Yonah, *The Jews of Palestine: A Political History from the Bar Kochba War to the Arab Conquest* (Oxford, 1976), 17.

groups in the Roman empire. J. North has outlined the gradual process between the second century B.C.E. and the fourth century C.E. by which pagan Romans came to view religion as a distinct aspect of life, in principle separable from other political and cultural aspects of society.[45] This new Roman attitude found expression in the early empire in the increasing efflorescence of *collegia* whose whole reason for existence was cultic worship by their members. The prime examples of such religious clubs were Christian communities which, as has been seen above (p. 135), were clearly recognized by the state as autonomous institutions by the mid-third century. Romans in the third century could most easily fit the Jews into such a model.

If all this is correct, it would not be so surprising that the Roman state should have allowed the *nasi* to exercise jurisdiction over Jews. If Jews were by definition only Jews through their voluntary adherence to Judaism, and they could apostatize at any time, their submission to the authority of the *nasi* could be seen as similarly voluntary—just as any Christian unhappy with his bishop could, if he so wished, cease to be a Christian. There is, I believe, no evidence that either non-Jews or lapsed Jews in the Galilee in this period had any reason to heed the views of the *nasi*: the earliest clear evidence that a *nasi* might have judged cases involving non-Jews is to be found much later, in the law of October 415 C.E. which restricted the authority of Gamaliel VI by forbidding him to try Christians.[46] Similarly, there is no evidence in the third century for the most striking aspect of the state's attitude to the *nasi* in the late fourth century, namely, support for the *nasi*'s authority outside Palestine and for his right to collect funds from all Jews in the Roman diaspora.[47] As L. I. Levine has correctly pointed out, the rights accorded the patriarch by the emperors in the fourth century may well have been modelled on

---

45 J. North, "Religious Toleration in Republican Rome," *Proc. Camb. Phil. Soc.* (n.s.) 25 (1979), 85–103.

46 *Cod. Theod.* 16.8.22.

47 Goodman, *State and Society*, 116–118. The Stobi inscription (J.-B. Frey, *Corpus Inscriptionum Iudaicarum* [2 vols.; Rome, 1939–52; vol. I reprint, New York, 1975], I, no. 694), which records the grant of part of a private house for use as a synagogue in the late second or third century C.E., stipulates a very large fine "payable to the patriarch" in case of contravention. How this was to be enforced is unclear; see comment and bibliography in Schürer, *History*, III, 67–68.

those granted to Christian clergy[48] and presumably would not have been in existence in the third century.[49]

What all this means for the history of the Galilee in the third century is that we should expect the Roman state to have treated this region in most aspects of life like any other part of the eastern empire, with local authorities dignified as city councillors, controlling and taxing their territories on behalf of Rome. The curious exception to this situation was only that, for spiritual reasons, some, perhaps many, inhabitants of the province voluntarily placed themselves, in some respects at least, under the religious and secular jurisdiction of an outstanding religious figure, the *nasi*.

[48] Levine, "Jewish Patriarch," 677.

[49] Most of the argumentation in this article depends on the unprovable hypothesis that the absence of evidence should be understood as significant. I do not think I could prove that the traditional composite picture of the role of the *nasi*, in which all evidence is lumped together to create a coherent whole, is impossible, but it seems to me much less plausible. The Romans in the High Empire did not need any single person to speak on behalf of Jews any more than they recognized such a representative of Thracians, Egyptians or Spaniards. It seems to me preferable to link the eventual empire-wide powers of the *nasi* to the policy of Theodosius the Great in the late 380s, whose insistence that the state impose the correct brand of Christianity on its subjects encouraged the process by which individuals were defined by the state primarily in terms of their religious affiliation.

*IV. RABBIS AND GALILEAN JEWRY
IN LATE ANTIQUITY*

Was There a Galilean Halakhah?*

LAWRENCE H. SCHIFFMAN

Many scholars have assumed that by the first two centuries of our era a distinctive pattern of halakhah covering a wide range of issues and aspects had evolved in the Galilee that was practiced by its inhabitants. This claim was based on a variety of tannaitic sources which distinguished regional customs or practices within the Jewish communities of Greco-Roman Palestine, and was used to explain in part the sympathy of Galileans for a variety of movements, including Sadduceeism, nascent Christianity, and the revolt against Rome.[1]

The entire notion of a Galilean halakhah is somewhat a misnomer, since the tannaitic halakhic system came to its literary fruition in the Mishnah, a document edited in the Galilee.[2] What we really mean by a Galilean halakhah is a system native to the Galilee which was already practiced in the first century C.E. and which, therefore, differed markedly from the "Judean" system of halakhah. According to this definition, the

* This study was completed during my tenure as a Fellow of the Institute for Advanced Studies of the Hebrew University in 1989. I gratefully acknowledge the assistance of the staff of the Institute.

1 These approaches are surveyed by A. Oppenheimer, *The 'Am Ha-aretz* (Leiden, 1977), 2–8, 200–202; and S. Freyne, *Galilee from Alexander the Great to Hadrian, 323 B.C.E. to 135 C.E.* (Wilmington, 1980), 307–309. Cf. also J. Schwartz, *Jewish Settlement in Judaea* (Jerusalem, 1986), 233–236 (Hebrew).

2 Indeed, M. Goodman, *State and Society in Roman Galilee A.D. 132–212* (Totowa, N.J., 1983), understands much of the tannaitic material as reflecting specifically Galilean conditions. We see this material as reflecting the common heritage of both Judean and Galilean Jews.

"Judean" halakhah would have been brought northward by the tannaim after the Bar-Kokhba revolt (132–135 C.E.). The existence of a Galilean halakhah would have required either that the Galileans had a completely different system for deriving their views on matters of Jewish law or that they differed on a large number of fundamental issues with the views held at that time by the emerging tannaitic movement.

This paper will reexamine all the passages in tannaitic literature referring explicitly to Galilean halakhic practices.[3] Each will be studied to clarify its textual basis, to determine its dating, and then to assess its relevance to the issue of a Galilean halakhah. We will seek to establish whether these tannaitic reports indicate differing approaches to the derivation of Jewish law or widespread differences in halakhic rulings among Galileans, or whether these varying practices are simply reflections of regional custom, often the result of differing political, social, and economic conditions. We will also inspect the evidence supporting the claim by some scholars of widespread laxity on the part of Galileans in the observance of Jewish law.[4] Such evidence, if evinced, would indicate the possibility that the halakhic system of the rabbis was new to the Galilee, but it would in no way provide support for the notion of a different halakhic system native to the north.

Our study will demonstrate that the claim for a Galilean halakhah has been highly exaggerated. The passages in question simply show that within the community of Jews which followed tannaitic traditions, those in the Galilee shared certain local customs. In the vast majority of matters, however, these Jews adhered to the same rulings as the tannaitic Jews of the south. The very nature of these differences and the manner in which they are presented in tannaitic sources show that they constituted the few areas in which such Galilean rulings or divergent customs existed.[5] Furthermore, we find no evidence of widespread laxity in the

---

3 Omitted here are references to weights and measures, agricultural or climatic conditions. Also omitted are amoraic deductions from tannaitic sources. See T Demai 1:1; J Demai 1, 1, 21d; B Shabbat 153a; J Mo'ed Qatan 3, 5, 82d; J Berakhot 2, 7, 5b; B Hullin 106a and 116a.

4 Goodman, *State and Society*, 107–108, describes Galilean Jewry in this period as basically observant, while minimizing the role of rabbinic authority in bringing about this state of affairs.

5 The very same conclusions were reached by Oppenheimer, *'Am Ha-aretz*, 200–217. His study approached the question in a different context and used a different method. Our replication of his results should settle the matter for once and for all. A similar approach is taken also by E. E. Urbach, "From Judea to the Galilee," in: *Jacob*

Galilee in tannaitic times or later. On the contrary, our study finds time and again that tannaitic sources attributed to the Galileans a higher degree of stringency in halakhic observance than to the Judeans.

This study does not claim to speak of the entire population of the Galilee. We must keep in mind that at this time tannaitic Judaism was still in the process of establishing itself as the dominant form of Judaism in the Galilee. Certainly, remnants of Hellenistic Judaism as well as the Judaism of the Galilean peasants still must have existed to a limited extent. Evidence points to close association of Galilean Jews with the Jerusalem Temple,[6] and the customs and rulings of the Galileans reported in the rabbinic corpus do not indicate a competing system of halakhah. Rather, they show the openness of the tannaitic system to differences of opinion and, within certain limits, to regional variation. Indeed, as rabbinic Judaism continued to develop within a widening geographic context, regional and local customs became one of the prime features of Jewish life both in the Land of Israel and in the Diaspora.

Marriage Customs

M Ketubot 4:12 discusses the conditions of the marriage contract regarding the support of widows:[7]

[If he did not write into the marriage contract:[8] "After my death] you shall dwell in my house and be supported out of my property, as long as you remain a widow in my house," [nonetheless] he [i.e., his estate] is [still] obligated, for it is a condition [of the marriage imposed] by the court [*bet din*]. Indeed, the people of Jerusalem used to write accordingly [in the marriage contract]. The people of the Galilee used to write in the same way as the people of Jerusalem. [But] the people of Judea used to write: "[You shall dwell in my house and be supported out of my property] up until such time

---

Friedman Memorial Volume, ed. S. Pines (Jerusalem, 1974), 61–66 (Hebrew); and S. Klein, *The Land of the Galilee* (Jerusalem, 1967), 174 (Hebrew). Klein provides a list of references in tannaitic halakhic material which mention the Galilee; see pp. 171–174. A similar list which also includes some amoraic material was compiled by S. Haggai, "Differences in *Halakha* between Judea and the Galilee," *Maḥanaim* 101 (1965), 15–17 (Hebrew).

6 Freyne, *Galilee,* 259–297; and S. Safrai, *Pilgrimage at the Time of the Second Temple* (Tel-Aviv, 1965), 115–117 (Hebrew).

7 Cf. M. A. Friedman, *Jewish Marriage in Palestine – A Cairo Geniza Study* (2 vols.; Tel-Aviv/New York, 1980), I, 428–435.

8 See M Ketubot 4:8, *loʾ katav lah.*

as the heirs shall desire to pay you your marriage contract settlement."
Therefore, if the heirs [in Judea] wanted to, they could pay her her marriage
contract settlement and send her away.

This mishnah testifies to a difference regarding the text of the marriage
contract. It begins with the blanket statement that the clause guarantee-
ing the widow support is required, and that even if omitted from the
contract it is still in force. It then indicates a difference of custom regarding the content of the clause, proffering the Jerusalem-Galilean version
and that of the Judeans. The mishnah then draws the conclusion that the
Jerusalem-Galilean contract provided for permanent support for the
widow (if this was what she preferred), whereas the Judean version permitted the heirs to pay a one-time settlement even against the will of the
widow.

Galilean and Jerusalemite widows enjoyed the option of permanent
support after the death of their husbands, what we would call an annuity
plan, or a lump sum payment. In the case of Judean widows, it was up to
the heirs to determine which form of payment would be made. It seems
that, in this case, the Galileans went much further in making sure that the
purpose of the marriage contract (*ketubah*), to protect the woman from
the financial vicissitudes of widowhood or divorce, would be effected.
This constitutes, therefore, a Galilean stringency.

M Ketubot 1:5 preserves another difference in marriage customs:

One who eats at the house of [ʾetzel] his father-in-law in Judea without [the
presence of] witnesses cannot make a claim of [non-]virginity, since he is
alone with her [his bride-to-be].

The normal procedure in Jewish marriage in the tannaitic period consisted of two steps. The first, betrothal (ʾerusin), meant that all aspects of
the marriage were effected, other than cohabitation. With the second
step, marriage (nissuʾin), usually a year later, the relationship was con-
summated and the couple shared a home. This mishnah indicates that if
the groom were to move into the house of his future father-in-law during
the period of betrothal, as was the custom in Judea (at least among some
Jews), and if he were left alone with his bride-to-be, he forever forfeited
the right to make a claim that she was not a virgin in accordance with
Deut. 22:13–21. It can be deduced from this mishnah that this problem
did not exist in the Galilee.

In a similar vein, M Yevamot 4:10 mentions another difference between Judea and the Galilee.[9] There the anonymous mishnah[10] rules that widows, whether from betrothal or marriage, are forbidden to marry for three months after the death of the "spouse," in order to establish the paternity of a child who might be born, and hence the responsibility of child support. An opposing opinion then follows:

> R. Judah says: Those who were married may be betrothed and those who had been betrothed may get married, except for the betrothed in Judea, because he is accustomed to [or: intimate with] her.

R. Judah takes the view that the anonymous ruling is excessively strict, since in some of the cases the possibility of pregnancy need not be considered: he is confident that a betrothed widow will not become pregnant with her new husband during her period of betrothal, and that a girl who had been betrothed but not married and whose future husband died would not have become pregnant during the period of betrothal. Yet he makes an exception of the betrothed in Judea, where the standards were much laxer and the possibility existed that intimacy may have led to sexual relations and pregnancy. Once again, the Galileans maintained a stricter standard than their Judean coreligionists.

T Ketubot 1:4 lists a number of differences in marriage customs between Judea and the Galilee which are related to this same problem.[11] Here again, the attribution is to R. Judah.

> Said R. Judah: At first [*ba-rishonah*] in Judea they used to search [examine?] the marriage canopy, the groom, and the bride [for?] three days before the wedding, but in the Galilee they were not accustomed [to do] so. At first in Judea they used to set aside the bride and groom [for] an hour before the wedding, so that he would become intimate with her,[12] but in the Galilee they were not accustomed [to do] so. At first in Judea they would set up two best men, one from the house of the groom and one from the house of[13] the

9   9 Cf. T Yevamot 6:6–7; and S. Lieberman, *Tosefta Ki-Fshuṭah* (10 vols.; New York, 1955–88), VI, 51–57.

10   From the Tosefta it appears that the anonymous mishnah is to be attributed to R. Meir, whose view is supported in the Tosefta with a statement attributed to R. Yoḥanan b. Beroqa, a second-generation tanna who was a contemporary of R. ʿAqiva.

11   Cf. J Ketubot 1, 1, 25a; B Ketubot 12a.

12   So M. Jastrow, *A Dictionary of the Targumim, the Talmud Babli and Yerushalmi, and the Midrashic Literature* (Philadelphia, 1903; reprint New York, 1985), s.v. *gws*.

13   Following ms. Erfurt and *ed. princ.*

bride, but even so [in Judea] they set up these best men only for the marriage [*nissu²in*] [itself], but in the Galilee they were not accustomed [to do]
so. At first in Judea two best men would sleep where the groom and the
bride slept, but in the Galilee they were not accustomed [to do] so. Whoever
does not follow this practice [*minhag*] cannot claim [lack of] virginity.[14]

Each of the customs related here was designed to ensure that neither the
bride nor groom in Judea was able to do anything to make possible a
false claim, or a fraudulent defense against a claim, that the bride had not
been a virgin upon marriage. It seems, however, that the Galilean bride
and groom did not practice these precautions, but generally relied on
each other's upstanding character and entered the marriage expecting no
dishonest claims. This was not the case in Judea, where such claims seem
to have been much more common and where there was greater suspicion
of fabricated claims or defenses.

In this case, the evidence shows that stricter observance and honesty
prevailed in the Galilee. Both Judea and the Galilee had the same laws
regarding the obligation of virginity for the unmarried, and both adhered
to the biblical injunction regarding claims of the bride's non-virginity.
Yet the Judeans, because of their laxer moral standards, had to employ
additional precautions unnecessary for the Galileans. Again, there is no
Galilean halakhah, just more stringent observance of the common set of
laws.

Vows

M Nedarim 2:4 mentions two differences between Judea and the
Galilee:

[If he took a vow, saying,] "May it [a certain object] be for me like *terumah*":
if he took the vow [intending it to be] like a contribution to the sanctuary
[*terumat ha-lishkah*], then it [the object] is forbidden [to him].[15] But if [he took
the vow intending it to be] like the portion [*terumah*] set aside at the threshing floor,[16] it [the object] is permitted.[17] But if [he took the vow] with no

---

[14] Cf. Deut. 22:13–19.

[15] That is, the vow is valid.

[16] Which is given to the priests.

[17] The vow is invalid, since he compared the object to an item which the Torah
forbade him to eat. See M Nedarim 2:1 and Albeck (below, n. 26).

specific intention [*setam*], then it is forbidden.[18] These are the words of R. Meir. [But] R. Judah says: [If he took a vow comparing an object to] unspecified *terumah*[19] in Judea, it is forbidden, but in the Galilee it is permitted, for the people of the Galilee are not familiar with [*she-ʾen . . . makkirin ʾet*] the contribution to the sanctuary [*terumat ha-lishkah*]. Unspecified consecration [*herem*] offerings, in Judea are permitted,[20] but in the Galilee they are forbidden since the people of the Galilee are not familiar with consecration offerings which are set apart for the priests.

In order for a vow [*neder*] to be valid, such that the vower is forbidden to make use of the object in question, he must vow that the object is considered by him to be forbidden like some object usually permitted but now consecrated. If instead he vows that the object should be like a forbidden object, then the vow is not valid. When the vower does not really have any specific intention, the beginning of the mishnah rules that the stricter approach is to be taken and it is assumed that the vow is valid. According to this approach, our passage reports the view attributed to R. Meir, that the ambiguous term *terumah* is to be assumed as referring to the offering of funds for communal sacrifices, the *terumat ha-lishkah*, thus rendering the vow valid. R. Judah is said to have added that this ruling is applicable only in Judea, where the phrase *terumat ha-lishkah* is often used. Hence, it is conceivable that people could intend it in a vow. But since in the Galilee, which is distant from the Temple, the term *terumah* always refers to the priestly portion, there the vow may be assumed to be invalid. Similarly, there is a difference in the usage of the term *herem*.[21] In Judea, this matter is ambiguous and the stricter approach is taken. It is assumed that this term refers to portions consecrated for the priests and hence the vow is valid. In the Galilee, however, due to the distance from the Temple, *herem* is used to refer only to offerings for refurbishing the Temple. Since these are always forbidden, the vow is not valid.[22]

T Nedarim 1:6 preserves a parallel to this passage in the Mishnah. It indicates that whereas the clause regarding the Galilee and *terumah* vows

18 The vow is valid according to the ruling at the beginning of the mishnah, that vows which are unspecified are to be understood in the strictest sense.

19 The one who took the vow had no specific intention, for if he had, his intention would determine the issue.

20 They are considered to be offerings for the priests and may be used by others after they have been transferred to the priests' ownership.

21 It is not certain if these are the words of R. Judah or an addition by later tradents or editors.

22 Cf. J Nedarim 2, 4, 37c.

is to be attributed to R. Judah, the clause regarding the *herem* is to be attributed to R. El'azar b. Zaddoq of the Yavnean period.

Some have taken this mishnah to indicate that the Galileans did not contribute to the sanctuary or give portions to the priests. Nothing could be farther from the truth. The discussion concerns the meaning of the terms *terumah* and *herem* in the various regions of Palestine. The entire system of oaths and vows was dependent on the common usages of the people.[23] This Yavnean debate informs us that since the Galileans were occupied regularly with priestly offerings, but due to the distance from the Temple they did not regularly encounter the other donations, the unspecified terms used in the Galilee could easily be defined as referring to priestly portions. Hence, in both cases the vows were considered valid. In any event, this passage may deal with a Galilean linguistic usage, but certainly not with a Galilean halakhah.

The same aspect of *herem* is taken up again in M Nedarim 5:4–5. M Nedarim 5:4 mentions a case of two individuals[24] who declare each other's possessions to be forbidden as *herem*. The mishnah is concerned with whether they may then use public property in which they are partners, and rules that they may continue to use that public property set aside by the returnees from Babylonia (*'ole Bavel*), since this property has been made the possession of all Israel and no declarations of *herem* have any validity regarding it. However, they may not use the property of their own city, since they are regarded as partners in the city's facilities.

After a definition of these two types of property, M Nedarim 5:5 states that the reciprocal *herem* can be vitiated by each of the two people deeding over his own portion in the city's property to the *nasi*. R. Judah takes the view that deeding the share to anyone is as valid as deeding it to the *nasi*, except that the latter does not require a formal act of acquisition. The sages require acts of acquisition even from the *nasi*. The mishnah notes that the earlier anonymous statement had simply reflected the normal condition in which such deeds were made over to the *nasi*.[25]

To this, R. Judah adds:

---

[23] See S. Lieberman, *Greek in Jewish Palestine* (New York, 1942), 115–143.

[24] Are they partners? See M Nedarim 5:1.

[25] Klein, *Land of the Galilee*, 23–24, takes the term *nasi* here as referring to one of the Hasmonean kings. He is followed by Urbach, "From Judea," 59–60, who identifies the *nasi* of this mishnah with Simon Maccabee. It may also be understood as referring to the Pharisaic-rabbinic *nasi*.

The people of the Galilee do not have to deed over their property [*likhtov*], since their forefathers already deeded it over on their behalf.

It should be emphasized that since R. Judah accepts the equal validity of deeding the share of city property to the *nasi* or to anyone else (provided that in the latter case there is an act of acquisition), his statement about the Galileans need not necessarily be taken as a reference to the *nasi*.[26]

Here we have an anonymous mishnah glossed in the Ushan period by R. Judah bar Ilai, who notes that the Galileans made a permanent deeding over of their share in the city property. A *baraita* in B Nedarim 48a suggests that the Galileans were quick to vow and deeded their property as a precaution against such *herem* declarations. Hence, this is not a Galilean halakhah, but simply a description by R. Judah of how the Galileans went about taking precautions to ensure compliance with a law, the specifics of which he and the sages had debated.

Tithes

The subject of tithes in Judea is discussed in M Ḥagigah 3:4.[27] While this passage does not explicitly mention the Galilee, it has implications for our study:

There is a greater stringency regarding *terumah* [the priest's share of the crop,[28] than regarding sacrifices], for in Judea they [the common people] are trusted regarding the purity of wine and oil [for sacrifices] all year round. And at the time of the wine presses and the olive presses [i.e., during the pressing], [they are trusted] even regarding the *terumah*. Once the time of the wine presses and the olive presses has passed, if they [the common people] brought to him [i.e., to a priest] a jug of wine of *terumah*, he should not accept it from him [i.e., them].[29] But he [the commoner] may leave it for the next wine-press[ing season].[30] But if he [the commoner] said to him [the

26 Cf. C. Albeck, *The Six Orders of the Mishnah* (6 vols.; Jerusalem, 1957–59), commentary and "Addenda," ad loc. (Hebrew).

27 Cf. the parallel in T Ḥagigah 3:30-33; and Lieberman, *Tosefta Ki-Fshuṭah*, V, 1331-1334.

28 So Jastrow, *Dictionary*, s.v. *terumah*.

29 T Ḥagigah 3:36 relates a story to the effect that R. Tarfon rejected this ruling and accepted *terumah* all year round. He cited Rabban Yoḥanan b. Zakkai as agreeing with him. Nonetheless, after receiving complaints, R. Tarfon accepted the ruling of the anonymous mishnah.

30 T Ḥagigah 3:32 in mss. Vienna and Erfurt (before the correction) rules that the priest should not accept the jug the following year. The correction in ms. Erfurt and

priest], "I have poured [lit., separated][31] into it [the jug] a quarter [log] of [wine which is sufficiently pure to be offered as a] sacrifice, then he is trusted [even regarding the ritual purity] of the *terumah*.

This mishnah sets forth the distinction regarding the reliability of Judeans to certify the ritual purity of wine and oil. They were always considered reliable regarding the purity of sacrificial offerings, since these restrictions were observed widely. Regarding the purity of *terumah*, they were assumed to be reliable only during the pressing season, when they were careful to separate the priestly portion that was in a state of ritual purity. Thereafter, until the time of the next pressing, the common people of Judea were not considered reliable regarding *terumah*.

Both the Palestinian and Babylonian Talmuds conclude that the reliability of the commoners accepted in this mishnah applies only in Judea and not in the Galilee.[32] Indeed, this contrast seems sensible in light of M Ḥagigah 3:5,[33] which indicates that the determining factor here is proximity to Jerusalem.[34] In Judea, where Temple offerings and practices were a large part of life, purity was maintained as regards offerings. In the Galilee, however, where produce was much less likely to be used for offerings, a lower level of reliability could be presumed.[35] This passage, therefore, does not reflect on the piety of the Galileans or their halakhic rulings. They accepted the same laws as the Judeans; it is simply because they were far from the Temple that they saw no reason to maintain Temple purity for all their produce.

That the Galileans held to the tithing laws, as did the Judeans, can be seen from other evidence as well. Josephus (*Life* 12, 62–63 and 15, 80)

---

various secondary witnesses omits *lo'* and permits acceptance of this jug by the priest; Lieberman, *Tosefta Ki-Fshuṭah*, V, 1332–1333). It is also possible to understand the Tosefta as prohibiting acceptance only when the priest is certain (*makkir*) that this is the same jug from last year.

31 The causative inflection (*hiph'il*) of *prš* is usually employed as a technical term for the setting aside of the priestly portion.

32 J Ḥagigah 3, 4, 79b; B Ḥagigah 25a. Note that the Babylonian material is of Palestinian provenance.

33 Cf. the parallel in T Ḥagigah 3:29, and Lieberman, *Tosefta Ki-Fshuṭah*, V, 1330–1331.

34 Oppenheimer, *'Am Ha-aretz*, 204–205.

35 The explanation of the amoraim that it was the intervening "strip of the Samaritans" (רצועה של כותים) which rendered the produce of the Galilee impure has been rightly questioned by Tosafot to B Ḥagigah 25a, and later by Safrai, *Pilgrimage*, 44–46. In any case, the context of the mishnah argues against it.

testifies to the observance of the priestly gifts in the Galilee during the Great Revolt of 66–73 C.E It appears, from the text of T Sanhedrin 2:6, that the Pharisaic sages were in contact with the Galileans in this regard:

> It happened that Rabban Gamaliel and the Elders were sitting on the stairs [*ʿal gav maʿalot*] on the Temple Mount, and Yoḥanan, that scribe, was before them. They said to him, "Write to our brothers, the people [*bene*] of the Upper Galilee and the people of the Lower Galilee: 'May you have great peace! We are informing you that the time of the removal has come, to take out the tithes from the vats of olives.'"

This letter concerns the requirement that on the Passover[36] of the fourth and seventh years of the sabbatical cycle all tithes and priestly portions set apart and not given to the Levites or the poor had to be given to them or destroyed in accordance with Deut. 14:28–29 (cf. 26:13). The sages are said to have written to the Galileans to remind them that this was a year for "the removal" of these offerings.

If indeed the setting is accurate, the letter would have been sent in the days of the Temple, and the Rabban Gamaliel mentioned would have been Gamaliel I. On the other hand, it is more likely that such a letter was sent after the destruction, under Gamaliel II of Yavneh, to encourage giving these gifts in the absence of the Temple. In either case, the passage still testifies to the regular participation of the Galileans in the agricultural rituals and gifts required by the halakhah.

Festivals and Fasts

M Pesaḥim 4:1–5 is a list of matters in which one is to follow local custom. The chapter begins with the difference in custom regarding the 14th of Nisan, the eve of Passover, on which the paschal sacrifice is offered in the afternoon. The mishnah tells us that in some places it was customary to do work (*melakhah*) up to noon, while in others it was not. In M Pesaḥim 4:5, the text returns to the main topic:

> Everywhere, scholars abstain [from work]. Rabban Simeon b. Gamaliel says: A person should always act as if he is a scholar [and abstain from work]. But the sages say: In Judea they worked on Passover eve until noon, but in the Galilee they did no work at all [that day]. As to the night [before], the House

---

36 There is some dispute as to whether this is on the first or last day of Passover. See *Talmudic Encyclopedia* (20 vols.; Jerusalem, 1955–91), IV, 46 (Hebrew).

of Shammai forbids [work], but the House of Hillel permits [it] up to sunrise.

This mishnah speaks of the start of both the Ninth of Av and Passover, where the same situation exists. Some do labor on the Ninth of Av whereas others do not; this is a matter of local custom. The dispute of the Houses of Hillel and Shammai seems to refer to the view of the Galileans, but it may also follow on the statement that it was customary in some locales to abstain. In this case, one cannot claim that the statement regarding the Galileans is to be dated to Temple times. In any case, the mishnah itself states that abstention from labor on the morning before Passover is a matter of local custom, in which the Galileans are among those adopting the stricter view. Note that the view of the sages who disagree with Simeon b. Gamaliel is that one may not be strict if his locale is lenient. It is in the context of this dispute with Simeon b. Gamaliel (probably II in the Ushan period) that we hear about the strictures of the Galileans in this matter.

An aspect of the celebration of the Day of Atonement is discussed in M Ḥullin 5:3:

> On four occasions during the year, one who sells an animal to his fellowman must inform him, "Its mother I [also] sold to slaughter," [or] "Its daughter I [also] sold to slaughter." And these are: the day before the last day of the festival [of Shemini Atzeret],[37] the day before the first day of Passover [i.e., the 14th of Nisan], the day before Sukkot, and the day before Rosh Ha-Shanah. But according to the words of R. Yose the Galilean, even the day before Yom Kippur in the Galilee. Said R. Judah: When [is the seller required to inform the buyer]? When he has no interval. But if he has an interval, he need not inform him.

This mishnah is concerned with avoiding violation of the prohibition on slaughtering a mother and its daughter on the same day (Lev. 22:28). Hence, on occasions when large numbers of animals were bought for immediate slaughter, the seller was required to inform the buyer if the mother or daughter had been sold. The mishnah indicates that the Galileans ate festival meals on the eve of the Day of Atonement on a scale not known in Judea. In R. Judah's statement, we are told that the need to make this declaration exists only when there is insufficient time for the

---

37 Cf. M Sukkah 4:8 (Albeck).

mother and daughter to be slaughtered on separate days. If there is time, however, the seller is not required to make such a declaration.

T Ḥullin 5:9 provides an additional explanation. First, it quotes the anonymous ruling and the words of R. Yose the Galilean, and then adds: "Because it is a festival [*yom tov*]." We learn from this that in the Galilee it was not simply the eating of a big meal before the fast that was in question. It was the notion that rejoicing was required on the eve of Yom Kippur either because that day itself was a festival or because the Day of Atonement was considered a festival, for which the festive meal had to be eaten the day before. Support for the latter view comes from the assertion in M Ta'anit 4:8 that "there were no festivals for Israel like the Fifteenth of Av and the Day of Atonement."[38]

T Ḥullin 5:10 also provides an interpretation of R. Judah's statement in the Mishnah:

Said R. Judah: To what case do these words refer? When the Day of Atonement occurs on Monday. But if it falls on any other day of the week, he [the seller] need not inform him [the buyer], since one might slaughter [his animal] today and the other might slaughter [his animal] tomorrow.

This clause in the Tosefta interprets the words of R. Judah in the Mishnah as referring to Yom Kippur[39] and therefore as a gloss on the words of R. Yose the Galilean. As it stands, the statement in the Mishnah could just as easily be a comment on the anonymous ruling ("On four occasions . . ."). Furthermore, the Tosefta explains accordingly that the interval of which the Mishnah speaks would have to be an extra day after the Sabbath in order to allow the mother and daughter to be slaughtered on separate days.

In any case, what is evident is that Galileans ate a special festive meal on the eve of Yom Kippur. This meal was most probably an attempt to eat the festive meal of the Day of Atonement on the day before, because otherwise it was curtailed by the fast. The Galileans thus sought to maintain the character of both the fast and the festival by imposing a stringent ruling to resolve one of the fundamental tensions regarding the character of the Day of Atonement.

---

38 See L. Finkelstein, *The Pharisees*[3] (2 vols.; Philadelphia, 1962), I, 54–58.
39 So Albeck, *Mishnah, Qodashim*, 378.

Conclusions

Our examination of the specific references in tannaitic sources to differences between the Galileans and Judeans has revealed that, in most cases, the Galileans were more stringent in regard to the law than their Judean coreligionists. Other instances indicate that differences of practice were minor or resulted from distance from the Temple. In no case did the sources portray the Galileans as lenient or less observant. These texts certainly do not testify to an alternative system of halakhah or to differing methods for the derivation of the law. Rather, the Galileans and Judeans shared a common heritage of Jewish legal tradition.

If Galileans differed substantially from Judeans in their patterns of observance in the first and second centuries C.E, it is not evident in the rabbinic materials. Rather, these texts provide a picture of a Galilean Jewry heavily influenced by tannaitic Judaism but preserving their own local variations on a few details. In this respect the Galileans did not differ at all from their fellow-Jews in Judea, whose local customs are sometimes alluded to, and from the "Southerners," whose traditions differed from those of the majority of tannaim. No, there was no Galilean halakhah!

The Place of the Rabbi in Jewish Society of the Second Century*

SHAYE J. D. COHEN

The Mishnah records the dicta of 54 figures who flourished between ca. 80 C.E. and the Bar-Kokhba war (the Yavnean period); of 29 figures who lived in the generation after the Bar-Kokhba war (the Ushan period); and of 16 figures who were contemporaries of R. Judah the Patriarch. The other tannaitic corpora provide some additional names.[1] By the third century C.E. the successors to these 100+ people emerged as an elite, and perhaps as *the* elite, in Jewish society of the Land of Israel. In this paper I shall try to show that in the second century the rabbinate neither was, nor had any interest in being, the leaders of Jewry, and that the nature of the rabbinate was radically transformed by Judah the Patriarch.

In order to minimize methodological difficulties, I shall restrict my investigation to the Mishnah and other tannaitic corpora (Tosefta, Mekhilta, Sifra, Sifre), ignoring for the most part the *baraitot* and other allegedly tannaitic material quoted by the Babylonian and Palestinian

---

* This paper is a condensation and revision of a much longer piece written in 1983, scheduled to appear in *Cambridge History of Judaism*, vol. 4. In particular I have tried to incorporate appropriate references to two monographs that have appeared since 1983 that deal directly with the topic of this paper: M. Goodman, *State and Society in Roman Galilee A.D. 132–212* (Totowa, N.J., 1983), and L. I. Levine, *The Rabbinic Class of Roman Palestine in Late Antiquity* (Jerusalem, 1989). In the writing of the original paper I benefited from several fruitful discussions with Professor Levine, and in its revision from the comments of Dr. I. Gafni.

1 C. Albeck, *Introduction to the Mishnah* (Jerusalem, 1959), 222–233 (Hebrew). (I do not follow Albeck's division of the Yavnean period into two.) Cf. Levine, *Rabbinic Class*, 66–69, for parallel statistics for the amoraic period.

Talmudim. All the tannaitic corpora were redacted in the third century
(or later!) and all of them undoubtedly contain some post-tannaitic material, but these works on the whole bring us much closer to the world of
the second-century rabbis than do the Talmudim.[2] As we shall see, in a
number of important areas the tannaitic material is consistent with itself
but is incompatible with the allegedly tannaitic material quoted by the
Talmudim. Whether these contrasts are the result of the varied literary
criteria by which the tannaitic and amoraic corpora were assembled and
redacted, or of pseudepigraphic activity by later rabbis, is not clear and
requires investigation.

A. Rabbinic Power

Tannaitic literature gives us frequent glimpses at the religious life of
second-century Jewry. For example, the Jews of Tiberias observed the
rabbinic Sabbath limits; "the people" followed R. Eliezer's opinion in the
laws of menstruation; landowners distributed certain crops to the poor
although they were not obligated to do so. Even the actions of the villagers of Kefar Sogane and Shihin were regarded as valid precedents in
rabbinic discussions. The literature also gives us glimpses at the irreli-
gious life of Jewry. A Jew in Caesarea once slaughtered an animal for
sacrifice to a pagan god; a murder was committed in order to gain an inheritance.[3]

Particularly important are those texts which describe the legal decisions rendered by the rabbis for Jews who were neither entitled "rabbis"
nor otherwise said to have belonged to the rabbinic class. In these texts
the rabbis were actively involved in the private lives of ordinary Jews.
Some texts use the formula "and the case came before Rabbi X" or "and
they came and asked Rabbi X." Some employ a simple past tense of a
verb of action to describe the rabbinic response to a given situation (e.g.,

---

2 I occasionally cite ʾAvot de Rabbi Nathan, although its tannaitic origins are debatable. Sifre Zutta and Midrash Tannaim are extant largely through quotations from
later works and are not cited here. Goodman also attempted to base his work on the
evidence of the tannaitic corpora alone, but did not fully succeed in doing so; see my
review in *American Historical Review* (1984), 1315–1316.

3 *Tiberias*: T ʿEruvin 5:2–3, Lieberman, p. 111; *R. Eliezer's opinion*: T Niddah 1:5,
Zuckermandel, p. 641; *landowners*: T Peʾah 2:21, Lieberman, p. 49; *villagers*: T Terumot
3:18, Lieberman, p. 121; and T ʿEruvin 3:17, Lieberman, p. 103; *Caesarea*: T Hullin 2:13,
Zuckermandel, p. 502; *murder for inheritance*: T Ketubot 11:4, Lieberman, p. 94. A full
collection and analysis of this material is a desideratum; in the interim, see Levine,
Rabbinic Class, 120–124, and Goodman, *State and Society*, 102–104.

"Rabbi X instituted the practice" or "Rabbi X ruled"). A substantial number do not use any set formulae. All together, tannaitic literature yields a total of 128 separate cases which present the rabbis as figures of authority in Jewish society.[4] Let us now investigate some aspects of this material.

1. Periodization

Of the 128 cases, 57 (or 44%) concern Yavnean figures. In addition, four cases which mention Yavneh as the site where unnamed sages rendered their verdict probably also date to the Yavnean period. By contrast, only 13 cases (10%) involve figures of the Ushan period, and only three involve a figure of the period of Judah the Patriarch (not by accident, Judah the Patriarch himself). The remaining cases, slightly less than half of the total, were adjudicated by anonymous sages or by the unidentified subjects of third person plural verbs. Why the tradition is so skewed in favor of the Yavneans is a phenomenon which requires explanation, but which will not be treated here. The material does not represent equally all the stages of the tannaitic period.[5]

2. Geographical Scope

Before the tenure of Judah the Patriarch the rabbinic movement was primarily rural, anchored in the towns and villages rather than the cities (see below). This view is confirmed by our corpus of texts. In 57 cases (or 44%) the incident which prompted the legal decision is assigned to a specific place. Of these 57 cases, 19 (exactly one third) are assigned to

---

[4] For a complete inventory of the material, see my essay in *Cambridge History of Judaism* (forthcoming). I omit from consideration those cases which involve only rabbis or rabbinic figures or which took place before 70 C.E. The importance of legal cases for an understanding of the social position of the rabbis was first highlighted by J. Neusner in his *History of the Jews in Babylonia* (5 vols.; Leiden, 1965–70). See also I. Gafni, "Court Cases in the Babylonian Talmud," *PAAJR* 49 (1982), 23–40 (Hebrew). Goodman, *State and Society*, 94–101, also appreciates the importance of the reported cases, but lumps all the material together and presents an incomplete picture. Levine, *Rabbinic Class*, 128, n. 123, makes a good statement about the methodological difficulties in determining the reality and social setting of the reported cases.

[5] The simplest explanation is that the Yavnean period is approximately twice as long as the two others, but I am not convinced that this explanation is adequate. In an unpublished study of the *ma'asim* of the Mishnah and Tosefta, Joel Gereboff points out that Ushans appear more frequently in the Tosefta than in the Mishnah. In some cases it is unclear what generation is under discussion because of manuscript variants or uncertainty of the date of the sage involved.

cities (6 in Lod,[6] 6 in Sepphoris, 2 in Akko-Ptolemais, 2 in Tiberias, 2 in Beth Shean-Scythopolis, and 1 in Caesarea), the other 38 to towns and villages. The only two cities where the rabbis had a considerable following in the Yavnean period, if not throughout the entire second century, were Sepphoris and Lod. Neither Tiberias, Caesarea, nor even Yavneh, the seat of the rabbinic court, was the source of a single case involving a Jew outside the rabbinic establishment.[7] By a 2:1 margin the rabbinic movement had its followers in the towns and villages, not the cities.

Many modern scholars assert that the Galilee was not part of the rabbinic orbit until after the Bar-Kokhba war. This view has come under increasing attack in recent years and is contradicted by our corpus.[8] The Yavnean rabbis rendered legal decisions in many Galilean settlements, notably Sepphoris, Tiberias, Sogane, Meiron, Kefar Mandi, Kefar Sisi, Rum Beth ʿAnat, Kefar ʿAris, ʾAriaḥ, and others.[9] The transfer of the patriarchal court from the south to the north undoubtedly had many important consequences for the propagation of rabbinic power, but rabbinic influence extended to the Galilee, at least to some degree, even before the Bar-Kokhba war.

3. Range of Authority

Of the 128 cases in our corpus, 122 treat single topics. The remaining six resist monothematic classification and seem to treat two topics

---

[6] I generously include Lod (Lydda) among the cities, although it did not become a *polis* until the early third century. See A. Oppenheimer, "Jewish Lydda in the Roman Era," *HUCA* 59 (1988), 115–136.

[7] The sages sat in Yavneh and cases were brought to them from elsewhere; see T Kilʾaim 1:4, Lieberman, pp. 203–204; T Ḥullin 3:10, Zuckermandel, p. 504; T Miqvaʾot 4:6, Zuckermandel, p. 656; T Parah 7:4, Zuckermandel, p. 636; cf. also M Kelim 5:4 and T Niddah 4:3–4, Zuckermandel, p. 644. In all these, the cases originated somewhere outside of Yavneh. Of the six cases originating in Lod, five involved a figure of the Yavnean period (M Taʿanit 3:9; T Taʿanit 2:5, Lieberman, p. 331; T Ḥagigah 2:13, Lieberman, p. 386; M Bava Metziʿa 4:3; T Oholot 4:2, Zuckermandel, p. 600), and one involved R. Judah the Patriarch (T Niddah 6:3, Zuckermandel, p. 647). Of the six cases originating in Sepphoris, four were Yavnean (T Kilʾaim 1:4, Lieberman, pp. 203–204; T Sheviʿit 4:13, Lieberman, p. 182; T Taʿanit 1:12, Lieberman, pp. 327–328; T Kelim, Bava Batra 2:2, Zuckermandel, p. 591), one was Ushan (M Bava Metziʿa 8:8), and perhaps another was Ushan as well (T Shabbat 15:8, Lieberman, p. 70). The prominence of Sepphoris is surprising since in amoraic times there was great tension there between the rabbis and the local aristocracy. See A. Büchler, *The Political and Social Leaders of the Jewish Community of Sepphoris* (London, 1909).

[8] S. Freyne, *Galilee from Alexander the Great to Hadrian* (Wilmington, 1980), 323–329; A. Oppenheimer, *The ʿAm Ha-aretz* (Leiden, 1977), 210–211.

[9] The identification of some of these towns and villages is unknown.

apiece,[10] thereby raising the total, for statistical purposes, to 134. I have compiled from both Palestinian and Babylonian amoraic literature a corpus of 45 cases which center upon R. Judah the Patriarch and whose topic profile can be compared with that of the tannaitic cases.[11] Which types of cases were addressed by the tannaim, primarily of the Yavnean period, and which by R. Judah the Patriarch?

The five topics most frequently treated by the tannaim were: purities (27.6%); marriage, divorce, and levirate marriage, especially the ability of a woman to marry after her husband's presumed but unverifiable death (19.4%); oaths and vows, especially the release of an oath-taker from his obligation (8.2%); avoidance of idolatry (7.4%); and agricultural tithes (including the second tithe and the fourth year offering of new plantings) and priestly offerings (5.9%). The large gap between the second and third topics is noticeable, as is the remarkably poor representation of: civil cases (4.4%); Shabbat, especially ʿeruv (4.4%); kosher slaughtering (2.2%); and festivals (2.2%). We obtain a completely different profile for the 45 cases attributed by the Talmudim and the 3 attributed by the Tosefta to Judah the Patriarch (a total of 48 cases):[12] marriage, divorce, and levirate marriage (18.8%); civil law, especially contracts (14.6%); kosher food, especially kosher slaughtering (12.5%); purities (12.5%); and Shabbat, especially ʿeruv (10.4%). The decline of purities from a strong first place to a tie for third, and the rise of civil cases from a low position to second place, are important developments. Remarkable, too, is the total absence of agricultural tithes, priestly offerings, and idolatry from the patriarch's casebook.

Differences are apparent even when R. Judah and the earlier tannaim adjudicated the same topics. The tannaim enforced virtually all aspects of the laws of purity—modes of purification, sources of impurity (especially menstruant women), and loci of impurity. The patriarch's range was much narrower: four of his six purity cases involved menstruation (or other bloody discharge), but the focal point was the sexual availability of the woman to her husband, not the impurity which she might have im-

---

10 M Shabbat 3:4; M Betzah 3:5; M Nedarim 9:5; T Niddah 5:16–17, Zuckermandel, pp. 646–647; T Toharot 8:15, Zuckermandel, p. 669.

11 For a complete inventory of the material, see my essay in *Cambridge History of Judaism* (forthcoming). In his unpublished study, Gereboff points out that the topic profile of the cases of the Mishnah differs somewhat from that of the Tosefta.

12 I am not sure that I have located all the cases involving Judah the Patriarch; in some talmudic discussions it is hard to know which Judah the Patriarch is meant. My assumption here that Judah's topic profile was not affected by his status as patriarch is debatable.

parted. The sexual aspect of a menstruant woman never came before the earlier tannaim. Similarly, of the nine marriage cases decided by the patriarch, three concerned sexual relations; of the 26 marriage cases decided by the tannaim, none concerned the sexual aspects of marriage. Two of the patriarch's marriage cases involved the eligibility of the woman to collect her marriage contract, another area that was avoided by the tannaim. R. Judah's authority in this matter probably stemmed from his authority in civil matters generally, an authority which had not been shared by his predecessors.

We do not know the criteria by which legal cases and other narratives were selected for inclusion in our rabbinic texts. Nor do we know whether the criteria for tannaitic corpora differ from those for amoraic corpora. Nor can we confirm (or deny) the authenticity of any individual case.[13] It seems reasonable to assume, however, that the extant cases accurately reflect the areas of legal interaction between the rabbis and the people. The Yavneans' obsession with purity laws and disregard for civil law are confirmed by mishnaic tradition.[14] Judah the Patriarch restricted the applicability and lessened the severity of the laws of tithing, purity, and separation from gentiles,[15] and it is probably no coincidence that few cases in these areas were brought before him. The rabbis prior to Judah the Patriarch were acknowledged experts in the laws of purity and personal status, legal relics of the sectarian past of the rabbinic movement. They also were sufficiently expert and holy to be able to cancel oaths and vows. However, in matters of personal piety, e.g., Shabbat, holidays, kosher food, marital relations, prayer, and synagogue rituals, and in civil matters the people apparently did not need the rabbis.[16] By contrast, R.

---

[13] Some of the cases of Judah the Patriarch seem legendary (B Nedarim 50b and B Menaḥot 37a); none of the tannaitic cases seems legendary.

[14] J. Neusner, *Judaism: The Evidence of the Mishnah* (Chicago, 1981), 95–97, 101–110.

[15] These are the "enactments" (*taqqanot*) of Judah the Patriarch. *Tithing*: M Sheviʿit 6:4 and T Sheviʿit 4:17, Lieberman, p. 183; J Demai 2, 1, 22c–d; *purity*: M Oholot 18:9 and T Oholot 18:18, Zuckermandel, p. 617; *separation from gentiles*: M ʿAvodah Zarah 2:6 and T ʿAvodah Zarah 4:11, Zuckermandel, p. 467.

[16] A similar conclusion is reached by Goodman, *State and Society*, 101. Contrast the opinion of S. Safrai, "The Recovery of the Jewish Settlement in the Yavnean Period," in: *Eretz Israel from the Destruction of the Second Temple to the Muslim Conquest*, eds. Z. Baras et al. (2 vols.; Jerusalem, 1982), I, 31 (Hebrew). The Palestinian Talmud contains two traditions for the date when the right to adjudicate civil law was "taken from Israel," in the time of either Simeon b. Shetaḥ (J Sanhedrin 1, 1, 18a) or Simeon b. Yoḥai (J Sanhedrin 7, 2, 24b). I assume that one of these is a textual corruption of the other, but I doubt whether either date has any historical value.

Judah the Patriarch adjudicated civil matters and dispensed guidance in marital affairs. Purity laws no longer had their sectarian prominence.

If second-century Jews rarely went to the rabbis for the normal day-to-day affairs of religion and commerce, to whom did they go? For religious matters, we do not know. Aside from the priests, the rabbis had no potential rivals about whom anything is known. For civil matters, however, there was an alternative: the municipal courts, at least in the Jewish areas of the country, would have consisted of Jewish judges. Tannaitic sources refer to "the judges of Sepphoris" and "the court of Tiberias."[17] These judges were Jews but were not (necessarily) members of the rabbinic estate, and their decisions were not (necessarily) consonant with rabbinic law. These courts were backed by the power of the state, and the rabbis in all likelihood had the status of arbitrators whose authority was based on moral suasion, nothing more. "Do you take it upon yourselves to accept the verdict which I shall pronounce for you?" is the question which R. Yosi purportedly asked two disputants who came before him for judgment.[18]

In religious matters the rabbis certainly could rely only upon their powers of persuasion and had no means of enforcing their decisions. "Shouldn't we be concerned about the decision of the sages?" is a question put in the mouth of a son of a wealthy landowner whose father was not following a rabbinic enactment. Although rabbinic power increased during and after the tenure of R. Judah the Patriarch, even third-century rabbis lacked the legal authority to enforce their decisions in religious matters. When a disciple of R. Judah the Patriarch was served a dish of peacock and milk, he had no means short of excommunication by which to compel his host to refrain from mixing fowl with milk. One rabbi was powerless to stop a Jewish butcher in Sepphoris from selling non-kosher meat. The most he could do was to express satisfaction when the butcher died accidentally one Friday night and to forbid his disciples from moving the corpse on the Sabbath, thereby exposing it to the dogs.[19]

---

17 *Sepphoris*: M Bava Batra 6:7; *Tiberias*: Sifre Deuteronomy 355, Finkelstein, p. 419. Rabbinic texts also refer to a wide variety of communal officials, but their exact functions and relationship to the rabbis are not clear; see Goodman, *State and Society*, 119–126.

18 J Sanhedrin 1, 1, 18a. On the municipal Jewish judges, see Goodman, *State and Society*, 126–128; on the conflicts of jurisdiction in Roman Palestine, see ibid., 155–171.

19 *Wealthy landowners*: T Pesahim 3:20, Lieberman, p. 157; *peacock and milk*: B Shabbat 130a = B Hullin 116a; *butcher in Sepphoris*: Leviticus Rabbah 5:6, Margulies, p. 119 = J Terumot 8, 5, 45c.

Thus, in spite of all the reported cases and decisions, the enactments (*taqqanot*) of the patriarchs and their courts, and the numerous references to judicial authority, appointment of judges, and supervision of the calendar,[20] the nature and status of the rabbinic "judiciary" are very obscure. Two crucial points, however, are clear. Firstly, many Jews were not committed to a rabbinic way of life and did not accept rabbinic authority. Second-century rabbis adjudicated purity cases far more frequently than any other type of case, but second-century rabbis also tell us that the ʿamme ha-ʾaretz, while observant in other respects, did not properly observe the laws of purity. Most of the laws about which the rabbis were consulted were precisely those laws which were practiced the least by a substantial segment of the population. Secondly, rabbinic authority depended on the social status, the powers of persuasion, the charisma, and the personality of the rabbi more than upon his institutional or bureaucratic setting.[21] It was a voluntary act for a Jew to accept the verdict of a rabbinic court or the authority of a rabbi. The tannaim had no means (aside from excommunication, about which they say little[22]) to enforce their decisions and decrees. They were neither agents of the state nor communal leaders.[23] In sum, the rabbis did not control the religious and civil life of second-century Palestinian Jewry.

---

[20] References to judicial authority (no case mentioned): Mekhilta de R. Ishmael, Neziqin 18, Lauterbach, pp. 141–142 = Horowitz-Rabin, p. 313; contrast ARN A 38 and ARN B 41, Schechter, p. 57b; Sifre Numbers 118, Horowitz, p. 143; Sifre Deuteronomy 16, Finkelstein, p. 27; T Yevamot 12:11, Lieberman, p. 43; M Gittin 9:8; T Niddah 6:8–9, Zuckermandel, pp. 647–648. *Appointment of judges*: Sifre Numbers 92, Horowitz, p. 93 and parallels; Sifre Deuteronomy 17, Finkelstein, pp. 27–28; on the phrase, "to seat in the session [or: school]" (להושיב בישיבה) see S. Lieberman, *Siphre Zutta* (New York, 1968), 87–88; *supervision of calendar*: M and T Rosh Ha-shanah, *passim*; M Yevamot 16:7.

[21] Cf. Levine, *Rabbinic Class*, 131. Tannaim are rarely portrayed as holy men, charismatics or magicians, although amoraim in both Palestine and Babylonia often are; see Levine, ibid., 105–109. Goodman, *State and Society*, 108–109, argues that tannaim, too, were regarded as holy men, but all the cited evidence comes from amoraic sources.

[22] The tannaim mention excommunication only in passing, for example, M Moʿed Qatan 3:1; M ʿEduyot 5:6; M Niddah 2:2. On excommunication, see Levine, *Rabbinic Class*, 97, n. 238.

[23] Tannaitic sources frequently refer to rabbis who were "appointed over [or: for] the community" (for example, Sifre Deuteronomy 41, Finkelstein, pp. 86–87 and T Taʿanit 1:7, Lieberman, pp. 324–325) or "involved in the needs of the community" (T Berakhot 1:2 and 2:6, Lieberman, pp. 2 and 7, respectively)—however, the institutional setting presumed by these phrases is not clear. J Peʾah 8, 7, 21a portrays

B. The Rabbis and the Masses

Tannaitic and, to the best of my knowledge, later Palestinian literature knows nothing of hatred between the rabbis and the non-rabbinic masses. Mutual disdain, perhaps, but not hatred.[24] Every day a rabbinic Jew was supposed to thank the Lord for not creating him "a gentile, an 'outsider' [*bur*], or a woman," three categories of people who could not experience rabbinic piety.[25] What exactly makes a *bur* an outsider is nowhere stated. Presumably his entire way of life was unrabbinic.[26] He is similar, perhaps, to the one "who is not immersed in Scripture, rabbinic tradition, and proper conduct." Such a person "has no part in the inhabited world."[27] When R. ʿAqiva remembered what he had done in his youth before becoming a rabbi, he said, "I thank You, Lord my God, that You have placed my lot among those who dwell in the rabbinic academy [*bet ha-midrash*] and You have not placed my lot among those who dwell on the corners [?] in the marketplace."[28] This prayer is quoted in order to elucidate the saying of another rabbi, "Sleep during the morning, wine during midday, talk with children, and sitting in the assemblies of the ʿamme ha-ʾaretz drive a man out of the world."[29] In the minds of many of the tannaim, the ʿamme ha-ʾaretz were almost synonymous with gentiles, as can be seen from the fact that legislation concerning relations with the former often merged imperceptibly with legislation concerning the latter.[30] Disdain towards the ʿam ha-ʾaretz is clearly in evidence.

R. ʿAqiva as a *parnas*. The rabbinic presence in synagogues was minimal; see S. J. D. Cohen, "Epigraphical Rabbis," *JQR* 72 (1981), 1–17.

[24] For example, the story in Genesis Rabbah 79:6, Theodor-Albeck, pp. 943–944, about the opposition of an ʿam ha-ʾaretz to R. Simeon b. Yoḥai's purification of Tiberias, lacks any pointed references to the hatred borne by the ʿamme ha-ʾaretz against the rabbis. Hatred between the rabbis and the masses is perhaps implied by Sifre Numbers 92, Horowitz, p. 93, but the reference to cursing and stoning may be exegetically derived.

[25] T Berakhot 6:18, Lieberman, p. 38. In his commentary, Lieberman (following previous scholars) compared this with Diogenes Laertius 1.33. Cf. also Gal. 3:28.

[26] "From the manner in which one recites the blessings we can discern whether a man is a *bur* or a sage" (T Berakhot 1:6, Lieberman, p. 3).

[27] M Qiddushin 1:10 and T Qiddushin 1:17, Lieberman, p. 281. "Proper conduct" is my translation of *derekh ʾeretz*, "inhabited world" of *yishuv* (= *oikoumene*?).

[28] ARN A 21, Schechter, p. 37b; cf. the prayer of Neḥunyah b. Haqqanah in M Berakhot 4:2, with the amplifications in the talmudim, ad loc.

[29] M ʾAvot 3:14; ARN A 21 = ARN B 34, Schechter, p. 37a.

[30] See T Demai 2 and 3, passim; and T ʿAvodah Zarah 3:9–10, Zuckermandel, p. 464.

But the disdain had its limits. In spite of their sinful inattention to certain rabbinic ordinances (notably the laws of tithing and purity),[31] *ʿamme ha-ʾaretz* did, the rabbis had to admit, observe many of the commandments, notably the prohibitions of eating priestly offerings and food grown during the sabbatical years. They also observed the Sabbath.[32] The rabbis encouraged cooperation with the *ʿamme ha-ʾaretz* (and the gentiles) "for the sake of peace."[33] The tannaim did not object to the marriage of *haverim* with the *ʿamme ha-ʾaretz* as long as it was stipulated in advance that the wife (and her family in its dealings with her and her husband) would adhere to the rabbinic laws of purity.[34] The tannaim were even capable of using the term *ʿam ha-ʾaretz* neutrally and without any perjorative connotations.[35] The document quoting R. ʿAqiva's prayer when remembering what he had done in his youth fails to mention in its "biography" of that sage that he had been a rabbi-hating *ʿam ha-ʾaretz* before becoming a rabbi himself. The tannaim did not pretend that the masses loved them or followed their every desire, but they gave no indication that they hated the *ʿamme ha-ʾaretz* or were hated by them.[36]

The evidence for hatred between the rabbis and the *ʿamme ha-ʾaretz* derives exclusively from the Babylonian Talmud.[37] The Babylonian rabbis, whose attempts to promulgate rabbinic Judaism met the resistance of many of their coreligionists,[38] were very receptive to Palestinian traditions about tensions and hatred between the tannaim and the masses. Perhaps they were inventive, too. An entire folio page of the Babylonian Talmud documents this hatred: he who would marry the daughter of an *ʿam ha-ʾaretz* or would give his daughter to an *ʿam ha-ʾaretz* is denounced severely; sexual relations with an *ʿam ha-ʾaretz* are akin to sexual relations with a donkey; R. ʿAqiva declares that when he was an *ʿam ha-ʾaretz* he could wish for no greater pleasure than sinking his teeth into the neck of

---

[31] See especially M Demai 2:2–3 with the Tosefta, ad loc.; T ʿAvodah Zarah 3:10, Zuckermandel, p. 464. R. Judah (in M Demai) defines the *ʿam ha-ʾaretz* as someone who does not observe rabbinic piety; cf. B Berakhot 47b.

[32] *Sabbath and priestly offerings*: T Demai 5:2, Lieberman, p. 85; *sabbatical year*: T ʿEruvin 5:10, Lieberman, p. 113. In general, see M Bekhorot 4:10.

[33] M Sheviʿit 5:9; M Gittin 5:9.

[34] See especially T ʿAvodah Zarah 3:9–10, Zuckermandel, p. 464.

[35] M Sotah 9:15 (an addition to the mishnah); T Sanhedrin 7:7, Zuckermandel, p. 426.

[36] Biography of R. ʿAqiva: ARN A 6 = ARN B 12–13, Schechter, pp. 14a–17a.

[37] The evidence is presented and discussed by Oppenheimer, *ʿAm Ha-aretz*, 172–188.

[38] Neusner, *History of the Jews in Babylonia*, passim.

a rabbi. Hyperboles of this type abound in the discussion. There is no way to verify the authenticity of this material, but the fact that these statements and the ethos they represent are completely absent from Palestinian texts raises serious doubts.[39]

Rabbinic disdain for the masses is evidenced also in the failure of the rabbis to mount any sort of outreach program to them. Perhaps the school of the patriarch was a real "academy," a perpetual institution with a corporate identity and a hierarchical structure,[40] but the schools of other rabbis were nothing more than disciple circles. A single master was surrounded at all times by a handful of apprentices who attended their master like servants in order to learn from his every action. When the master died, the circle disbanded and the students were left to fend for themselves. Needless to say, a limited number of masters teaching a limited number of disciples in a limited number of disciple circles was not the vehicle for mass education. Furthermore, there is no indication that the tannaim ever attempted to propagate their teachings among the masses. On the contrary, Judah the Patriarch, in whose time the rabbinic establishment entered the cities and broadened its social base, decreed that Torah was not to be taught in the marketplace. Like the thighs of a woman, Torah was to be kept covered in public. Presumably he was afraid of casting pearls before swine.[41]

Rabbinic law, both tannaitic and amoraic, and in both disciple circles and academies, was also studied orally. Perhaps students used notes in their private studies, but in their formal sessions neither masters nor disciples ever consulted a written text of rabbinic law.[42] Oral teachings were often secret teachings, hallmarks of esoterica. The tannaim enjoined that

39 B Pesaḥim 49a–b. Most scholars do not question the authenticity of this material; see, for example, S. Lieberman, "The Discipline in the So-Called Dead Sea Manual of Discipline," *JBL* 71 (1952), 204–205, and Levine, *Rabbinic Class*, 112–117.

40 T Sanhedrin 7:8–10, Zuckermandel, pp. 426–427. See I. Gafni, "The Babylonian *Yeshiva* as Reflected in Bava Qamma 117a," *Tarbiz* 49 (1980), 292–301 (Hebrew), and S. J. D. Cohen, "Patriarchs and Scholarchs," *PAAJR* 48 (1981), 57–85.

41 B Mo'ed Qatan 16a–b. The patriarchal academy would probably have been more open to outsiders than were the rabbinic disciple circles, but even here an exclusivistic ethic might have prevailed. In B Berakhot 28a, R. Gamaliel declares, "He whose inside is not like his outside shall not enter into the study hall." See Cohen, "Patriarchs and Scholarchs," 76–79. The type-stories about the education of the great masters, Hillel (B Yoma 35b), R. Eliezer, and R. 'Aqiva (ARN A 6 and ARN B 12–13, Schechter, pp. 15b–16b), are set in academies, not disciple circles.

42 S. Lieberman, *Hellenism in Jewish Palestine* (New York, 1950; reprint 1962), 83–99. The prohibition of the writing of the "Oral Law" first appears in amoraic corpora; tannaitic texts know nothing about written copies of rabbinic lore.

certain sections of the Bible which were difficult or easily misunderstood were to be taught only to a few people at a time and not to the public. Were other portions of rabbinic Torah kept secret from the Jews at large?[43] Would the rabbis teach the same law in public as they did in private?[44] If a Jew or gentile asked a difficult question, would he always receive a truthful answer?[45] We cannot be sure. Thus, while the tannaim had neither the means nor the inclination to propagate their Torah among the masses, they had both the means and, to some extent, the inclination to keep their Torah secret.[46] Although rabbinic ideology obligated all Jews to study Torah, the tannaim did not create any social mechanism to implement this ideology.

In sum, the rabbis were an easily differentiated element within second-century Jewish society. They had their own organizations (*havurot*), modes of piety, and way of life. They could be recognized in the marketplace "by their walk, their speech, and their dress."[47] They were distinct from the masses of the Jews and looked down upon all those who did not share their outlook and follow their observances. They did not create institutions or mechanisms by which they could tutor the unlettered masses in the ways of Torah.

---

43 M Ḥagigah 2:1 and T Ḥagigah 2:1, Lieberman, p. 380. T Berakhot 6:23–24, Lieberman, pp. 39–40, seems to recommend keeping Torah secret under certain circumstances. Cf. B Pesaḥim 49b (not to teach Torah to an *'am ha-'aretz* and not to reveal secrets to him) and J 'Avodah Zarah 2, 8, 41d (to study Torah only before people who are worthy).

44 Rav did not; see J Shabbat 3, 1, 5d and B Ḥullin 15a.

45 The Romans are said not to have thought so; they sent spies to disclose what the rabbis were teaching. See Sifre Deuteronomy 344, Finkelstein, p. 401 and B. J. Bamberger, *Proselytism in the Talmudic Period* (Cincinnati, 1939), 233–234. There are many stories about rabbis who answered a gentile's question in a manner which the former knew to be unsatisfactory. The students would object, remarking, "This one [the gentile] you turned away with a [broken] reed, but to us what will you say?," that is, "What is the *real* answer to the question?" See, e.g., J Berakhot 8, 1, 11d = Genesis Rabbah 8:9, Theodor-Albeck, pp. 62–63, and B Ḥullin 27b.

46 Secrecy in rabbinic Judaism needs further study; see the partial collection of material in G. A. Wewers, *Geheimnis und Geheimhaltung im rabbinischen Judentum* (Berlin/New York, 1975).

47 Sifre Deuteronomy 343, Finkelstein, pp. 399–400. Cf. M Yevamot 16:7: a rabbinic student on his journey carries, and can be recognized by, a Torah scroll, cloak, and staff. On the distinctiveness of the rabbinic class, see Levine, *Rabbinic Class*, 47–53.

C. Judah the Patriarch and His Impact

The tenure of Judah the Patriarch had a major impact on the development of the rabbinate. The rabbis became more involved in their ambient society and more broadly representative of the Jews as a whole only in the third century, in large measure as a result of the work of Judah the Patriarch.[48] I have already noted above that the scope of rabbinic jurisdiction seems to have changed and, in some ways, increased during his tenure (a point that requires verification),[49] and I shall briefly survey three other important developments.

1. In the period of Judah the Patriarch the power of the central rabbinic office advanced greatly. R. Judah was asked by the people of Simonias to appoint for them a man who would "deliver sermons, serve as judge, deacon [*hazzan*] and scribe [or: teacher of children, *sofer*], teach us [rabbinic tradition], and fulfill all our desires"—quite a request! A suitable Pooh-Bah was found. R. Judah also sent R. Romanus to check the family purity of the Jews in a certain distant place.[50] No such traditions are recorded for any of the previous patriarchs.[51] Before R. Judah, at least, the rabbis were not communal functionaries.

2. In the period before Judah the Patriarch the rabbis were well-to-do, associated with the well-to-do, and interested themselves in questions which were important to the landed classes.[52] Perhaps some tannaim

---

[48] Thus, J. Neusner suggests that the Mishnah is primarily a book of "philosophy" while the Jerusalem Talmud is a book about "Judaism and Society." See Neusner, *Evidence of the Mishnah*; idem, *Judaism in Society: The Evidence of the Yerushalmi* (Chicago, 1983).

[49] A great desideratum is a complete collection and analysis of the legal cases that appear in the Jerusalem Talmud.

[50] *Simonias*: J Yevamot 12, 7, 13a = Genesis Rabbah 81:2, Theodor-Albeck, p. 969; cf. J Ḥagigah 1, 7, 76c and J Sheviʿit 6, 1, 36d; *R. Romanus*: J Yevamot 8, 2, 9b.

[51] According to one tradition, R. Gamaliel removed from office the "head" of Gader (Gezer?), but the Talmudim also record a conflicting tradition, rendering the matter very obscure. See J Rosh Ha-shanah 1, 6, 57b = B Rosh Ha-shanah 22a. In any case, it is nowhere reported that R. Gamaliel appointed anyone to a communal position.

[52] Second-century rabbis dined with people who seem to have been wealthy: Sifre Deuteronomy 41, Finkelstein, p. 85; T Shabbat 2:5, Lieberman, p. 7; T Shabbat 13:2, Lieberman, p. 57; T ʿEruvin 6:2, Lieberman, pp. 118–119; T Pesaḥim 10:12, Lieberman, pp. 198–199; T Sukkah 1:9, Lieberman, p. 258. The rabbis also associated with the well-to-do: Mekhilta de R. Ishmael, Pisḥa 15, Lauterbach, p. 127 = Horowitz-Rabin, p. 57; T Terumot 2:13, Lieberman, p. 115; T ʿEruvin 1:2, Lieberman, p. 87; T Ḥagigah 2:13, Lieberman, p. 386. Some scholars have suggested that these texts refer to

were poor, but their poverty has been rendered invisible by the tannaitic documents. No tannaitic document (except for *Fathers according to Rabbi Nathan*, in a series of paradigmatic rags-to-riches stories[53]) implies that any second-century rabbi was poor. Those tannaim about whose economic status anything is known seem to have been *ba'ale batim*, landowners. They even shared the eternal prejudice of landowners against shepherds and goatherds, whom the rabbis regarded as inveterate thieves and contumacious liars.[54] Some of the Jews buried at Joppa were remembered as X the Baker, Y the Peddler, Z the Flax-Seller,[55] but rabbinic literature, both tannaitic and amoraic, rarely bestows such cognomens upon the tannaim.[56]

---

charity—needy rabbis were given a place at the tables of the wealthy—but there is no indication of this in the texts themselves.

53 ARN A 6 and ARN B 12–13, Schechter, pp. 14b–17a.

54 *Prejudice against goatherds and shepherds, goats and sheep*: M Bava Qamma 7:7; T Bava Qamma 8:10–15, Lieberman, pp. 38–40; T Bava Metzi'a 2:33, Lieberman, p. 72; T Sanhedrin 5:5, Zuckermandel, p. 423; M Rosh Ha-shanah 1:8. By the third century rabbinic views had shifted; R. Yohanan preferred sheep to land (B Hullin 84a). Social prejudice adequately explains the rabbinic attitude toward shepherds and there is no need for the complicated political explanations advanced by A. Gulak, "Shepherds and Breeders of Small Cattle after the Destruction of the Second Temple," *Tarbiz* 12 (1940–41), 181–189 (Hebrew). See G. Alon, *The Jews in Their Land in the Talmudic Age*, ed. and trans. G. Levi (2 vols.; Jerusalem, 1980–84), I, 277–285.

55 J.-B. Frey, *Corpus Inscriptionum Iudaicarum* (2 vols.; Rome, 1939–52), II, nos. 902, 928, 929, 931, 937, 940, 945, 949. It is perhaps significant that none of the rabbis buried at Joppa bore this type of nomenclature. The Murabba'at documents refer to a Josephus the Scribe; see P. Benoit, J. T. Milik and R. de Vaux, *Discoveries in the Judaean Desert*, II: *Les Grottes de Murabba'at* (Oxford, 1961), 232, no. 103.

56 The only clear cases known to me are Yohanan the Sandalmaker, Judah the Baker, and Judah b. Isaiah the Perfumer (I assume that the perfumer was Judah, a contemporary of R. 'Aqiva). Several pre-70 figures were remembered by their crafts: Nahum the *libellarius*, Zecharia son of the butcher, Nehunya the Ditch-digger, and Tobiah the Physician. The reference to "the son of the blacksmith" in T 'Eruvin 5:7, Lieberman, p. 112, is probably corrupt; see apparatus there and cf. T Ketubot 5:1, Lieberman, p. 72. Various cognomens are obscure and may refer to a trade or craft: Simeon the *pequli*, Yosi the *horem*, Joshua the *garsi*, Levi the *sadar* (or: *sarad*), Eleazar *hisma* (the explanation of this name in Leviticus Rabbah 23:4, Margulies, pp. 531–532, is obviously fictional), and Eleazar the *qappar*. A great deal of work needs to be done on rabbinic nomenclature and cognomens; see R. Hachlili, "Names and Epithets of the Jews in the Second Temple Period," in: *Eretz Israel*, XVII (Jerusalem, 1984), 188–211 (Hebrew); J. Naveh, "Nameless People?," *Zion* 54 (1989), 1–16 (Hebrew).

Amoraic traditions refer to the poverty of R. Joshua (and others) who allegedly were employed in menial occupations,[57] but these traditions receive no confirmation from tannaitic sources. The tannaim encouraged Jews to support the poor, tried to regulate the collection and disbursement of charity, and perhaps even served as charity agents themselves;[58] they never said that charity should be given to needy rabbis and never reported that poor students actually received any charity.[59] The Babylonian Talmud mentions that R. Gamaliel appointed two needy students to public positions in order to give them a livelihood, but the "make-work" aspect of the appointment and the reference to the poverty of the students are absent from the tannaitic version of the story.[60]

Tension between the well-to-do and the rabbis, patriarchal appointments of rabbis to salaried posts, and the distribution of the "poor tithe" to needy students are securely attested for the period of Judah the Patriarch. During his tenure and afterwards, the patriarchate enlarged its power and the rabbinic movement was compelled to expand its social horizons, to come to terms with wealthy judges, and to find ways to include the poor among its numbers. The numerous amoraic testimonies about poor tannaim and organized charity for needy students of second-century rabbis are best explained as throwbacks ("retrojections") from the amoraic period.[61]

---

57 *R. Joshua*: B Berakhot 28a and J Berakhot 4, 1, 7d. In general, see E. E. Urbach, "Class Status and Leadership in the World of the Palestinian Sages," in: *Proceedings of the Israel Academy of Sciences*, II (Jerusalem, 1968), 24 and 31, who accepts the amoraic testimony. Goodman, *State and Society*, 93, asserts that many tannaim were manual laborers, but adduces no tannaitic evidence to support his assertion.

58 *Encourage Jews to support the poor*: T Pe'ah 4:18–21, Lieberman, p. 61; *regulations*: M Pe'ah 8:7–9; T Pe'ah 4:8–17, Lieberman, pp. 57–60; T Shabbat 16:22, Lieberman, pp. 79–80; T Megillah 1:5 and 2:15, Lieberman, pp. 344–345 and p. 352, respectively; T Demai 3:17, Lieberman, pp. 77–78; *rabbis served as charity agents*: M Ma'aser Sheni 5:9 (ambiguous); ARN A 3, Schechter, p. 9a (Benjamin the Righteous); and a string of amoraic traditions.

59 The only possible exception known to me is T Pe'ah 4:10, Lieberman, p. 58.

60 Cf. Sifre Deuteronomy 16, Finkelstein, p. 26 with B Horayot 10a–b (I am following Rashi rather than the Tosfot Ha-Rash).

61 *Tension between the well-to-do and the rabbis, and appointment to salaried posts*: G. Alon, *Jews, Judaism and the Classical World* (Jerusalem, 1977), pp. 344–353 and 374–435; L. I. Levine, "The Jewish Patriarch (Nasi) in Third Century Palestine," in: *ANRW*, II, 19.2, eds. H. Temporini and W. Haase (Berlin/New York, 1979), 649–688; R. Kimelman, "The Conflict between R. Yohanan and Resh Laqish on the Supremacy of the Patriarchate," in: *Proceedings of the Seventh World Congress of Jewish Studies – 1977: Studies in the Talmud, Halacha, and Midrash* (Jerusalem, 1981), 1–20. Cf. the prayer of the school of R. Yannai, "Do not [O God] bring us to need the gift of men and do not

3. Before Judah the Patriarch the rabbinate was primarily a rural phenomenon, in Judea and especially in the Galilee. Most of the legal cases addressed by the tannaim originated in rural settlements, not the cities (see above). Forty or so of the post-70 tannaim were identified to posterity by their names and geographical origins. Some hailed from the Diaspora (e.g., Simeon the Yemenite, Nathan the Babylonian, Abba Gurion a man of Sidon, Theudas a man of Rome), but the vast majority were from the rural towns and villages of Judea and the Galilee (e.g., 'Ono, Hadar, Yanuaḥ, Bartota, Tiv'on).[62] Similarly, tannaitic (and amoraic) traditions place many of the prominent tannaim in small towns and villages: R. Ishmael in Kefar 'Aziz, R. Joshua in Peqi'in, R. Yoḥanan b. Nuri in Beth She'arim, R. Simeon in Teqo'a, and R. Meir in 'Ardasqus.[63] The tradition quoted by the Babylonian Talmud on the peregrinations of the Sanhedrin is of doubtful historicity, but it agrees with this portrait of a rural rabbinate.[64]

The urbanization of the rabbinic movement is the work of R. Judah the Patriarch. When he moved his seat from Beth She'arim to Sepphoris, the rabbinic movement found itself headquartered in a city for the first time since its golden days at Yavneh. R. Judah the Patriarch attempted to establish the ritual purity of the cities of Palestine and to free their inhabitants of the priestly tithes, both reforms clearly intended to facilitate the entrance of rabbis and rabbinic Jews into the cities. Probably not by coincidence, Palestine entered a new phase of urbanization during R.

---

entrust our support into the hands of men, for their gift is small but their abuse is great" (J Berakhot 4, 2, 7d), with the analysis of A. Oppenheimer, "Those of the School of Rabbi Yannai," *Studies in the History of the Jewish People and the Land of Israel* 4 (1978), 137–145 (Hebrew); *distribution of poor tithe*: J Pe'ah 8, 8, 21a; *amoraic testimonies about organized charity*: Levine, *Rabbinic Class*, 69–71, 162–167.

62 R. Ḥananya a man of 'Ono (near Lod), R. Yaqim a man of Hadar (near Lod), Abba Yosi b. Ḥanin a man of Yanuaḥ (in Lower Galilee; the name is variously spelled), R. Eleazar a man of Bartota (location unknown), Abba Yosi HLYQPRI a man of Tiv'on and R. Ḥananya a man of Tiv'on (near Haifa), and more. Many of these place-names are obscure or corrupt. The standard aids are *Sefer ha-Yishuv*, ed. S. Klein (Jerusalem, 1939; reprint 1978) (Hebrew); M. Avi-Yonah, *The Holy Land: A Historical Geography* (Grand Rapids, 1979); and idem, *Gazetteer of Roman Palestine* (Qedem 5; Jerusalem, 1976).

63 *R. Ishmael*: M Kil'aim 6:4 and M Ketubot 5:8; *R. Joshua*: T Sotah 7:9, Lieberman, pp. 193–194; R. Yoḥanan b. Nuri: T Terumot 7:14, Lieberman, p. 147 and T Sukkah 2:2, Lieberman, p. 260; *R. Simeon*: T 'Eruvin 5:24, Lieberman, p. 116; *R. Meir*: T Nazir 5:1, Lieberman, p. 141 = T Oholot 4:14, Zuckermandel, p. 601 and T 'Eruvin 6:4, Lieberman, p. 119; cf. B Sanhedrin 32b.

64 B Rosh Ha-shanah 31a–b.

Judah's tenure: Lod and Beth Guvrin were elevated to the status of *poleis* by Septimius Severus, as was Emmaus by Elagabalus.[65]

Conclusion: The Elusive Rabbis of the Second Century

The elite status of the rabbis depended as much, if not more, upon their wealth and birth as upon their intellectual and pietistic achievements. They had little inclination and availed themselves of few opportunities to propagate their way of life among the masses. Their judicial authority extended to a few circumscribed topics only. The rabbis were but a small part of Jewish society, an insular group which produced an insular literature. They were not synagogue leaders. Most of them were of rural, not urban, origin. Despite their small numbers and aloofness, there is no evidence (aside from some allegedly tannaitic material quoted by the Babylonian Talmud) for hatred between them and the *ᶜamme ha-ʾaretz*—disdain yes, but not hatred.

The social standing of the rabbinic movement changed dramatically under the leadership of Judah the Patriarch. In his time the rabbinic movement expanded its base socially, economically, and politically. The rabbis moved into the cities of the Galilee, Judea, and the coast; they began to find ways to include the poor among their number, and achieved unambiguous recognition from the Romans. This period marks a major transition in the development of the rabbinate in the Land of Israel.

---

65 On R. Judah and the cities, see A. Büchler, "The Patriarch R. Judah I and the Graeco-Roman Cities of Palestine," in: *Studies in Jewish History*, eds. I. Brodie and J. Rabbinowitz (Oxford, 1956), 179–244; and L. I. Levine, *Caesarea under Roman Rule* (Leiden, 1975), 64–68. On urbanization, see Levine, *Rabbinic Class*, 25–26.

R. Ḥanina bar Ḥama at Sepphoris

STUART S. MILLER

R. Ḥanina b. Ḥama's role at Sepphoris has been discussed by the major talmudic historians, most of whom have concentrated on the early third-century sage's[1] supposed difficulties with the Sepphorians, or *Ẓipporaʾei*, as they are called in the Jerusalem Talmud.[2] Ḥanina is depicted as a colorful figure who attained substantial recognition as a scholar, but who was embroiled in the politics of the academy and was subject to the criticism and resentment reserved at times by the masses for the scholarly class.[3]

This paper will focus on Ḥanina's relationship to the *Ẓipporaʾei* and will attempt to present a comprehensive assessment of those passages in which the two appear together in order to obtain a balanced appreciation of the sage's role at Sepphoris.[4] Much attention will be directed to the

---

[1] According to the Iggeret of Rav Sherira Gaon, ed. Lewin, p. 59, Ḥanina was both a tanna and an amora, presumably because he bridged the tannaitic and amoraic periods.

[2] See A. Büchler, *The Political and Social Leaders of Sepphoris in the Second and Third Centuries* (Oxford, 1909), 53f., and esp. S. Lieberman, "Palestine in the Third and Fourth Centuries," *JQR* 36 (1946), 329–370 = *Texts and Studies* (New York, 1974), 144–147. Cf. S. Mendelsohn, "Ḥanina b. Ḥama," *JE* (12 vols.; New York/London, 1901–06), VI, 217. The most comprehensive treatment of Ḥanina can be found in I. S. Zuri, *History of Hebrew Public Law: The Reign of the Patriarchate and the Vaʿad* (Paris, 1931), III/1, 93–110 and III/2 (*The Academy of R. Ḥanina Bar Ḥama at Sepphoris*) (Hebrew).

[3] See L. I. Levine, *The Rabbinic Class of Roman Palestine in Late Antiquity* (Jerusalem, 1989), 117–127.

[4] This work does not purport to be an exhaustive study of Ḥanina nor does it suggest that a biography of the sage can be written. Recently articulated strictures on the writing of rabbinic biography are precisely the reason for the selective approach and

Zippora'ei themselves, in order to understand better who they were and to clarify further their role in Sepphorian society. Only then can their connection to Ḥanina be fully appraised.

Consideration should be given at the outset to the other passages in rabbinic literature that associate Ḥanina with Sepphoris.[5] Thus, we find Ḥanina deciding halakhic issues both independently and in consultation with two younger scholars who once lived at Sepphoris, R. Yoḥanan and Resh Laqish,[6] interpreting Scripture in the city,[7] and introducing (*hinhig*) various practices that follow the halakhic opinion of a tanna, either Simeon b. Gamaliel or Simeon b. Yoḥai.[8] Likewise, Ḥanina reports a mourning practice of Jews in Sepphoris and invokes a relevant *taqqanah* issued earlier by the well-known Sepphorian tanna, Yose b. Ḥalafta.[9] He also exhibits great respect for his mentor, R. Judah ha-Nasi, another prominent resident of Sepphoris from whom he learned much.[10] Ḥanina expresses his satisfaction with the academic achievements of his disciple, Yoḥanan, at Sepphoris.[11] The respect is, in fact, mutual; thus, upon hearing the great commotion attending the funeral arrangements for a scholar at Sepphoris, Yoḥanan presumes (rightly) that it is Ḥanina who has died and immediately mourns for him.[12]

Other facets of Ḥanina's life at Sepphoris are also revealed. The scholar is regarded as a scrupulously ethical businessman and is remembered for using the proceeds from his sale of honey to build a *bet midrash*

---

topic adopted here. On the difficulties posed by the writing of biographies of talmudic sages, see J. Neusner, *In Search of Talmudic Biography: The Problem of the Attributed Saying* (Chico, 1984), and W. S. Green, "What's in a Name? – The Problematic of Rabbinic 'Biography'," in: *Approaches to Ancient Judaism: Theory and Practice*, ed. W. S. Green (Missoula, 1978), 77–96.

5 The assumption in this paper is that Ḥanina b. Ḥama is intended whenever a rabbinic text mentions "Ḥanina" in connection with Sepphoris or the *Zippora'ei*. This is reasonable, especially when the text can be dated to the first half of the third century. For a discussion of the four different Ḥaninas who appear in the Jerusalem Talmud, see Z. W. Rabinovitz, *Sha'are Torath Eretz Yisrael* (Jerusalem, 1940), 458.

6 J Niddah 2, 50b. Cf. J Rosh Ha-shanah 2, 58b and J Sanhedrin 1, 18c.

7 Exod. 22:30 in Leviticus Rabbah 5:6; J Terumot 8, 45c and J 'Avodah Zarah 2, 41a; Job 24:16 in J Ma'aser Sheni 5, 55d.

8 See J Megillah 1, 71a (= J Sheqalim 1, 46a); cf. J Demai 5, 24d (= J Gittin 4, 46b) where Simeon b. Yoḥai seems to be intended.

9 J Sanhedrin 2, 20c and J Berakhot 3, 6b.

10 See J Niddah 2, 50b. Cf. discussion below and nn. 97, 98 and 106.

11 J Horayot 3, 48b.

12 J Bava Metzi'a 2, 8d.

at Sepphoris.[13] Ḥanina also has a reputation for knowing the secret pronunciation of the Divine name, which others came to Sepphoris to learn from him.[14] A comment assigned to Ḥanina concerning the prevalence of deaths due to the cold is attributed to his familiarity with the climate in Sepphoris.[15] Finally, a discussion pertaining to the *kashrut* of a slaughtered goat that Ḥanina finds between Tiberias and Sepphoris suggests that the rabbis regarded as noteworthy even trivial incidents that involved the sage.[16]

Ḥanina and the Zippora'ei

Introduction

Of the eighteen traditions in the Jerusalem Talmud that refer to the Zippora'ei,[17] eight or possibly nine mention Ḥanina. No other sage is associated with the Zippora'ei to the same extent. Those passages that do not mention Ḥanina will be considered first, however, as they, too, may help to establish the identity of the Zippora'ei.

The Zippora'ei were at times Jewish residents of Sepphoris who apparently had no significant connection with the rabbinic class. It is they who were intended when R. Mana, a fourth-century Sepphorian sage, is said to have permitted the sale of already rented homes "for the sake of the Zippora'ei," whose sons would have been forfeited to the Roman *numerus* had they been unable to pay the *aurum tironicum*.[18] We also hear of Zippora'ei who disguised themselves to avoid being caught in the days of

---

13   J Pe'ah 7, 20b relates that Ḥanina once informed his customers when they unwittingly bought date honey instead of bees' honey from him. Cf. J Megillah 4, 75c and B Ketubot 23a, which also mention a *bet midrash* associated with Ḥanina.

14   Following Ecclesiastes Rabbah 3:11 and Mattenot Kehunah, ad loc. See, however, J Yoma 3, 40d. Cf. E. E. Urbach, *The Sages – Their Concepts and Beliefs* (Jerusalem, 1979), II, 739, n. 45.

15   J Shabbat 14, 14c.

16   B Bava Metzi'a 24b. Cf. J Ta'anit 4, 68a on Ḥanina's trips between Tiberias and Sepphoris.

17   Although this term appears elsewhere, such as in Genesis Rabbah, for the most part its use is exclusive to the Jerusalem Talmud. The instances in Genesis Rabbah, in fact, have parallels in the Jerusalem Talmud. Note, however, Genesis Rabbah 27:3, Theodor-Albeck, p. 257, where the term seems to have been introduced into a passage that lacks it in the talmudic version.

18   J Pesaḥim 4, 31b, following Lieberman, "Palestine in the Third and Fourth Centuries," 136. Cf. S. S. Miller, *Studies in the History and Traditions of Sepphoris* (Leiden, 1984), 43f.

Ursicinus "the king."[19] Finally, it is reported that the *Zippora'ei* prevented
one another from installing looms between their homes because of the
noise caused by the weaving process.[20] In these instances, too, the
Zippora'ei were ordinary Jewish inhabitants of the city of Sepphoris.

In most of the other passages that do not involve Hanina, the
Zippora'ei are part of the rabbinic milieu, although they do not seem to
have been sages or even disciples. Thus, they challenged Yose b.
Halafta's assertion that R. Meir was a great man, principally because the
latter seemed to be ignorant of local mourning customs.[21] Similarly, R.
Mana was compelled to explain to the *Zippora'ei* why he did not mourn
for R. Abun during *hol ha-mo'ed*.[22] Elsewhere, the *Zippora'ei* dramatically
convinced Rabbi to include the leek among the vegetables that he permitted to be purchased after the sabbatical year.[23] We also learn of Bar Qappara's metaphorical announcement before the *Zippora'ei* of Rabbi's
death.[24]

In two instances, the *Zippora'ei* seem to have been more closely associated with the rabbis. In the first of these, they suggest the distance that
new shoes should be walked in before they could be worn on the Sabbath.[25] Their view appears alongside the opinions of the *Tibera'ei*
(Tiberians) and the "members of the house" (*benei beteih*)[26] of Bar Qappara. The latter probably constituted a school associated with Bar Qappara.[27] Each opinion is presented with the usual technical formula, "so

19 J Sotah 9, 23c and J Yevamot 16, 15c. Cf. J Megillah 3, 74a, where the same Ursicinus is said to have burned the Torah scroll of the *Sinbara'ei* (Sennabrians). They
then ask R. Judah and R. Yose whether the burnt scroll may be used for a public service. Clearly, these *Sinbara'ei* were ordinary Jewish residents who were close enough
to the rabbis to ask them halakhic questions.

20 J Bava Batra 2, 13b.

21 J Berakhot 2, 5b and J Mo'ed Qatan 3, 82d. Cf. Genesis Rabbah 100:57.

22 J Mo'ed Qatan 3, 83a–b.

23 J Shevi'it 6, 37a.

24 J Kil'aim 9, 32b. Interestingly, the parallel in Ecclesiastes Rabbah 7:12 has Bar
Qappara address the *Zippora'ei* as *benei Yeda'yah*, i.e., priests. This appears to be an in-
terpolation. See Miller, *Studies*, 120–122.

25 J Shabbat 6, 8a and J Sanhedrin 10, 28a. The concern is that new shoes may be
uncomfortable so the wearer may come to carry them on the Sabbath. See Pene
Moshe to J Shabbat 6, 8a.

26 Following the reading in J Sanhedrin 10, 28a. See S. Lieberman, *Hayerushalmi
Kiphshuto* (Jerusalem, 1934), 444.

27 *Bet* is frequently used in reference to schools. Besides the obvious examples (*bet
midrash, bet* Hillel, etc.), cf. also the designation, *'ein de-vei Rabbi Yannai*. On the latter,
see A. Oppenheimer, "'Those of the School of Rabbi Yannai'," *Studies in the History of*

and so says (ʾamrin) . . . ," where the verb ʾamar signifies an opinion put forward among the rabbis.[28]

In the other instance, R. Ḥiyya b. Abba declared (derash) before the Zipporaʾei that they need not continue to observe the mourning prohibitions associated with the week of the 9th of Av following the day itself, but the latter refused to accept his opinion (ve-loʾ qiblu ʿaleihon).[29] While a public declaration seems to have been intended here,[30] later in the passage the customs of the Zipporaʾei, the Tiberaʾei, and the Deromaʾei (Southerners) are presented. Here the groups intended seem to have been closely connected with the rabbanan,[31] who are also mentioned in the passage.

For the most part, however, the Zipporaʾei who interact with the rabbis may have been part of a rabbinic setting, but they do not play an active role in the circles of the sages. Although at times they have opinions of their own, for instance with regard to the sabbatical year, and while they appear to have been knowledgeable of mourning practices pertaining to the Sabbath and ḥol ha-moʿed, their reactions and views are usually presented in an aggadic context rather than one that assumes their presence and active participation in an academy or, better, rabbinic session.

The Ḥanina Passages

Our discussion of the Zipporaʾei traditions that involve Ḥanina begins with those texts in which the sage decides laws (horei) either in Sepphoris or, more specifically, for the Zipporaʾei. J Maʿaserot 1, 49a reads:[32]

A. It was taught [in a baraita]: R. Ishmaʿel b. R. Yose [said] in the name of his father, "Bitter almonds, behold they are exempt, and sweet almonds do not require [tithing] until their outer shells separate."

B. R. Ḥanina decided the law [horei] in Sepphoris in accordance with [the view of] R. Ishmaʿel b. R. Yose.

---

the Jewish People and the Land of Israel 4 (1978), 137–145 (Hebrew). Also see the discussion of bei rav and related expressions by D. Goodblatt, Rabbinic Instruction in Sasanian Babylonia (Leiden, 1975), 108–154.

28 On the use of ʾamar, see D. W. Halivni, Midrash, Mishnah, and Gemara: The Jewish Predilection for Justified Law (Cambridge, 1986), 74 and 139f., n. 20.

29 See J Taʿanit 4, 69b.

30 On the use of derash/darash, see the discussion below.

31 According to D. Halivni, "ספקי דנברי," PAAJR 46–47 (1979–80), 81f., this term refers to amoraim in the Jerusalem Talmud. Cf. Goodblatt, Rabbinic Instruction, 286–288.

32 Unless otherwise indicated, translations of texts from the Jerusalem Talmud are the writer's and follow ms. Leiden.

C. With regard to what did he decide the law [*horei*]?

D. The *Zippora'ei* say [*'amri*], "[With regard to] bitter almonds."

E. R. Ze'ira said [*'amar*], "[With regard to] sweet [almonds]."

F. Said [*'amar*] R. Yoḥanan, "[When] they descended to this place they [the bitter almonds] required [tithing]; [when] they ascended, they were already exempted."

M Ma'aserot 1:4 states that small bitter almonds must be tithed but sweet almonds that are not fully grown need not be because they are not suitable for eating. The mishnah also asserts that full-grown bitter almonds are inedible, so they do not require tithing whereas large sweet almonds do. In our passage, Sepphorian and Tiberian views are clearly juxtaposed and contrasted. Thus, the *baraita* has R. Ishma'el report in the name of his father, Yose b. Ḥalafta, that bitter almonds of all sizes are exempt from tithing, and sweet ones need to be tithed only once their outer shells have fallen away. The fact that Ḥanina actually decided the law in Sepphoris in accordance with this *baraita* becomes the focal point of the views that follow.

First the *Zippora'ei* claim that Ḥanina followed Yose only where bitter almonds are concerned. The views of the second- and third-generation Tiberians, Ze'ira and Yoḥanan, are then presented. Ze'ira maintains that Ḥanina's decision complied with Yose's view with respect to sweet almonds. Yoḥanan seems to be saying that when one goes down to Tiberias, one does not follow Yose's view and therefore is obligated to tithe small bitter almonds. A person who goes up to Sepphoris, however, need not do so, as Ḥanina had decided there that Yose's view was the halakhah. Although another Tiberian, Ze'ira, claims that Ḥanina's decision refers to the sweet almonds, both he and Yoḥanan would agree that small bitter almonds need to be tithed. That apparently was the Tiberian viewpoint.[33]

By assuming that Ḥanina's decision pertains to bitter almonds and by further clarifying that there are regional differences on the issue, Yoḥanan clearly establishes that the matter was discussed for a while and came to a head during his own and Ze'ira's time. The opinions expressed here appear to be presented in chronological as well as geographical order. The view of the second-century tanna of Sepphoris, Yose, is first

---

[33] See the comments of Ephraim Dov Ha-Kohen, *Gilyon 'Ephraim*, ad loc. and those of Jacob David Willowski (Ridbaz) on the passage. Also see Rabinovitz, *Sha'are Torath Eretz Yisrael*, 105. For a completely different understanding of the passage, see the comments of Elijah of Vilna, ad loc., and those of M. Margolies in his commentaries, *Pene Moshe* and *Mar'eh ha-Panim*.

quoted by his son, Ishmaʿel. Ḥanina, of the early third century, is then said to have ruled on the matter in Sepphoris. Once the understanding by the *Zipporaʾei* of Ḥanina's decision is presented, the views of the Tiberians, Zeʿira and Yoḥanan, follow.³⁴ It is reasonable to assume that the *Zipporaʾei* here are mid- to late third-century contemporaries of Yoḥanan and Zeʿira. The fact that the Babylonian Talmud (B Ḥullin 25a and B ʿEruvin 28b) has the third generation amora, R. Ila, report Ḥanina's ruling at Sepphoris would lend further support to this conclusion.

The *Zipporaʾei* here are full-fledged representatives of the Sepphorian point of view. Curiously, the gemara does not have Ḥanina decide the law for the *Zipporaʾei* per se. Rather, their view is formulated just as that of Zeʿira, i.e., "so and so *ʾamrin / ʾamar.*"³⁵ Moreover, the use of the term *horei* suggests that Ḥanina ruled on the matter in a rabbinic session.³⁶ While these *Zipporaʾei* may have been amongst those who heard his decision, it seems more likely that they were participants in a later discussion of its implications, perhaps in Tiberias itself. In any case, the *Zipporaʾei* are presumed to have been knowledgeable about the views of Ḥanina and are regarded as legitimate interpreters of his position. Clearly, they are presented here as active members of a rabbinic circle.

In the next instance of *horei* with reference to Ḥanina, the sage resolves issues for the *Zipporaʾei* directly. J Betzah 1, 60a reads:

A. R. Ḥanina decided the law [*horei*] for the *Zipporaʾei* with regard to the [purchase of] aftergrowth of mustard [seeds in the sabbatical year] and the egg in accordance with [the view of] R. Judah.³⁷

B. R. Yoḥanan came and declared [*ʿaʾal u-derash*] to them in accordance with the *rabbanan* here [in the case of the egg] and in accordance with the *rabbanan* there [in the case of the aftergrowth of mustard seeds].

---

³⁴ Although Zeʿira was the younger contemporary of Yoḥanan, the chronological presentation is not necessarily thrown off despite the fact that Zeʿira's view is presented first. After all, Yoḥanan is not simply responding to the question at C ("With regard to what did he decide the law?") but is glossing the entire discussion. Note how his view is presented somewhat differently (*ʾamar R. Yoḥanan*).

³⁵ On this usage, see above, n. 28. For the formula used for Yoḥanan's view, see previous note.

³⁶ According to Halivni, *Midrash, Mishnah, and Gemara,* 139, n. 16, the use of *horei* implies either a public or private session. The point here, however, is that these sessions were attended by the rabbis, their colleagues and students. Cf. Zuri, *Reign,* I, 288f.

³⁷ The parallel in J Sheviʿit 9, 38c omits Ḥanina's statement but the entire *sugiaʾ* is out of place there and was incorrectly copied from its original source in J Betzah 1, 60a. See the critical discussion in I. Francus, *Jerusalem Talmud: Tractate Betzah* (New York, 1967), 32f., 72 (Hebrew).

Ḥanina is said to have decided (*horei*) two laws for the *Ẓipporaʾei*, both in accordance with the views of the mid-second century tanna, R. Judah.[38] The first pertains to the purchase of the aftergrowth of mustard seed during the sabbatical year. Unlike the *rabbanan*, Judah did not suspect the seller of having sold mustard that had really grown during the sabbatical year itself.[39] Judah also disagreed with the *rabbanan*, who maintained that an egg laid on a festival may be eaten on an adjoining Sabbath day (or vice versa).[40]

Ḥanina is not the only one who reportedly addressed these matters before the *Ẓipporaʾei*. Yoḥanan, too, got into the act, but, interestingly, he declared (*derash*), as opposed to *horei* in the case of Ḥanina, to the *Ẓipporaʾei* that the views of the *rabbanan* were correct. The choice of terms may be significant. *Darash/derash* is commonly reserved for exegetical lessons and halakhic pronouncements of a public nature,[41] usually made in either a synagogue or a *bet midrash*.[42] *Horei*, as already indicated, is used where decisions on practical concerns are rendered by a sage in a rabbinic session.[43] The verb *derash* is used elsewhere in the Jerusalem Talmud to describe Yoḥanan's activity in a *bet midrash* in Sepphoris.[44]

---

[38] Ḥanina again adopts a view of R. Judah in a passage connected with the *Ẓipporaʾei* in J Yevamot 1, 2d, which is discussed below.

[39] See M Sheviʿit 9:1.

[40] See the preceding material in the gemara and cf. T Betzah 1:3, both of which indicate that this issue was already debated by the houses of Hillel and Shammai. The question is whether or not the adjoining festival day and Sabbath constitute distinct days of holiness or one such period (*qedushah ʾaḥat*). If the latter is the case, then the egg certainly could not have undergone any "preparation" (*hakhanah*) in advance of the festival or Sabbath and, consequently, would have been prohibited. Cf. B Betzah 4a, where the understanding that the issue of *shetei qedushot ʾo ʾaḥat* is rejected. Instead, the suggestion is made that the dispute resulted from different views regarding "the preparation of Rabbah" (*hakhanah de-Rabbah*), which prohibited the eating of something that was prepared, even of itself (such as an egg), on a festival following a Sabbath or a Sabbath following a festival.

[41] Cf. Halivni, *Midrash, Mishnah, and Gemara*, 74 and below, n. 42. Note that B Betzah 4a has innkeepers and landlords raising the same issues pertaining to the egg. So, at least in the Babylonian Talmud, ordinary persons are concerned about these matters.

[42] See D. Urman, "The Synagogue and Beth ha-Midrash – Are They One and the Same?," in: *Synagogues in Antiquity*, eds. A. Kasher, et al. (Jerusalem, 1987), 57 (Hebrew).

[43] See discussion above and n. 36. It should be noted that these concerns could have been purely academic. See Halivni, *Midrash, Mishnah, and Gemara*, 139, n. 16.

[44] See J Horayot 3, 48b and 48c (= J Shabbat 12, 13c), where Yoḥanan is found teaching, apparently on two separate occasions, in the *bet midrash* of R. Benayah in

What is particularly significant is that Ḥanina is the only authority, let alone Sepphorian, whose teachings to the *Zipporaʾei* are characterized by the term *horei*.

The terminological shift in this passage makes it particularly difficult to identify the *Zipporaʾei* intended. Those whom Ḥanina is said to have addressed could have been members of his circle whereas those before whom Yoḥanan taught the halakhah may very well have been a larger audience, including lay members of the Jewish community of Sepphoris.[45]

Precisely because the recipients of Ḥanina's decision and Yoḥanan's declaration have a passive role in the passage, they cannot be positively identified. What is evident is that they are presumed to have been close to both Ḥanina and Yoḥanan. Yoḥanan, like many other tannaim and amoraim, may have delivered public discourses and pronouncements (*derash*) in Sepphoris,[46] but only Ḥanina decided (*horei*) practical issues for the *Zipporaʾei* in the rabbinic session. In fact, Ḥanina appears to have

---

Sepphoris. Cf. PRK 18, Mandelbaum, p. 297, where he lectures in the *kenishtaʾ rabbataʾ de-Zipporin*. Forms of *drsh* are used in each of these instances to describe his activity.

45 In Babylonia, scholars often attended public sessions know as *pirqaʾ*. In fact, the rabbis demanded that their students attend when they lectured publicly. Interestingly, the activity of the sage addressing a *pirqaʾ* is often described as *derash*. See D. Goodblatt, *Rabbinic Instruction*, 171–196, passim. For the situation in Palestine, see the famous story regarding Rabban Gamaliel and R. Joshua in J Berakhot 4, 7c–d and J Taʿanit 4, 67d. There Rabban Gamaliel "sits and lectures" (*yoshev ve-doresh*) in a schoolhouse (*bet ha-vaʿad*) and "all the people" (*kol ha-ʿam*) complain about his treatment of R. Joshua. Cf. I. Gafni, "Yeshiva and Metivta," *Zion* 43 (1973), 17 (Hebrew). The gloss of the late third – early fourth century amora, Abba b. Zamina, that follows our passage uses the difference of opinion between Yoḥanan and Ḥanina as the reason for the former's departure to Tiberias. The words attributed to Yoḥanan by Abba suggest that Yoḥanan addressed a public assembly, but one that was certainly interested in rabbinic matters. In any case, his statement serves to confirm that Ḥanina and Yoḥanan did, in fact, maintain different halakhic perspectives on the issues mentioned. On Yoḥanan's departure, see R. Kimelman, "Rabbi Yoḥanan of Tiberias: Aspects of the Social and Religious History of Third Century Palestine" (doctoral dissertation, Yale University; New Haven, 1977), 11–13.

46 R. Yose is said to have lectured openly (*darash/derash*) at Sepphoris in B Moʿed Qatan 21a (in a *bet midrash*) and B Sanhedrin 113a–b. Amoraim who did the same include Bar Qappara in B Sanhedrin 93a–b and 94a and R. Ḥelbo in J Megillah 3, 74a. The tradition regarding R. Judah (b. Simon?) in ed. Venice of Genesis Rabbah 28:3 seems faulty. See Theodor-Albeck, p. 261. Evidently, public discourses of both a halakhic and exegetical nature were commonplace at Sepphoris. Cf. the other uses of *drsh* where Yoḥanan is concerned, in the sources referred to above, n. 44.

been the only sage to resolve such matters for the *Zippora'ei* as well as to teach in public (*derash*) in Sepphoris.[47]

The last occurrence of *horei* involving Ḥanina is in J Bava Metzi'a 10, 12c:

A. R. Justa [said] in the name of Resh Laqish, "The one who lives below provides the joists and the boards, and the one who lives above provides the plaster."

B. Which type of plaster [should he provide]?

C. R. Jacob b. Aḥa [said] in the name of R. El'azar, "Thick plaster."

D. R. Abbahu [said] in the name of R. El'azar, "Medium plaster."

E. They only said this with regard to the rinsing of cups. However, if he [the one who lives above] wanted to wash garments, even R. Abbahu [who said] in the name of R. El'azar agrees [that he must provide] thick plaster.

F. R. Ḥanina decided the law [*horei*] for those [*'ilein*] *Zippora'ei*[48] [as follows]: both of them [the occupants of both stories] would have to provide the joists and the boards, since they [those who live above] need to bring up their donkeys there and to bring their fruits there.

In M Bava Metzi'a 10:3, R. Yose states that should the floor of a tenant's apartment be in disrepair, the landlord provides the joists and the tenant supplies the plaster which goes upon them.[49] The gemara expands the subject by referring to the views of three late third-century amoraim, and resolves the different views attributed to R. El'azar (C and D) by explaining that the type of plaster to be contributed by the tenant depends upon whether he washes garments in his apartment. Ḥanina's ruling, which certainly is earlier than the opinions expressed here, is introduced precisely because he, too, deals with unusual circumstances, i.e., the keeping of animals and fruits by the upstairs tenant.

Once again, Ḥanina rules on a practical matter for the *Zippora'ei*. If, indeed, the practice among many residents of Sepphoris was to keep animals and fruits in their second-floor apartments, one could easily understand how the issue arose, even among the sages, as the term *horei* would imply. Nevertheless, one cannot say with certainty what role these

---

47 See J Ma'aser Sheni 5, 55d.

48 Ms. Escorial has *Zippora'* here, which Lieberman emends to read *Zippora'ei*. See his comments in *Yerushalmi Neziqin: Edited from the Escorial Manuscript with an Introduction by E. S. Rosenthal* (Jerusalem, 1983), 173. The phrase *'ilein Zippora'ei* also appears in J Bava Batra 2, 13b. Cf. the phrase *'ilein de-vei Rabbi Yannai* (above, n. 27).

49 R. Yose's view is repeated before our excerpt in the gemara.

Ẓippora^ʾei played in Ḥanina's circle of colleagues and students, only that they evidently heard him discuss the issue.

On two or probably three occasions the Jerusalem Talmud has a sage hold the *Ẓippora^ʾei* responsible for a view that they evidently transmitted in the name of Ḥanina. In each instance the formula used is, "You say in the name of R. Ḥanina," *ʾatun ʾamrin be-shem R. Ḥanina*. The first of these occurs in J Sheviʿit 7, 37b:

A. The *Ẓipporayei* = *Ẓippora^ʾei* asked [*sha^ʾalun*] R. Immi [Ammi], "What is [the law] with regard to the moistening [of wheat kernels] by means of [moist, thorny] grasses [*hohim*50]?"

B. He replied to them, "You [yourselves] say in the name of R. Ḥanina [*ʾatun ʾamrin be-shem R. Ḥanina*],51 'even with the leaves of the *cynara* [artichoke]52 plant it is permitted'."

---

50 Following the emendation of Feliks, *Jerusalem Talmud: Tractate Sheviʿit* (2 vols.; Jerusalem, 1979–86), II, 115 (Hebrew). On the identification of *hohim*, see ibid., II, 99, 103.

51 Ms. Rome has R. Yusah (Yose) b. R. Ḥanina instead of R. Ḥanina, but the better mss. and editions have R. Ḥanina. Many of the commentators do not understand the *Ẓippora^ʾei* to be the subject of Immi's statement (B). Instead, they translate *ʾatun ʾamrin* as "they [i.e., students] came and said," taking the word *ʾatun* as the third person plural of *ʾata^ʾ*, "to come." See, for example, the text and comments of Solomon Sirilio, ad loc. Cf. Y. Levi and A. Carmel, *Jerusalem Talmud: Tractate Sheviʿit with the Commentary Qav Naqi* (Jerusalem, 1979), 138 (Hebrew); and Feliks, *Tractate Sheviʿit*, II, 116. The translation suggested here follows the rendering of Pene Moshe, ad loc., where *ʾatun* is understood to be the second person plural pronoun, "you," to wit, the *Ẓippora^ʾei*. In the other two passages in which the formula appears, there is no possibility of any other translation. The fact that, in this instance, another rendering is possible does not mean that it is necessarily correct, even if it does obviate the difficulty of the *Ẓippora^ʾei* asking a question to which they already should have known the answer. The similarity of the phraseology found here and elsewhere cannot be a mere coincidence. Indeed, as will be argued below, it is entirely possible that the *Ẓippora^ʾei* were regarded as the transmitters of the sayings of R. Ḥanina. Moreover, where *ʾatun ʾamrin* does mean, "they came and said," the two verbs are usually connected by the conjunction *ve-* and the usage is usually followed by the pronoun *le-*, i.e., the person being addressed is indicated. See the many examples of this form and the similar *ʾatun ve-sha^ʾalun le-* in M. Kosovsky, *Concordance to the Jerusalem Talmud* (Jerusalem, 1979–), II, 250f. Kosovsky lists the usage in our passage as a pronoun but indicates that it is difficult; ibid., I, 884. However, the formula *ʾatun ʾamrin be-shem . . .* does not occur with *ʾatun* meaning "they came." In addition to the occurrences involving the *Ẓippora^ʾei* and Ḥanina, there are other examples of this usage. See, for example, J Terumot 1, 44a for *ʾatun ʾamrin be-shem R. Yohanan* and J Makkot 2, 31d for *ʾatun ʾamrin be-shem Rav*.

52 See Feliks, *Tractate Sheviʿit*, II, 116 for the identification of this plant.

C. R. Josiah said, "[R. Ḥanina ruled thus] in an actual instance [*le-ʿovadah*] and one may rely on it."

This passage begins with the question of the *Zipporaʾei* as to whether moist grasses (*hoḥim*) may be used during the sabbatical year to dampen wheat kernels that were eventually to be ground.[53] Produce of the sabbatical year may be used only for its usual purpose, i.e., that which is normally consumed by humans may not be fed to animals or put to other uses, and that which is usually eaten by livestock may not in any way be utilized by people. The *Zipporaʾei* are concerned that once the grasses are used to moisten the kernels they will no longer be suitable for their ordinary function as food for animals.[54] R. Immi, a leading amora in Tiberias at the end of the third century,[55] seems to respond directly to the *Zipporaʾei*. He apparently reminds them that they have reported in the name of Ḥanina that even the leaves of the *cynara* plant may be used for this very purpose, although generally they, too, are regarded as food.[56] R. Josiah, a contemporary of R. Immi and also a Tiberian, then indicates (C) that one may regard Ḥanina's view as the halakhah.[57]

The *Zipporaʾei* who ask R. Immi a technical halakhic question are clearly his contemporaries. They could very well be Sepphorian farmers for whom this matter is important. Alternatively, they may be participants in a rabbinic discussion who are aware of a common practice and wish to determine whether it is permissible. Immi's response suggests that the *Zipporaʾei* pass on traditions as do other sages. The implication is that the *Zipporaʾei* are asking a question concerning which they or others of their group had passed on a relevant tradition earlier. In any event, they clearly belong to the late third century, they raise technical halakhic questions, and transmit traditions in the name of Ḥanina—all of which indicate that they moved within rabbinic circles. Finally, the fact that R. Immi and R. Josiah were Tiberians suggests that the matter was addressed in Tiberias. Once again, it would appear that the *Zipporaʾei* asso-

---

[53] This aided the grinding process. See Feliks, ibid.

[54] See M Sheviʿit 7:1, where *hoḥim* are considered *maʾakhal behemah*.

[55] See A. Hyman, *A History of the Tannaim and Amoraim* (3 vols.; reprint; Jerusalem, 1964), I, 221f. (Hebrew).

[56] The leaves of the artichoke plant are edible. Apparently *hoḥim* and *cynara* leaves are similar, hence they are compared here. See Feliks, *Tractate Sheviʿit*, II, 116, esp. n. 56.

[57] Following the interpretation of Pene Moshe. Cf. the comments of Elijah of Fulda to the passage.

The *Zipporaʾei* are found in a similar predicament in J Yevamot 1, 2d:

A. R. Hezekiah [said] in the name of R. Abbahu . . . "It was taught [in a *baraita*]:[58] Until when can the [fatherless] daughter refuse [to stay with a husband she was married off to by her mother or brothers while yet a minor]? Until she brings forth two [pubic] hairs, so R. Meir [maintains]."

B. "R. Judah said, 'Until the black [pubic hair] predominates'."

C. "R. Simeon said, 'Until the crest[59] begins to flatten'."

D. R. Zeʿira [and] R. Hiyya [said] in the name of R. Simeon ben Laqish, "Until the crest begins to flatten and the black [i.e., dark hair] is greater than the white [skin, i.e., the bare areas]."

E. R. Abbahu [and] R. Elʿazar [said] in the name of R. Hoshʿayah, "The halakhah is according to R. Judah."

F. R. Joshua b. Levi said, "The halakhah is according to R. Judah."

G. A case came before R. Yose (*Ysʾ*). He said, "Go before R. Abbahu since he has a tradition that the halakhah [is according to] R. Judah. We do not have a tradition that the halakhah is according to R. Judah."

H. R. Ḥanina said, "The halakhah is according to R. Judah."

I. R. Yoḥanan said to the *Zipporayeiʾ* [= *Zipporaʾei*], "You say in the name of R. Ḥanina [*ʾatun ʾamrin be-shem R. Ḥanina*], 'The halakha is according to R. Judah', but it is not so."

J. How is it then [i.e., how do we know that R. Ḥanina could not have said this]?

K. The *ḥavrayaʾ* [said] in the name of R. Ḥanina, "R. Judah admits that if she had intercourse after she has brought forth two hairs, she cannot refuse."

L. R. Zeʿira [said] in the name of R. Ḥanina, "R. Judah admits that if she was betrothed after she has brought forth two hairs, she cannot refuse."

A fatherless girl who had been married off by her mother or brothers while she was yet a minor could refuse to remain married to her husband. This *sugiaʾ* is concerned with the time limitation placed upon this right of refusal (*miʾun*). A *baraita* containing the opinions of the tannaim Meir, Judah, and Simeon is quoted by the early fourth-century amora, R. Hezekiah, in Abbahu's name. The opinions of several third-century sages

---

58 See T Niddah 6:5.

59 M. Jastrow, *A Dictionary of the Targumim, the Talmud Babli and Yerushalmi, and the Midrashic Literature* (reprint; New York, 1971), 657, renders *kaf* as "the crest (fleshy elevation) over the genitals."

follow, several of whom, including Ḥanina, assert that the halakhah accords with the view of R. Judah, who maintains that a minor may refuse "until her black [pubic hair] predominates."

The remainder of the *sugia*ʾ is devoted to the ascription of this opinion to Ḥanina. After Yoḥanan questions the accuracy of the attribution, different versions of Ḥanina's saying are presented by Zeʿira and by the *havraya*ʾ (K–L). The latter, according to M. Beer, were a group of *talmidei ḥakhamim* associated with Tiberias during the third and fourth centuries.[60] Here it is likely that they are contemporaries of the Tiberians, Zeʿira and Yoḥanan.

Earlier (G) we learn that an actual case came before Yoḥanan's disciple, R. Yose, and he sent the party to Abbahu, presumably in Caesarea, because "we do not have a tradition that the halakhah is according to R. Judah." Unlike the Caesarean Abbahu, the Southerner Joshua b. Levi, and the *Zipporaʾei*, the Tiberians (Yoḥanan, Zeʿira, and the *havraya*ʾ) did not have a ruling indicating that the halakhah followed Judah. Moreover, they had different accounts of Judah's view as reported by Ḥanina.

Interestingly, Yoḥanan holds the *Zipporaʾei* accountable for reporting Ḥanina's assertion that Judah's view was the halakhah. Indeed, it is not until Yoḥanan takes the *Zipporaʾei* to task (ʾatun ʾamrin be-shem R. Ḥanina . . .ve-leit hiʾ khen) that we learn that they are responsible for reporting Ḥanina's view.[61] Although they do not in turn respond to Yoḥanan, it is apparent that they must have been knowledgeable about, or at least aware of, the complexities of the issue under discussion. It is assumed that these *Zipporaʾei* were participants in deliberations concerning a theoretical issue,[62] so they certainly were not ordinary Sepphorians.

Once again, the *Zipporaʾei* are credited with an attribution to Ḥanina and appear to be members of a rabbinic gathering. Yoḥanan's assumption that the *Zipporaʾei* are responsible for Ḥanina's view, and the prevalence of Tiberian opinions, suggest Yoḥanan's circle at Tiberias as a *Sitz im Leben*. The *Zipporaʾei* are the ones remembered in Tiberias for assigning the words, "the halakhah is according to R. Judah" to Ḥanina; Yoḥanan did not hear his mentor Ḥanina state so directly. The predomi-

---

60 See M. Beer, "On the 'Ḥevraya' in the *Talmudim*," *Bar Ilan* 20–21 (1983), 80–82, 88 and 94 (Hebrew).

61 We would expect instead of "R. Ḥanina said . . ." (H), "the *Zipporaʾei* said in the name of R. Ḥanina . . . ."

62 Cf. the report at G where an actual case is said to have come before R. Yose. In contrast, the statement attributed to the *Zipporaʾei* is not invoked in the context of a particular case.

nance in the *sugia*ʾ of late third-century amoraim suggests that these *Zipporaʾei* belong to the same period.

The final passage of this type appears in J Gittin 1, 43b–c:

A. R. Yoḥanan said to the *Zipporayeiʾ* [= *Zipporaʾei*], "You say in the name of R. Ḥanina [*ʾatun ʾamrin be-shem R. Ḥanina*][63]: 'Even one who brings [a divorce document] from Babylonia to here [Eretz Israel] is not required to say: before me it was written and before me it was signed'."

B. "And I say that he is required [to say it] because it [is in accordance with the] Mishnah [Gittin 1:2, which states]: R. Judah says, 'from Reqem and to the East. And Reqem is considered like the East'."

C. And even if you say that they differed[64] with R. Judah, that is, that Reqem was not considered like the East, could it really be that from Babylonia to here [is also considered part of the Land [of Israel, with regard to *gittin*]?

D. Rav said, "We have made ourselves like the Land of Israel with regard to *gittin*."

E. And Samuel said, "Even from neighborhood to neighborhood [one who delivers a *get* in Babylonia needs to say, 'before me it was written, etc.]'."

Although ms. Leiden has R. Yoḥanan comment to the *Zipporaʾei*, "You say in the name of *R. Yoḥanan*" (*ʾatun ʾamrin be-shem R. Yoḥanan*), the editors of the printed editions and some of the commentators sensed the difficulty in this reading and, taking J Yevamot 1, 2d into account, emended the text to read, "R. Ḥanina."[65] It is at least possible that R. Yoḥanan would have been correcting a mistaken impression of something he said. Nevertheless, that the text is faulty seems more likely and the substitution of "Ḥanina" for "Yoḥanan" is reasonable.

Assuming that the *Zipporaʾei* report in the name of Ḥanina, we then have another instance of their association with the sage. Again, the *Zipporaʾei* function as tradents of Ḥanina's view. This time the issue is whether one who brings a *get* from Babylonia to the Land of Israel needs to state, "Before me it was written, before me it was signed." Perhaps

63 Ms. Leiden actually has R. Yoḥanan instead of R. Ḥanina. The text has been emended here in accordance with the versions discussed below.

64 Pene Moshe and Qorban ha-ʿEdah point out that R. Meir disagrees with R. Judah in the Mishnah. So it is R. Meir who is intended by "they differed."

65 See ed. Zhitomir and the comments of Pene Moshe, ad loc. D. Fraenkel, Qorban ha-ʿEdah, changes the text to "Rabbi" instead. In his Sheyarei ha-Qorban he explains that it is Judah ha-Nasi who is intended, as he, like the *Zipporaʾei*, came from Sepphoris. But so did Ḥanina! Fraenkel does not make the connection with the similar readings in J Sheviʿit 7, 37b and J Yevamot 1, 2d.

Hanina's Babylonian origins influenced his view that his native land was to be treated as though it were Eretz Israel.[66] In any event, Yohanan objects that Babylonia is, in fact, one of the areas where the saying is required, as implied by R. Judah's statement in the Mishnah. Rav and Samuel, Babylonian contemporaries of Hanina, disagree on the matter, with Rav maintaining a view similar to that of Hanina .

This case is like those presented earlier inasmuch as, once again, we are dealing with a theoretical halakhic issue where Hanina's view à la *Zipporaʾei* generates the entire discussion. There can be no question that here again the *Zipporaʾei* are assumed to be legitimate members of a rabbinic circle. The only difference is that, in this instance, the appearance of Yohanan and the *Zipporaʾei* alongside Rav and Samuel would push up the activity of the *Zipporaʾei* as tradents in Hanina's name to, say, the mid-third century. As in the other cases, a Tiberian milieu is possible, if not probable, since Yohanan is again the respondent.

Three Hanina/*Zipporaʾei* texts remain for consideration. We begin with J Shabbat 4, 7a:

A. The [opinion] of R. Ba b. Hanah is in agreement with that of R. Hanina.

B. For R. Hanina said, "We were going up [before the Sabbath] to Hammath Gader[67] with Rabbi [Judah ha-Nasi] and he said to us, 'Select some stones and you will be permitted to handle them tomorrow'."

C. R. Zeʿira said [ʾamar],[68] "Once he [the person intending to use the stones on the Sabbath] has scraped [them]."

D. The *havrayaʾ* say [ʾamri], "Once he has cleaned off [the stones]."

E. The *Zipporaʾei* say [ʾamrin], "Once he has thought [about using the stones]."

F. R. Yohanan said [ʾamar], "Once they have taken on the appearance of a vessel."

G. Consequently, Rav Hanah b. Abba,[69] R. Yohanan, and R. Yonatan are one [i.e., they share the same opinion].

---

66 This is another reason to assume that the emendation accepted here is correct. But cf. the attitudes of later amoraim who rejected their native Babylonia. See Kimelman, "Rabbi Yohanan of Tiberias," 140f. Also note that another Babylonian, Samuel, differs with Hanina here. On the latter's origins, see J Peʾah 7, 20a and J Sotah 1, 17b.

67 Ms. Leiden has *grr*, but Hammath Gader is obviously intended. See B. Ratner, *ʾAhavat Zion vi-Yerushalayim* (10 vols.; reprint; Jerusalem, 1967), *Shabbat*, 62.

68 The word *ʾamar* appears in ms. Leiden above the line, after Zeʿira's name.

69 There is some confusion here, as it is R. Ba b. Hanah whose opinion appears earlier. See Ratner, *ʾAhavat Zion, Shabbat*, 62.

H. Rav, R. Zeʿira, and R. Ishmaʿel b. R. Yose are one.

I. The *Zipporaʾei*, R. Yose b. Saul and R. Ḥalafta b. Saul are one.

J. The *ḥavrayaʾ* do not have a pair [of scholars who agree with them].

This passage is embedded in a *sugiaʾ* concerning the handling of materials on the Sabbath that were made for purposes that are inappropriate for that day. Thus, R. Ba b. Ḥanah (early third century) maintains that dried branches that have been cut for the purpose of making either bedding or tenting need to be tied together before the Sabbath if one would like to handle them on the Sabbath. The gemara then proclaims that this agrees with what R. Ḥanina had once seen R. Judah ha-Nasi do on a trip to Ḥammath Gader. Different opinions are then presented as to what Rabbi had actually intended when he said, "*Select* some stones and you will be able to handle them tomorrow."

Among these opinions, all of which are presented in the usual "so and so *ʾamar/ʾamrin*" manner, is that of the *Zipporaʾei*. Once again, views assigned to Zeʿira, Yoḥanan, and the *ḥavrayaʾ* appear alongside that of the *Zipporaʾei*, and here, too, a mid- to late third century Tiberian context seems likely. Moreover, as in many of the previous instances, Ḥanina himself is not a participant in the debate. Instead, the *Zipporaʾei* and others interpret his comments. In this respect the *Zipporaʾei* function much as they do in J Maʿaserot 1, 49a.[70] Like the *ḥavrayaʾ*, the *Zipporaʾei* are treated as sages in the breakdown of all the opinions that appear in the *sugiaʾ* (G–J).

Curiously, the parallel in the Babylonian Talmud (Shabbat 125b) has the early fourth-century amora, R. Dimi, or, alternatively (*ʾamrei lah*), R. Zeʿira, report the incident involving Rabbi in the name of Ḥanina.[71] This version has Rabbi state to his unspecified companions that they should "go out" and "think about" the stones which they intend to use on the Sabbath for sitting purposes. Here Ḥanina claims, contra Yoḥanan, that Rabbi did not require any action indicating that the stones were to be used on the morrow. Thus, the view of the *Zipporaʾei* in the Jerusalem Talmud (i.e., "Once he has thought about using the stones") is entirely in agreement with that presented by Zeʿira/Dimi *in Ḥanina's name* in the Babylonian Talmud! Two late third-century Tiberian amoraim, Ammi and Assi, who were both students of Yoḥanan, take up their mentor's

---

70 See discussion above.

71 The attribution to Zeʿira seems more likely since Ammi and Assi, whose views follow, were his contemporaries in Tiberias.

position and explain exactly how Rabbi expected the stones to be prepared.[72]

Thus, these *Zippora'ei* appear to belong to the mid- to late third century. Their opinion is presented like that of any other sage. Indeed, their
understanding of Ḥanina's point is as valid as anybody else's, no more,
no less. Furthermore, it presupposes an appreciation for the subtleties of
halakhic practice. The *Zippora'ei* here function no differently than the
ḥavraya' who, as already indicated, were a rabbinic group mostly associated with Tiberias.[73]

The two remaining Ḥanina/*Zippora'ei* passages seem to discredit the
sage to some degree. J Taʿanit 3, 66c reads:

A. There was a pestilence in Sepphoris that did not spread to the street
on which R. Ḥanina lived.

B. And the *Zippora'ei* were saying [*ve-havun Zippora'ei 'amrin*], "What
does this elder lose [i.e., what difference does it make to him]?[74] For
he sits in health together with his neighborhood while the city per-
ishes in illness."

C. He [R. Ḥanina] came and said before them, "There was one Zimri in
his generation but twenty four thousand fell of Israel. And among us,
how many Zimris are there in our generation, and you grumble?"

D. One time they needed to institute a fast [because of a drought], but
rain [still] did not fall.

E. R. Joshua instituted a fast in the South and rain fell.

F. And the *Zippora'ei* said, "R. Joshua b. Levi causes rain to fall for the
Deroma'ei [Southerners] and R. Ḥanina prevents water [from falling]
for the *Zippora'ei*."

G. They [the *Zippora'ei*] needed to institute [a fast] a second time. He [R.
Ḥanina] sent for and brought R. Joshua b. Levi.

H. He said to him, "Would my master mind going out with us [to the
city square] to fast?"

I. And the two of them went out for the fast and rain did not fall.

---

[72] Cf. the view of Assi, which is exactly that of the *ḥavraya'* in the Jerusalem Talmud. This is what one would expect if the latter were mostly Tiberians, as Beer
claims (see above, n. 60), rendering the views of Ḥanina/*Zippora'ei* and Assi/*ḥavraya'*
thoroughly consistent.

[73] See above, n. 60.

[74] See S. Lieberman, "Emendations," *Tarbiẕ* 4 (1934), 110 (Hebrew), who follows
the reading of the Geniza text published in L. Ginzberg, *Geniza Studies* (3 vols.; New
York, 1928–29), I, 420.

J. He [R. Ḥanina] came and said before them, "It is not R. Joshua b. Levi who brings down the rain for the *Deroma²ei*, nor is it R. Ḥanina who prevents rain [from falling] for the *Zippora²ei*."[75]

K. "Rather the hearts of the *Deroma²ei* are soft and when they hear a word of the Torah they humble themselves."

L. "But the hearts of the *Zippora²ei* are obstinate and when they hear a word of the Torah they do not humble themselves."

M. When he [Ḥanina] went on his way, he lifted his eyes and saw the air was clear.

N. He said, "Is it still so?"

O. Immediately rain fell.

Here we have two straightforward stories in which the *Zippora²ei* interact with Ḥanina. In the first (A–C), the sage counters the criticism of the *Zippora²ei* by alluding to the many Zimris who plague the present generation. In the second (D–O), Ḥanina castigates the *Zippora²ei* because they fail to humble themselves to the teachings of the Torah.

In the ensuing narrative two late third-century amoraim[76] offer proof texts expressing the thought that a community is judged by the majority of its residents. The preceding Ḥanina stories certainly support this deduction and probably served as its basis.[77] Thus, these stories about Ḥanina were certainly in circulation before the end of the century, at which time they were probably formulated as they appear in the Jerusalem Talmud.

More importantly, the emphasis on communal responsibility certainly enhances the impression that the *Zippora²ei* depicted in the stories were everyday residents of Sepphoris. Nevertheless, these *Zippora²ei* recognize Ḥanina's greatness and assume that he is a holy man with wonder-working abilities.[78]

---

75 According to Büchler, *Political and Social Leaders*, 10 and 54, it was *R. Joshua* who defended R. Ḥanina in this way.

76 R. Zeʿira in the name of R. Ḥanina and R. Jacob b. Idi in the name of R. Joshua b. Levi.

77 Note that the proof texts are provided in the name of Ḥanina and Joshua b. Levi, the protagonists of our passage. See previous note.

78 Elsewhere I have shown that the term *Zippora²ei* is really used to refer to three groups: (1) everyday Jewish residents of Sepphoris who have no real relationship with the rabbis; (2) others who had a casual relationship with the rabbis; and (3) actual members of the rabbinic class. See S. S. Miller, "*Zippora²ei, Tibera²ei* and *Deroma²ei*: Their Origins, Interests and Relationship," in: *Proceedings of the Tenth World Congress of Jewish Studies*, Division B, II (Jerusalem, 1990), 15–22.

The final Ḥanina/Ẓippora'ei passage is found in J Taʿanit 4, 68a:[79]

A. Rabbi used to make two appointments [*minnuyin*][80] [annually].

B. If they were worthy, they would retain [their appointment]; if not, they would resign.

C. When he [Rabbi] was about to die, he instructed his son, saying, "Do not do thus [as I have done], rather appoint them all at once, and appoint R. Ḥanina b. Ḥama[81] at the head [*be-re'shah*]."

D. And why did he [R. Judah ha-Nasi] not appoint him?

E. R. Derosa[82] said, "Because the Ẓippora'ei shout [*tzavḥin*, i.e., complain] against him."

F. But because of a "shout" [*tzevaḥah*] do we act [why should "shouting" make a difference]?

G. R. Elʿazar b. R. Yose said, "Because he publicly refuted the rendering [of a verse as given by R. Judah ha-Nasi]."

H. And which rendering did he refute?

I. Rabbi was sitting and teaching [Ezek. 7:16], "[And if any survive] they shall take to the mountains; they shall be like doves of the valley moaning [*homiot*] together [every one for his iniquity]."[83]

J. He [Ḥanina] said to him, "[It should read]: *homot*."

K. He [Rabbi] replied to him, "Where did you read it [in this manner]?"

L. He responded, "Before R. Hamnuna of Babylonia."

M. He [Rabbi] said to him, "When you go down there, tell him that I appointed you a sage [*manitakh ḥakim*]."[84]

N. And he knew that he would not be appointed in his [Rabbi's] lifetime.

---

79 The text here follows that found in Ginzberg, *Geniza Studies*, I, 427.

80 Transliteration follows ms. Leiden. This word is also rendered as "ordination." See J Sanhedrin 1, 19a, where it is explained that *minnuy* is the same as *semikhah*, which was the more usual term in Babylonia.

81 Ms. Leiden has R. Ḥama b. Ḥanina, but cf. Ecclesiastes Rabbah 7:7 and B Ketubot 103b. See Ratner, 'Ahavat Zion, Taʿanit, 96.

82 The parallel in Ecclesiastes Rabbah 7:7 has R. Yose b. Zeveda instead of R. Derosa. Yose was a Palestinian amora who lived in the early part of the fourth century.

83 Trans. Jewish Publication Society (Philadelphia, 1985).

84 Cf. Qorban ha-ʿEdah: ". . . tell him to appoint you . . . ." This rendering is not supported by the text in the Jerusalem Talmud. Cf. Ecclesiastes Rabbah 7:7, which has *she-manitikha*. For the Aramaic form of *mny* with pronominal suffixes, see G. Dalman, *Grammatik des jüdisch-palästinischen Aramäisch* (Darmstadt, 1960), 386. For the understanding here, cf. Pene Moshe, and S. S. Miller, "Yerushalmi Taanit," in: *In the Margins of the Yerushalmi*, ed. J. Neusner (Chico, 1983), 29.

The exact nature of Ḥanina's appointment or "ordination" has been subject to dispute.[85] In any event, appointment "at the head" was clearly a greater honor than to be designated ḥakim.[86] The Ẕipporaʾei enter the picture when the mid-fourth century amora, R. Derosa, explains Judah's failure to appoint Ḥanina. Derosa explains that the Ẕipporaʾei protested or "shouted against" Ḥanina. When an objection is raised to this reason (F), R. Elʿazar b. R. Yose's explanation, that Ḥanina had once refuted the Patriarch's reading of a biblical verse, is offered as an alternative.[87]

---

[85] The apparent meaning of be-reʾshah (lit., "at the head") is "first." That is, Ḥanina deserved to be ordained before anybody else. The reading in B Ketubot 103b, yeshev ba-roʾsh, has led many scholars to conclude that the appointment was to a special position. Zuri and Alon have suggested that Ḥanina was appointed av bet din. See Zuri, Reign, III/1, 95 and G. Alon, The Jews in Their Land in the Talmudic Age, ed. and trans. G. Levi (2 vols.; Jerusalem, 1980–84), II, 726–728. Cf. H. Mantel, Studies in the History of the Sanhedrin (Cambridge, 1961), 127. According to H. Graetz, Geschichte der Juden[4] (11 vols.; Leipzig, 1897–1911), IV, 282, Ḥanina was to sit at the head of the first row of ḥakhamim. I. H. Weiss, Dor Dor ve-Dorshav (5 vols.; Vilna, 1904), III, 40f. (Hebrew), maintains that Ḥanina became the roʾsh yeshivah after Rabbi. C. Albeck, "Semikha and Minui and Bet Din," Zion 8 (1943), 88f. (Hebrew), would agree that that was the intent of the version in the Babylonian Talmud. The question as to why Ḥanina was not ordained by Rabbi does not appear in B Ketubot 103b since the assumption there is that the appointment was as Head of the Great Academy (yeshivah gedolah) of the Nasi. Thus, the question did not arise simply because Ḥanina could not possibly have been appointed Head while the Nasi was alive, as he himself fulfilled this function. The understanding in the Jerusalem Talmud, which Albeck claims is correct, is that Ḥanina was appointed to be the head of one of the other academies in Sepphoris. Thus, the question as to why the Nasi did not appoint Ḥanina earlier is relevant there. Cf. Mantel, Studies, 208–211. On the distinctions between the versions of the Babylonian and Jerusalem Talmuds, see Levine, The Rabbinic Class, 73, n. 149, and Gafni, "Yeshiva and Metivta," 19f. Gafni also discusses ordination in the sense of raising a student to the rank of member of the sanhedrin.

[86] Cf. I. Halevy, Dorot haRischonim (7 vols.; Frankfurt, 1901; reprint; Jerusalem, 1974), V, 264–266. Ḥanina is referred to as ḥakim in J Niddah 2, 50b and B Niddah 20b, where the term is usually understood as an adjective meaning "wise." See the standard commentaries to these passages. Some scholars have suggested that the title of ḥakham/ḥakim was of lower authority and status than "rabbi." See B Bava Metziʿa 86a and cf. H. Zucker, Studien zur jüdischen Selbstverwaltung im Altertum (Berlin, 1936), 135f. Curiously, the parallel in Ecclesiastes Rabbah 7:7 has zaqen instead of ḥakim. Cf. the use of zaqen in the similar story regarding the appointment of Bar Elʿasa in J Moʿed Qatan 3, 81c.

[87] Lieberman posits a connection between the reasons given by Derosa and Elʿazar. He does this by reading, "But merely because of a shout do we remove [ʿavrin] one from ordination?" as opposed to, "But because of a shout do we act [ʿavdin]?" Accordingly, Elʿazar offers a more substantial reason for Ḥanina's removal from the ordination list (pitqaʾ). See S. Lieberman, "Emendations," Tarbiẕ 3 (1932), 207 (Hebrew).

Lieberman emphasizes R. Derosa's explanation and explains that the underlying reason for Ḥanina's difficulties with the *Ẓipporaʾei* was his well known wealth.[88] The practice among the later patriarchs was to sell ordinations to the highest bidders. The wealthy had the most to gain from the tax exemptions that came with ordination. The *Ẓipporaʾei*, Lieberman contends, "would naturally begrudge" Ḥanina the exemption. Lieberman further calls attention to the use of the word "shout" (*tzevaḥah*) which parallels the *boe* or *ekboesis* found in reference to the clamor of the masses in Greek literature.[89] Accordingly, the "mob at Sepphoris" protested Ḥanina's appointment, as indeed it had the right to do.[90]

Lieberman undoubtedly understands *Ẓipporaʾei* to be the people of Sepphoris in general. His understanding of Derosa's statement is, however, difficult, as one wonders why Ḥanina, who was known for his business ethics and was remembered for building a *bet midrash* in Sepphoris,[91] would all of a sudden engender the resentment of his neighbors. To be sure, this objection could also be raised to the suggestion that the *Ẓipporaʾei* belonged in some way to the school(s) of Sepphoris. After all, the disciples, scholars, and students would have directly benefited from Ḥanina's wealth, if in fact he had built a *bet midrash* for them. Presumably, the poorer academicians would have had the most to complain about if indeed Lieberman is right that they often were passed over for ordination in favor of their wealthier colleagues.

Still, Lieberman's explanation, as ingenious as it is, is not entirely convincing. First of all, there is no reason to assume that the view of Derosa, a fifth-generation amora, is any more authoritative than that of his contemporary, Elʿazar. The gemara itself (F) finds Derosa's explana-

---

In view of the fact that Derosa and Elʿazar appear together elsewhere, where they offer entirely distinct opinions, it seems likely that their views here are also unrelated. Thus, Derosa is simply offering his view as to why Ḥanina was not ordained. The comment at (F) that suggests a link between the two statements (with or without Lieberman's emendation, which makes the connection more obvious) appears to be editorial. See the ensuing discussion.

88 Lieberman notes the tradition that Ḥanina built a *bet midrash* in Sepphoris (see above) and points out that this would have been an exceptional contribution in the third century. See Lieberman, "Palestine in the Third and Fourth Centuries," 146.

89 Cf. I. I. Halevy, *The Amoraic Aggadot: The Biographical Aggadah of Palestinian and Babylonian Amoraim in Light of Greek and Latin Sources* (Tel-Aviv, 1977), 17 (Hebrew).

90 Lieberman, "Palestine in the Third and Fourth Centuries," 146f.

91 See J Peʾah 7, 20b and above, n. 13.

tion difficult.92 Indeed, his understanding may have been premised upon the poor relations between the *Zippora⁾ei* and Ḥanina referred to in the pestilence and fast day incidents that appear earlier in J Taʿanit.93 As such, it would have been a fourth-century inference.94 Furthermore, Derosa and Elʿazar appear together elsewhere in the Jerusalem Talmud, where they offer alternative explanations for events that were supposed to have happened in the early third century.95 Finally, *tzavḥin* is not used elsewhere in talmudic literature to characterize the remonstrance that tax exemptions awarded to wealthy rabbinic appointees might have elicited.

Nevertheless, Lieberman's assumption that the *Zippora⁾ei* to whom Derosa is referring are ordinary residents of Sepphoris is at least reasonable. These *Zippora⁾ei* do not offer halakhic opinions or interpretations and they do not pass on traditions attributed to Ḥanina. Nor do others treat them as though they belong to Ḥanina's circle. Yet, it cannot be denied that Derosa's perception of them, albeit from the perspective of the fourth century, has them involved and interested in rabbinic politics, particularly where Ḥanina is concerned.96

Ḥanina may once again be the focus of criticism but, at the same time, his greatness is clearly recognized in the passage. For some reason he was not appointed "at the head" in Rabbi's time, but that he deserved this honor is clearly indicated by Rabbi's instructions to his son. Later sages such as Elʿazar may have surmised that there were difficult relations between Rabbi and Ḥanina, but that, in fact, is not the image portrayed in rabbinic literature.97 Indeed, Ḥanina reports many of the cases (*maʿasim*) that came before Rabbi and passes on several decisions in his name.98

---

92 See the even more emphatic objection in the version in Ecclesiastes Rabbah 7:7.

93 Cf. Halevy, *The Amoraic Aggadot*, 17 and Bacher, *Aggadot Amorai Eretz Israel* (3 vols.; Tel-Aviv, 1925–30), I, 3 (Hebrew).

94 This would be true even if the explanation is to be attributed to R. Yose b. Zeveda and not to R. Derosa. See above, n. 82.

95 J Shabbat 1, 3a and J Kilʾaim 9, 32a.

96 See above, n. 78.

97 Cf. Rabbi's declaration regarding Ḥanina before Antoninus in B ʿAvodah Zarah 10b: *leit dein bar nash.*

98 *maʿasim*: J Terumot 10, 47b; J Sheqalim 7, 50c and J Ketubot 1, 28a. Other attributions to Rabbi or reports of his activities made by Ḥanina: J Berakhot 3, 6d; J Maʿaserot 1, 49a; J Shabbat 14, 14d; J Moʿed Qatan 3, 82a; J Niddah 1, 49c; J Yevamot 8, 8d; B Berakhot 24a; B Shabbat 47a, 52a, 125b; B Megillah 5a; B Bava Batra 130b; B Menaḥot 88b and B Ḥullin 57b.

Ḥanina at Sepphoris: A Reappraisal

Surely, it is no coincidence that at least half of the *Zippora'ei* traditions that occur in the Jerusalem Talmud mention Ḥanina. A comparison of these *Zippora'ei* traditions with those that do not refer to Ḥanina is revealing. The latter often include the *Zippora'ei* in a rabbinic setting but rarely have them actively pursue halakhic matters with the sages. In contrast, the *Zippora'ei* of the Ḥanina traditions frequently offer opinions on technical halakhic matters, receive decisions from the master, and transmit his views.

Obviously, Ḥanina was a key figure at Sepphoris. On three occasions he is said to have rendered decisions (*horei*) either in the city or, more specifically, for the *Zippora'ei*. In one instance the *Zippora'ei*, probably in Tiberias, interpret Ḥanina's earlier decision regarding the tithing of almonds. In another, the *Zippora'ei* are contemporaries of Ḥanina and Yoḥanan, both of whom resolve for them issues pertaining to the sabbatical year and festivals, very possibly in two distinct settings in Sepphoris. Finally, they are the recipients of a decision of Ḥanina pertaining to a tenant's responsibilities. In these last two examples, the *Zippora'ei* seem to have been associated with Ḥanina's circle at Sepphoris. The use of the term *horei* may, in fact, indicate some form of rabbinic session as the place where Ḥanina issued these decisions.

In the passages that have either Immi or Yoḥanan respond to the *Zippora'ei*: "*'atun 'amrin be-shem R. Ḥanina*," the *Zippora'ei* are clearly members of a rabbinic circle who transmit the opinions of their town's leading sage, Ḥanina b. Ḥama, possibly in Tiberias. In all three instances, the halakhic opinions they pass on in Ḥanina's name are technical and theoretical. These *Zippora'ei* belong to the mid- to late third century. Zuri has suggested that the *Zippora'ei* passed on traditions of Ḥanina after his death.[99] The dating of these uses of the term *Zippora'ei* leaves this as an intriguing possibility, reports of Ḥanina's longevity notwithstanding.[100]

One lone tradition (J Shabbat 4, 7a) juxtaposes the *Zippora'ei* with other mid- to late third-century sages, including the *ḥavraya'*, and has them interpret an incident that involved Ḥanina and Rabbi. Here again, the issue as it is taken up in the gemara is theoretical. What is particularly interesting, however, is that Ḥanina himself is clearly out of the picture once his recollection of the incident is recalled. Here we may very well have *Zippora'ei* who function after Ḥanina's death. In any event, the

---

[99] Zuri, *Reign*, III/2, 160.
[100] See J Taʿanit 4, 68a and B Ḥullin 24b.

Zippora'ei were certainly regarded by later authorities, particularly at Tiberias, as both conveyors and interpreters of Ḥanina's opinions. That these *Zippora'ei* included actual disciples of Ḥanina seems reasonable.[101]

Were the *Zippora'ei* the official transmitters of Ḥanina's halakhic opinions? Possibly. It seems more likely, however, that the term was used loosely in Tiberian circles to refer to those scholars from Sepphoris who were in the habit of reporting Ḥanina's views. What is important from our perspective is the fact that Ḥanina's views are passed on by the *Zippora'ei*. This more than anything attests to Ḥanina's pre-eminence as the scholar par excellence from Sepphoris in the early amoraic period.

This profile of Ḥanina so far corresponds well with what we already know from the traditions that place the sage in the city but make no mention of the *Zippora'ei*. Thus, the Ḥanina who introduces (*hinhig*) certain halakhic practices and decides cases both alone and with his disciples, Yoḥanan and Resh Laqish, in Sepphoris,[102] also resolves issues (*horei*) for the *Zippora'ei*. Surely, the importance that Yoḥanan and Immi give to the reports attributed to Ḥanina by the *Zippora'ei* stems from the fact that Ḥanina was a formidable halakhic authority. Ḥanina also appears in both types of traditions as an exegete who learns important lessons from the biblical text.

The perception of Ḥanina as a wealthy and powerful sage who engendered the disdain of his neighbors in Sepphoris must be countered by the overall impression gained from the sources. These portray the sage as a prominent scholar whose following and reputation were quite well established. Stories that detracted from his reputation eventually circulated, but so did others that presented him in a very positive light. Thus, we hear how Ḥanina was extremely honest in his business relations and generously used his earnings to build a *bet midrash* in Sepphoris.[103] Likewise, "all the people" of the city were said to have tended to the

---

101 References to *talmidei de-R. Ḥanina* appear in J Shabbat 6, 8d, B ʿEruvin 65b and B Niddah 52a. All of these are accounts of various incidents that occurred to them. They do not report in the name of Ḥanina as the *Zippora'ei* do, so there is no way of knowing whether they are identical with the latter. For a list of most of the sages who report in Ḥanina's name, see Hyman, *History*, II, 489–491 and cf. Zuri, *Reign*, III/2, passim. It would seem that these would not be intended by the term *Zippora'ei*, as many of these sages are more actively involved in rabbinic circles. Thus, many of them render decisions, something the *Zippora'ei* do not do. Whether the *Zippora'ei* are "rabbis" of a lesser status or teachers lacking ordination is certainly possible. If so, they would resemble the *ḥavraya'*. See my study, "*Zippora'ei, Tibera'ei* and *Deroma'ei*."

102 See discussion above and nn. 6 and 8.

103 See J Peʾah 7, 20b and above, n. 13.

funeral arrangements for the scholar.[104] Great sages were evidently subject to praise and abuse precisely because of their position and visibility
within the community.

The third century was an important period in the history of the Jewish community of Sepphoris.[105] Judah ha-Nasi's presence in the city at the
beginning of the century certainly enhanced its reputation as a rabbinic
center. But Judah spent only the remaining seventeen years of his life
there, according to the Jerusalem Talmud.[106] Much work was left to his
disciples, foremost among whom was Ḥanina b. Ḥama, whose presence
at Sepphoris undoubtedly further augmented the city's prestige. Indeed,
the academies of third-century Sepphoris attracted scholars from beyond
the city, including Tiberias, its noteworthy neighbor.[107] Ḥanina b. Ḥama
and the Zipporaʾei were no doubt largely responsible for assuring Sepphoris a prominent place in the annals of amoraic Eretz Israel.

---

[104] J Bava Metziʿa 2, 8d.

[105] This has clearly been corroborated by the recent excavations at Sepphoris which
testify to the vitality of the city during this period.

[106] J Kilʾaim 9, 32b and J Ketubot 12, 35a and parallels. Interestingly, Ḥanina ap-
pears in connection with Sepphoris much more frequently than Rabbi. Perhaps
Rabbi's earlier association with Beth Sheʿarim is the reason for the relative silence
about his activities at Sepphoris. After all, Rabbi dwelled for a longer period at Beth
Sheʿarim than at Sepphoris. The sources allude to his varied activities in Beth
Sheʿarim. See S. Safrai, "Bet Sheʿarim in Talmudic Literature," in: Eretz Israel, V
(Jerusalem, 1959), 210 (Hebrew).

[107] On the relationship between the two cities during this period, see S. S. Miller,
"Intercity Relations in Roman Palestine: The Case of Sepphoris and Tiberias," AJS Review 12 (1987), 1–24.

The Sages and the Synagogue in Late Antiquity: The Evidence of the Galilee

LEE I. LEVINE

The nature and extent of rabbinic contact with, involvement in, and influence on the synagogue of late antiquity is an issue which has commanded scholarly attention over the past decades. On the one hand, the synagogue was the central institution in Jewish communal life, serving as a community center and a setting for varied religious, educational, and social activities both in Israel and the Diaspora.[1] Who shaped and controlled this institution, who gave it direction? Who decided upon its design and artwork, its liturgy and educational agenda? On the other hand, the rabbis, who constituted the most important religious elite within Palestinian Jewry at the time,[2] have left us the overwhelming majority of literary sources that we possess today from this period. To what degree did the sages' interests and activities take them beyond the walls of the

[1] On the synagogue in antiquity in Palestine and the Diaspora, see S. Krauss, *Synagogale Altertümer* (Vienna, 1922); S. Baron, *The Jewish Community* (3 vols.; Philadelphia, 1942), I, 55–117; S. Safrai, "The Synagogue," in: *The Jewish People in the First Century*, eds. S. Safrai and M. Stern (2 vols.; Assen, 1974–76), II, 908–944; L. I. Levine, "The Second Temple Synagogue: The Formative Years," in: *The Synagogue in Late Antiquity*, ed. L. I. Levine (Philadelphia, 1987), 7–31; A. T. Kraabel, "The Diaspora Synagogue: Archaeological and Epigraphic Evidence since Sukenik," in: *ANRW*, II, 19.1, eds. H. Temporini and W. Haase (Berlin/New York, 1979), 477–510.

[2] See, for example, E. E. Urbach, "Class-Status and Leadership in the World of the Palestinian Sages," in: *Proceedings of the Israel Academy of Sciences and Humanities*, II (Jerusalem, 1968), 54–74; idem, *The Sages: Their Concepts and Beliefs* (2 vols.; Jerusalem, 1979), I, 593–648; L. I. Levine, *The Rabbinic Class of Roman Palestine in Late Antiquity* (Jerusalem, 1989).

bet midrash (academy) and into the lives and institutions of Jewish society at large? What role did they play in the synagogue in particular? To phrase the issue in somewhat different terms: were the rabbis the dominant religious, political, and social force in Jewish society of late antiquity?[3] Or is this indeed an idealized picture, the sages having been but one of many groups whose influence on Palestinian Jewry was relatively circumspect and peripheral?[4] Most opinions in this regard fall somewhere between the above alternatives. The sages were not the universally recognized authorities of the period, but neither were they without influence. Much depended on the particular sage, his locale, the issue at hand, and the time frame involved. Our present inquiry hopes to contribute towards determining the nature and extent of rabbinic involvement in and influence on the life of the community, and, more specifically, with respect to the ancient synagogue.

The relative abundance of rabbinic sources at our disposal and the richness of the material therein are matched by the wealth of archeological remains from the scores of ancient synagogues discovered throughout Roman Palestine. Evidence also can be marshalled from a number of ancient extra-rabbinic writings, such as the Theodosian Code and works of pagan writers and Church fathers. The study of the relationship of the rabbis to the ancient synagogue is particularly relevant to the Galilee, for much of our archeological and literary evidence comes from this region: in addition to the remains of some fifty synagogues in the Galilee alone,[5] the rabbinic literature of this period—the Mishnah and Tosefta, early midrashim, and the Jerusalem Talmud—was created there; most Palestinian sages lived in the Galilee, and others frequented it, since the

---

3 G. Alon, *Jews, Judaism and the Classical World*, trans. I. Abrahams (Jerusalem, 1977), 22, n. 11. While Alon makes this statement with regard to the Pharisees, it is assumed in all of his writings and in those of his students. See, for example, idem, *The Jews in Their Land in the Talmudic Age* (2 vols.; Jerusalem, 1980–84), I, 308; S. Safrai, "Recovery of the Jewish Settlement in the Yavnean Generation," and A. Oppenheimer, "Renewal of the Jewish Settlement in the Galilee," in: *Eretz Israel from the Destruction of the Second Temple to the Muslim Conquest*, eds. Z. Baras et al. (2 vols.; Jerusalem, 1982–85), I, 27, 80ff., respectively (Hebrew).

4 E. Goodenough, *Jewish Symbols in the Greco-Roman Period* (13 vols.; New York, 1953–68), XII, 184–198.

5 Cf. the slightly varying lists compiled by S. J. Saller, *A Revised Catalogue of the Ancient Synagogues of the Holy Land* (Jerusalem, 1969); G. Foerster, "The Ancient Synagogues of the Galilee," in this volume, pp. 289–319; Z. Ilan, *Synagogues in the Galilee and Golan* (Jerusalem, 1987) (Hebrew).

primary rabbinic academies of late antiquity were located in Tiberias and Sepphoris.

Before addressing the question at hand, two assumptions generally accepted today in scholarly circles ought to be clearly stated, as our ensuing argument is contingent upon them. First, the primary social, intellectual, and religious setting of the rabbis in late antiquity was the *bet midrash*. It is there that the sages spent most of their time and it was the *Sitz im Leben* for most of their sayings and stories recorded in rabbinic literature. They controlled the agenda, composition, and proceedings of the *bet midrash*, and, quite naturally, ranked it foremost among the institutions in Jewish society.[6]

To note but a few representative examples of rabbinic preference for the *bet midrash*: the second-century sage, R. Yosi, praised those who functioned within this institution, saying, "Let my portion be among those who seat [others] in the *bet midrash* and not among those who make [others] rise [i.e., depart] from the *bet midrash*."[7] Several centuries later, R. Zeʿira, on wondering how he merited to live such a long life, speculated, among other things, ". . . and I never slept in the *bet midrash*, neither a deep sleep nor a short nap."[8] A second-century source, oft-quoted in later compilations, notes the occasions on which a *bet midrash* should be closed out of respect for sages of different rank who had passed away:

> Our rabbis taught: when a sage (*ḥakham*) dies his academy is closed; when the head of a local court (*av bet din*) dies all the academies in his city are closed, and they enter the synagogue and change their places: those who [usually] sit in the north [now] sit in the south, those who [usually] sit in the south [now] sit in the north. When a *nasi* dies all academies are closed, and members of the synagogue enter the synagogue and read seven [sections, i.e., *ʿaliyot*] and [then] leave.[9]

Thus, the institution regularly affected by the death of a sage was the academy. Regular sessions were cancelled out of respect for a deceased colleague, and only when a person holding public office died (e.g., the head of a court or the *nasi*) did the community officially acknowledge his loss in the synagogue, the communal—not rabbinic—institution par excellence.

---

6 For example, B Megillah 26b–27a places the academy (*be rabbanan*) at the top of the mishnaic list of places and objects organized by sanctity and holiness.

7 B Shabbat 118b.

8 B Megillah 28a.

9 B Moʿed Qatan 22b–23a.

Throughout rabbinic literature, the sages appear to have been the sole party responsible for the operation of the *bet midrash*. This stands in marked contrast to the synagogue for which we have abundant evidence of widespread participation of the community at large: the *nasi*, the wealthy, and community members generally, as well as the sages themselves. The academy functioned first and foremost as a place of study, an activity of undisputed primacy among the sages.[10] R. Levi b. R. Ḥiyya is quoted as having said that one who leaves the synagogue and goes to the academy to study Torah is worthy of receiving the Divine Presence;[11] in the late third century, R. Ami and R. Asi of Tiberias are said to have preferred praying in the place where they studied, i.e., the academy, and not the synagogue.[12] Even with regard to donations for the building of academies (a subject rarely mentioned in our sources), the only noted donors were sages. R. Abun is said to have contributed (*ʿavad*)[13] the gates (or doors) of the Sidra Rabbah, presumably the main academy in Tiberias,[14] and R. Ḥanania is noted as having built a *bet midrash* in third-century Sepphoris.[15]

The second assumption concerns the relationship between the academy and the synagogue; these are in no way to be construed as one and the same institution. This is already implied in the statement of R.

10 See my *Rabbinic Class*, 43–47; Urbach, *Sages*, 603–620, as well as M. Aberbach, *Jewish Education in the Mishnaic and Talmudic Periods* (Jerusalem, 1983), 33–92 (Hebrew).

11 B Berakhot 64a.

12 B Berakhot 8a, 30b. See, however, the opposite statement attributed to the fourth-century Babylonian sage, Abbaye (B Megillah 29a): "At first I used to study at home and pray in the synagogue. When I realized [the implications] of what David said, 'O Lord, I loved Your temple abode' [Psalms 26:8], I began studying in the synagogue." This statement, however, contradicts B Berakhot 8a and, in general, would seem to stand in contrast with what we generally know regarding the role of the synagogue in amoraic Babylonia; see I. Gafni, "Synagogues in Talmudic Babylonia," in: *Synagogues in Antiquity*, eds. A. Kasher et al. (Jerusalem, 1987), 155–162 (Hebrew).

13 On the term *ʿavad* as used in dedicatory inscriptions, see J. Naveh, *On Stone and Mosaic* (Jerusalem, 1978), 9–10 (Hebrew).

14 J Sheqalim 5, 6, 49b.

15 J Peʾah 7, 4, 20b. In several instances we do find sages fundraising, although never explicitly connected with a building. They invariably sought support for the *bet midrash* and for those studying Torah (Leviticus Rabbah 5:4, Margulies, pp. 110–114; J Horayot 3, 7, 48a; Deuteronomy Rabbah 4:8; Tanḥuma, Ki-Tisa, 15). The second-century Theudas of Rome was singled out for his support of the sages; see J Pesaḥim 7, 1, 34a (and parallels); B Pesaḥim 53b. On the religious value that the sages placed in support of their class, see Urbach, *Sages*, 627–628; M. Beer, "Issachar and Zebulun," *Bar-Ilan Studies* 6 (1968), 167–180 (Hebrew).

Pappi, namely, that it is permissible to turn a synagogue into an academy but not vice versa,[16] as well as that of R. Joshua b. Levi, that one can sell a synagogue in order to buy an academy but not vice versa.[17] Although these two institutions are often mentioned together in rabbinic literature, it is quite clear that each functioned autonomously. The Talmud distinguishes between a place where one promotes Torah-study (מקום שמגדלין בו תורה), i.e., the academy, and a place where one promotes prayer (מקום שמגדלין בו תפילה), i.e., the synagogue.[18] So, too, the statement of R. Isaac is indicative of this distinction: ". . . Thus God moves from synagogue to synagogue, from academy to academy."[19] A statement from Midrash Psalms makes the same point:

> Thus our sages taught us: anyone who leaves the synagogue and enters the academy is referred to by the verse, "They will go from strength to strength" [Ps. 84:8]. Moreover, such a person is considered worthy of receiving the Divine Presence.[20]

Keeping in mind the above two assumptions, that the academy was exclusively a rabbinic institution and that it was not to be identified with the synagogue, we may now proceed to define the nature of the relationship between the sages and the synagogue.

*　　　　　*　　　　　*

Throughout late antiquity rabbinic attitudes towards the synagogue were undeniably positive; the sages accorded a great measure of respect for this institution:

> One is not to conduct himself disrespectfully in synagogues, one should not enter them in the heat because of the heat, nor in the cold because of the cold, nor in the rain because of the rain, and one does not eat therein, nor drink therein, nor sleep therein, nor stroll therein, nor derive pleasure therein,[21] but rather read [Scriptures], learn [the laws, i.e., Mishnah], and

---

16 B Megillah 26b–27a.

17 J Megillah 3, 1, 73d.

18 B Megillah 27a.

19 PRK, Mandelbaum, p. 90.

20 Midrash Psalms 84:4, Buber, p. 371. See also T Sukkah 2:10, Lieberman, p. 265 and parallels.

21 Rashi explains: "nor dress up in them" (אין מתקשטין בהן).

deliver sermons [expound biblical readings] therein. A public eulogy can be delivered therein.[22]

Abba Benjamin remarked in the second century: "One's prayer is heard only in the synagogue,"[23] and according to another rabbinic source the synagogue is to be included among the ten institutions vital to any town.[24] In the third and fourth centuries rabbis sometimes studied at the entranceway of a synagogue; both R. Judah I and R. Yoḥanan are mentioned as having studied in front of the large Babylonian synagogue in Sepphoris.[25] R. Isaac claimed that God Himself was to be found in the synagogue: "From where do we learn that the Holy One Blessed be He is to be found in the synagogue? As it is written: 'God stands in the divine assembly' [Ps. 82:1]."[26] The fourth-century sage, R. Zeʿira, once eulogized one of his colleagues in a synagogue,[27] and R. Pinḥas compared prayer in the synagogue to a pure meal offering at the Temple.[28]

Nevertheless, the nature and extent of rabbinic contact with the synagogue in late antiquity were not uniform. Some rabbis appear to have been regularly involved in synagogue affairs, others not. Some frequented the synagogue, others seem to have avoided it studiously, preferring the *bet midrash* instead (see n. 12 above). This variety of attitudes vis-à-vis the synagogue is altogether natural given the diversity of rabbinic opinions and actions on a plethora of subjects.[29] Furthermore, careful examination of our sources indicates that there was a marked increase in rabbinic involvement in synagogue affairs from the mid-third century on. This trend seems especially significant and demands attention.

Rabbinic ties to the synagogue in the second century are scarcely mentioned; only a few accounts note a rabbinic presence there. One instance speaks of R. Meir teaching in the synagogue of Ḥammath Tiberias on Friday evenings. One woman who regularly came to hear his sermons would incur the wrath of her husband since her attendance meant that

---

[22]   T Megillah 2:18, Lieberman, p. 353. See also J Megillah 3, 4, 74a; B Megillah 28a–b, as well as M Megillah 3:3.

[23]   B Berakhot 6a.

[24]   B Sanhedrin 17b.

[25]   Genesis Rabbah 33:3, Theodor-Albeck, p. 305; J Berakhot 5, 1, 9a; see also PRK, Mandelbaum, p. 297.

[26]   B Berakhot 6a.

[27]   B Megillah 28b.

[28]   J Berakhot 5, 1, 8d.

[29]   See my *Rabbinic Class*, 83–97.

the Sabbath meals were not prepared on time.[30] Even if this report is historical (and it ought be noted that the story appears only in the Jerusalem Talmud, redacted over two centuries after R. Meir lived; it may possibly be a retrojection from a later period), it practically stands alone in drawing a clear connection between a rabbi and his role in a synagogue. The only other tannaitic source which might be invoked in this regard refers to R. El'azar b. R. Simeon, who reputedly was a teacher of Bible and Oral Law,[31] a reciter of different types of *qerovot* and *piyyut*,[32] and an expounder of Scriptures. R. El'azar probably functioned as such within the context of a synagogue, but we cannot be sure; a *bet midrash* setting is likewise possible. The very limited contact of sages with the synagogue during the second century is possibly reflected in the Mishnah itself, which mentions the synagogue on only twelve occasions, often with regard to issues which have no particular connection with the sages.[33] Each of the tannaitic midrashim (Mekhilta, Sifra and Sifre) mentions the synagogue but once.[34]

The inescapable conclusion of the evidence at hand—despite the fact that we are primarily invoking an argument *ex silencio* and dealing mostly with halakhically oriented sources—is that this dearth of information is far from coincidental. It would appear that there existed a minimal involvement of the sages in the workings of the second-century synagogue.

In contrast, from the mid-third through the fourth centuries the number of sources attesting to rabbinic involvement in synagogue affairs increases dramatically, undoubtedly reflecting a more significant presence. The issues with which the sages dealt were varied. In the mid-third

---

30 J Sotah 1, 4, 16d.

31 PRK 27:1, Mandelbaum, pp. 403–404. Leviticus Rabbah 30:1, Margulies, p. 690, and Song of Songs Rabbah 3:5:7, omit the word *dorshan*. Cf. PRK, Buber, p. 179a, n. 23 and S. Lieberman, "Hazzanut Yannai," *Sinai* 4 (1939), 223 (Hebrew). See J. N. Epstein, *Introduction to the Mishnaic Text*[2] (2 vols.; Jerusalem, 1964), II, 688 (Hebrew), who interprets *tanne* as a public reciter (*sheliah tzibbur*) of oral tradition.

32 On these various types of liturgical poetry, see the *EJ*, s.v. "piyyut"; J. Heinemann and J. Petuchowski, *Literature of the Synagogue* (New York, 1975), 205–213; I. Elbogen, *Jewish Prayer*, trans. J. Heinemann (Jerusalem, 1972), 153–173 (Hebrew); E. Fleischer, *Hebrew Liturgical Poetry in the Middle Ages* (Jerusalem, 1975), 67–76, 137–247 (Hebrew).

33 See, for example, M Nedarim 5:5. For additional references, see C. Y. Kasovsky, *Thesaurus Mishnae* (4 vols.; Jerusalem, 1956–60), s.v. "bet knesset" (Hebrew).

34 Mekhilta de R. Ishmael, Yitro, 2:11, Horowitz-Rabin, p. 243; Sifra, Vayiqra, 11, 8, 6, Weiss, p. 22, col. c; Sifre Deuteronomy 306, Finkelstein, p. 342.

century, several sages were consulted about the re-use of stones from one synagogue in order to build another; the residents of Migdal sought the advice of Resh Laqish regarding re-using stones from one city in another, and the Jews of Beth Shean asked R. Ami about re-using stones within the same town.[35] In the mid-fourth century, the inhabitants of Sinbarri asked R. Yonah and R. Yosi about using a Torah scroll which was damaged in all probability during the Gallus Revolt.[36] On at least one occasion—and perhaps on two—a third-century rabbi saw fit to remove a prayer leader who bowed for too long a time.[37] R. Yohanan once issued an order to the synagogue of Kifra, a district in or near Tiberias,[38] and several generations later R. Yosi instructed bar 'Ulla, the *hazzan* of a synagogue of Babylonians, as to the proper practice for reading from one or two Torah scrolls when two separate scriptural readings were required.[39] Similarly, in the fourth century R. Abun was consulted regarding synagogue procedure when a prayer leader named Batitiya suddenly stopped in the middle of a prayer and a replacement had to be sought. The sage was asked whether the new leader should continue from where Batitiya left off or at the beginning of that section.[40]

This increased rabbinic involvement in synagogue affairs is reflected not only in the larger number of incidents preserved in our sources, but also in the sheer number of rabbinic sources dealing with the synagogue and its activities. The third-century Tosefta mentions the synagogue on twenty-five occasions, often regarding specific customs and practices. The Jerusalem Talmud and later aggadic midrashim are infinitely richer in such material relative to second-century tannaitic sources. However, despite this increase in source material, rabbinic involvement in synagogue activities nevertheless appears sporadic and limited in scope.

Three areas seem to have constituted the major foci of their activity, and it was primarily in these areas that the sages made their impact on

---

35 J Megillah 3, 1, 73d.

36 J Megillah 3, 1, 74a. On the Gallus Revolt and its effects, see M. Avi-Yonah, *The Jews of Palestine* (New York, 1976), 176–184; S. Lieberman, "Palestine in the Third and Fourth Centuries," *JQR* 36–37 (1946), 335–341 (= *Texts and Studies* [New York, 1974], 118–124); and more recently, J. Geiger, "The Gallus Revolt," in: *Eretz Israel from the Destruction*, I, 202–208 (Hebrew).

37 J Berakhot 1, 8, 3d. See L. Ginzberg, *A Commentary on the Palestinian Talmud* (4 vols.; New York, 1941–60), I, 189.

38 J Rosh ha-Shanah 4, 4, 59c; J Ta'anit 4, 5, 68b.

39 J Yoma 7, 1, 44b; J Megillah 4, 5, 75b; J Sotah 7, 6, 22a; Tractate Soferim 11:3, Higger, p. 220.

40 J Berakhot 5, 3, 9c.

the ancient synagogue. The first is that of teacher or preacher, and several sages are specifically mentioned in this capacity. Most notable is the third-century Palestinian amora, R. Yoḥanan, who regularly preached in the synagogue of Sepphoris:

> "R. Yoḥanan was sitting and expounding in the great synagogue of Sepphoris . . . a seafaring *min* [one who has deviated from rabbinic norms] spoke up . . . . On another occasion, he came upon and found R. Yoḥanan sitting and expounding on the same matter . . . ."[41]

His student, R. Abbahu, was likewise a noted speaker, often appearing at the Maradata synagogue in Caesarea and elsewhere.[42] Another Caesarean, R. Isaac b. R. Elʿazar, also functioned in the Maradata synagogue and was compared on one occasion to "God in His holy sanctuary" (Hab. 2:20).[43] R. Samuel b. R. Naḥman is mentioned as having preached in Lydda at the Tarsian synagogue (alternatively, synagogue of the weavers or coppersmiths).[44]

In one instance from the fourth century, R. Jeremiah expounded Scriptures (*darash*) in the synagogue of the *boule* while R. Aḥa did the same in the academy.[45] The account is reminiscent of the well-known story regarding R. Abbahu and R. Ḥiyya b. Abba; upon arriving at a certain town, R. Ḥiyya addressed halakhic subjects while R. Abbahu spoke on aggada. The people flocked to hear the latter, leaving R. Ḥiyya with practically no audience and hurt feelings. R. Abbahu subsequently sought to console his colleague by according him the respect due a great teacher.[46] Although not specifically indicated, the settings of their talks may well have been the *bet midrash* and the synagogue, respectively.

---

[41] PRK 18:5, Mandelbaum, pp. 297–298. On the presence of a *min* in the synagogue and the nature of his exchange with R. Yoḥanan, see E. E. Urbach, "Heavenly and Earthly Jerusalem," in: *Jerusalem Through the Ages: The Twenty-fifth Archaeological Convention* (Jerusalem, 1968), 170 (Hebrew); R. Kimelman, *Rabbi Yoḥanan of Tiberias: Aspects of the Social and Religious History of Third Century Palestine* (University Microfilms; Ann Arbor, 1980), 175ff. and especially 187–188. On the term "seafaring" (*prs*), see S. Lieberman, *Tosefta Ki-Fshuṭah*, I (New York, 1955), 54, n. 84.

[42] See, for example, J Nazir 7, 2, 56a; Pesiqta Rabbati, Friedmann, p. 196b (where his name is spelled אבוהו).

[43] J Bikkurim 3, 3, 65d; Midrash Samuel 7:6, Buber, p. 68; Midrash Hagadol, Exodus 20:20, Margulies, p. 443.

[44] Leviticus Rabbah 35:12, Margulies, pp. 830–831.

[45] J Taʿanit 1, 2, 64a.

[46] B Sotah 40a. In contrast to the preceding one (n. 45), the venue of these addresses in this source is not given. Nevertheless, it is most likely that R. Abbahu

Not only were some sages noted for their public teaching in the synagogue, but others close to their circles functioned in a similar capacity. In two instances recorded in rabbinic literature sermons in defense of rabbinic rights and privileges were delivered by people who were not rabbis. In a synagogue in Tiberias Yosi of Maʿon spoke out against the heavy taxes imposed by the Patriarch, a situation which, he claimed, prevented people from donating a larger amount of money to the sages.[47] The fourth-century Jacob of Kefar Nevoraya preached at the Maradata synagogue in Caesarea, advocating that sages, and not the wealthy, ought to be appointed judges.[48]

A second aspect of rabbinic activity within the confines of the synagogue was the adjudication of halakhic matters. On one level, rabbis were asked to make decisions in numerous areas of law; whether this was done in an official capacity (if any) is unclear. So, for example, R. Yoḥanan was questioned on numerous halakhic issues in the synagogue of Maʿon near Tiberias and in a synagogue in Caesarea.[49] In another instance, a question arose in the Maʿon synagogue and was referred to him. There were a number of instances when sages served in an official capacity in a court that met regularly in the synagogue, as was the case with R. Abbahu in the Maradata synagogue of Caesarea.[50]

A third area of rabbinic involvement concerned education of the young. Schooling is often mentioned together with primary school teachers (lit., teachers of Bible), and such instruction took place for the most part in the synagogue precincts. Rabbinic involvement in this area was twofold: on the one hand, many sages, such as R. Yoḥanan, R. Ami, and R. Samuel b. R. Isaac, issued directives to these teachers;[51] on the other hand, these teachers often referred their questions to various sages, as was the case with R. Jeremiah, R. Isaac, and R. Mana.[52] In one instance R. Abbahu showed a teacher how to conduct himself through his own

---

spoke in the synagogue (as he did on numerous occasions; see below) and R. Ḥiyya in the *bet midrash*.

47 J Sanhedrin 2, 6, 20d; Genesis Rabbah 80:1, Theodor-Albeck, pp. 950–952.

48 J Bikkurim 3, 3, 65d; Midrash Samuel 7:6, Buber, p. 34b.

49 *Tiberias* – B Bava Qamma 99b; B Yevamot 64b; B Ḥullin 97a; *Caesarea* – B Yevamot 65b.

50 J Sanhedrin 1, 1, 18a.

51 J Megillah 3, 4, 74a; Midrash Psalms 91:3, Buber, pp. 397–398.

52 J Megillah 3, 6, 74b.

personal example.[53] The following account clearly indicates a facet of rabbinic involvement in the education of the young:

> R. Judah Nesiah sent R. Ḥiyya, R. Asi and R. Ami to tour the towns of Palestine in order to check on teachers of Scriptures and Oral Law. In one place they found neither teacher of Scriptures nor of Oral Law, whereupon they said to them [the residents]: "Bring us the guardians of the city." They brought them the sentries of the city. The sages responded: "These are not the guardians of the city, but rather its destroyers!" "And who are its guardians?" they asked. "The teachers of Scriptures and Oral Law."[54]

Two important points ought to be highlighted in this tradition. First, sages at times were intimately involved in the educational activities of Jewish communities throughout Roman Palestine. Second, the sages who functioned in this capacity operated under the auspices of the Patriarch, for it was the latter who was officially and formally in charge of Jewish education. The sages thus served as representatives and emissaries of the Patriarchal office.

That the above-mentioned functions might have been filled by sages or by those close to them is indicated in two very similar accounts from third-century Palestine. Around the turn of the century, the inhabitants of Simonias[55] solicited the help of R. Judah I in finding someone for their community who could be "a preacher, a judge, a synagogue administrator, a teacher [of Bible], a teacher [of Oral Law], and one who fills all of our needs"; R. Judah recommended one Levi b. Sisi.[56] A similar list of functions appears again in a tradition associated with the mid-third-century amora, Resh Laqish, who, when approached by the people of Bostra for someone to fill such a position, considered recommending a Babylonian (sage?) for the post.[57]

*   *   *

The crucial issue which remains to be examined is the nature and extent (if any) of rabbinic influence within the ancient synagogue. The fact that the sages were involved in certain activities related to this institution

---

53 J Megillah 3, 4, 74a. According to A. D. York, the *safra* was (primarily?) in charge of Torah-reading and also served as *meturgeman*; "The Targum in the Synagogue and in the School," *JSJ* 10 (1979), 74–86.

54 J Ḥagigah 1, 7, 76c.

55 A village in the Lower Galilee, near Sepphoris.

56 J Yevamot 12, 7, 13a.

57 J Sheviʿit 6, 1, 36d.

does not necessarily indicate that they played a dominant role there. In the first place, it must be remembered that throughout antiquity, and well into the Middle Ages, the rabbis never played an official role *per se* in the synagogue. They were not employees of this institution; such an arrangement, which is commonplace today, evolved only a millennium later. Moreover, the ancient synagogue was primarily a local institution. It was built by local donors, governed by a local body, and its practices and cultural proclivities reflected local tastes. Thus, when the town of Simonias turned to R. Judah I to find someone who would fulfill a variety of the community's needs, the latter did not recommend a known sage, but rather one Levi b. Sisi. When Levi failed to meet these requirements he risked being dismissed.[58] A similar situation occurred with regard to one R. Simeon, the Bible teacher of Tarbanat, who would translate the weekly scriptural reading verse by verse. When the congregation asked him to translate half of one verse at a time so they could relate its contents to their children, R. Simeon refused on the grounds that it deviated from rabbinic practice. After consulting with R. Ḥanina, who reaffirmed that the rabbinic injunction should indeed be followed scrupulously, the community promptly dismissed him.[59]

That many sages probably found the synagogue setting less congenial to their spiritual needs at the time of prayer is reflected in the many statements urging sages to pray in the synagogue.[60] Our sources cite numerous examples of rabbis who looked with askance upon certain synagogue practices. Some, for example, objected vehemently to the existence of the synagogues of the *ʿamme ha-ʾaretz*, as well as to their practice of referring to the holy ark as *ʾarona* and to the synagogue as *bet ha-ʿam*.[61] A

---

58 J Yevamot 12, 7, 13a; Genesis Rabbah 81:1, Theodor-Albeck, p. 969. A similar job definition was given by the people of Bostra when asking Resh Laqish to recommend a candidate; see J Sheviʿit 6, 1, 36d; Deuteronomy Rabbah, Lieberman, pp. 60–61.

59 J Megillah 4, 5, 75b. The identification of Tarbanat is disputed. It has been identified as: (a) a place in the Jezreel Valley – Darbanat (I. Press, *Encyclopedia of Eretz-Israel* [4 vols.; Jerusalem, 1951–55], II, 380 [Hebrew]); (b) a village in the Lower Galilee near Simonias (S. Klein, "R. Simeon the Sofer of Tarbanat," in: *Minḥa le-David – Festschrift in Honor of D. Yellin* [Jerusalem, 1935], 96–99 [Hebrew]; idem, *Land of the Galilee*[2] [Jerusalem, 1967], 110 [Hebrew]); (c) Tarichaeae, on the western shore of the Sea of Galilee (I. Horowitz, *Eretz-Israel and Its Neighbors* [Vienna, 1923], 305 [Hebrew]); and (d) Trachonitis (M. Schwartz, *Torah-Reading in the Ancient Synagogues* [University Microfilms; Ann Arbor, 1975], 288).

60 J Berakhot 5, 1, 8d; B Berakhot 6b–8a.

61 M ʾAvot 3:10; B Shabbat 32a. Such references to the ark have been found at Dura Europos and perhaps at Naveh as well. *Dura*: C. Kraeling, *The Excavations at Dura Europos: The Synagogue*[2] (New Haven, 1979), 269; *Naveh*: Y. Breslavski, "A Hebrew-Ara-

number of rabbis were troubled by the fact that during prayer they would have to bow down on a synagogue floor exhibiting figural representations; the Talmud describes how each of them tried to resolve this dilemma; one simply avoided going to the synagogue, another changed his usual place of worship in the synagogue, and yet another prostrated himself in an unusual manner. Only R. Abbahu of Caesarea—probably the most acculturated of Palestinian amoraim—remained unperturbed by this situation and maintained his usual practice.[62]

The Mishnah lists a series of prayers, undoubtedly recited in local synagogues, which the rabbis found objectionable as well. Repeating "we give thanks" (*Modim*) twice raised suspicions of dualism, as did adding a prayer for God's mercy on a bird's nest or that His name be associated (only) with the good.[63] A prayer leader who insisted on wearing only white was declared unacceptable, as was he who insisted on being barefoot. Any deviation in the way one placed the phylacteries on his head and hand was declared invalid and specifically termed sectarian (*derekh ha-minut or derekh ha-hitzonim*).[64] R. Yoḥanan and R. Yose—the latter despite the vigorous objections of R. Aḥa—chose not to object when the *Shemaᶜ* was recited more than three hours after sunrise on a fast day, contrary to their practice.[65] In Babylonia as well, local custom was unfamiliar to Rav who had just arrived from Israel. In one particular synagogue the entire congregation bowed down, but Rav did not. Despite the attempts

---

maic Inscription from Naveh," *Yediᶜot* 4 (1936), 8–12 (Hebrew); J. -B. Frey, *Corpus Inscriptionum Iudaicarum* (2 vols.; Rome, 1939–52), II, 93. More recently, J. Naveh has questioned this reading; see his *On Stone and Mosaic*, 64.

62　J ᶜAvodah Zarah 4, 1, 43d. G. Blidstein, "Prostration and Mosaics in Talmudic Law," *Bulletin of the Institute of Jewish Studies* 2 (1974), 33–37. See S. Lieberman, *Greek in Jewish Palestine* (New York, 1942), 21ff. Another interesting case of diversity among the sages regarded prayer—although not related specifically to the synagogue. The Mishnah established that the third paragraph of the *Shemaᶜ* (Numbers 15:37–41) should be recited in the evening as well as the morning; however the Talmud relates that this practice was followed neither in Babylonia nor in Palestine (J Berakhot 1, 6, 3d). The rabbis in each place had customs different from each other as well as from the mishnaic ruling.

63　M Berakhot 5:3. See A. Segal, *Two Powers in Heaven* (Leiden, 1977), 98–108.

64　M Megillah 4:8–9. The distinction made by the sages between these two types of sectarians is not altogether clear. See the comments of Rashi and Rambam, loc. cit. Some of the practices mentioned recall sectarian behavior; see Josephus, *War* II, 8, 3, 123 (wearing white) and B Sotah 40a (barefoot priests). See also S. Krauss, *Talmudic Antiquities (Qadmoniot Ha-Talmud)*, II/2 (Tel-Aviv, 1945), 89 (Hebrew).

65　J Berakhot 1, 5, 3c.

of later authorities to explain this discrepancy, clearly Rav was confronted by a local custom which was unknown to him.[66]

Torah-reading practices in the synagogue likewise might have encountered rabbinic criticism. The Jerusalem Talmud has preserved a series of stories about local practices regarding the translation of the Bible
into Aramaic which ran counter to rabbinic prescriptions. The account
noted above concerning R. Simeon of Tarbanat demonstrates that local
preferences were the determining factor; woe to anyone who dared defy
the will of the congregation.[67] In this regard, the Talmud records three
separate traditions involving R. Samuel b. R. Isaac: in the first, he re-
buked a *meturgeman* for translating the scriptural reading while standing
by a column (instead of next to the Torah-reader); in the second, one and
the same person (instead of two different people) both read from the
Torah and translated the Torah portion; in the third, the *meturgeman* read
the scriptural translation from a book (instead of giving a spontaneous
translation).[68] Moreover, scholars have long recognized the many dis-
crepancies between targumic literature and rabbinic sources.[69] Formerly
it was assumed that the Targum reflects either a private opinion[70] or an
early version of the halakha.[71] It is also quite possible that it reflects non-
rabbinic conceptions and practices widespread in Jewish society.[72] Finally, we know of several instances in which actions in express violation
of rabbinic dictates were taken in synagogues. R. Isaac b. El'azar was

---

66 B Megillah 22b.

67 J Megillah 4, 5, 75b.

68 J Megillah 4, 1, 74d. Rabbinic objections to the use of a written translation clearly
indicate that Targums existed at this time. See, for example, M Yadaim 4:5; T Shabbat
13:2, Lieberman, p. 57; B Shabbat 115a, and the evidence from Qumran. This same R.
Samuel b. R. Isaac instructed teachers (ספרא ומתנינא) on other occasions as well;
Numbers Rabbah 12:3; Midrash Psalms 91:3, Buber, pp. 397–398.

69 JE, XII, 58; Lieberman, "Ḥazzanut Yannai," 222–223; P. S. Alexander, "The Rabbinic Lists of Forbidden Targumim," JJS 27 (1976), 177–191.

70 C. Albeck, "Apocryphal Halakha in the Palestinian Targums and the Aggada,"
in: B. Lewin Jubilee Volume, ed. J. L. Fishman (Jerusalem, 1940), 93–104 (Hebrew).

71 P. Kahle, The Cairo Geniza[2] (Oxford, 1959), 206; A. Diez-Macho, "The Recently
Discovered Palestinian Targum: Its Antiquity and Relationship with the Other Targum," VT 7 (1960), 222–245; J. Heinemann, "Early Halakhah in the Palestinian Targumim," in: Studies in Jewish Legal History, ed. B. Jackson (London, 1974), 114–122; J.
Faur, "The Targumim and Halakha," JQR 66 (1975–76), 19–26; and generally A. York,
"The Dating of Targumic Literature," JSJ 5 (1974), 49–62; M. McNamara, "Targums,"
in: The Interpreter's Dictionary of the Bible – Supplement (Nashville, 1976), 856–861.

72 A number of rabbinic objections to the Targum can be found in Targum
Jonathan. See, for example, J Berakhot 5, 3, 9c and Tg. J. to Lev. 22:28.

involved in one such incident in Sepphoris, and R. Jeremiah in an incident in Bostra; neither was consulted in these matters nor did they see fit to object.[73]

The synagogue is mentioned, albeit infrequently, by John Chrysostom and Jerome, two fourth-century Church fathers. They take note of various synagogue practices—daily prayers, with their anti-Christian references; the presence of the sacred Torah scrolls; Christian attendance at synagogue services; blowing of the *shofar*; magical cures, etc.[74] However, Jewish leaders or groups are rarely identified: Jerome notes the *magistrorum synagoge,* Pharisees, *praepositi sapientissimi,* priests, as well as the apostoli of the Patriarch, who had the authority to remove each of the above.[75] Epiphanius mentions *archisynagogoi,* elders, the *ḥazzan,* and priests.[76] The sages, individually or collectively, are never mentioned. The same holds true for the Theodosian Code, which lists synagogue functionaries—the Patriarch, elders, priests, *archisynagogoi,* and *pater synagogoi*—but never mentions the sages.[77]

The case against rabbinic dominance within the ancient synagogue is further strengthened by archeological evidence. Of all the inscriptions appearing in ancient synagogues, none mentions any of the sages known

---

73 B Shabbat 29b.

74 See R. L. Wilken, *John Chrysostom and the Jews* (Berkeley, 1983), 97–127; Chrysostom's *Homilia Adversus Judaeos* in English translation in: W. Meeks and R. L. Wilken, *Jews and Christians in Antioch in the First Four Centuries of the Common Era* (Missoula, 1978), 83–127. See also S. Krauss, "The Jews in the Works of the Church Fathers," *JQR* 5 (1893), 122; 6 (1894), 82–99, 225–261.

75 *magistrorum synagoge – In Zach.* II, 6:9, *CCSL* 76a, 796; Pharisees – *Epistle* CXII, *PL* 22, 924; *praepositi sapientissimi – Epistle* CXXI, 10, 19–20, *CSEL* 56, 48–49. This last reference in Jerome comes the closest to pointing to the rabbis. Jerome defines the *praepositi* as those who teach Pharisaic traditions (*deuterosis – mishnah*). Such traditions, he claims, are binding on the Jews; those who do not accept them are liable to attack (*Comm. in Isa.* 59:25, *PL* 24, 581).

On the use of the above-mentioned titles throughout the Roman Diaspora, see J. Juster, *Les juifs dans l'empire romain* (2 vols.; New York, 1914), I, 442–456.

76 *Panarion* 30.11.4, *PG* 41, 424.

77 *Codex Theodosianus* 16.8.4; 8; 13; 15. See A. Linder, *The Jews in Roman Imperial Legislation* (Detroit, 1987), 186–189, 201–204, 220–222; see also S. J. D. Cohen, "Pagan and Christian Evidence on the Ancient Synagogue," in: *The Synagogue in Late Antiquity,* 159–181. Similarly, with regard to other ancient sources, functionaries and officials are mentioned, but never sages. See, for example, Libanius, in M. Stern, *Greek and Latin Authors on Jews and Judaism* (3 vols.; Jerusalem, 1974–84), II, 589–597; *Scriptores Historia Augustae,* in: Stern, ibid., II 630, 636–641; Palladius, *Dialogue on the Life of John Chrysostom, PG* 47, 50.

to us from rabbinic literature.[78] Synagogues were built and run by people other than the rabbis. Moreover, the art in the synagogue does not reflect rabbinic attitudes of late antiquity. Art *per se* is not often a subject of discussion in rabbinic literature, but when mentioned it is usually with regard to questions of idolatry and related matters. The relatively few sources that address the subject of figural representation indicate that the rabbis generally were either vehemently opposed or, at best, grudgingly accepting of this phenomenon. Certain symbolic Jewish art was regarded as problematic, such as representations of the seven-branched menorah as it had once existed in the Temple; other symbols, such as the globe and sceptre, which were associated with the emperor cult, were considered offensive.[79] Notwithstanding, examples of such depictions are not infrequent in ancient Jewish art.

The seven-branched menorah is the most popular form of this symbol in Jewish art and is found in a large number of synagogues throughout Israel and the Diaspora.[80] As regards the symbols of the emperor cult, the most striking example comes from Hammath Tiberias. In the center of the zodiac design, Helios is clearly carrying a globe and a whip or sceptre, holding his hand high in a gesture of triumph, and crowned with a halo. These attributes were taken from representations of the emperor and his cult during the third and particularly the fourth centuries![81] The famous passage in the Jerusalem Talmud is quite explicit about rabbinic attitudes toward figural representation:

---

[78] S. J. D. Cohen, "Epigraphical Rabbis," *JQR* 72 (1981–82), 1–17. See also H. Shanks, "Is the Title 'Rabbi' Anachronistic in the Gospels?," *JQR* 53 (1962–63), 337–345; idem, "Origins of the Title 'Rabbi'," *JQR* 59 (1968–69), 152–157; S. Zeitlin, "A Reply," *JQR* 53 (1962–63), 345–349; idem, "The Title Rabbi in the Gospels is Anachronistic," *JQR* 59 (1968–69), 158–160.

[79] B Rosh ha-Shanah 24a–b and parallels; M ʿAvodah Zarah 3:1; J ʿAvodah Zarah 3, 1, 42c. See E. E. Urbach, "The Rabbinical Laws of Idolatry in the Second and Third Centuries in the Light of Archaeological and Historical Facts – II," *IEJ* 9 (1959), 238ff.

[80] A. Negev, "The Chronology of the Seven-Branched Menorah," in: *Eretz Israel*, VIII (Jerusalem, 1967), 193–210 (Hebrew); R. Hachlili, *Ancient Jewish Art and Archaeology in the Land of Israel* (Leiden, 1988), 236–256; R. Hachlili and R. Merhav, "The Menorah in the First and Second Temple Times in the Light of the Sources and Archaeology," in: *Eretz Israel*, XVIII (Jerusalem, 1985), 256–267 (Hebrew).

[81] Hachlili, *Ancient Jewish Art*, 301–309; idem, "The Zodiac in Ancient Jewish Art: Representation and Significance," *BASOR* 228 (1977), 61–77. See also M. Dothan, *Hammath Tiberias* (Jerusalem, 1983), 39–43.

In the days of R. Yohanan they began to make figural representations on the walls and he did not object; in the days of R. Abun they began making such figures on the mosaic floors and he did not object.[82]

The difference between rabbinic attitudes towards figural representation and another view current in antiquity can be understood from the well-known targumic passage to Lev. 26:1:

And you shall not place a figural stone in your land for the purpose of pros-tration, but you may place a stoa [here, probably a mosaic pavement with figures and human images] impressed in the ground [i.e., floors] of your sanctuaries [i.e., synagogues], though not to bow down to it [i.e., not for purposes of worship], for I am the Lord your God.[83]

Even the language used in many synagogues seems to have been different from that which the rabbis would have used or would have even approved. The Greek names of donors in the inscriptions from Sepphoris and Tiberias reflect circles in Jewish society quite different from those of the rabbis.[84] An extreme example of a synagogue practice which was contrary to rabbinic tastes is related in an account of a Caesarean synagogue where it was customary to recite the *Shema* in Greek. Two rabbis who happened to attend reacted in very different ways; one was openly hostile, the other more understanding. Levi bar Ḥiyta was so incensed that he considered disrupting the service; R. Yosi responded that it was preferable that these people recite the *Shema* in Greek than not recite it at

---

[82] J ʿAvodah Zarah 3, 3, 42d. The text follows the more probable version of the tradition preserved in a Genizah fragment and published by Epstein in *Tarbiẓ* 3 (1932), 20 (Hebrew). On the non-rabbinic character of some aspects of Jewish art, especially the zodiac and Helios scenes, see E. E. Urbach, "The Rabbinical Laws of Idolatry," 238–245; J. Baumgarten, "Art in the Synagogue: Some Talmudic Views," *Judaism* 19/2 (1970), 196–206. G. Foerster has argued that the zodiac signs are endemic to Jewish tradition from the Second Temple period onward. He is probably correct; however, the real issue is not the zodiac signs *per se* (see Deuteronomy Rabbah, Lieberman, p. 16), but their artistic representation and, even more, the representation of Helios and his accoutrements; see his "The Zodiac and Ancient Synagogues and Its Place in Jewish Thought and Liturgy," in: *Eretz Israel*, XIX (Jerusalem, 1987), 225–234 (Hebrew).

[83] Ginzberg, *Commentary*, III, 116–123; Blidstein, "Prostration," 37–39; M. Klein, "Palestinian Targum and Synagogue Mosaics," *Immanuel* 11 (1980), 44–45. See also: Z. A. Steinfeld, "Prostration in Prayer and the Prohibition of the Paving Stone," *Sidra* 3 (1987), 53–79 (Hebrew).

[84] L. Roth-Gerson, *The Greek Inscriptions from the Synagogues in Eretz-Israel* (Jerusalem, 1987), 58–75, 105–110 (Hebrew). See also B. Lifshitz, *Donateurs et fondateurs dans les synagogues juives* (*Cahiers de la Revue Biblique* 7; Paris, 1967), 59–66.

all. Interestingly, neither statement reflects the even more lenient position of the Mishnah, which explicitly allows the *Shema*ᶜ to be recited in
any language.[85]

The gap between the world of the sages and the synagogues in Israel
excavated to date is likewise reflected in some of the descriptions of synagogues and synagogue practices recorded in rabbinic literature. The
latter are at times quite different from what we find in archeological remains. To cite but three examples. First, the Tosefta states that synagogue
entrances should face east.[86] However, to date very few Galilean synagogues (or any other, for that matter) subscribe to this guideline, although it should be noted that four synagogues found in southern Judea
were indeed built in this manner.[87] Second, in times of mourning the
rabbis prescribed changing their usual seating arrangements within the
synagogue; those sitting in the north would sit in the south and vice
versa.[88] However, it is difficult to anchor this tradition in any known
archeological reality: since entrances were almost always oriented towards Jerusalem in the northern and southern parts of the country,
benches were invariably placed on the eastern and western walls of the
synagogue. Finally, the statement that the elders are to sit with their
backs to "the Holy" (referring either to the Torah shrine or to Jerusalem)
while facing the congregation does not find expression in practically any
of the synagogue remains.[89] Only in the few pre-70 buildings did benches
line the wall facing Jerusalem.[90] In synagogues of late antiquity these
walls rarely had benches.[91]

---

[85] J Sotah 7, 1, 21b and M Sotah 7:1.

[86] T Megillah 3:22, Lieberman, p. 360.

[87] In addition to the well-known examples at Susiya and Eshtemoa (see *Ancient
Synagogues Revealed*, ed. L. I. Levine [Jerusalem, 1981], 120–128), two others from the
same area have been discovered in recent years, at Maᶜon and ᶜAnim. See reports of
Z. Ilan and D. Amit in: *Archaeological News of the Department of Antiquities, Israel* 93
(1989), 86–89 (Hebrew).

[88] See above, n. 9.

[89] T Megillah 3:21, Lieberman, p. 360.

[90] See the articles of Y. Yadin, G. Foerster, S. Gutman and Z. Maᶜoz in: *Ancient Synagogues Revealed*, 19–41.

[91] An exception to this rule, from the Diaspora, is the synagogue of Dura Europos,
where benches line each of its four walls; Kraeling, *Dura Europos*, 16–17. In many respects, however, the Dura phenomenon is unusual. Most synagogues from the Roman Diaspora were very similar—in basilical plan, mosaic floors, extensive and frequent use of menorahs, permanent Torah shrine, and donor inscriptions—to those
found in Israel, and may point to some sort of common tradition. See Kraabel, "The
Diaspora Synagogue," 477–510; A. Seager, "The Architecture of the Dura and Sardis

*   *   *

If rabbinic influence was indeed peripheral to the actual operation of the ancient synagogue, who, then, exercised control over these institutions? Although information in this regard is scant, it is still possible to single out three different groups that wielded significant authority. First, there is the local community, especially in the rural areas, referred to as *bene ha-qehillah* (members of the community) or *bene ha-knesset* (members of the congregation); these people built and supported their synagogue[92] and undoubtedly had ultimate power to determine its course and direction. Indeed, the synagogue is referred to in the Mishnah as communal property.[93] A second group that exercised control in synagogal matters was the wealthy urban aristocracy; it was this group which produced the many individual donors who built and maintained these institutions.[94] The *nasi* (or Patriarch) was a third source of authority. Rabban Gamaliel II was approached by members of a Tiberian synagogue to resolve an issue,[95] while his son, R. Ḥanina, probably representing the Patriarchal house, appears to have played an authoritative role regarding an issue which arose in the synagogue in Kabul.[96] As already noted, the Theodosian Code makes it clear that the Patriarch had some sort of role in synagogue affairs, and this seems to be borne out by the late third-century inscription from Stobi as well.[97]

*   *   *

What, then, are the historical implications of our discussion with regard to the sages of Roman Palestine? In trying to delineate the nature and degree of rabbinic involvement in the ancient synagogue, we have

---

Synagogues," in: *The Dura Europos Synagogue*, ed. J. Gutmann (Missoula, 1973), 79–116.

92 See the references to the community in general at the synagogues of Maʿon, Jericho, and Susiya, in: Naveh, *On Stone and Mosaic*, 92, 104, 123, as well as N. Wieder, "The Jericho Inscription and Jewish Liturgy," *Tarbiz* 52 (1983), 557–579 (Hebrew).

93 M Nedarim 5:5.

94 See Baumgarten, "Art in the Synagogue," 204–206; Lifshitz, *Donateurs et fondateurs*; Levine, *Rabbinic Class*, 178–181; Z. Safrai, "Financing Synagogue Construction in the Period of the Mishna and the Talmud," in: *Synagogues in Antiquity*, 80–86.

95 M ʿEruvin 10:10.

96 B Megillah 25b.

97 M. Hengel, "Die Synagogeninschriften von Stobi," *ZNW* 57 (1966), 145–183; Levine, *Rabbinic Class*, 138, 140, 191; and the bibliography listed in: J. -B. Frey, *Corpus Inscriptionum Iudaicarum*, I (KTAV reprint; New York, 1975), 504–507.

claimed that the rabbis had no control of this institution.[98] Nevertheless, it has been noted that during the third and fourth centuries their involvement in synagogue affairs increased significantly in certain areas. A number of factors seem to have been at play here. On the most immediate level, this trend may have been linked in some way to the figure of the most outstanding Palestinian amora, R. Yoḥanan (d. ca. 280), who is prominently mentioned in almost every area of rabbinic involvement in synagogue life.[99] A wider view, however, would claim that rabbinic penetration into the synagogue was part of the sages' increasing involvement in Jewish communal institutions generally from the turn of the third century on. As noted elsewhere,[100] from the time of Rabbi Judah I the rabbinic class underwent a transformation from a relatively isolated elite centered in Judean villages to one much more active in the Jewish community at large, based in the major Galilean cities.

It is also possible, however, that increased rabbinic involvement was connected to the gradual transformation of the synagogue in the first centuries C.E. from a general communal institution to one with a more prominent religious character. In its early stages of development, the synagogue had been primarily a community center which also housed liturgical activities on the Sabbath and holidays.[101] Although the communal aspect of the synagogue continued throughout late antiquity, beginning in the third century we are witness to a more distinctive religious character adopted by the institution, one which is clearly expressed in its architecture and art. Synagogues now faced Jerusalem, as is evident either in the orientation of their facades and entrances (as in the Galilee) or in the direction of their apses and *bimas*, which contained the permanent Torah shrine and were located in the Jerusalem-oriented wall.[102]

---

[98] See the article by S. J. D. Cohen in this volume, p. 162, n. 16.

[99] On R. Yoḥanan, see the doctoral thesis of R. Kimelman, "Rabbi Johanan of Tiberias: Aspects of the Social and Religious History of Third Century Palestine" (University Microfilms; Ann Arbor, 1980); idem, "The Conflict between R. Yoḥanan and Resh Laqish on the Supremacy of the Patriarchate," in: *Proceedings of the Seventh World Congress of Jewish Studies* (Jerusalem, 1981), 1–20.

[100] See my *Rabbinic Class*, 23–42 and Cohen (above), pp. 169ff.

[101] For the Second Temple period, see Levine, "The Second Temple Synagogue," 7–31.

[102] Y. Tsafrir, "The Byzantine Setting and Its Influence on Ancient Synagogues," in: *The Synagogue in Late Antiquity*, 147–157; idem, *Eretz Israel from the Destruction*, II, 165–189, 285–300; Hachlili, *Ancient Jewish Art*, 143–192. See also A. Ovadiah, "Mutual Influences of Synagogues and Churches in Byzantine Palestine," in: *Between Hermon and Sinai*, ed. M. Broshi (Jerusalem, 1977), 163–170 (Hebrew).

Even the art forms used in synagogues changed significantly from the third century on, exhibiting many more Jewish religious symbols than before. Furthermore, synagogues in the Byzantine period were often referred to as a "holy place" (*ʾatraʾ qadisha*), both in inscriptions[103] and in the Targums (*bet qudsha*).[104]

This transformation in the religious character of the ancient synagogue is in all likelihood part of an overall pattern ubiquitous in late antiquity. P. Brown has argued that the concern for the holy (be it a person, place or object) and its impact on daily life took on increased importance at this time.[105] The successful incursion of the Church into Byzantine Palestine from the fourth century on, as well as the prominent role played by bishops, did not go unnoticed by the Jews; these developments may have affected rabbinic attitudes regarding the synagogue and the community's increased acceptance of the rabbis as their religious leaders.

Another implication of the above discussion regards the status of the rabbis in Jewish society in general. While the sages clearly had an influence, it is safe to assume that they did not wield institutionalized control over any part of the Jewish community. In the context of late antiquity, the standing of the sages lay somewhere between that of the bishops on the one hand and that of the saints or holy men of Christian society on the other, between those who headed institutions and those on the periphery of society who operated in an entirely spontaneous, unstructured, and charismatic fashion. The rabbis fit neither mould neatly. While enjoying their own private world of the *bet midrash*, they at the same time demonstrated a willingness and desire to become involved in mainstream Jewish institutions, such as the synagogue.

Limited rabbinic influence in Jewish society of late antiquity stemmed in part both from the absence of any central rabbinic body at the time[106] and from the rabbis' lack of control over any specific office within the Jewish communal structure. If such a central rabbinic body had existed, the sages might well have wielded considerably more influ-

---

103 As in Kefar Ḥananiah, Ḥammath Tiberias, Beth Shean and Naʿaran; see Naveh, *On Stone and Mosaic*, passim.

104 Tg. Ps.-J. to Gen. 11:1; 31:47; 32:3; 42:23; 45:12; Deut. 25:7–8. Tg. Neof. to Gen. 2:19; 11:1; 22:1; 38:10; 45:12; 46:2; Exod. 3:4. My thanks to Dr. A. Shinan for these references. See his article in this volume, pp. 241–251, and idem, "'Lishan Bet Qudsha' in the Aramaic Targums to the Torah," *Bet Miqra* 3(66) (1976), 472–474.

105 P. Brown, *Society and the Holy in Late Antiquity* (Berkeley, 1982), 163–165; idem, *The World of Late Antiquity AD 150–750* (London, 1971), 49–57.

106 See my *Rabbinic Class*, 76–83.

ence than they actually did. In both regards, however, precisely what the sages lacked, the bishops had, i.e., regularly convened central bodies and an official position in local churches. Undoubtedly, the authority of the bishop in Church affairs was a direct result of the nature and structure of his office.

For Jews throughout Palestine, the synagogue was first and foremost an institution of the local community. This may account for the significant differences in language, art forms, and building plans that existed among the synagogues of late antiquity. As a communal institution, the synagogue was clearly responsive to the local needs and individualized proclivities of the various communities. This phenomenon is reflected not only in material remains but also in synagogue practices: the Torah-reading, the use of *piyyut* (liturgical poetry), the form and content of the prayers, the types of *derashot* (exegetical comments), and the different genres among the Aramaic Targums. Whatever authority was wielded by the Patriarch in local affairs (about which we know very little), we can safely assume that Jewish communities were largely autonomous, and this was certainly the case after the disappearance of the Patriarchate ca. 429.[107] The synagogue always retained its indigenous roots, thereby reflecting its own particular constituency, needs, desires, and proclivities. The rabbis were but one of a number of elements in Jewish society of late antiquity which had a hand in shaping the course and destiny of this central Jewish communal institution.[108]

[107] J. Cohen, "Roman Imperial Policy towards the Jews from Constantine until the End of the Palestinian Patriarchate (ca. 429)," *Byzantine Studies* 3 (1976), 1–29.

[108] For a comprehensive treatment of many of the issues discussed in this article, see my forthcoming book, *The Ancient Synagogue*.

V. LANGUAGE AND LITERATURE IN THE GALILEE

The Galilean Background of Mishnaic Hebrew

GARY A. RENDSBURG

All scholars today agree that Mishnaic Hebrew (MH) represents a colloquial dialect used in Eretz-Israel in late antiquity[1] and that its literary counterpart was the continuum represented by Late Biblical Hebrew (LBH) and Qumran Hebrew (QH).[2] These conclusions have resulted in the widely-accepted theory that the Hebrew language in late antiquity was characterized by diglossia.[3]

---

[1] The first scholar to recognize this was M. H. Segal. See his standard grammars: *A Grammar of Mishnaic Hebrew* (Oxford, 1927); *A Grammar of Mishnaic Hebrew* (Tel-Aviv, 1936) (Hebrew).

[2] The grouping of BH and QH as one continuum is accepted by most scholars. See, e.g., H. Yalon, *Studies in the Dead Sea Scrolls* (Jerusalem, 1967), 71 (Hebrew). For a full treatment, see the grammars by E. Qimron, "The Hebrew of the Dead Sea Scrolls" (doctoral dissertation, Hebrew University; Jerusalem, 1976) (Hebrew); *The Hebrew of the Dead Sea Scrolls* (Atlanta, 1986). This position has been challenged recently by S. Morag, "Qumran Hebrew: Some Typological Observations," *VT* 38 (1988), 148–164. The data utilized by Morag are undeniable, but in the main it is still true that QH is closer to BH than it is to MH. On the other hand, see my closing comments below, p. 237.

[3] I use the term diglossia according to its original meaning as defined by C. A. Ferguson, "Diglossia," *Word* 15 (1959), 325–340. Since Ferguson's introduction of the term, diglossia has come to mean different things to different people; see J. A. Fishman, "The Sociology of Language," in: *Current Trends in Linguistics*, ed. T. A. Sebeok (14 vols.; The Hague, 1967–76), XII, 1689–1701. On the diglossia of Hebrew in late antiquity, see E. Y. Kutscher, "The Language of Ḥazal," in: *Hanoch Yalon Jubilee Volume*, eds. S. Lieberman et al. (Jerusalem, 1963), 247–248 (Hebrew); J. Fellman, "On Diglossia," *Language Sciences* 34 (1975), 39; C. Rabin, "Hebrew and Aramaic in the First Century," in: *The Jewish People in the First Century*, eds. S. Safrai and M. Stern (2 vols.;

I will attempt here to advance the discussion by addressing the issue of the specific origins of MH. Scholars have previously opined that MH or an early form thereof was also the colloquial variety of Hebrew in biblical times,[4] and that BH served as a literary language only.[5] Accordingly, the diglossia of Hebrew attested to in late antiquity can be projected back to the biblical period as well.[6]

I accept this hypothesis wholeheartedly.[7] Now, however, due to recent studies in the dialect geography of ancient Hebrew we are able to refine the above conclusion regarding MH. I propose that MH is more specifically the colloquial dialect of the northern regions of Eretz-Israel, i.e., the Galilee.

This view was once suggested in passing by C. Rabin. In a discussion of the relationship between Aramaic and MH, he wrote:

> Of the many similarities with Aramaic there can be no doubt, but it is not easy to establish which of these are due to the effect of contract [*sic!*] of fully-formed Hebrew, which ones may be due to a northern origin of the parent dialects of Mishnaic Hebrew, in an area where they had common isoglosses with Aramaic, and which are the result of parallel development of Middle Aramaic and Middle Hebrew.[8]

This is the only statement about the Galilean background of MH I have encountered in the secondary literature. However, Rabin appears to have retracted from this view several years later, when he wrote that "the basis of mishnaic Hebrew . . . was the spoken language of the Judaean population."[9]

Assen, 1974–76), II, 1015–1016; and S. J. Lieberman, "Response to Professor Blau," in: *Jewish Languages: Themes and Variations*, ed. H. H. Paper (Cambridge, MA, 1978), 26.

[4] Segal, *Grammar*, 11; E. Ullendorff, *Is Biblical Hebrew a Language?* (Wiesbaden, 1977), 11 (= *BSOAS* 34 [1971], 249). Apparently this view is also stated very clearly by A. Bendavid, *Biblical Hebrew or Mishnaic Hebrew?* (Tel-Aviv, 1951), 69–73 (Hebrew) [unavailable to me, cited from C. Rabin, "Hebrew," in: *Current Trends in Linguistics*, VI, 314]. This approach appears less explicitly, though certainly implicitly, in the book's second edition; A. Bendavid, *Biblical Hebrew and Mishnaic Hebrew* (2 vols.; Tel-Aviv, 1967–71) (Hebrew).

[5] Note the comment by J. Blau, *A Grammar of Biblical Hebrew* (Wiesbaden, 1976), 1, that BH "was always a *literary* language" (Blau's italics).

[6] See G. A. Rendsburg, "*Laqṭîl* Infinitives: Hiphʿil or Yiphʿil?" *Orientalia* 51 (1982), 235–236; Ullendorff, *Is Biblical Hebrew a Language?*, 11; and W. Chomsky, *Hebrew: The Eternal Language* (Philadelphia, 1964), 161.

[7] G. A. Rendsburg, *Diglossia in Ancient Hebrew* (New Haven, 1990).

[8] Rabin, "Hebrew," 322–323.

[9] Idem, "Hebrew and Aramaic in the First Century," 1015.

However, I would like to return to Rabin's earlier suggestion and attempt to supply the evidence to substantiate it. Before doing so, a few prefatory words about the recent research in regional dialects of ancient Hebrew are in order.

The vast majority of biblical literature was composed in Judah in general, or in Jerusalem in particular, or by exiles from Judah and Jerusalem. Thus, the regional standard of the Bible may be called Judahite Hebrew (JH). Stories which emanate from the north, such as those concerning the northern judges or the northern kings, often reflect different grammatical usages[10] and may be attributed to a northern Hebrew dialect, Israelian Hebrew (IH).[11] Moreover, most of these same usages are paralleled in the languages spoken to the north of Israel (Aramaic, Phoenician, and Ugaritic[12]) and in Transjordan (Deir ʿAlla, Ammonite, and Moabite).[13] This line of investigation now allows us to isolate Israelian texts in the Bible[14] and to begin to write a grammar of IH.[15]

---

[10] Many have been collected in the two commentaries by C. F. Burney, *Notes on the Hebrew Text of the Books of Kings* (Oxford, 1903), 208–209; and *The Book of Judges* (London, 1918), 171–176. These two books have been reprinted in one volume with a prolegomenon by W. F. Albright (New York, 1970). The material from Kings is mentioned briefly by M. Cogan and H. Tadmor, *II Kings* (*AB* 11; Garden City, 1988), 9.

[11] I have coined this term based on the usage of H. L. Ginsberg, *The Israelian Heritage of Judaism* (New York, 1982). S. Gevirtz, "Of Syntax and Style in the 'Late Biblical Hebrew' – 'Old Canaanite' Connection," *JANES* 18 (1986), 25 and n. 1, independently adduced the same term.

[12] I accept the classification system of H. L. Ginsberg, "The Northwest Semitic Languages," in: *Patriarchs*, ed. B. Mazar (New Brunswick, 1970), 102–106, which places Phoenician and Ugaritic together in his "Phoenic" group.

[13] A convenient and very useful summary of most of the information (though not the Ugaritic data) is W. R. Garr, *Dialect Geography of Syria-Palestine, 1000–586 B.C.E.* (Philadelphia, 1985).

[14] For an illustration of this method, see G. A. Rendsburg, "The Northern Origin of 'The Last Words of David' (2 Sam 23, 1–7)," *Biblica* 69 (1988), 113–121; and idem, "Additional Notes on 'The Last Words of David' (2 Sam 23, 1–7)," *Biblica* 70 (1989), 403–408. For a much more comprehensive work, see idem, *Linguistic Evidence for the Northern Origin of Selected Psalms* (Atlanta, 1990). Other Israelian texts are noted below, in the course of the discussion.

[15] Idem, "Morphological Evidence for Regional Dialects in Ancient Hebrew," in: *Linguistics and Biblical Hebrew*, ed. W. Bodine (Winona Lake, forthcoming). For the theoretical framework, see B. Halpern, "Dialect Distribution in Canaan and the Deir Alla Inscriptions," in: *"Working With No Data": Semitic and Egyptian Studies Presented to Thomas O. Lambdin*, ed. D. M. Golomb (Winona Lake, 1987), 119–139. Note especially his comment that "Canaan was linguistically cantonized" (p. 139).

My own investigations of ancient Hebrew dialects have made it clear that MH shares many of the same properties as IH. Twelve such instances, taken collectively, point to the Galilean origin of MH (see Figure 1 for a convenient summary of the data).

1) The origin of the MH relative pronoun *še-* has been widely discussed, but one will agree with E. Y. Kutscher that "its use was common in the vernacular of Northern Eretz-Israel."[16] This conclusion is reached on the basis of the cognate evidence and on the distribution of this form in IH texts. The cognate form אש occurs in Phoenician and Ammonite,[17] and perhaps at Deir ʿAlla.[18] In pre-exilic biblical texts, *še-* is limited to northern contexts: the Song of Deborah (Judg. 5:7 – twice), the Gideon cycle (Judg. 6:17, 7:12, 8:26), and the Elisha cycle (II Kgs. 6:11). Not until exilic and post-exilic times did *še-* penetrate Judah (Lam. 2:15, 2:16, 4:9, 5:18; Ezra 8:20; I Chr. 5:20, 27:27; etc.). Even in the later period its most frequent appearance is in Ecclesiastes and Song of Songs, both of which are most probably northern compositions.[19]

2) The MH feminine singular demonstrative pronoun *zô* is another characteristic of IH, as again may be seen both in the cognate evidence and in its distribution in the Bible. In Phoenician and Aramaic the corresponding form is either *z* or *zʾ*.[20] The vocalization of these forms is not known but, at the very least, their consonantism aligns with the MH form *zô*. In the Bible, *zô* (or the alternate spelling *zōh*) appears in Hos. 7:16, a northern prophet; Ps. 132:12, a northern psalm;[21] II Kgs. 6:19, in

---

16 E. Y. Kutscher, *A History of the Hebrew Language* (Leiden, 1982), 32.

17 See Garr, *Dialect Geography*, 85–86.

18 This is the interpretation of J. A. Hackett, *The Balaam Text from Deir ʿAlla* (Chico, 1980), 31.

19 On Ecclesiastes, see M. Dahood, "Canaanite-Phoenician Influence in Qoheleth," *Biblica* 33 (1952), 30–52, 191–221; and J. R. Davila, "Qoheleth and Northern Hebrew," in: *Sopher Mahir: Northwest Semitic Studies Presented to Stanislav Segert = Maarav 5–6* (1990), 69–87. On Song of Songs, see S. R. Driver, *An Introduction to the Literature of the Old Testament* (New York, 1906), 448–449; and Y. Avishur, "Stylistic Common Elements between Ugaritic Literature and Song of Songs," *Beth Mikra* 59 (1974), 508–526 (Hebrew). See also the discussion in M. H. Pope, *Song of Songs* (AB 7C; Garden City, 1977), 33–34, 362. See also the Excursus, p. 238.

20 Garr, *Dialect Geography*, 83–84. An exceptional case is *zʾt* in the Tell Fekheriyeh inscription, which forms an isogloss with JH and Moabite.

21 The linguistic evidence is presented in Rendsburg, *Psalms*, 87–90. Note the statement of F. M. Cross, *Canaanite Myth and Hebrew Epic* (Cambridge, MA, 1973), 97: "the traditions of Psalm 132 are wholly independent of the traditions in the Deuteronomic history." I would go one step further and claim that this independence results from the psalm's Israelian provenance.

the Elisha cycle; six times in Ecclesiastes (2:2, 2:24, 5:15, 5:18, 7:23, 9:13); and Ezek. 40:45. This last example is problematic but may be explained as a northern grammatical feature in exilic and post-exilic literature due to the reunion of northern and southern exiles in Mesopotamia in the sixth century B.C.E.[22] Again, our conclusion was anticipated by Kutscher: "It is probable that the form *zô/zōh* existed from early times as a dialectal form mainly in the Northern speech."[23]

3) The MH plural demonstrative pronoun *ʾēllû* is only slightly different from the corresponding BH form *ʾēlleh*. This minor difference is significant, however, as the MH pronunciation probably is paralleled in Phoenician. Our evidence is meager, but the spelling *ily* by Plautus in *Poenulus* 938 apparently points to a *u*-class vowel at the end of the word.[24]

4) The *nomen actionis* form *qĕṭîlah* is very common in MH but is relatively rare in BH. However, when it occurs in the latter, *qĕṭîlah* appears disproportionately in northern contexts, for example: Judg. 5:16 (Song of Deborah), Judg. 14:12, 14:19 – twice (Samson story), I Sam. 13:21 (history of Saul), I Kgs. 19:8 (Elijah cycle), Job 41:10,[25] Eccl. 12:12, II Chr. 30:17. The last example is especially interesting, as this chapter, which has no parallel in Kings, is specifically concerned with the remnant of Israelians residing in the north during the reign of Hezekiah of Judah. This list points to a northern home for the *qĕṭîlah* form, as was already recognized by M. H. Segal: "The fact that in earlier BH it occurs only in the Song of Deborah and in the story of Elijah may, perhaps, tend to show that it was originally a Northern dialectal form."[26]

5) The 3rd feminine singular perfect of IIIy verbs in MH bears the termination *-āt* (as opposed to BH *-āh*).[27] Historically, the MH ending is

---

[22] C. H. Gordon, "North Israelite Influence on Postexilic Hebrew," *IEJ* 5 (1955), 85–88. This view has been accepted by Kutscher, *History*, 55.

[23] Ibid., 31.

[24] S. Segert, *A Grammar of Phoenician and Punic* (Munich, 1976), 56, 107.

[25] I accept the hypothesis of D. N. Freedman, "Orthographic Peculiarities in the Book of Job," in: *Eretz-Israel*, IX (Jerusalem, 1969), 35–44, esp. p. 43, concerning the northern provenance of the book of Job. In addition, style-switching or code-switching is at work in Job, whereby the author has intentionally colored the language of the book to enhance its non-Judahite setting. See S. A. Kaufman, "The Classification of the North West Semitic Dialects of the Biblical Period and Some Implications Thereof," in: *Proceedings of the Ninth World Congress of Jewish Studies* (Jerusalem, 1988), 55.

[26] Segal, *Grammar*, 103. This statement is absent in his later Hebrew edition.

[27] Idem, *Grammar*, 91–92; Kutscher, *History*, 128; and G. Haneman, *A Morphology of Mishnaic Hebrew* (Tel-Aviv, 1980), 342–343 (Hebrew).

older than its BH counterpart. It appears, therefore, that MH springs from a dialect which preserved this ancient feature.[28] Since the ending -*āt* is standard in Aramaic,[29] northern Israel would be the home of such a dialect. This is borne out by the use of *hyt* in II Kgs. 9:37 in a story set in the Jezreel Valley. Unfortunately, the picture is more complicated. Other IIIy verbs which retain the ending -*āt* in BH appear in Lev. 25:21, 26:34, Jer. 13:19, Ezek. 24:12, and in line 3 of the Siloam Tunnel inscription. The date of Leviticus is a moot point, but the two forms in this book may be explained as archaic survivals. The forms in Jeremiah and Ezekiel may be understood as true Aramaisms, since both of these books have many such examples. The last example is still problematic, since one would not expect to find a form with -*āt* in eighth-century Jerusalemite Hebrew. Do we assume that the scribe was an Israelian who had come south after the fall of Samaria? Or do we assume that this, too, is an Aramaism, based on our knowledge that Jerusalemite officials already knew Aramaic by this time (II Kgs. 18:26 = Isa. 36:11)?[30] Despite these difficulties, I maintain that the ending -*āt* in IIIy verbs was a characteristic of IH which continued into MH.

6) Another common trait of MH is the "double plural" construction, e.g., *rā'šê šānîm*, whereby both *nomen regens* and *nomen rectum* in a construct chain are morphologically plural.[31] S. Gevirtz has noted recently that this grammatical usage is characteristic of Phoenician, Ugaritic, Byblos Amarna texts, and IH.[32] Examples from the Bible are to be found in Gen. 49:23 (blessing to Joseph), Judg. 5:6, 5:10 (Song of Deborah), Pss. 29:1, 45:10, 47:10, 74:13, 77:6, 78:49 (all northern psalms[33]). It is true that double plurals occur elsewhere in the Bible where northern provenance

---

[28] See Kutscher, *History*, 128.

[29] See, e.g., R. Degen, *Altaramäische Grammatik* (Wiesbaden, 1969), 76; and F. Rosenthal, *A Grammar of Biblical Aramaic* (Wiesbaden, 1974), 51, 66.

[30] In more general terms, see Kutscher, *History*, 67.

[31] Segal, *Grammar*, 187; and Kutscher, *History*, 129. Although there are ample illustrations of this usage in Segal, *Grammar* (Hebrew), 97–100, there is no explicit statement concerning the phenomenon.

[32] Gevirtz, "Of Syntax and Style," 28–29; and idem, "Asher in the Blessing of Jacob (Genesis xlix 20)," *VT* 37 (1987), 160.

[33] For full documentation, see Rendsburg, *Psalms*. Also, consult the following references. For Psalm 29: H. L. Ginsberg, "A Phoenician Hymn in the Psalter," in: *Atti del XIX Congresso Internazionale degli Orientalisti (Roma 1935)* (Rome, 1938), 472–476. For Psalm 45: M. Buttenweiser, *The Psalms* (Chicago, 1938), 85–89. For Psalm 47 (within the Koraḥ collection): M. J. Goulder, *The Psalms of the Sons of Korah* (Sheffield, 1982). For Psalms 74, 77, 78 (all within the Asaph collection): M. J. Buss, "The Psalms of Asaph and Korah," *JBL* 82 (1963), 382–392, esp. 384.

is not indicated, e.g., in Chronicles,[34] but the overall picture still favors Gevirtz's conclusion. Accordingly, the use of the double plural is another trait which links MH and northern dialects.

7) The noun *pōᶜēl*, "worker," the active participle from the verbal root *pᶜl*, "work, do," is much more common in MH than it is in BH.[35] This verb is standard in Phoenician,[36] and although the inscriptions are not vocalized it is clear in several instances that *pᶜl* is the active participle meaning "worker."[37] Ugaritic uses the by-form *bᶜl*,[38] and now *pᶜl* is attested in the Deir ᶜAlla texts (Combination I, line 2).[39] In none of these languages, in fact, does the verb *ᶜšy* occur. It therefore may be concluded that *pᶜl* is a northern lexeme. This is borne out by the distribution of this verb in the Bible;[40] a significant proportion of the attestations of *pᶜl* occurs in IH texts such as Hosea (7:10), Job (34:32, 36:23), Proverbs (16:4, 30:20),[41] Deuteronomy 32 (v. 27),[42] the Korah psalms (44:2), and the Asaph psalms (74:12). In addition, one example occurs in the Balaam oracles (Num. 23:23) where style-switching is clearly in effect. In light of this evidence, we are now in a position to answer the question posed by Kutscher: "Is it

34 R. Polzin, *Late Biblical Hebrew: Toward an Historical Typology of Biblical Hebrew Prose* (Missoula, 1976), 42.

35 For a list of occurrences in MH, see C. H. Kasovsky, *Thesaurus Mishnae* (4 vols.; Jerusalem, 1956–60), IV, 1484–1485; idem, *Thesaurus Thosephtae* (6 vols.; New York, 1932–61), V, 565–567; and B. Kosovsky, *Concordantiae Verborum quae in Mechilta D'Rabbi Išmael* (4 vols.; New York, 1967–69), IV, 1493–1494.

36 R. S. Tomback, *A Comparative Semitic Lexicon of the Phoenician and Punic Languages* (Missoula, 1978), 267–268.

37 Ibid. Note examples h), i), j) in Tomback's list.

38 C. H. Gordon, *Ugaritic Textbook* (Rome, 1967), 375.

39 Hackett, *The Balaam Text from Deir ᶜAlla*, 25, 34–35.

40 I exclude from my calculations the construct plural participle *pōᶜălê*, which is quite frequent in the idiom *pōᶜălê ʾāwen*, and the noun *pōᶜal*, "labor, work," which likewise is a common word in the Bible. For similar reasons, A. Hurvitz, "Linguistic Criteria for Dating Problematic Biblical Texts," *Hebrew Abstracts* 14 (1973), 75, excluded *pōᶜălê ʾāwen* from his investigations.

41 For the northern affinities of Proverbs, see W. F. Albright, "Some Canaanite-Phoenician Sources of Hebrew Wisdom," in: *Wisdom in Israel and in the Ancient Near East*, eds. M. Noth and D. W. Thomas (*SVT* 3; Leiden, 1960), 1–15; Ginsberg, *The Israelian Heritage*, 36; and Y. Avishur, *Stylistic Studies of Word-Pairs in Biblical and Ancient Semitic Literatures* (*AOAT* 210; Neukirchen-Vluyn, 1984), 440 and n. 6.

42 On the northern provenance of this poem, see O. Eissfeldt, *Das Lied Moses Deuteronomium 32.1–43 und das Lehrgedicht Asaphs Psalm 78 samt einer Analyse der Umgebung des Mose-Liedes* (Berlin, 1958), 42; and E. Nielsen, "Historical Perspectives and Geographical Horizons: On the Question of North-Israelite Elements in Deuteronomy," *ASTI* 11 (1977–78), 82.

possible that here, too, we should look for its origin in Canaanite where it is employed as a standard root?"[43] The answer is yes, with the qualification that it is specifically a northern Canaanite trait.

8) The verbal root *ṣrk*, "need," is very common in MH.[44] In BH it appears only once, in II Chr. 2:15, but its context—a letter sent by King Hiram of Tyre to Solomon—is most significant. The root *ṣrk* has not yet been found in a Phoenician inscription,[45] but the evidence nonetheless points to the northern home of this verb. The widespread use of this root in Aramaic dialects supports this conclusion.[46]

9) The syntagma of *hyh* + participle, sometimes called the progressive tense, is a distinctively MH usage.[47] It appears commonly in Aramaic,[48] and in the Bible it appears frequently in northern settings. II Sam. 3:6, 17 concern Avner of the house of Saul; I Kgs. 22:35, II Kgs. 6:8, 17:33 (twice), 41, and II Chr. 18:34 all concern the northern kingdom of Israel; Job 1:14 is in a non-Judahite setting.[49] This evidence permits us to view this construction as a grammatical feature linking Israelian and Aramean territory.[50] The region in which MH developed is to be located within this area as well.

10) The verbal root *nwm*, "speak" in MH,[51] is to be identified with BH *nʾm*. In the former, *nwm* is simply an ordinary word for "speak," an alternate to the usual verb *ʾmr*. In the Bible, *nʾm* is restricted to Divine

43 Kutscher, *History*, 135.

44 Kasovsky, *Thesaurus Mishnae*, IV, 1534–1536; idem, *Thesaurus Thosephtae*, VI, 32–38; Kosovsky, *Concordantiae Verborum quae in Mechilta*, IV, 1537–1538; and M. Moreshet, *A Lexicon of the New Verbs in the Tannaitic Hebrew* (Ramat-Gan, 1980), 312–313 (Hebrew).

45 According to Kutscher, *History*, 136, *ṣrk* occurs in Ugaritic, but this is most doubtful. J. Aistleitner, *Wörterbuch der ugaritischen Sprache* (Berlin, 1967), 270, included an entry for this word, which he translated as "versagen," but his lone example is spurious. The form *yṣrk* in 1 Aqht 43 is almost certainly the 3rd person masculine singular imperfect of the root *ṣrr* with the 2nd person masculine singular pronominal suffix -*k*, to be translated, "may he [Baal] afflict you."

46 See the convenient survey by Moreshet, *Lexicon*, 313, n. 18**.

47 Segal, *Grammar*, 156; and Segal, *Grammar* (Hebrew), 182.

48 See the survey by J. C. Greenfield, "The 'Periphrastic Imperative' in Aramaic and Hebrew," *IEJ* 19 (1969), 206–207.

49 The many examples in post-exilic books (Dan. 8:5, 7; 10:2, 9; Neh. 3:26, 5:18, 6:14, 19 [twice]) are to be considered true Aramaisms.

50 For discussion of this phenomenon and other examples of it, see C. Rabin, "The Emergence of Classical Hebrew," in: *The Age of the Monarchies: Culture and Society*, ed. A. Malamat (Jerusalem, 1979), 72.

51 Kasovsky, *Thesaurus Mishnae*, III, 1188; idem, *Thesaurus Thosephtae*, V, 36; and Moreshet, *Lexicon*, 223–224.

speech, except in four instances—all in northern contexts. The four places where *nʾm* is predicated of humans are Num. 24:3–4, 15–16, both in the Balaam oracles; II Sam. 23:1, in a poem of undoubtedly northern origin;[52] Ps. 36:2, in a poem with other IH characteristics;[53] and Prov. 30:1, in words ascribed to Agur of Massa, located by most authorities in the Syrian Desert.[54] Accordingly, the use of *nwm* for human speech in MH is to be explained as a feature of a northern dialect.

11) In MH the plural construct of *yôm*, "day," is usually *yĕmê*, but the alternative form *yĕmôt* appears quite frequently.[55] This latter form is standard in Phoenician,[56] suggesting that *yĕmôt* is a northern usage.[57] Support for this conclusion is found in the fact that one of the two biblical attestations of *yĕmôt*, in a poem in Deut. 32:7,[58] is widely believed to be northern in origin.[59]

12) The MH Nitpaʿal is often used in a passive sense.[60] The corresponding BH Hitpaʿel has this meaning in only three instances (Mic. 6:16, Prov. 31:30, Eccl. 8:10),[61] all in northern contexts. The first of these is from a southern prophet, but this verse specifically mentions Omri and Ahab; the latter two appear in northern compositions, as noted above. It is most

---

52 See above, n. 14.

53 For full treatment, see Rendsburg, *Psalms*, 39–43. Note the comment of C. A. Briggs, *A Critical and Exegetical Commentary on the Book of Psalms*, I (ICC; New York, 1906), 315: "The author of v. 7 was familiar with Lebanon and Hermon and the Mediterranean Sea, and possibly had his home in northwestern Galilee, where these were in view."

54 See, for example, I. Ephʿal, *The Ancient Arabs* (Jerusalem, 1982), 218–219.

55 Kasovsky, *Thesaurus Mishnae*, II, 846; idem, *Thesaurus Thosephtae*, III, 499–501; and Kosovsky, *Concordantiae Verborum quae in Mechilta*, III, 929.

56 Tomback, *Phoenician and Punic*, 125.

57 For a different explanation, see Kutscher, *History*, 134.

58 The second attestation is in Ps. 90:15. Since there is no concentration of IH features in this psalm, it cannot be considered a northern composition. There is another IH characteristic, the use of the root *nʿm*, "pleasant, good"; see Rendsburg, "Additional Notes on 'The Last Words of David'," esp. p. 407, n. 38, but this is insufficient to ascribe northern provenance to Psalm 90. The form *yĕmôt* was used in Ps. 90:15, probably to evoke a similar sound to the form *šĕnôt*, "years of," in the next stich. One might compare the manner in which American poets occasionally employ British usages (lorry = "truck," lift = "elevator," flat = "apartment," etc.) for metrical or rhyming purposes.

59 See above, n. 42.

60 Segal, *Grammar*, 67.

61 E. Kautzsch, *Gesenius' Hebrew Grammar* (Oxford, 1910), 150. Only two of the three examples are cited there; perhaps Mic. 6:16 is excluded because it is often emended by critics. See D. R. Hillers, *Micah* (Philadelphia, 1984), 81, note s.

probable, therefore, that the passive connotation of the Nitpaʿal/Hitpaʿel conjugation was a feature of northern Hebrew reflected in both MH and IH.

These twelve points of morphology, syntax, and vocabulary are a representative sampling of the nexuses linking MH and IH.[62] To these points may be added the larger issue of the relationship between MH and Aramaic. Scholars have noted previously the strong Aramaic coloring of MH. While many of these judgments have been grossly exaggerated, it is obvious that MH has more ties to Aramaic than does BH. This phenomenon, however, is not to be attributed to any Aramaic influence over MH, rather it is the result of dialect geography. IH/MH was used in a region of Israel with close ties to Aramean and Phoenician territory. Accordingly, the isoglosses, which may be traced on a map, will frequently link IH/MH with Aramaic and Phoenician to the exclusion of standard BH (= JH). These data point to the Galilean origin of Mishnaic Hebrew, which should not be surprising given the Galilean provenance of the Mishnah itself. Moreover, this also explains the "striking points of contact" between MH and Punic (a North African branch of Phoenician) noted by J. T. Milik.[63]

While it is true that IH is attested mainly before 721 B.C.E. and that MH is attested only from ca. 200 C.E. onward, we simply have very little evidence of northern language in the millennium which separates these two dates (an exception would be Nehemiah 9, on which see below, n. 67). Indeed, "we hear very little about further developments on the territory of the state of Israel after the fall of Samaria."[64] But there are sufficient clues in the Bible and elsewhere to support our assumption that Israelians continued to populate the region even after 721 B.C.E. A sketch of the evidence follows.

---

[62] I am inclined to view the data presented by B. A. Levine, "Survivals of Ancient Canaanite in the Mishnah" (doctoral dissertation, Brandeis University; Waltham, 1962), and J. C. Greenfield, "Amurrite, Ugaritic, and Canaanite," in: *Proceedings of the International Conference on Semitic Studies* (Jerusalem, 1969), 99, as further support for the Galilean background of MH. Even though Ugaritic words serve as the springboard for these avenues of research, as noted above, n. 12, Ugaritic and Phoenician are to be classified together within Northwest Semitic.

[63] J. T. Milik, *Ten Years of Discovery in the Wilderness of Judaea* (Naperville, 1959), 131.

[64] S. Herrmann, *A History of Israel in Old Testament Times* (Philadelphia, 1981), 252.

First of all, the annals of Sargon II inform us that only 27,290 inhabitants of Samaria were exiled.[65] This relatively small number suggests that a large population remained behind. Secondly, stories such as those in II Chr. 30 and Jer. 41:4–5 imply that Israelians continued to dwell in their homeland and were even loyal to Jerusalem.[66] Thirdly, the survey of history in Neh. 9:5–37 is written from the perspective of a northerner some years after the fall of Samaria, as can be seen in the expression, "from the days of the kings of Assyria unto this day" (v. 32).[67] Finally, our post-biblical sources (e.g., Josephus) attest to the existence of a substantial Jewish population in the Galilee and Samaria but give no impression that they migrated there from Judah. Accordingly, despite the fact that II Kgs. 17:24 refers to the transfer of Mesopotamians to Samaria, and notwithstanding the complex problem of the origin of the Samaritans, "it can be stated with assurance that the Assyrians did not annihilate the Israelite population of the North, and that the rural population of Samaria and Galilee remained and continued to exist."[68] Furthermore, we may assume, having no evidence to the contrary, that IH continued to be used in the region and that MH was its eventual successor.

To return now to matters of linguistics. From the list of twelve features which link IH and MH, it must be stressed that IH and MH are not identical. As stated at the outset, not only did regional varieties of ancient Hebrew exist, but diglossia did as well. I believe, as did earlier scholars in the field of Hebrew linguistics, that IH (as part of what we call BH) was a literary dialect and that MH was a colloquial one. One important point should suffice to illustrate the distinction between the two: the consecutive tenses were characteristic of the written dialect,

---

[65] A. L. Oppenheim, "Babylonian and Assyrian Historical Texts," in: *Ancient Near Eastern Texts Relating to the Old Testament*, ed. J. B. Pritchard (Princeton, 1969), 284–285.

[66] Concerning II Chr. 30, I agree with J. Bright, *A History of Israel* (Philadelphia, 1972), 281, that "there is no reason whatever to question the historicity of this incident."

[67] The northern provenance of Neh. 9 was first posited by A. C. Welch, "The Source of Nehemiah IX," *ZAW* 47 (1929), 130–137. Welch, however, assumed that the text came from ca. 721 B.C.E., probably because he never considered the possibility of a continued Israelian presence in the northern part of the country. See G. A. Rendsburg, "The Northern Origin of Nehemiah 9," *Biblica* (forthcoming), where the linguistic evidence to support Welch's northern hypothesis will be presented.

[68] S. Japhet, "People and Land in the Restoration Period," in: *Das Land Israel in biblischer Zeit*, ed. G. Strecker (Göttingen, 1983), 103–125, esp. 105. I thank Professor Japhet for bringing this article to my attention.

northern (IH) or southern (JH), but they were not used in spoken Hebrew (e.g., MH).[69]

Similarities and differences between IH and MH can be understood only within the larger picture of Hebrew dialectology. Accordingly, I conclude with a brief presentation of the different varieties of ancient Hebrew known to date (see Figure 2). We may distinguish a southern literary dialect (JH) and a northern literary dialect (IH) in the biblical period.[70] About 80 per cent of the Bible is written in the former, but we are able to isolate texts composed in the latter. In contrast to these written regional varieties were the spoken dialects of Eretz-Israel, which are obviously much harder to reconstruct, though sufficient colloquialisms have penetrated the biblical corpus to afford us a glance at ancient spoken Hebrew.[71]

We have determined that MH was a spoken dialect native to the northern region of Israel in the post-biblical period, or late antiquity. Little can be said about the written dialect of the north. It is possible, however, that the language of certain prose tales imbedded in rabbinic literature (e.g., the story of the sons of Levi in M Yevamot 16:7) represents the written dialect of the north, especially since these stories include grammatical features (infinitive absolute, consecutive tenses, etc.) more reminiscent of BH than of MH.[72]

In the southern part of the country, particularly in Jerusalem, we assume a continuation of JH, especially in its LBH garb. Unfortunately, we have no demonstrably Jerusalemite texts from the first century C.E. by which to test this assumption. QH, with its many links to BH, especially

---

69 On this dichotomy, see G. A. Rendsburg, "Diglossia in Ancient Hebrew as Revealed Through Compound Verbs," in: *Bono Homini Donum: Essays in Historical Linguistics in Memory of J. Alexander Kerns*, eds. Y .L. Arbeitman and A. R. Bomhard (Amsterdam, 1981), 665–677. The discussion of the progressive tense there needs alteration in light of the present article.

70 Even this is an oversimplification. Presumably there were many local varieties: Galilean, Ephraimite, Gileadite, Benjaminite, Judahite, Negevite, etc. But given the information at our disposal, it is sufficient and convenient to distinguish two main regional standards: JH and IH.

71 The data are assembled in Rendsburg, *Disglossia in Ancient Hebrew*.

72 For discussion of these stories, though without any assignment of them to a northern literary dialect, see C. Rabin, "The Historical Background of Qumran Hebrew," in: *Aspects of the Dead Sea Scrolls*, eds. C. Rabin and Y. Yadin (*Scripta Hierosolymitana*, IV; Jerusalem, 1965), 155–156; and Rabin, "Hebrew and Aramaic in the First Century," 1015–1017.

LBH, is obviously a literary dialect of the southern part of the country, but one hesitates to equate it with the regional standard of Jerusalem.[73]

The spoken language of the southern region of Israel is another enigma and should perhaps be associated with such texts as the Copper Scroll (3Q15) and Miqṣat Maʿaśe ha-Torah (= MMT) (4Q394–399) from Qumran and the Bar-Kokhba letters. The language of these texts is similar to MH but not identical with it.[74] The minor differences which separate the Copper Scroll, MMT, and the Bar-Kokhba letters from the language of the Mishnah are probably due to regional variation.[75] The linguistic cantonization of Eretz-Israel assumed for the biblical period no doubt continued into late antiquity as well. Rabbinic literature itself advises us of local variations;[76] it is also important to recall Jerome's observation about the Hebrew he encountered in Eretz-Israel ca. 400 C.E.: "According to the discretion of readers and the different regions the same word is pronounced with different sounds and accents."[77]

---

[73] This is the most important conclusion I derive from Morag, "Qumran Hebrew: Some Typological Observations."

[74] On the Copper Scroll, see J. T. Milik, "Le rouleau de cuivre provenant de la grotte 3Q (3Q15)," in: *Les 'petites grottes' de Qumrân*, eds. M. Baillet, J .T. Milik, and R. de Vaux (*DJD*, III; Oxford, 1962), 221–225. This material should be read in conjunction with the important review article by J. C. Greenfield, "The Small Caves of Qumran," *JAOS* 89 (1969), 136–137. A full treatment of MMT is still forthcoming; in the meantime, see E. Qimron and J. Strugnell, "An Unpublished Halakhic Letter from Qumran," in: *Biblical Archaeology Today* (Jerusalem, 1985), 404–406. On the Bar-Kokhba letters, see E. Y. Kutscher, "The Language of the Hebrew and Aramaic Letters of Bar Kosiba and his Contemporaries, Second Study: The Hebrew Letters," *Leshonenu* 26 (1961), 7–23 (Hebrew); idem, *History*, 142.

[75] This was recognized by Milik, *Les 'petites grottes'*, 222, who considered the language of the Copper Scroll to be an "hébreu populaire, parlé effectivement par les Juifs résidant en Judée, au sud-ouest et au sud de la Palestine, ainsi que dans la vallée du Jourdain."

[76] See Kutscher, *History*, 141–142.

[77] Quoted by Kutscher, ibid., 142.

Excursus on Ecclesiastes and Song of Songs

As a result of this study, I propose a compromise position regarding the language of Ecclesiastes and Song of Songs. Dahood argued for a northern provenance of Ecclesiastes on the basis of the many affinities between the book and Phoenician.[78] He was challenged, in many ways correctly, by R. Gordis, who claimed that the language of Ecclesiastes was closer to MH than it was to Phoenician.[79] The same conclusion was reached by Bendavid.[80] In light of the above, I claim that both views are correct. The Hebrew of Ecclesiastes is similar to *both* Phoenician and MH because all three comprise what we may tentatively label the Israelian-Phoenician dialect bundle. A very similar conclusion was reached independently by Davila.[81] D. C. Fredericks also argued for a northern origin of Ecclesiastes but placed it in pre-exilic times, presumably because he did not take into consideration the possibility of Israelians remaining in Eretz-Israel in post-exilic times.[82]

There has been less controversy concerning Song of Songs, but we may contrast the view of Driver and Avishur favoring a northern origin[83] with that of Bendavid favoring connections with MH.[84] Again, the Hebrew of Song of Songs may be *both* northern and close to MH, in light of the Israelian-Phoenician dialect bundle.

---

[78] Dahood, "Canaanite-Phoenician Influence."

[79] R. Gordis, "Was Koheleth a Phoenician?" *JBL* 74 (1955), 103–114.

[80] Bendavid, *Biblical Hebrew and Mishnaic Hebrew*, 77–80.

[81] Davila, "Qoheleth and Northern Hebrew."

[82] D. C. Fredericks, *Qoheleth's Language: Re-evaluating Its Nature and Date* (Lewiston, NY, 1988).

[83] See above, n. 19.

[84] Bendavid, *Biblical Hebrew and Mishnaic Hebrew*, 74–76.

Fig. 1: Summary of MH Features and Their Cognates

MH Features	IH	Phoenician	Aramaic	Other
1. relative pronoun *še-*	*še-*	*ʾš*	—	Ammonite: *ʾš* Deir ʿAlla: *ʾš* (?)
2. fem. sg. demonstrative pronoun *zô*	*zô(h)*	*z(ʾ)*	*zʾ*	—
3. plural demonstrative pronoun *ʾēllû*	—	Plautus: *ily*	—	—
4. *qĕṭîlah* form	*qĕṭîlah*	—	—	—
5. 3rd fem. sg. perfect of IIIy verbs in *-āt*	*-āt*	—	*-āt*	—
6. "double plural" construction	dbl. pl.	dbl. pl.	—	Ugaritic: dbl. pl. Amarna: dbl. pl.
7. root *pˁl*, "work, do"	*pˁl*	*pˁl*	—	Deir ʿAlla: *pˁl* Ugaritic: *bˁl*
8. root *ṣrk*, "need"	—	(see Other)	*ṣrk*	II Chr. 2:15: *ṣrk*
9. *hyh* + participle	*hyh* + part.	—	*hyh* + part.	—
10. root *nwm*, "speak"	*nʾm*	—	—	—
11. plural construct *yĕmôt*, "days"	*yĕmôt*	*ymt*	—	—
12. Nitpaʿal in passive sense	Hitpaʿel in passive sense	—	—	—

Fig. 2: Varieties of Ancient Hebrew

	BIBLICAL		POST-BIBLICAL	
	Spoken	Written	Spoken	Written
N O R T H	isolated colloquialisms	IH	MH	isolated stories (e.g., M Yevamot 16:7)
S O U T H	isolated colloquialisms	JH	MMT Copper Scroll Bar-Kokhba	JH? QH?

The Aramaic Targum as a Mirror of Galilean Jewry

AVIGDOR SHINAN

A comprehensive description of any society, which is essential for a full understanding of the socio-historical and cultural events of a people in a specific area, may be obtained through the study of the historical and legal documents, archeological evidence, and, to a lesser degree, literary works of the period. Using literature (poems, stories, sermons, parables, and the like) for this purpose requires careful and sensitive treatment of texts, taking into consideration such factors as their form, purpose, language, mode of speech, audience, and so forth. Ancient Jewish literature is no exception.

The literature of Galilean Jewry in late antiquity and thereafter (from the fourth–fifth to the seventh–eighth centuries) is composed of various groups of texts, originating in at least two different centers of cultural and literary activity: the house of learning (*bet midrash*) and the synagogue (*bet knesset*). The distinction between the two institutions is not physical—in many places, especially in small villages, the same building served as both—but functional, each serving different needs for different audiences. The *bet midrash* served primarily the learned men, rabbis, and their students, those who devoted most of their time to study, developing the halakha, and discussing theological and moral issues. The gates of the *bet midrash* were almost never closed to the general public, yet the people's presence there was casual and what transpired therein had little impact upon them. The *bet midrash* in the Galilee produced most of the material found in the Palestinian Talmud and in numerous midrashim, such as Leviticus Rabbah,[1] Pesiqta de-Rav Kahana,[2] and others. The synagogue, on the other hand—as its Hebrew (*bet knesset*), Aramaic (*kenishta*), and Greek (*synagoge*) names imply—was a place of gathering, where all segments of society took an active and significant part in its activities.

The synagogue in the late rabbinic period produced four kinds of texts: (1) a vast liturgical literature which later became the core of the Jewish prayerbook;[3] (2) thousands of *piyyutim*, which were composed mainly as poetical substitutes for part of the regular prayer;[4] (3) the translations of Scriptures into Aramaic (the Targums), primarily those biblical units that were read in public,[5] e.g., the Pentateuch, certain chapters from the Prophets, and the five scrolls; (4) different types of public sermons, the best known of which is the Proem (*petihta*),[6] which were eventually incorporated into the talmudic-midrashic corpus side by side with material that originated in the *bet midrash*. In short, the Palestinian Talmud, midrashim, Targums, prayers, and *piyyutim* were the main components of Galilean literature in late antiquity. Surely, the learned circles of rabbis, teachers, and scribes, who had both the knowledge and the means, were responsible for creating these texts.

Where, then, can we find the literary heritage of the *common people*—those in the markets and in the fields, farmers as well as small craftsmen, uneducated men and women? Where can we learn about their stories and songs, proverbs and fables, words of wisdom and jokes? The masses undoubtedly had their own literary traditions: grandmothers in Tiberias

---

1 On the Galilean origin of this midrash, see M. Margulies, ed., *Leviticus Rabbah* (5 vols.; Jerusalem, 1960), V: *Introduction, Supplements and Indices*, xxvii–xxxi (Hebrew).

2 The Pesiqta was composed in Palestine. See *Pĕsiḳta dĕ-Raḇ Kahăna*, trans. by W. G. Braude and I. J. Kapstein (Philadelphia, 1975), xlvi. Its close relationship to Leviticus Rabbah (ibid., xlix–li) also points to a Galilean origin.

3 Galilean prayers from the period under discussion are recorded in the Palestinian Talmud and midrashim and are found—although later—in the Babylonian geonic prayerbooks and scattered manuscripts, most of them originating in the Cairo Genizah. See E. Fleischer, *Eretz-Israel Prayer and Prayer Rituals* (Jerusalem, 1988) (Hebrew).

4 Such as the poetical compositions of Yannai, who lived in the Galilee (Tiberias?) in the fifth–sixth centuries. See Z. M. Rabinovitz, *The Liturgical Poems of Rabbi Yannai* (2 vols.; Jerusalem, 1985–87) (Hebrew).

5 See below for a discussion of the Galilean origin of the Targums.

6 See J. Heinemann, "The Proem in the Aggadic Midrashim – A Form-Critical Study," *Scripta Hierosolymitana* 22 (1971), 100–122. The Galilean midrashim (cf. above, nn. 1 and 2) preserve dozens of proems attributed to sages from different parts of the Galilee.

sang to their grandchildren, and shepherds sitting around the fire on chilly Galilean nights shared witty stories. This literature, which was transmitted orally outside the walls of the *bet midrash* and the synagogue, was recorded only randomly and very partially in talmudic-midrashic literature. Sometimes we find an Aramaic proverb preceded by the phrase, "that is what the people used to say";[7] at other times we come across a story exhibiting some of the literary and linguistic features frequently found in folktales.[8] Here and there some popular beliefs are recorded, and from time to time one comes across evidence of a popular custom,[9] but, on the whole, there is little doubt that most of the popular literature was never recorded and thus disappeared into oblivion. While the literary activity of the *bet midrash* and the synagogue is strongly represented in our sources, the literature and culture of the general populace are, unfortunately, hardly at hand and are sorely felt in any attempt to portray Galilean Jewry in late antiquity.

In an effort to overcome this deficiency we should examine the so-called "Palestinian" Aramaic translations (the Targums[10]) of the Bible, especially those of the Pentateuch, which, more than any other text created in the synagogue or the *bet midrash*, were consciously directed toward the masses. Scholars have never seriously questioned this hypothesis,[11] which is a cornerstone of targumic studies, although it seems to be somewhat romanticized and oversimplified. This view is not expressed in rabbinic literature itself but in geonic literature, for example in Rav Hai Gaon's definition of Targum Esther as a "targum of the common people,"[12] and later in Rashi's famous statement that the

---

[7] See, for example, B Taʿanit 23a; B Bava Qamma 92b; Genesis Rabbah 86:7.

[8] See, for example, the ten stories discussed by D. Noy, "Galilean Folk Stories," *Mahanaim* 101 (1968), 18–25 (Hebrew).

[9] For but a few of the many examples, see S. Lieberman, "Jewish Life in Eretz-Israel as Reflected in the Palestinian Talmud," in his *Texts and Studies* (New York, 1974), 180–190.

[10] The targumic texts discussed in this article are as follows: *Frg. Tg.*: M. L. Klein, *The Fragment Targums of the Pentateuch* (Rome, 1980); *M. Neof.*: The marginal notes in the ms. of Targum Neofiti I; *Tg. Ps.-J.*: E. E. Clarke, *Targum Pseudo-Jonathan of the Pentateuch – Text and Concordance* (Hoboken, 1984); *Tg. G.*: Genizah fragments of Targums, according to M. L. Klein, *Genizah Manuscripts of Palestinian Targums to the Pentateuch* (2 vols.; Cincinnati, 1986); *Tg. Neof.*: A. Diez Macho, *Neophiti 1* (Madrid/Barcelona, 1968–79).

[11] For a summary, see A. Shinan, *The Aggadah in the Aramaic Targums to the Pentateuch* (Jerusalem, 1979), 26–29 (Hebrew).

[12] See M. H. Goshen-Gottstein, "The Third Targum on Esther and Ms. Neofiti 1," *Biblica* 56 (1975), 303.

"targum is meant to be heard by women and the common people."[13] This hypothesis was accepted and has been explicitly stated more than once by scholars of targumic literature who use it to explain different phenomena in the Targums, such as its tendency not to translate some verses in order to preserve the honor of the Patriarchs[14] or its treatment of various theological questions, such as the various epithets assigned to God.[15] A specific midrashic statement could have been directed toward the well-defined circle of students in the *bet midrash*, but a targumic saying had to be understood *prima facie* by the masses. True, the Targums cannot be described as popular literature par excellence; after all, these texts were composed by learned men in the religious atmosphere of the synagogue. Their status as popular literature is granted by virtue of their audience .

The geographical region and historical setting in which these texts were composed and flourished are yet another consideration. The phenomenon of the Aramaic Targum is, of course, very early and can be traced back to the Second Temple period,[16] while the extant manuscripts of Targum are relatively late: a few were copied as early as the ninth century, but most of them—and especially the more extensive ones— were copied or edited in the fourteenth and as late as the sixteenth centuries.[17] We are therefore confronted with one of the most complicated issues in targumic studies, that of dating each targumic tradition individually and each targum corpus as a whole.[18] The fact that the targumic texts underwent all kinds of changes and emendations in the process of transmission places yet another obstacle before the scholar wishing to set any targumic tradition in a specific time or setting. Scholars agree, however, that these texts were in use primarily before Arabic replaced Aramaic as the vernacular, a process which took place in Palestine during the seventh and

13 Rashi to B Megillah 21b.

14 See M. Ginsburger, "Verbotene Thargumim," *MGWJ* 44 (1900), 1–7; P. S. Alexander, "The Rabbinic Lists of Forbidden Targumim," *JJS* 27 (1976), 177–191; M. L. Klein, "Not to be Translated in Public – לא מתרגם בציבורא," *JJS* 39 (1988), 80–91.

15 See the material gathered by A. Chester, *Divine Revelation and Divine Titles in the Pentateuchal Targumim* (Tübingen, 1986). See also below, n. 45.

16 See Y. Komlosh, *The Bible in the Light of the Aramaic Translations* (Tel-Aviv, 1973), 17–18 (Hebrew).

17 Regarding the only manuscript of Tg. Ps.-J., see E. Levine, "British Museum Additional Aramaic Ms. 27031," *Manuscripta* 16 (1972), 3–13. Regarding Tg. Neof., see, for example, Goshen-Gottstein, "The Third Targum."

18 For a systematic treatment of this issue, see A. D. York, "The Dating of Targumic Literature," *JSJ* 5 (1974), 49–62.

eighth centuries. Moreover, there is no basis for dating any targumic texts *a priori* earlier than the fourth century, mainly because of the date of the sources used by the Targums. The core of the Targum texts may therefore be dated between the fourth and eighth centuries.[19] Since the Palestinian origin of these texts is unquestionable, as proven by their language and other internal hints, there is little doubt that they were composed in the Galilee, the only region in Palestine at the time where the flourishing Jewish community could produce such texts.

If all the above-mentioned assumptions are correct, i.e., that these texts are remnants of the activity in the Galilean synagogues of late antiquity intended mainly for the Jewish community at large, then the Targum texts may contribute to our knowledge of Galilean Jewish life at the time, as demonstrated in the following pages.

Popular Customs and Beliefs

References to popular customs and beliefs, some of them superstitions, are to be found in the Targums where additional text accompanies the translation of the various verses. Such, for example, is the targumic rendering of Deut. 24:6: "A handmill or an upper millstone shall not be taken in pawn, for that would be taking someone's life in pawn."[20] The preceding verse concerns a man who takes a bride and is therefore exempt from military service for one year. The juxtaposition of these two laws is probably the basis for the Targum's understanding of our verse as dealing with the newlywed as well: "My people, My people, O Israelites,[21] you shall not take in pawn a handmill or an upper millstone, for that is taking in pawn the requisites of life; nor shall you bind grooms and brides, for anyone who does these things denies life in the world to

---

19 Dating the core of the extant targumic texts to the fourth–eighth centuries does not, of course, exclude the possibility of finding an ancient targumic tradition here and there, such as Tg. Ps.-J. to Deut. 33:11; see R. Syren, *The Blessing in the Targums* (Abo, 1986), 165–166. The possibility of a late addition should also not be overlooked.

20 For recent literature on the Targums to this verse, see A. Shinan, "Miracles, Wonders and Magic in the Aramaic Targums to the Pentateuch," in: *Isaac Leo Seeligmann Volume* (2 vols.; Jerusalem, 1983), II, 424–425 (Hebrew). See also B. B. Levy, *Targum Neophyti 1: A Textual Study* (2 vols.; Lanham, 1987), II, 262–263.

21 This formula (ʿami ʿami bene yisraʾel), or a similar one, is found dozens of times throughout the Palestinian Targums, frequently at the beginning of a halakhic ruling, which is directed toward the common Jew, not only judges and courts. A list of verses which are preceded by this formula is found in: M. M. Kasher, *Torah Shelemah*, XXXV (Jerusalem, 1983), 154–160 (Hebrew).

come."[22] Most commentators of Targum agree that this addition hints at a popular belief in or custom of using some kind of witchcraft for preventing the groom from fulfilling his marital obligations on the first night or nights of his marriage. Such a magical technique is not mentioned in the vast talmudic-midrashic literature but is attested, as scholars have noted, in a geonic responsum in which someone explains his inability to cohabit by being "tied."[23] This custom seems to have been one of many superstitions concerning the wedding ceremony and the first night and was most probably still in practice at the time of the Targum's composition. This explains its probable emotional appeal to its listeners to refrain from such a habit lest they risk their share in the world to come.

Some other popular customs or beliefs found in the Targums are:[24] the fetus in his mother's womb lives in water mixed with fire (Num. 12:12); a woman may have a miscarriage if she hears a terrifying noise (Gen. 44:18); the appropriate use of a spell could extinguish a fire (Gen. 11:28); uttering the Divine Name could enable man to fly, uncover secrets, and be saved from all dangers (Num. 31:8 and Exod. 28:30); rivers from the Garden of Eden still yield precious stones (Exod. 14:9); swarms of ants come out of the body of a murdered man and march straight to the house of the murderer, thus revealing his identity (Deut. 21:8); the "one who casts spells" can protect from snakes and scorpions (Deut. 18:11). This list is by no means exhaustive,[25] but suffices to demonstrate the treasure of folk-beliefs incorporated in the targumic literature. Many of these traditions are well known from other ancient (including Greco-Roman) and even contemporary societies, and this fact indeed strengthens the argument for their popular origin.

The last tradition we shall mention in this context is a peculiar one, found only in the Tg. Ps.-J. to Gen. 31:19: "and Rachel stole her father's household idols." The Targum finds it necessary to explain the nature of the "household idols" (*terafim*):[26] "They used to slaughter a first-born, cut off his head and marinate it with salt and spices and then they used to

22 Cf. ms. Paris of Frg. Tg. as well as Tg. Neof., M. Neof., and Tg. Ps.-J.

23 The text was published by L. Ginzberg, *Geonica*, II (New York, 1909), 152.

24 For the sake of brevity, references in the following paragraph are according to biblical verse and not the various Targums.

25 See A. Shinan, "Folk Elements in the Pseudo-Jonathan Targum," in: *Studies in Aggadah and Jewish Folklore . . . Presented to . . . D. Noy*, eds. I. Ben-Ami and J. Dan (Jerusalem, 1983), 155 (Hebrew).

26 See J. Dan, "Teraphim: From Popular Belief to a Folktale," *Scripta Hierosolymitana* 27 (1978), 99–106.

write magic words on a golden plate and put it under its tongue and hang it on the wall and it would talk to them." As this tradition is also found in some midrashim,[27] the question is raised whether we are dealing here with an ancient and fossilized literary tradition shared by these sources or with evidence for a popular belief (practice?) in daily life which was still known to the Targum and its audience. It is almost impossible to answer this question but, in any case, the existence of such a tradition in a targumic text offers a glimpse at the people before whom it was delivered.

This last tradition raises two methodological problems. The first deals with the origin of traditions—in rabbinic literature as well as in the Targums—which do not pronounce themselves as popular: how can we distinguish in these cases between a tradition that was taken from the vast treasure of folk-beliefs and a tradition which was created by a skilled writer, who might have used his imagination to make his work more appealing to his listeners or readers? We must therefore differentiate between three types of traditions: (1) those which are unique to the Targums,[28] (2) those which are recorded in the Talmuds and midrashim only, and (3) those which are found in both corpora of sources. The methodological rule to be followed in treating this problem is that traditions which are found only in the targumic literature should be treated as popular in origin, unless otherwise proven; traditions which are recorded only in the Talmuds and midrashim should be considered as non-popular in origin, unless otherwise proven; the traditions shared by the Targums and the talmudic-midrashic literature must be discussed without any bias. Most scholars and commentators assume that in the above-mentioned cases the Targums derived their ideas from the midrash, but this is a hasty and unsubstantiated assumption.

The second methodological issue concerns the fact that the description of the "household idols" (*terafim*) and some other traditions designated as "popular" are recorded only in the relatively late Tg. Ps.-J. We will not discuss here the nature, date, and origin of this targumic text, which abounds in accretions on the biblical story and which, more than

---

[27] Such as Midrash Tanḥuma or Pirke de-Rabbi Eliezer. See L. Ginzberg, *Legends of the Jews* (7 vols.; reprint, Philadelphia, 1954), V, 301, n. 218.

[28] For a partial list of unparalleled targumic traditions, see M. M. Broyer, "Studies in Targum Pseudo-Jonathan" (doctoral dissertation, Yeshiva University; New York, 1950), 82–91; for one example, see below, n. 31.

any other Targum, demonstrates popular characteristics.[29] Suffice it to say that the Tg. Ps.-J. should be dealt with very cautiously; nonetheless, for our purposes this text is found to be most useful and very rich.[30]

Linguistic Usage

The linguistic usage peculiar to the Targum texts also better acquaints us with Galilean Jewry of late antiquity. For example, the term *lishan bet qudsha* (לישן בית קודשא, "the language of the sanctuary") appears sixteen times in the targumic texts:

(1)   Gen. 2:19 (Tg. Neof.) – the first man, Adam, gave the animals their names in *lishan bet qudsha*.[31]

(2)   Gen. 11:1 (Tg. Neof., M. Neof., Frg. Tg., Tg. Ps.-J.) – the world was created by God in *lishan bet qudsha*.[32]

(3–8)   Gen. 22:1 (Tg. Neof.), 22:11 (Frg. Tg., M. Neof.), 31:11 (Tg. G., p. 55; Frg. Tg., M. Neof.), 37:13 (fragment published by M. Klein, *Sefarad* 49 [1989], 131), 46:2 (Tg. Neof.), Exod. 3:4 (Tg. Neof.) – In these six verses the Hebrew word *hineni* (הנני, "here I am") is translated: ". . . answered in *lishan bet qudsha* and said, *hineni*."

(9)   Gen. 31:46 (M. Neof.) – "Jacob said to his brothers" is translated, "and Jacob said to his sons, whom he called in *lishan bet qudsha* 'his brothers'."[33]

(10–12) Gen. 31:47 (Tg. G., p. 63; Tg. Neof., Tg. Ps.-J.), 32:2 (Tg. Ps.-J.), 35:18 (Frg. Tg., Tg. Neof.) – In these three verses a place or a person is given a Hebrew name; the Targum indicates this by saying that the name was given in *lishan bet qudsha*.[34]

(13)   Gen. 42:23 (Frg. Tg., Tg. Ps.-J.) – Joseph understood his brothers when they stood before him in Egypt because he knew *lishan bet qudsha*.

---

[29] For a recent summary of the main issues concerning Tg. Ps.-J., see R. Hayward, "The Date of Targum Pseudo-Jonathan: Some Comments," *JJS* 40 (1989), 7–30. Cf. A. Shinan, "The Date of Targum Pseudo-Jonathan: Some More Comments," *JJS* 41 (1990), 57–61.

[30] See above, n. 25.

[31] This tradition is exclusive to the targumic texts.

[32] For numerous parallels, see Ginzberg, *Legends*, V, 205, n. 91. See also Levy, *Targum Neophyti 1*, 124.

[33] The identity of Jacob's "brothers" is similarly established in Genesis Rabbah 74:13 and parallels.

[34] The necessity for this note is clear, since the Hebrew name is based on a play on words which is lost in the Targum.

(14)   Gen. 45:12 (Tg. Neof., Tg. Ps.-J.) – Joseph proves his identity to his brothers by speaking *lishan bet qudsha*.[35]

(15–16) Deut. 25:7–8 (Tg. Ps.-J.) – the ceremony of removing the sandal of the brother-in-law in the law of levirate is to be performed in *lishan bet qudsha*.[36]

This term is therefore found quite frequently in all extant "Palestinian" Targums (but never in Targum Onqelos). In a few instances the term *lishan bet qudsha* is replaced by *lishan qudsha* (= *leshon haqqodesh*), a phrase known in Hebrew from rabbinic literature; this change is apparently to be attributed to scribes who had difficulties with the uncommon term and replaced it with a more familiar one. As some of the examples clearly demonstrate, *lishan bet qudsha* designates the Hebrew language. Some scholars[37] regard this term as the linguistic remnant of the Second Temple period, when it referred to the language used in that holy place, as opposed to Aramaic, which was spoken outside the Temple. I have some doubts regarding this assumption, since the Targums always refer to the Temple as *bet miqdasha*, *miqdash* or *bet muqdasha*, but never as *bet qudsha*. *Bet qudsha* is the translation of *qodesh* or *haqqodesh* (in phrases such as *sheqel haqqodesh* [Exod. 30:13] or *le-sharet baqqodesh* [Exod. 28:30]).[38] Disregarding its origin for the moment, I would suggest that *bet qudsha* be understood as a popular term for the synagogue, wherein Hebrew was used mainly for prayer and *piyyutim*. While I have not as yet found another literary source or archeological find from the period which designates synagogue as *bet qudsha* or *bet haqqodesh*, lack of evidence does not prove to the contrary. The synagogue is called a number of names in various sources: *oikos*, *hagios topos*, *beta*ʾ, *bet* ʾ*elohim*, ʾ*atra qadisha*, and the like.[39] The similarity between *bet* ʾ*elohim* and *bet qudsha* is very strong, since *qudsha* denotes God Himself, as in the terms *ruaḥ haqqodesh* and *haqqodesh barukh hu*ʾ. These terms therefore have the same meaning. The distance between the common Greek designation for the synagogue, *ha-*

---

35 For parallels, see Ginzberg, *Legends*, V, 355, n. 281.

36 This tradition is already found in Sifre Deuteronomy 191, Finkelstein, p. 310.

37 E. Levine, "Some Characteristics of Pseudo-Jonathan Targum to Genesis," *Augustinianum* 11 (1971), 97; P. Schäfer, *Die Vorstellung von heiligen Geist in der rabbinischen Literatur* (Munich, 1972), 137–139. See also Kasher, *Torah Shelemah*, 150–151 and Klein, *Genizah Manuscripts*, II, 21.

38 For examples, see Kasher, *Torah Shelemah*, 152–153.

39 See J. Naveh, *On Stone and Mosaic* (Tel-Aviv, 1978), 1–3 (Hebrew); L. Roth-Gerson, *The Greek Inscriptions from the Synagogues in Eretz-Israel* (Jerusalem, 1987), 160–161 (Hebrew).

gios topos, the Aramaic one, *ʾatra qadisha*, and the term *bet qudsha* is just a few steps away.

Furthermore, a tannaitic statement in the Babylonian Talmud mentions that the common people (*ʿamme ha-ʾaratzot*) had liturgical and sacred terms of their own: "For two things the common people are sentenced to death: because they call the Holy Ark in the synagogue *ʾarona* and because they call the synagogue *bet ʿam*."[40] The exact "sin" which is described here is far from obvious, but it is clear that the common people used their own terminology to describe the synagogue and elements within it. I would confidently add *bet qudsha* to the list of popular linguistic terms.

The Targums also contain a small number of popular proverbs not mentioned in rabbinic literature, as, for example, an addition found in Tg. Neof. and Frg. Tg. (ms. Vatican only) to Gen. 49:1. These concern Jacob's last words and claim that he wanted to reveal heavenly secrets to his sons, but "as soon as the secret was revealed to him it was concealed from him, and after the gate was opened for him it was shut on him."[41] This phrase is apparently a popular proverb which was used to describe someone who has almost achieved his goal: the gate had already opened before him but at that very moment it closed and all efforts were in vain.

Another popular proverb may be found in Tg. Ps.-J. to Num. 25:3: "Thus Israel attached itself to Baʿal Peʿor." The Targum reads, "And the people of Israel were attached to Baʿal Peʿor as a nail that cannot be taken out of the wood without taking some wood with it," i.e., a wrongdoing cannot be corrected without some painful consequences, and therefore the sin of Israel with the Moabite idol had to cause the loss of some lives.[42] Proverbs such as these were familiar to the people who heard the Targum and therefore facilitated the translator in making his point.

---

[40] B Shabbat 32a.

[41] This proverb contains a play on words between תרעא and איטרד. See also Klein, *Genizah Manuscripts*, I, 163, and the following note .

[42] This proverb contains a play on words between קיסא and קיסמא. It has a Hebrew parallel in Sifre Numbers 131, but the Aramaic version is more concise and seems to be the original. My colleague, Dr. Galit Hasan-Rokem, who is conducting a long-term study of Jewish proverbs, confirms my intuition regarding the two targumic sentences which I describe as proverbs.

Reflections on Daily Life

The Targum, through the minute details added to the biblical story, can be utilized for drawing a detailed portrait of daily life among Galilean Jewry in late antiquity. In this group of additions[43] we may include statements, such as: only trees bearing no fruit are to be used for building and heating (Gen. 1:29); women use make-up (Gen. 6:2) and are permitted to shave their armpits (Deut. 22:5); a week of mourning is customary after someone's death (Gen. 7:10). Targumic statements that people used to fall on their face while praying (Gen. 17:3), that the proper time for the daily meal is "as the day is growing hot" (Gen. 18:1), that treasures are hidden in caves (Gen. 41:36), and that in the ceremony of circumcision it is customary to cite Gen. 48:20, "May God make you like Ephraim and Manasseh," and so forth are reflections of customs of the period. Moreover, the famous words of the Targum concerning decorating the synagogue with *tziyyurin ve-diyoqnin* (pictures and portraits—Lev. 26:1),[44] reference to the *dukhan* (platform, stand) in the synagogue (Num. 6:23), a *mezuzah* in the house (Deut. 20:5), a coffin and shrouds for the dead (Deut. 26:14), and, in a different realm, theaters and circuses in the city (Deut. 28:19) are all mirrors of daily life—customs, beliefs, and linguistic usages—of the common people in Galilean Jewish society of late antiquity.

A number of topics may be added to the three briefly explored above, such as the ways in which the Targums treat theological, moral, and philosophical issues.[45] The picture I have sketched here fully warrants further investigation of the possible contribution of the Aramaic Targum to our knowledge of the Galilee and its inhabitants in late antiquity.

---

[43] See above, n. 24.

[44] See M. L. Klein, "Palestinian Targum and Synagogue Mosaics," *Immanuel* 11 (1980), 33–45.

[45] For example, the Targums' view of the angelic world; see A. Shinan, "The Angelology of the Palestinian Targums to the Pentateuch," *Sefarad* 43 (1983), 181–198; or their attitude toward the doctrine of reward and punishment; idem, "Live Translation: On the Nature of the Aramaic Targums to the Pentateuch," *Prooftexts* 3 (1983), 46–47. See also above, nn. 14 and 15.

Rabbinic Views on the Practice of Targum, and Multilingualism in the Jewish Galilee of the Third–Sixth Centuries

STEVEN D. FRAADE

I. Introduction

Anyone who approaches ancient rabbinic texts with the intention of using them to reconstruct some aspect of ancient Jewish history, society or practice must confront the challenges posed by their deeply rhetorical nature. The literature of the rabbis is not so much one which simply seeks to represent the world outside it; it ultimately seeks to transform that world by the force of an illocutionary world, or web, of representations, both halakhic and aggadic, into which it dialogically and, hence, transformatively, draws its society of students in the very process of creating and conveying its meanings. By no means do I wish to deny the possibilities of using rabbinic literature for purposes of historical reconstruction, but to caution that such uses are fraught with great difficulty. Even as rabbinic texts might be critical of and seek to transform the contexts of which they provide fragmentary and often contradictory representations, they are nevertheless culturally rooted in those contexts, in relation to which they would have had to have made communicative sense for them to have been rhetorically effective.[1]

---

[1] For the theoretical and bibliographical underpinnings of this opening statement, see the introductory chapter and the introductions to the successive chapters of my book, *From Tradition to Commentary: Torah and Its Interpretation in the Midrash Sifre to Deuteronomy* (Albany, 1991).

In what follows, I wish to offer one case-in-point for consideration: the practice of Aramaic translation of Scripture, or Targum, in the ancient Jewish social contexts of worship and study. For descriptions of such practice, both legal and narrative, we have only one source—rabbinic literature. Notwithstanding speculation about the practice of Targum in pre-rabbinic times (i.e., pre-70 C.E.) or in extra-rabbinic contexts, we have no direct evidence for such practice from pre-rabbinic or extra-rabbinic sources. Although we have fragments of an Aramaic translation of two non-continuous sections of Leviticus (4Q156) and parts of two copies of an Aramaic translation of the book of Job (11QtgJob and 4Q157) from Qumran, both of these being fairly literal in their translations, we have no way of knowing what their purpose or what their function (not necessarily lectionary) would have been within that community or its larger movement; and although we have several descriptions in Josephus, Philo, and the New Testament of the reading and interpretation of Scripture in the synagogues of Palestine and the Diaspora, none of these mentions the rendering of Hebrew Scripture into Aramaic as a way of conveying its meaning or interpretation to a synagogue audience.[2] This is not to deny that such a practice could have existed in pre-rabbinic times, but simply to state that we have no direct evidence for it.[3] By contrast, our earliest rabbinic documents, having been created in their present forms beginning in the early third century C.E., contain a rather large corpus of both legal and narrative representations of such practices, which were well established already in the so-called tannaitic collections.[4]

---

[2] See Philo, *Hypothetica* 7, 12–13; *Spec. Leg.* 2, 62; *Quod. Omnis.* 82; *Somn.* 2, 127; *Leg.* 156–157; *Mos.* 2, 215–216; Josephus, *Ant.* XVI, 2, 4, 43; *Ag. Ap.* 2, 17, 175; Luke 4:16–22; Acts 13:13–16, 27; 15:21.

[3] Rabbinic traditions which trace Targum to the time of Ezra (e.g., B Megillah 3a [= B Nedarim 37b]; J Megillah 4, 1, 74d; Genesis Rabbah 36:8) are all amoraic or later, whereas tannaitic passages which mention the recitation of Scripture in Second Temple times make no mention of the practice of Targum in such settings. However we understand *mephorash* of Neh. 8:8 (for the scholarly view that it denotes translation, see H. H. Schaeder, *Esra der Schreiber* [Tübingen, 1930], 51–59), this passage as it stands refers to a one-time event of covenantal renewal. The later rabbinic texts, however, view it as the origin and prototype of the practice that they knew and sought to validate and regulate: weekly Torah readings accompanied by oral translation/explication. Cf. M. Fishbane, *Biblical Interpretation in Ancient Israel* (Oxford, 1985), 113, who argues that a lectionary ceremony like that described in Neh. 8 was already the established practice of regular Jewish communal worship during the Babylonian exile. This is unprovable and improbable.

[4] To give a rough sense of the extent of this wealth of rabbinic texts relevant to the status of targumic texts, the practice of Targum, the *meturgeman*, and the statuses of

What picture of the practice of Targum emerges from these rabbinic sources? First, it is important not to homogenize, as is often done, rabbinic representations of targumic practice in diverse rabbinic collections that span close to a millennium and derive from both Palestinian (by which we generally mean Galilean) and Babylonian contexts. Here, however, space will only permit a summary of the results of my analysis of the rabbinic evidence, with particular attention to the rather large number of sources deriving from the Galilee from the early third through late fifth centuries. Finally, I shall consider extra-rabbinic types of evidence, both literary and archeological, that will allow us to view the rabbinic portrayal of the practice of Targum in the broader language setting of the Galilee of this period, a setting which I shall argue was much more multilingual (Aramaic, Greek, and Hebrew) than has heretofore been appreciated. The resulting picture will call into question a conventional view of the function of Targum as serving a popular Jewish synagogue audience that no longer understood Hebrew and needed to be provided with an Aramaic rendering of Scripture as its substitute. For an illustration of this conventional view, a single citation will suffice:

> The Targums—or early Aramaic translations of the Bible—have their origin in the synagogue, in a period when the Aramaic-speaking masses of Jewish people no longer understood biblical Hebrew, and had to have the weekly Pentateuchal reading translated into their vernacular. This is similar to the Septuagint (Greek translation of the Bible), which originated in the Greek-

---

Aramaic and Hebrew, the following discussion is based on 46 passages from tannaitic texts (Mishnah, Tosefta, and tannaitic midrashim), 20 from talmudic *baraitot*, 21 from the Palestinian Talmud, 20 from the Babylonian Talmud, 6 from the amoraic midrashim, 10 from extra-canonical talmudic tractates, 8 from post-amoraic midrashim, and 8 from geonic sources. These sources are collected, translated, and analyzed in greater detail in my forthcoming book, *Targum and Torah: Early Rabbinic Views of Scriptural Translation in a Multilingual Society*. It needs to be stressed that the evidence of rabbinic sources can only tell us how those sources chose to portray the practice of Targum. To what extent these are representations of what actually was the contemporary practice, which in any case must have varied over place and time, and to what extent these are portrayals of what the "authors" of these sources thought that practice ought to be is impossible to determine in the absence of any evidence external to rabbinic literature. See the example given below, n. 9. For another survey of many of these same sources, coming to both similar and different conclusions, see P. S. Alexander, "The Targums and Rabbinic Rules for the Delivery of the Targum," in: *Congress Volume: Salamanca, 1983* (*Vetus Testamentum Supplement*, 36), ed. J. A. Emerton (Leiden, 1985), 14–28.

speaking Alexandrian Jewish community of the early Hellenistic period (3rd Century BCE).[5]

II. Legal Traditions

To begin with, several tannaitic sources presume the existence and legitimacy of written Targums. Their interest, especially in the Mishnah and Tosefta, is in clarifying the liminal status of such texts. Scrolls of translated Scriptures, like scrolls of Scripture, are considered "holy writings" (*kitve qodesh*) and therefore require *genizah*, or withdrawal from circulation, when they become unfit for use.[6] As we now know from the Cairo Geniza, many targumic texts, to our good fortune, were so withdrawn rather than destroyed. Furthermore, according to most interpretations of a difficult mishnah (Shabbat 16:1), such texts of translation, like texts of Scripture, may be removed from a burning building on the Sabbath, even if it involves the performance of an otherwise prohibited act of work.[7] Yet, if Targum texts share with scriptural texts the status of "holy writings," they are still of a lower canonical and hence ritual status than Scripture itself, as indicated by M Yadayim 4:5: they do not "defile the hands." The very fact that texts of translation do not "defile the hands" and therefore do not require being copied and handled in the limiting manner prescribed for scriptural scrolls may even have facilitated their broader circulation and utilization for purposes that will be considered below.

While the tannaitic sources presume both the existence and acceptance of texts of Targum, the same sources suggest that such texts were not to be employed in the synagogue service for the recitation of the Aramaic translation that accompanied the reading of the Torah and the Prophets from scrolls. However, it should be noted that while this distinction is clearly implied in the tannaitic sources, it is only stated

---

[5] M. L. Klein, "The Palestinian Targum and Synagogue Mosaics," *Immanuel* 11 (1980), 33–45.

[6] E.g., T Shabbat 13:1–3; M Shabbat 16:1.

[7] T Shabbat 13:2 makes the rescue and withdrawal of texts of Targum, per se, obligatory. For the famous story of Rabban Gamaliel I having ordered a Targum of Job to be withdrawn from circulation, perhaps because it was not part of the lectionary cycle and therefore would cause people in their private reading of it to neglect the house of study, see T Shabbat 13:2–3, and parallels in J Shabbat 16, 1, 15b–c; B Shabbat 115a; Tractate Soferim 5:17; 15:2. Alternatively, Rabban Gamaliel might have had it removed since it was a defective or unapproved translation.

explicitly in amoraic and post-amoraic sources.[8] The basic procedure for the targumic rendering of Scripture in the synagogue, as specified in the Mishnah and Tosefta, is as follows: the reader recites a verse of Torah from the scroll, after which the translator renders the same verse in Aramaic, followed immediately by the reader's recitation of the next verse in Hebrew. In the case of the reading of the Prophets, three verses at a time could be so read and translated. It is repeatedly stressed, at least with respect to the Torah, that the reading and translation be conducted in such a way that the two voices, of reader and translator, be clearly distinguishable from each other, each in its successive turn, with neither rising in volume above the other.[9] The combined effect of the implementation of these rules would be for the audience to experience the aural equivalent of an interlinear or parallel-column bilingual text, with the two alternating voices complementing one another in their counterpointal reading.

8 Note especially M Megillah 4:6, where a blind person is allowed to translate but not to read the Torah as part of the synagogue service. Such a person would certainly translate without a text before him. Similarly, T Sukkah 2:10 implies that while one needed to free one's hands in order to read Scripture, this was not necessary for translation. For an amoraic text that explicitly precludes the reading from a targumic text in the context of the synagogue lection, see especially J Megillah 4, 1, 74d. In B Megillah 32a, the view is ascribed to ʿUlla that the reader cannot assist the translator lest the synagogue audience think that the targumic translation is written in the Torah scroll. Although it is generally assumed that the rule not to read the translation from a text already applied in tannaitic times, it should be noted that B Megillah 18a interprets M Megillah 2:1 ("One who recites it [the Scroll of Esther] in Targum does not fulfill his obligation") to refer to the reciting of the Targum from a written targumic text. Does this presume that such a practice existed, even though it could not substitute for reading the Scroll of Esther in Hebrew, or is this simply raised as a hypothetical possibility? Similarly, according to B Shabbat 115a, R. Huna understood it to have been a matter of dispute among tannaim whether one could read from a written text of Targum of the Writings (at least on the Sabbath). In both cases, however, it is unclear whether the reference is to public reading in the synagogue or to the private reading of such targumic texts.

9 See M Megillah 4:4; T Megillah 4 (3):20; J Megillah 4, 1, 74d; B Megillah 23a–b; B Sotah 38b (in R. Ḥisda's name); and the *baraita* cited in B Berakhot 45a. On the question whether these rules were actually followed in ancient synagogues (see above, n. 4), note the story told in J Megillah 4, 5, 75b, about R. Simeon the Scribe of Terakhon in Transjordan: the congregation wished him to read only half a verse of the Torah at a time, presumably followed by its Targum (see commentaries), so that their children could follow along better. When, after seeking rabbinic advice, he refused to bend the rabbinic rule to accommodate the community's desire, they forthwith fired him.

All of these rules presume (even if ideally) an audience that was attentive both to the Hebrew reading and to the Aramaic translation, which together constituted the publicly performative recitation of Scripture. The Aramaic translation could never substitute for the Hebrew reading which it accompanied. Nor is it ever stated or presumed in a single Galilean rabbinic source that the Aramaic translation was intended for a common crowd which did not understand Hebrew.[10] This is in contrast to the translation of the Torah and the Scroll of Esther into other languages, especially Greek, which, according to tannaitic rules, could be performed from written texts in lieu of the reading from a Hebrew scroll in congregations in which the Hebrew original was not understood or in which a competent Hebrew reader could not be found.[11]

But if the practice of public Aramaic translation was placed almost on a par with that of Hebrew reading (at least for the Torah) as its accompaniment and not substitute, even as it was distinguished from it, its status was still a notch lower. Thus, our rabbinic sources require that a person of lesser status, such as a minor or student, recite the Targum in response to the reading by a person of a higher status, such as an elder or teacher, just as Aaron acted, it is said, as Moses' "translator" before Pharaoh.[12] This is consistent with the proximate yet inferior status of targumic texts relative to those of Scripture.

---

10 The idea that the Targum was intended for the unlearned "women and ʿamme ha-ʾaretz" is a view commonly expressed since medieval times. See, for example, Rashi to B Megillah 21b. Note also Qorban Ha-ʿedah to J Megillah 4, 1, 74d, but this view receives no expression in tannaitic sources. Only one amoraic source, and a Babylonian one at that, raises this possibility, only for it to be rejected. See B Megillah 18a, to be discussed below. See also Tosafot to B Berakhot 8a–b. The view that the targumic translation was intended for the common people, the women, and the children is also found in Tractate Soferim 18:6, Higger, p. 317, but, as Higger indicates in his introduction (p. 29), this is a later addition from a Babylonian source.

11 See M Megillah 2:1; T Megillah 2:6; 4 (3):13; and *baraitot* in B Megillah 18a. For subsequent discussions, see J Megillah 2, 1, 73a; 4, 3, 75a; J Sotah 7, 1, 21b; B Megillah 8b–9a; 18a. There remains a division of opinion whether a Greek speaker who understands Hebrew but hears the Scroll of Esther read in Greek from a Greek scroll has fulfilled his obligation. For the special status of the Greek translation, especially for the Torah but also, according to some, for the Scroll of Esther, see M Megillah 1:8 (the view of R. Simeon b. Gamaliel); J Megillah 1, 11(9), 71c; B Megillah 8b–9a (*baraita*), 9b (the view of R. Yoḥanan), 18a (the view of Rav and Samuel); Genesis Rabbah 36:8; Deuteronomy Rabbah 1:1.

12 T Megillah 4 (3):21. Some take this to refer to people not of lesser and greater age but to lower and higher status. See S. Lieberman's discussion in *Tosefta Ki-Fshuṭah* (10 vols.; New York, 1955–88), V, 1195. Either interpretation suits my argument. For the minor allowed both to read Torah and to translate, see M Megillah 4:6. However, that

Not only was the synagogue *meturgeman*, or translator, not to read from a text, but his rendering was not to be a recitation of an established text of translation that he had memorized; he was to render the Hebrew into Aramaic as he heard it. However, his freedom of translation was to be governed and constrained by certain traditions and principles of translation which, if not fully spelled out in our sources, are at least exemplified: certain changes could be made to clarify the meaning of Scripture, but others which might distort that meaning, as the sages understood it, could not. As an example of the latter, it is stated that if the translator sought to blunt Scripture's reproof of those who engage in unacceptable sexual conduct by changing the second person ("your father") of Lev. 18:7 to the third ("his father"), he could be silenced.[13] The difficult line that the public translator had to tread, between fidelity to the biblical text and the freedom to render it for his audience, is summed up by the famous dictum of R. Judah b. ʾElʿai: "One who translates literally (*ke-tzurato*) is a liar while one who adds is a blasphemer."[14] As this example and

---

same text permits a blind person and one poorly dressed (in torn clothes) to translate but not to read the Torah. For the targumic rendering of "prophet" of Exod. 7:1 as *meturgeman*, see Tg. Onq., Tg. Neof. ad loc. On the age of the *meturgeman*, cf. B Ḥagigah 14a, where the following opinion is attributed to R. Abbahu (ca. 280): "They do not appoint a *meturgeman* over the public who is less than fifty years old." The *meturgeman* referred to here, however, is most likely not one who translates Scripture in the synagogue but one who communicates a sage's homily to the public as a professional duty (also known as an amora). See Rashi ad loc. On the *meturgeman* to the sage, see below, n. 20.

13 See M Megillah 4:9. That the reference is to the translator and not to the reader, see C. Albeck, *Six Orders of the Mishna, Moʿed* (Jerusalem, 1959), 505. For the understanding of M Megillah 4:9 as referring to a change of "your father" to "his father," etc., see J Megillah 4, 10, 75c; B Megillah 25a. The Mishnah offers as a second example of a forbidden translation a rendering of Lev. 18:21 (forbidding passing one's children [seed] through a fire for Molech) so as to refer to impregnating a gentile woman (as we find in Tg. Ps.-J.). For another example of an unacceptable translation (of Lev. 22:28), see J Megillah 4, 10, 75c and J Berakhot 5, 3, 9c; cf. M Megillah 4:9. But the Palestinian Talmud specifically states that such forbidden translations (and, we may assume, other constraints on the *meturgeman*) apply to the public translation of Scripture, whereas in private study and teaching such explanations are permitted.

14 T Megillah 4 (3): 41. Much has been written on the tension between free and literal translation. For recent treatments of this theme in relation to the ancient translation of Scripture, see S. P. Brock, "The Phenomenon of the Septuagint, " in: *The Witness of Tradition, (OTS* 17; Leiden, 1972), 11–36; idem, "Aspects of Translation Technique in Antiquity, " *Greek, Roman and Byzantine Studies* 20 (1979), 69–87; J. Barr, "The Typology of Literalism in Ancient Biblical Translation," *Nachrichten der Akad. der Wissenschaften in Göttingen* 11 (1978), 279–335. In antiquity, cf. in particular Cicero, *De Optimo Genere Oratorum* 5, 14 (trans. H. M. Hubbell, *LCL*, p. 365):

others suggest, while rules and traditions of translation could only serve to guide the *meturgeman* in his translation, it was he who had to make difficult translation decisions in the live, public context of the synagogue lection.

A further way in which the recitation of the Targum is distinguished from that of Scripture is that certain embarrassing sections of the Torah, notably Reuben's indiscretion with Bilhah (Gen. 35:22) and the second account of the golden calf incident, in which Aaron bears responsibility for the people's sin (Exod. 32:21–25, 35), are "read but not translated" in public.[15] The public translation of such texts was problematic since to translate them literally would only reinforce the public dishonor which they communicated, whereas to provide a translator's cover-up would be recognized as such. Although it has been suggested that these passages were not translated so that the synagogue audience (presumed not to understand Hebrew) would be unaware of their contents,[16] the Tosefta, in the name of R. Simeon b. Elʿazar (ca. 200 C.E.) implies the opposite: in publicly translating the second account of the golden calf one might, like Aaron, try to justify what happened, perhaps leading some to believe that what happened was not so terrible after all.[17] In such cases it is better simply to acknowledge what Scripture says without either interpreting or enunciating it in the form of translation.

This restriction, it should be stressed again, applies only to the public translation of Scripture. Thus, the Tosefta, after listing passages which are not to be translated and, in the case of some passages in the Prophets, are not to be read either, states: "But the teacher of Scripture [*sofer*]

And I did not translate them as an interpreter, but as an orator, keeping the same idea and the forms, or as one might say, the 'figures' of thought, but in language which conforms to our usage. And in so doing, I did not hold it necessary to render word for word, but I preserved the general style and force of the language. For I did not think I ought to count them out to the reader like coins, but to pay them by weight, as it were.

In a similar vein, see Cicero, *De Finibus* 3, 4, 15.

15 See M Megillah 4:10; T Megillah 4 (3):31–38; J Megillah 4, 11, 75c; B Megillah 25b; Tractate Soferim 9:9, 10. On these rules and their relation to extant targumic texts, see P. S. Alexander, "The Rabbinic Lists of Forbidden Targumim, " *JJS* 27 (1976), 177–191; M. L. Klein, "Not to be Translated in Public – לא מתרגם בציבורא," *JJS* 39 (1988), 80–91. Cf. Josephus' skipping of the golden calf incident entirely in his retelling of the events at Sinai in *Ant*. III, 5, 8, 99; see note "c" there, *LCL*, pp. 362–363.

16 See Albeck's note to M Megillah 4:10. Cf. above, n. 10.

17 T Megillah 4 (3):37. For discussion, see Lieberman, *Tosefta Ki-Fshuṭah*, ad loc. A slightly different version, cited as a *baraita*, appears in B Megillah 25b.

teaches [these passages] in his usual way." Here an important distinction is drawn between the translating of scriptural passages in the public context of the synagogue liturgy and the interpretation (including perhaps translation) of those same passages in the less public context of the school or the house of study.[18] At issue, it would appear, is not whether the synagogue audience understood biblical texts which dishonor Israel's forebears, but what the effect of public translations of such passages would have been upon an audience which understood both Aramaic and Hebrew and was attentive both to the reading of Scripture and the recitation of its Targum. If these passages must be read publicly, better they be read without either the literal enunciation or apologetic elucidation of translation.[19]

Given the fact that the synagogue translator had the difficult task of rendering the Hebrew of Scripture into Aramaic as he heard it recited, without being either too literal or too free, it is surprising that we find no evidence in our early rabbinic sources for this translator serving as a "professional" synagogue functionary, as is often presumed.[20] Just as a

18 T Megillah 4 (3):38. Thus, while Reuben's deed (Gen. 35:22) is not to be translated in the context of the synagogue service, it is apologetically translated in Tg. Ps.-J. (as well as to Gen. 49:4) and similarly whitewashed in B Shabbat 55a. See above, n. 10, as well as the following note. The cited passage from the Tosefta may suggest that elementary education included not simply the ability to recite correctly Scripture in Hebrew, but also to translate it "correctly" into Aramaic. For a *sofer* functioning as a *meturgeman*, see J Megillah 4, 1, 74d.

19 The extant targumic texts treat these passages differently, either by translating them fairly literally (Tg. Onq.), by repeating the Hebrew of the lemma (the Palestinian Targums) or by providing a euphemistic paraphrase (Tg. Ps.-J.). Marginal or interlinear glosses to these texts, and the Masora to Tg. Onq., specify that such passages—and there are several others—are not to be translated "in public." Where translations are found in our extant Targums, they are to be used in study or preparation but not as part of the synagogue service. See the important evidence marshalled by Klein, "Not to be Recited in Public," especially a Cairo Geniza fragment containing a masoretic notation to a Palestinian Targum of Exod. 32:22 (Leningrad Antonin Ebr. III B 32, first published by G. E. Weill in *Textus* 4 [1964], 45 and cited by Klein, ibid., 88): "For those verses which are not translated in public there is [nevertheless written] targum."

20 Here, once again, it is important to distinguish between the *meturgeman* to the synagogue reader and the *meturgeman* to the rabbinic sage, although there is some overlap between them in amoraic times. For the *meturgeman* to the sage being paid for his services, even on the Sabbath, see B Pesaḥim 50b (*baraita*). Note that while synagogue inscriptions contain several references to the office of ḥazzan (see J. Naveh, *On Stone and Mosaic* [Jerusalem, 1978], 40–41 [Hebrew]), there is no reference in any inscription to a *meturgeman*. The arguments by S. Lieberman ("*Ḥazzanut Yannai,*" *Sinai*

qualified member of the congregation could be called upon by the synagogue supervisor (*ḥazzan*) to read or "pass before the ark," so, too, a qualified member of the congregation, including a minor, could be called upon to translate.[21] Finally, while the Mishnah prohibits one who finds a lost scroll of Scripture from studying from it, lest he causes it damage, the Tosefta defines such study either as reading the weekly lection and then repeating or reviewing it or reading the lection and translating it, perhaps verse by verse, into Aramaic.[22] Although such reading and translating from a found scroll is not likely to have occurred in the context of the synagogue service, this passage reinforces the idea that the ability to read Scripture and render it in Aramaic was not limited to a specific group of synagogue functionaries but could be presumed to have been a commonly cultivated skill, at least within the circles to which such rabbinic rules were expected to apply. Persons with facility in the reading and proper translation of Scripture could be called upon from among the congregation to provide a responsive yet rule- and tradition-governed Aramaic translation as an accompaniment to the reading of the weekly lection in Hebrew from a scroll.

This brings us to our next topic, one often ignored in the discussion of Targum—the place of targumic text practice within the rabbinic

---

4 [1939], 223–224 [Hebrew]) and E. Y. Kutscher (*Words and Their History* [Jerusalem, 1961], 47 [Hebrew]), citing J Megillah 4, 1, 74d, that one of the regular functions of the *ḥazzan* official in amoraic times was to translate Scripture in the synagogue, are unconvincing. For different conclusions regarding the synagogue *meturgeman* as a professional functionary of the synagogue, see A. Shinan, "The Form and Content of the Aggadah in the 'Palestinian' Targums on the Pentateuch and Its Place within Rabbinic Literature" (doctoral dissertation, Hebrew University; Jerusalem, 1977), 23–25 (Hebrew). For a broader and more detailed discussion of the *meturgeman* to the sage, see my forthcoming book, *Targum and Torah*.

21 See especially T Sukkah 2:10, in the name of R. Zadoq (ca. 100 or 150 C.E.): the same person who came to synagogue with his *lulav* in hand could be called to recite the *ʿAmidah* on behalf of the congregation, read from the Torah, recite the priestly blessing (if a priest), and translate. A parallel but variant *baraita* in B Sukkah 41b and J Sukkah 3, 14 (11), 54a (where it is cited as a Babylonian *baraita*) does not mention translating. Similarly, T Megillah 4 (3):30 associates those who translate, read, pass before the ark, and raise their hands. For other early sources that presume that one competent to read Scripture in the synagogue might be expected to be able to translate it into Aramaic, see the *baraita* cited in B Qiddushin 49a, with the opinion of R. Judah. See also above, n. 18, for the possibility that elementary teaching of Scripture may have included instruction in its Aramaic translation.

22 M Bava Metziʿa 2:8; T Bava Metziʿa 2:21. This appears, with slight variation, as a *baraita* in J Bava Metziʿa 2, 9 (10), 8d and B Bava Metziʿa 29b–30a.

curriculum of Torah study both in private and in schools.[23] Here we find
our evidence not so much in the Mishnah and Tosefta, with their concern
for differentiating between Torah and Targum in the public space of the
synagogue, as in the so-called tannaitic midrashim, with their frequent
delineation of the rabbinic curriculum of Torah-study as comprising
miqra², *mishnah*, and *talmud* (or *midrash*), plus others.[24] In Sifre Deuteronomy 161 we find: *miqra²* (recitation of Scripture from a text) leads to
targum (Aramaic translation), which leads to *mishnah* (oral teaching),
which leads to *talmud* (engaged study), which leads to *ma²aseh*
(performance), which leads to *yir²ah* (the fear of God). Thus, the rabbinic
study of Scripture begins with its translation before proceeding to its
more advanced and dialectically complex forms.[25] Thus, Targum is
poised between scriptural reading (*miqra²*) and oral teaching (*mishnah*).
This liminal position is also expressed by a passage from the Sifra, in
which it is asked whether Targum belongs with *midrashot, halakhot*, and
talmud as a form of (oral) "instruction" (*hora²ah*). According to R. Yose b.
Judah (ca. 200 C.E.), Targum, unlike Scripture (*miqra²*), is considered oral
teaching.[26] The mere fact that R. Yose's question needed to be asked suggests the Targum's gray position between Scripture and oral teaching.

The place of Targum as the first step in the study of Scripture is
spelled out more clearly in two, admittedly later, texts, where it is said

---

23 For earlier recognitions of Targum's pedagogic function, see A. D. York, "The
Targum in the Synagogue and in the School," *JSJ* 10 (1979), 74–86; and D. M. Golumb,
A Grammar of Targum Neofiti (Chico, 1985), 2–8; P. S. Alexander, "Jewish Aramaic
Translations of Hebrew Scriptures," in: *Mikra: Text, Translation, Reading and Inter-
pretation of the Hebrew Bible in Ancient Judaism and Early Christianity*, ed. M. J. Mulder
(Assen and Philadelphia, 1988), 238–241; idem, "The Targums and the Rabbinic Rules
for the Delivery of the Targum," 22–23.

24 See L. Finkelstein, "Midrash, Halakhah and Aggadot," in: *Yitzhak F. Baer Jubilee
Volume on the Occasion of His Seventieth Birthday*, eds. S. W. Baron et al. (Jerusalem,
1960), 28–47 (Hebrew); J. Goldin, "The Freedom and Restraint of Haggadah," in:
Midrash and Literature, eds. G. H. Hartman and S. Budick (New Haven, 1986), 57–58.
For other examples, see my book, *From Tradition to Commentary*, chapter 3, nn. 92, 96,
and 111.

25 Deut. 17:19, upon which this passage is a commentary, reads, "And it [the Torah
scroll] shall be with him [the king], and he shall read from it all the days of his life,
that he may learn to fear the Lord his God." Thus, his "learning" is midrashically
fleshed out to include targum, mishnah, and talmud, in that order, all of which lead
to fulfillment in practice and fear of God.

26 See Sifra, Shemini, 1:9, according to early manuscripts and not the printed editions, which have been corrupted under the influence of B Keritot 13b. For a fuller
treatment of this text, with a discussion of its variants, see my forthcoming book, *Targum and Torah*.

that R. ʿAqiva the student would enter the school house where he would first learn a scriptural section (from a tablet), then its Targum, and then its derived halakhot, aggadot, etc.[27] It is not clear from such passages whether the pedagogical exercise implied here is the recitation of Targum, like Scripture, from a text, or its oral generation.[28]

A similar ambiguity underlies the well-known rule found in the Babylonian Talmud but attributed to two third-century Palestinian amoraim, R. Joshua b. Levi (ca. 230) and R. Ami (ca. 300): "A person should always complete his [private study of the] weekly lection together with the public: twice Scripture and once Targum." Whereas later, and especially Babylonian, traditions understood the fulfillment of this dictum to involve the recitation of both Scripture and Targum from authorized texts, this need not have been the original intent of the Palestinian (Galilean) practice.[29] As a previously cited tosefta dealing with the study of a found scroll suggests, private scriptural study, at least in Palestine, may have involved the reading of the weekly lection, its repetition (either from the scroll or from memory), and its unaided rendering into Aramaic, perhaps verse by verse.[30] However, since it is clear that the

---

[27] ARN B 12 and 28, Schechter, pp. 29 and 58, respectively. The latter text also appears in Tractate Soferim 16:6, Higger, p. 289. In the first passage, R. ʿAqiva goes to the school to learn the weekly lection of the Torah. He begins by reading Scripture from a tablet. After he has learned the written text he proceeds to its Targum, then its halakhot, then its aggadot (according to some mss. but not others), and then to other types of derived interpretations. In the second passage, it is said that R. Yoḥanan b. Zakkai did not fail to learn a single weekly lection of the Torah. He would first master the written text, then its Targum, halakhot, aggadot, etc. For related texts which do not include Targum, see ARN A 14; B Sukkah 28a; B Bava Batra 134a. For the possible inclusion of scriptural translation in elementary school training, see above, n. 18.

[28] For the existence of written aids in the study of the rabbinic oral Torah, see S. Lieberman, *Hellenism in Jewish Palestine*[2] (New York, 1962), 87–88.

[29] B Berakhot 8a–b; see, e.g., Tosafot ad loc. Similarly, the medieval codes (e.g., Maimonides, *Mishneh Torah, Hil. Tefillah* 13:25; *Shulḥan Arukh, Oraḥ Ḥayyim* 285, 2) rephrase the talmudic text so as to denote a threefold reading, twice from Scripture and once from a text of Targum, in accord with what had become the practice, even though this is not stated in the talmudic text.

[30] T Bava Metziʿa 2:21. It is clear from the formulation *parashiyyotav*, "his [weekly] lections," in B Berakhot 8a–b, that a person's private reading, reviewing, and translating of the lection is intended. By geonic times, however, there developed the custom in some places of fulfilling this requirement communally by reading the lection twice in Hebrew and once in Aramaic in the synagogue on Sabbath morning before reading it liturgically from the Torah scroll. See *ʾOtzar Ha-geʾonim*, Lewin, p. 19, responsa to Berakhot 8b. R. Judah b. Elʿai's opinion, that to be a *qoreʾ*, "reader," is to read *and* translate Scripture, is later interpreted in the Babylonian Talmud (Qiddushin 49a) to

existence of written Targum texts are both attested and accepted in tannaitic sources (at least for scriptural texts which were part of the synagogue lectionary practice), it may be that such texts were used for private study and preparation even though they could not be read from as part of the synagogue service. In either case, private preparation of the weekly lection meant recitation both of its Hebrew text and its Aramaic translation. Clearly, the latter could not replace the former, and the obligation to recite the former twice while the latter only once, may serve again to reinforce the superior status of the former even as it was accompanied by the latter. Such a practice not only presumes the individual's knowledge of Hebrew and Aramaic and his ability to move freely between the two, but also serves to reinforce such facility.[31] In other words, comprehension of both Scripture and its language, at whatever level, is reinforced in private as well as in school study by shuttling between the biblical Hebrew of Scripture and the Aramaic of its translation. This would be the textual equivalent of the oral synagogue practice of interlinear translation previously described. Such pedagogic employment and strengthening of literary bilingualism would not have been unusual in the ancient world.[32]

---

refer to translating according to "our Targum" (Onqelos) and not "on one's own"; it is precisely the latter that is more likely to have been the intent of the earlier tannaitic tradition. This Babylonian transformation of a Palestinian teaching reflects a Babylonian tendency to restrict the practice of Targum to the reading of an authorized text. It should not be surprising, therefore, that the conferring of authority on particular texts of Targum is found in the Babylonian Talmud (Megillah 3a) but not in any Palestinian rabbinic sources.

[31] Note in this regard that many of the Palestinian targumic texts recently published from the Cairo Geniza contain not a continuous targumic (Aramaic) text, as we find in the texts of Targum among the Dead Sea Scrolls, but each scriptural verse appears first in Hebrew, in its entirety, and then in Aramaic. For such texts, see M. L. Klein, *Geniza Manuscripts of Palestinian Targum to the Pentateuch* (2 vols.; Cincinnati, 1986). Other Geniza texts, and later manuscripts of the other Targums, usually have simply the first word or words of the scriptural verse before its Aramaic renderings. But they still suggest that, unlike the continuous Aramaic translations from Qumran, these were to be keyed to the reading or studying of the Hebrew original and not to substitute for it. The same point is made by S. P. Brock, "Translating the Old Testament," in: *It is Written: Scripture Citing Scripture – Essays in Honor of Barnabas Lindars*, eds. D. A. Carson and H. G. M. Williamson (Cambridge, 1988), 92–95.

[32] See, for example, C. H. Moore, "Latin Exercises from a Greek Schoolroom," *Classical Philology* 19 (1924), 317–328 (Virgil and Cicero in Latin and Greek in facing columns). For further discussion, see V. Reichmann, *Römische Literatur in griechischer Übersetzung* (Leipzig, 1943), 28–61; H. I. Marrou, *A History of Education in Antiquity*, trans. G. Lamb (New York, 1956), 342–356. On the phenomenon of translation for a

III. Narrative Traditions

Thus far, I have concentrated on Palestinian legal traditions relating to the practice of Targum in the synagogue and in study. To understand not simply that practice but its purpose, or how the rabbis conceived of its purpose, we need to consider some narrative traditions, also from Palestinian sources although somewhat later (third–fourth centuries), that are often attached to the legal sources for elucidation.

First of all, the practice of Targum as it mediates the reading of Scripture in the synagogue is compared in several texts to what is rabbinically understood to have occurred at Mt. Sinai, of which, in a sense, it is a performative reenactment. Just as God's word was "given in reverence and fear," and just as it was "given by way of a middleman (*sirsur*)," being Moses, so, too, the public reading of Scripture must be reverently mediated by a *meturgeman*. In order to maintain this dramatic experience of scriptural reception through its live mediation, the *meturgeman* must be distinct from the reader; unlike the reader, he may not recite from a written text. Yet, like the reader, he must conduct himself in a manner befitting the importance of his role.[33] A similar tradition relates that just as God's voice and Moses' voice complemented each other at Sinai, so, too, the voices of Torah-reader and translator must accommodate one another so that neither rises above the other. Thus, both at Sinai and in the synagogue it is by a dialogical combination of voices that revelatory communication is effected.[34] It is curious that Moses' mediation of God's word at Sinai should be taken as a model for the practice of Targum in the synagogue, given the fact these rabbinic sources presume that at Sinai both God and Moses spoke Hebrew. But it is not so strange when we consider that it is the mediated or translated nature of revelation, even if within the same language (what is called "internal translation"), that is here

---

bilingual audience, especially for didactic purposes, see Brock, "The Phenomenon of the Septuagint," 29–31; L. Forster, "Translation: An Introduction," in: *Aspects of Translation*, eds. A. D. Booth et al. (London, 1958), 9–11. Since, as we saw, lay members of a congregation as well as minors could serve as synagogue translators, such weekly preparation of Scripture with its Aramaic translation, whether in private or in school, would have prepared them to assume such public roles.

33 See the three stories, all of late third–early fourth-century Palestinian amoraim, found in J Megillah 4, 1, 74d. On Moses' role as middleman at Sinai, see Josephus, *Ant.* III, 5, 3, 87, as well as the rabbinic sources listed in Lieberman, *Hellenism in Jewish Palestine*, 81–82, n. 271.

34 See B Berakhot 45a, in the name of R. Simeon b. Pazi (Palestine, ca. 280), with an attached *baraita* on the rule that the translator cannot raise his voice over that of the reader.

taken to be the Sinaitic model for the synagogue lection, as it is for the sage's teaching by way of his *meturgeman*.[35]

Yet, in other Palestinian texts revelation itself is conceived of as having been multilingual. That is, the Torah is said to have been issued at Sinai in many languages even though it was textually recorded in one. Thus, Sifre Deuteronomy 343 interprets Deut. 33:2 to mean that God revealed himself to Israel not by speaking to them in one language, as might have been expected, but in four languages—Hebrew, Latin, Arabic, and Aramaic—just as he revealed himself to them from all four directions.[36] Later texts speak of God's utterances issuing at Sinai in seventy languages.[37] Since the numbers four and seventy are whole numbers, totality of revelation is expressed in the totality of its linguistic expression, which is understood here as a multilingual expression.

[35] There is no indication, as is sometimes presumed, that the rabbinic *meturgeman* to the sage (or amora), in mediating the latter's teachings to his students or to the public, translates from Hebrew to Aramaic. It was befitting a sage, and particularly one of great stature, that his teachings be mediated to an audience. In fact, several Palestinian sources (e.g., Sifre Numbers 140; Sifre Deuteronomy 305) stress that the very presence of a *meturgeman* to a sage was a sign of the sage's importance. Thus, rabbinic teaching, like divine revelation, is mediated communication. The expression "internal translation," to denote the interpretive "reading" of any text out of one's own language and literature, is borrowed from G. Steiner, *After Babel: Aspects of Language and Translation* (New York/London, 1975), 28–30, 45–47.

[36] This is based on taking Sinai to represent Hebrew, Se‘ir (= Edom) to represent Latin (*leshon romi*) (see Gen. 32:4), Paran to represent Arabic (on the basis of Gen. 21:21), and the word *'atah* to represent Aramaic. Notice that in the Sifre's subsequent interpretations, this word is interpreted through word plays as if it were Hebrew.

[37] See B Sanhedrin 88b; Midrash Psalms 92:3; and Exodus Rabbah 5:9; 28:6. On the multiplicity of voices, see also Mekhilta, Yitro, 9; PRK, Bahodesh hashelishi, 25; Yalqut Shim‘oni, Psalms 709 and 843 (*Yelammedenu*). The understanding that the seventy Sinaitic languages were intended each for a different nation is only expressed in the later formulation of Exodus Rabbah 5:9. But cf. next note. For seventy languages as the totality of linguistic expression, see also J Megillah 1, 11 (9), 71b, where there is a debate between R. El‘azar (ca. 300) and R. Yohanan (ca. 280) as to whether humankind prior to Babel spoke seventy languages and understood one another or one language (Hebrew). According to the former view, Sinai would represent a brief return to the primeval ideal of multilingualism. On seventy languages, note also that according to B Sanhedrin 17a (with which cf. T Sanhedrin 8:1 and J Sheqalim 5, 1, 48d), B Menahot 65a, and B Megillah 13b, a qualification for membership in the Sanhedrin was knowledge of the "seventy languages." In B Sotah 33a it is said that the archangel Gabriel taught Joseph seventy languages so he could rule. Cf. the requirement that the Qumran "Overseer" (*mevaqqer*) know "all the languages of their families" (*kol leshon mishpehotam*). But cf. Josephus, *Ant.* XX, 12, 1, 264.

Thus, to translate a text of Scripture into one of these languages may be thought of not so much as a distancing from Sinai as a return to it. As one mishnaic passage suggests, to fully comprehend the written record of revelation, in a sense, to penetrate its seemingly unilingual writing, requires reverting it to the fullness of the seventy languages in which it was originally heard by Israel. Thus, in retelling the account in Deut. 27 of the covenantal ceremony in which the people, after crossing the Jordan, were to build an altar and write upon its stones "all the words of this Torah very plainly (*ba'er hetev*)" (Deut. 27:8), the Mishnah interprets these words as follows: "They inscribed on [the altar] all the words of the Torah in seventy languages." The biblical expression *ba'er hetev* is taken to mean not the physical clarity with which the words of the Torah were to be inscribed, but their translation into all seventy languages. The implication is that to articulate fully the meaning of the Hebrew text of the Torah would require its translation into the totality of human language.[38] Thus, translation is itself a form of explication, and no less so for those who "understand" the language of its source. In a sense, then, the original, pre-literary "text" of revelation is itself multilingual, and translation is one means of apprehending another one of its many faces.

---

[38] The biblical verb *be'er* is mishnaically construed not in its root meaning, to incise or articulate (see Z. Ben-Ḥayyim, "The Contribution of the Samaritan Inheritance," in: *Proceedings of the Israeli Academy of Sciences and Humanities* 3 [1969], 166–168), but in its extended post-biblical meaning, to interpret (here, multilingually). The same interpretation of Deut. 27:8 is repeated in B Sotah 36a. For the view that the translation into seventy languages made the Torah, or some part thereof, accessible to the seventy nations, see T Sotah 8:6–7; Mekilta to Deuteronomy (ed. S. Schechter in: *Tif'eret Yisra'el: Festschrift for Israel Lewy* [Breslau, 1911], 189); J Sotah 7, 5, 21d; B Sotah 35b. The idea of multilingual translation as a form of explication is similarly applied to Moses' teaching of the people in Tanḥuma, Deuteronomy 2, and Midrash Petirat Moshe (*Bet Ha-Midrasch*, Jellinek, I, p. 122). Compare the following text of M Sheqalim 5:1:

> And these are the ones who were appointed to serve in the sanctuary: . . . Petaḥiah over the bird offerings. Petaḥiah is also called Mordechai. [If so,] Why is he called Petaḥiah? For he would explain [*poteaḥ*] matters [or words] and interpret [*doresh*] them, for he knew seventy languages.

The source of the explanation of the name Petaḥiah-Mordechai is Neh. 7:7 and Ezra 2:2, where Mordechai, one of those who returned from the Babylonian exile, is immediately followed by Bilshan. If the two are taken as one name, then by a word play it could mean Mordechai, the master of languages (*ba'al lashon*). Cf. B Menaḥot 65a; B Megillah 13b; Pirke de-Rabbi Eliezer 50. The mishnaic passage clearly associates the skill of interpretation with a knowledge of seventy languages.

Just as different languages may correspond to different "faces" of the divinely revealed Torah, so, too, different languages may better suit different types of human discourse. Thus, the Palestinian Talmud attributes to R. Jonathan of Beth Guvrin (ca. 300) the view that there are "four languages which are pleasant for the world to use . . . Greek [*la'az*] for song, Latin for battle, Syrian [Palestinian Aramaic][39] for dirges, and Hebrew for speech [*dibbur*]."[40] I will return to the significance of the last two shortly, but for now simply note that once again we have four languages and once again we have languages with which the Jews of Palestine would have been familiar, albeit to differing degrees, in rabbinic times.

If it goes without saying that among all the languages Hebrew, as the "language of holiness," has a special status, then it needs to be stressed,

---

39 That *sursi* designates Aramaic (in particular Galilean Aramaic) is clear from J Sotah 7, 2, 21c and B Sotah 49b (and its parallel in B Bava Metzi'a 82b–83a).

40 J Megillah 1, 11 (9), 71b. The text next explains how the Israelites combined the Hebrew language with the Assyrian (Samaritan) script. I shall return to this tradition shortly. The same statement of R. Jonathan of Beth Guvrin is also cited in Esther Rabbah 4:12, but there the attribution is to R. Nathan of Beth Guvrin, and in place of Aramaic (*sursi*) we find Persian (*parsi*). E. Y. Kutscher, "The Language of the Hebrew and Aramaic Letters of Bar-Kosiba and His Generation," *Leshonenu* 26 (1961–62), 22 (Hebrew), comments that since R. Jonathan flourished in the second half of the third century, his statement may reflect the continued use of Hebrew as a spoken language that late, at least in southern Palestine (in Judea, where Beth Guvrin is located). But since R. Jonathan's saying is transmitted, without dissent, in a Galilean Palestinian source, there is no reason to assume that its sentiment would not have been endorsed in the north. For the obligation to teach one's child to speak Hebrew (*leshon haqqodesh*), and the rewards thereof, see Sifre Deuteronomy 46, Finkelstein, p. 104, introduced by *mikkan ameru*. For Palestinian parallels, see Sifre Zutta 15:38, Horowitz, p. 288; and T Hagigah 1:2, Lieberman, p. 375; and perhaps J Sukkah 3, 15, 54a (*leshon Torah*). In all of the parallel Babylonian passages (B Sukkah 42a; B Qiddushin 29a), however, the teaching of Hebrew is omitted from the list of what a father should teach his son. For the importance and reward of speaking Hebrew oneself, see Sifre Deuteronomy 333, Finkelstein, p. 383, in the name of R. Meir (ca. 150 C.E.). For parallels, see J Sheqalim 3, 4 (3), 47c; J Shabbat 1, 3c. Although some (e.g., E. Y. Kutscher, *The Language and Linguistic Background of the Isaiah Scroll* [Leiden, 1974], 8–15) have interpreted these passages conversely, as last-ditch efforts to preserve Hebrew from death as a spoken language, there is no reason, it seems to me, not to take them at their face value, especially in light of other evidence that I shall present below. S. Lieberman, in: *Archive of the New Dictionary of Rabbinical Literature*, eds. E. Y. Kutscher and M. Z. Kaddari (2 vols.; Ramat Gan, 1972–74), I, 107 (Hebrew), explains that Aramaic, as the Jewish "mother tongue" of the time, would have been a more spontaneous vehicle for the expression of mourning grief than Hebrew, but he does not reconcile this with the view of Hebrew as the preferred language of speech. On the use of Aramaic for dirges we now have new evidence, to be discussed below.

as do our rabbinic sources, that among all the languages Aramaic is closest but not quite equal in status to that of Hebrew, even as it accompanies Hebrew in several usages.[41] Thus, the Palestinian Talmud attributes to R. Yoḥanan (ca. 280) the view that Aramaic (*sursi*) should be treated with respect since it is employed in the Torah, the Prophets, and the Writings.[42] But Aramaic also has a special status close to that of Hebrew, as a revealed language and as a language of revelation, through its association with Ezra. According to the Tosefta, in a tradition attributed to R. Yose (ca. 150), the Torah would have been given through Ezra had he not been preceded by Moses, since both of them ascended in order to become teachers of Torah. Instead, Ezra gave Israel the Aramaic language and script (the square Assyrian letters), just as Moses gave them the Hebrew language and script (the cursive Samaritan letters).[43] Later reframings of this tradition in both Talmuds describe how Israel, when confronted in the time of Ezra with two Torahs in different revealed languages and scripts, chose to combine the Hebrew language of one with the Aramaic

[41] For example, both Hebrew and Aramaic are used in blessing and prayer, even though Hebrew is dominant in both of these usages. On Hebrew and Aramaic in blessing, see B Shabbat 12b. On the use of Aramaic in personal petitionary prayer, see B Sotah 32b, as well as B Shabbat 12b. Similarly, although the primary language in use in the Temple may be presumed to have been Hebrew, Aramaic is said to have been used for some functions (see M Sheqalim 5:3; 6:5). It is also stated (B Sotah 32b) that the intermediary divine voice (*bat qol*) communicates with humans both in Hebrew and in Aramaic. Note also the debate (B Sanhedrin 38b) whether Adam spoke Hebrew (Resh Laqish) or Aramaic (Rav). It may be coincidental, but the view that Adam spoke Aramaic is attributed to a Babylonian amora, while the view that he spoke Hebrew is attributed to a Palestinian amora (cf. the preceding note regarding a favorable attitude toward the teaching of Hebrew to one's children in Palestinian but not Babylonian sources). On the mishnaic distinction (Sotah 7:1–5) between those ritual recitations which are to be said in Hebrew and those which can be said in any language, see J Sotah 7, 2, 21c, where it is debated whether this distinction is a function which predates the giving of the Torah (and hence can be said in any language) or postdates the giving of the Torah (and hence must be said in Hebrew). Thus, there is an ambiguity whether Hebrew, the language of creation, was used immediately from creation or only after the revelation of the Torah, or, alternatively, whether it was spoken by Adam, subsequently suspended (with the fall or flood), and only restored at Sinai.

[42] J Sotah 7, 2, 21c. Examples are given from each: Gen. 31:47; Jer. 10:11; Dan. 2:4. For rabbinic texts in which it is emphasized that Targum (Aramaic) occurs within the text of Scripture, see M Yadaim 4:5 and J Sanhedrin 10, 1, 27d. Note that according to the following texts, the Aramaic parts of Scripture would lose their sacred (scriptural) status were they to be translated into Hebrew: M Yadaim 4:5; a *baraita* in B Megillah 8b–9a; a *baraita* in B Shabbat 115b.

[43] T Sanhedrin 4:7–8.

(Assyrian) script of the other.[44] Thus, the Aramaic language is elevated to a status approaching that of Hebrew, only to be lowered from that position by Israel themselves.[45]

From these rabbinic sources we see that Aramaic has something of an anomalous status, accompanying Hebrew in many usages but distinct from it, a revealed and scriptural language whose religious status is somewhat less than that of Hebrew, even as its script was combined with the language of Hebrew to constitute Scripture. But the anomaly of Aramaic, not in its scriptural status but in its common usage in rabbinic times, is also noted in a statement attributed to R. Judah the Patriarch in a *baraita* in the Babylonian Talmud: "Why [use] Aramaic [*sursi*] in the Land of Israel? Either *leshon haqqodesh* ["the language of holiness," i.e., Hebrew] or Greek."[46] The normal expectation would have been for the Jews of Palestine, especially in the Galilee, to either stick by their ancestral language or adopt that of the ruling culture, with Aramaic being neither. But, in a sense, while Aramaic was neither it was also something of both: a close cognate to Hebrew but also shared with the surrounding non-Jewish cultures among whom Israel dwelt.

---

44 J Megillah 1, 11 (9), 71b; B Sanhedrin 21b–22a. We find the same in J Sotah 7, 2, 21c. According to R. Judah the Patriarch, the Torah was first revealed in the Aramaic (Assyrian) script, was changed to the Hebrew (Samaritan) script when Israel sinned with the golden calf, and was finally restored to the Aramaic script in the days of Ezra.

45 None of these passages speaks of Targum per se, even though both Talmuds know of the association of Ezra's teaching activity with the origins of Targum. For this association, based on Neh. 8:8, see above, n. 3. This association is not found, however, in any tannaitic sources. For Ezra as a second Moses for his receiving of revelation, see also IV Ezra 14. Contrast B Sukkah 20a, which states that Ezra only reestablished what had been forgotten by the people. Only Babylonian rabbinic sources identify Ezra as the author of or authority behind a particular targumic text (Tg. Onq.).

46 B Bava Qamma 82b–83a. In the printed edition of the Talmud, the *baraita* continues with a similar statement attributed to R. Yose, asking about the reason for using Aramaic in Babylonia where either Hebrew or Persian would be the logical choices. But most manuscripts (including the Munich ms.) have Rav Joseph (b. Ḥiyya, ca. 300), a Babylonian amora who is the major Babylonian tradent of the Targum to the Prophets (see B Pesaḥim 68a; B Bava Qamma 3b). It would appear that his statement, not originally part of the *baraita*, has been appended to it. Kutscher's claim (*Language and Linguistic Background of the Isaiah Scroll*, 13) that our passage is irrefutable proof that Aramaic had replaced Hebrew as the spoken language of the Galilee by the time of R. Judah the Patriarch is, it seems to me, unwarranted, especially in light of other Palestinian rabbinic texts, and extra-rabbinic evidence, which presume their coexistence along with Greek.

Implicit in the Palestinian sources considered here is the rabbinic understanding that Targum is intended for an audience, whether in worship or in study, that comprehends both Hebrew and Aramaic but nonetheless is served in their reception of Hebrew Scripture through the mediating interpretation of its Aramaic translation. This is not to suggest that the rabbis or their students experienced no language gap with the Hebrew of Scripture. Quite the contrary, they admitted that the Hebrew they employed in their discourse was different from that of the Bible. R. Yoḥanan is reported to have stated, "The language of the Torah is one thing and the language of the sages is another."[47] Furthermore, we have stories of rabbis who were uncertain as to the meaning of biblical words and phrases and sought their meanings through parallel usages in Aramaic.[48] Thus, Aramaic, being close to yet still distinct from Hebrew,

[47] B ʿAvodah Zarah 58b and B Ḥullin 137b. This is not to deny that the Hebrew of Scripture was rabbinically read and interpreted in terms of rabbinic (mishnaic) Hebrew idioms, or to claim that either was a monolith, but simply to state that they were distinguishable languages, even as they were intertwined in rabbinic discourse.

[48] See the story in Genesis Rabbah 79:7, Theodor-Albeck, pp. 946–948, about two third-century sages who went to an Arab market to learn the Aramaic equivalents of some scriptural words by listening to equivalent expressions in Hebrew and Aramaic spoken there. For this understanding, see Theodor's notes ad loc. Frequently cited in this regard is the story about the handmaid of R. Judah the Patriarch and his students: B Megillah 18a = Rosh ha-Shanah 26b. But the earlier Palestinian version in J Megillah 2, 2, 73a and J Sheviʿit 9, 1, 38c is quite different. The sages come in search of the meaning of two mishnaic words and an answer to a question of rabbinic priority (age or learning). They learn the answers to all three from the handmaid's incidental comments to them (in Hebrew) regarding their manner of entering the house. The narrative voice of the story is in Aramaic. These stories denote not so much a general ignorance of Hebrew, whether biblical or rabbinic, as a phenomenon common in all societies: we learn the meanings of words from their application in social contexts. To the extent that such social contexts are multilingual, we learn the meanings of words of one language from their juxtapositions with those of another. Note also B Megillah 18a, where the view that only women and the unlearned are unable to understand Scripture is vigorously rejected: "Do we [sages] ourselves understand: הָאֲחַשְׁתְּרָנִים בְּנֵי הָרַמָּכִים (Esth. 8:10)?" For another Babylonian source that stresses the interpretive importance of Targum to the sages themselves (who certainly knew Hebrew and shifted freely between it and Aramaic), see B Megillah 3a (= B Moʿed Qatan 28b), where R. Joseph (ca. 300 C.E.) says of Zech. 12:11: "Were it not for the Targum of this verse we would not have understood it." His problem with the verse is not with the meaning of its words but with its seemingly elliptical contents, which the extant Targum to the Prophets fills out. For a similar statement, see B Sanhedrin 94b. The medieval Tosafot (to B Berakhot 8a–b) build upon R. Joseph's comment, as follows: "Targum clarifies what could not be learned from the [original] Hebrew [even for those who know Hebrew]." Note G. Steiner's comment (*After Babel*, 17) that, "Any

both in language and in status, provided a medium of interpretive reception, but only in dialogical accompaniment to the Hebrew original. Unlike translations into other languages (especially Greek) for audiences ignorant of Hebrew, the public translation of Scripture into Aramaic was, according to the rabbinic evidence, intended for an audience which could follow both the reading of Scripture in Hebrew and its responsive rendering into Aramaic, with the latter never upstaging or supplanting the former but drawing both interpretive and dramatic attention to it.[49] Thus, to Walter Benjamin's rhetorical question, "Is translation meant for readers who do not understand the original?"[50] we could have expected a negative rabbinic response.

IV. Rabbinic Literature Itself is Bilingual

I shall return now to my opening methodological caveat. If the picture that I have painted from Palestinian rabbinic sources of the practice of Targum both in the synagogue and in the context of study is correct, we need not assume that it is a simple representation of what actually took place in the synagogues and study houses of the ancient Jewish Galilee of the same time. Perhaps this is simply a picture that the rabbis sought to project onto those contexts—or how they sought to transform

---

thorough reading of a text out of the past of one's own language and literature is a manifold act of interpretation." The question that remains, then, and to which I shall return shortly, is: if such translation was necessary, even for those who knew Hebrew, why not translate the old Hebrew of Scripture into the new Hebrew of the sages?

49 For the possibility of rendering Scripture into other languages for those who did not understand Hebrew, and of those people using such translations as the texts of their readings, that is, as their Scriptures, especially in the case of Greek, see in particular B Megillah 18a, which treats the issue with respect to the Scroll of Esther. See as well M Megillah 1:8; 2:1; T Megillah 2:6; 4 (3):13; J Megillah 1, 11 (9), 71c; 2, 1, 73a; 4, 3, 75a; J Sotah 7, 1, 21b; B Megillah 8b–9a. It is clear from the various stories regarding the origins of the Septuagint that it was regarded as Scripture by the Jews of Alexandria, and eventually by other Greek-speaking Jewish communities and early Christianity. See in particular Philo, *Mos.* 2, 26–44, who claims not only that the translators were divinely inspired but that the resulting translation is the equivalent, "both in matters and words" (2, 40), of the Hebrew. Compare, however, the view of Ben Sira's grandson in his preface to his Greek translation of Ben Sira's wisdom (ca. 132 B.C.E.), that the Greek translation of "the law, the prophets and the other writings" does not accurately represent the Hebrew original. For the rabbinic practice of having Targum accompany Scripture rather than replace it, see also above, n. 31.

50 W. Benjamin, "The Task of the Translator: An Introduction to the Translation of Baudelaire's Tableaux Parisiens," *Illuminations* (New York, 1955), 69.

the practice of Targum as it had developed apart from rabbinic control—
and even if they did so with some success, we cannot assume that they
were equally successful in all places. Since we have no contemporary
non-rabbinic sources for the practice of Targum against which we could
check our picture so as to determine to what extent it is representative
and to what extent it is rhetorical, we may have to remain content to say
that this is how our Palestinian texts (with some important differences
from their Babylonian kin) viewed targumic practice.

But there is another side to our picture, relating not so much to what
our rabbinic texts assert as to what they seem to presume, and for which
we have other types of evidence with which to compare. The presump-
tion is that the targumic setting, both in study and in worship, was a
bilingual one, wherein both Hebrew and Aramaic (besides Greek, of
course) were widely used in Palestine as vehicles of creative expression
and comprehension in the period, not simply up to the Bar-Kokhba revolt, as is now commonly held, but significantly thereafter as well. Since
no ancient tape recorders have survived until our day, the question of
what people "really" spoke is one we cannot answer with any certainty.
However, even if we could, it is likely that we would find different answers at different times in different places among different classes and
under different circumstances, and that even for a given time, place,
class, and circumstance we could possibly hear a mixture of tongues,
whether Hebrew and Aramaic, Aramaic and Greek, or even all three. All
of our evidence is literary of some sort and, hence, with some rhetorical
coloring—whether it be a rabbinic text, an inscription or a letter.

Having examined all the rabbinic stories and sayings which, when
interpreted as simple representations, are said to prove that Hebrew had
already died among all except the sages, and among them it had weak-
ened, I find that each and every one can just as easily be interpreted to
suggest that Hebrew and Aramaic continued to coexist, even as they
were in competition with one another, and therefore significantly inter-
penetrated each other.[51] But here we are, still caught in the dilemma of
rabbinic literature's dual nature of rhetorical representation.

---

[51] For the most comprehensive assemblage of such sources, see E. Ben-Yehuda,
"Until When Did They Speak Hebrew?," in: *A Complete Dictionary of Ancient and Mod-
ern Hebrew. Prolegomena* (Jerusalem, 1948), 83–254, esp. 201–254 (Hebrew). See also A.
Bendavid, *Biblical Hebrew and Mishnaic Hebrew* (2 vols.; Tel-Aviv, 1967–71), I, 153–165.
For examples, see above n. 48. Another such case is B ʿEruvin 53a–b, often cited as
evidence for the demise of Hebrew in the Galilee, which, in fact, simply attests to a
Galilean tendency not to distinguish clearly between gutterals and other letters, not

Yet, even before we leave the rabbinic evidence, it is important to remind ourselves that rabbinic literature is itself bilingual: it employs both Hebrew and Aramaic, not just in different texts but in the same texts, albeit to different extents. I speak here not so much of Hebrew influences on rabbinic Aramaic or of Aramaic influences on rabbinic Hebrew, of which there are many, but of the way in which some rabbinic texts alternate between Hebrew and Aramaic: the two Talmuds, the amoraic midrashim, and parts of the liturgy. Especially in the Talmuds, Hebrew and Aramaic are assigned particular functions by the redactors of those documents. Hebrew is generally the language of teaching, be it in the form of a *baraita* or a saying of an amoraic sage, or even of an amora of the later generations, while Aramaic is the language of debate, question and answer, as well as the editorial connecting and framing structures. It is as if the text were written in two colors, or two scripts, so as to distinguish its layered voices, those of the tannaitic and amoraic teachers from those of the anonymous redactors who interwove their teachings so as to create a cross-generational dialectic.[52] Similarly, texts of

---

only in Hebrew but also in Aramaic. The same passage is followed by a series of riddles, by both sages and R. Judah the Patriarch's handmaid, which in some cases depend on Hebrew/Aramaic word plays, and hence knowledge of both. While it is often noted that rabbinic Hebrew displays signs of Aramaic influence, this being a mark of Hebrew's weakening, the converse is as true: Galilean Aramaic, unlike its eastern Aramaic cousins, displays the active influence of a living Hebrew. See Z. Ben-Ḥayyim, "The Contribution of the Samaritan Heritage to the Study of the History of Hebrew," in: *Proceedings of the Israel Academy of Sciences and Humanities*, III (Jerusalem, 1968), 63–69 (Hebrew); ibid. (Jerusalem, 1969), 162–174 (English); idem, *The Literary and Oral Tradition of Hebrew and Aramaic amongst the Samaritans*, V (Jerusalem, 1977), 251–259 (Hebrew); A. Tal, "Between Hebrew and Aramaic in the Writings of the Samaritans," in: *Proceedings of the Israel Academy of Sciences and Humanities*, VII (Jerusalem, 1987–88), 239–255 (Hebrew).

52 See E. Margoliot, "Hebrew and Aramaic in the Talmud and Midrash," *Leshonenu* 27 (1962–63), 20–33 (Hebrew). Abba Bendavid (*Biblical Hebrew and Mishnaic Hebrew*, 134–135) follows Margoliot in this regard, going on to draw a connection between the bilingualism of the Talmud and that of those who attended the synagogue. However, as much as Hebrew and Aramaic are somewhat functionally differentiated in the Talmud, they are also more complexly intermixed than Margoliot's study would suggest. See in this regard, S. Friedman, "A Critical Study of *Yevamot X* with a Methodological Introduction," in: *Texts and Studies of the Jewish Theological Seminary of America*, I (New York, 1977), 301–302 (Hebrew) in criticism of H. Klein, "Gemara and Sebara," *JQR* 38 (1947), 67–91. I am not familiar with a similar treatment of the mix of Hebrew and Aramaic in the Palestinian Talmud, but would expect it to be pretty much the same yet with a higher proportion of Hebrew. While it is sometimes presumed that the *gemara* of both Talmuds is in Aramaic while the Mishnah upon which

aggadah, whether talmudic or midrashic, often switch languages as they shift from a story frame to its contained dialogue, sometimes with the frame being in Aramaic, sometimes in Hebrew, depending on the text. Similar language shifting between Hebrew and Aramaic can be seen in the liturgy, going back to rabbinic times, as well.[53] Literary bilingualism (and socio-linguists would extend this to language in general) constitutes a complex code in which switches between languages performatively denote switches in signification as well.[54] Such texts, of course, presume audiences which understand both Hebrew and Aramaic and are able to shift easily and unconsciously between the two, whatever their uses in other domains.

---

they comment is in Hebrew, this is not true: the *gemara* itself, even when we discount scriptural citations and *baraitot*, is still about half Hebrew and half Aramaic. This was confirmed by Prof. M. Bar-Asher of the Academy for the Hebrew Language in Jerusalem. Similarly, Prof. M. Sokoloff, in a lecture at the Tenth World Congress of Jewish Studies in Jerusalem on August 22, 1989, estimated that only ten per cent of the Palestinian Talmud overall is in Aramaic.

[53] To my knowledge, no systematic study has been made of the interrelation of Aramaic and Hebrew in the Palestinian homiletical midrashic collections of the period we are considering. They presume a reading audience with facility both in Hebrew and in Aramaic. But if these texts go back ultimately to oral preaching and teaching settings in the Galilean synagogues and study houses of the third through sixth centuries, are we to presume that the oral homilies upon which they are ultimately based were delivered in Hebrew, Aramaic or some combination of the two? Similarly, what language knowledge do they presume for their audience in order for their linguistically-based exegeses to have been understood? For one case of a halakhic homily that presumes knowledge of Hebrew on the part of its popular audience, see B Pesaḥim 42a (in the name of R. Mattena), cited in this regard by E. Y. Kutscher, "Some Problems of the Lexicography of Mishnaic Hebrew and Its Comparison with Biblical Hebrew," in: *Archive of the New Dictionary of Rabbinical Literature*, I, 55 (Hebrew). For the use of targumic Aramaic in dialogical juxtaposition with scriptural Hebrew in ancient prayers, especially the *qedusha de-sidra*, see D. Boyarin, "The Song and the Praise: Dual Meaning and the Art of Song in Fixed Prayer," in: *Eshel Beer-Sheva*, III: *Essays in Jewish Studies in Memory of Prof. Nehemiah Alloni*, eds. G. J. Blidstein et al. (Beersheva, 1986), 91–99 (Hebrew). For the bilingualism of the synagogue service more generally, see A. Shinan, "Hebrew and Aramaic in the Literature of the Synagogue," in: *Tura: Studies in Jewish Thought – Simon Greenberg Jubilee Volume*, eds. M. Ayali et al. (Tel-Aviv, 1989), 224–232.

[54] For a much broader discussion of recent research on bilingualism in relation to the present topic, see my forthcoming book, *Targum and Torah*.

V. Extra-Rabbinic Evidence for Bilingualism in the Galilee of Late Antiquity

One important extra-rabbinic source for language usage in the Galilee during the third through sixth centuries is the many inscriptions in Aramaic, Hebrew, and Greek found at ancient synagogues and related sites. It would be wrong to read such inscriptions as being simple markers of what language the people of a particular place "actually" spoke, since they are stylized and often two or more languages are used within a single location, even within a single inscription. Such inscriptions, no less than texts, are literary and hence convention-bound. Therefore, why a particular inscription appears in one language and not another, or in one language alongside another, may be a function of local conventions that governed the appropriateness of a particular language for conveying a particular type of information in a particular functional setting.

While the vast majority of synagogue inscriptions are in Aramaic, these are mainly dedicatory inscriptions, marking the building, repair or expansion of synagogue edifices, and crediting the donors who made these possible. Yet, at least seven synagogues have dedications in Hebrew and at least one synagogue (Kefar Barᶜam in the Upper Galilee) has a dedicatory inscription in both Hebrew and Aramaic. In one synagogue (ᶜAlma in the Upper Galilee) we have a bilingual inscription on a lintel containing a blessing in Hebrew for inhabitants of that place and other places in Israel, and then, switching to Aramaic, the artist's identification of himself: "I am Yose bar Levi the Levite, the artist who made [this lintel]." Yet this very same artist "signs" the exact same Hebrew blessing at nearby Barᶜam in Hebrew, speaking of himself in the third person: "Yose the Levite the son of Levi made this lintel." Perhaps when he wished to identify himself in a more personal way (first person) he employed Aramaic, but when he wished to be more formal (third person) he employed Hebrew. Nevertheless, in both cases we may presume that he knew both languages and expected those who attended the synagogue to know both as well (although we cannot infer their level of fluency in either).[55]

---

55 I have culled this survey from Naveh, *On Stone and Mosaic*. See also the comments of J. Yahalom in his review of the same, in *Kiryat Sefer* 53 (1978), 349–355 (Hebrew); and in an expanded English version of the same, "Synagogue Inscriptions in Palestine: A Stylistic Classification," *Immanuel* 10 (1980), 47–56. For additional inscriptions following much the same pattern from the Golan, see D. Urman, "Jewish Inscriptions of the Mishna and Talmud Period from Kaẓrin in the Golan," *Tarbiẓ* 53 (1983–84), 513–545 (Hebrew); idem, "Jewish Inscriptions from Dabbura in the Golan," *IEJ* 22 (1972), 16–23. Although I will not focus here on the Greek synagogue inscriptions, their presence is not insignificant, although appreciably less common in Pales-

Perhaps an analogous case, but now in a switch from Greek to Aramaic, can be seen in the synagogue at Hammath Tiberias. There we find, centrally located, a two-part inscription which, first in Greek, singles out two leading members of the community for having contributed to the completion of the synagogue renovations (as do other Greek inscriptions in this synagogue), and then switches to Aramaic to bless all the members of the congregation who have made or will make (so it is hoped) contributions to the synagogue.[56] Those who attended such synagogues are assumed to have been multilingual, with such multilingualism being literarily employed within the synagogue in order to differentiate between the distinct types of information communicated within it.

Equally interesting is the fact that what have been called "literary" inscriptions, that is, inscriptions whose language appears to be drawn from texts, are uniformly in Hebrew, whether they be biblical quotes ('En-Gedi and Beth Alpha),[57] an extensive halakhic text (Rehov) or lists of priestly cycles of service in the Temple (*mishmarot*).[58] Similarly, mosaic zodiacs contain the names of signs and seasons in Hebrew (Hammath Tiberias, Beth Alpha, Na'aran, and 'En-Gedi). In most cases, these Hebrew inscriptions are found in synagogues which also have Aramaic dedicatory inscriptions. Of particular interest is the sixth–seventh century halakhic inscription in the Rehov synagogue, in which place names and names of fruits and vegetables are in Aramaic and aramaicized Greek, while the connecting phrases and other comments are in Hebrew, which is the overall language of the inscription. Such an inscription was to be read and understood—so as to be applied—by those who attended

---

tine than in the Diaspora and more common in certain regions of the former (coastal and major cities) than in others (e.g., the Golan). As we shall soon see, Greek inscriptions in Palestinian synagogues can be found alongside Hebrew and Aramaic ones. For the Greek synagogue inscriptions, see B. Lifshitz, *Donateurs et fondateurs dans les synagogues juives* (Paris, 1967), nos. 64–81; and now, L. Roth-Gerson, *The Greek Inscriptions from the Synagogues in Eretz-Israel* (Jerusalem, 1987) (Hebrew).

56 For this dual inscription, set within a single *tabula ansata*, see M. Dothan, *Hammath Tiberias: Early Synagogues and the Hellenistic and Roman Remains* (Jerusalem, 1983), 53–54, 60, Pls. 21.1–2, 35.3. Much the same pattern of Greek-Aramaic switching can be seen in a dual inscription at the entrance to the synagogue of Beth Alpha: first the two artists are blessed in Greek, then the members of the village as a whole are blessed in Aramaic for having contributed the cost of the inscription. In Hammath Tiberias the zodiac captions are in Hebrew, as are the biblical captions at Beth Alpha.

57 Whereas at Dura Europos similar scriptural captions are in Aramaic.

58 For the *mishmarot*, see Naveh, *On Stone and Mosaic*, nos. 51, 52, 56, 106.

this synagogue, unless, of course, we consider it to have been merely decorative.[59] In the recently published synagogue inscriptions from the synagogue and what is said to have been a study hall at Meroth in north-ernmost Galilee (fifth–seventh centuries), we find a prominently dis-played blessing in Hebrew (Deut. 28:6) for all who enter, the recording of a donor's or artist's name in Aramaic, a scriptural caption in Hebrew (Isa. 65:25), and an amulet which begins in Hebrew, switches to Aramaic for the body of its magical incantation, and concludes in Hebrew.[60] Thus, it would appear from Palestinian synagogue inscriptions that, while Ara-maic predominates, Hebrew and Aramaic (as well as Greek) were em-ployed alongside each other, even while somewhat functionally differ-entiated in their usage, and that in many places some knowledge of both languages (as well as Greek) on the part of those who frequented the synagogues may be presumed.

Another sort of recently expanded literary evidence, whose relation to rabbinical authority is uncertain but whose locus is generally thought to be the Galilean synagogue, is the literature of *piyyut* (liturgical poetry), beginning as early as 400 C.E. but certainly by 500 C.E. and largely un-known until it was brought to light from the Cairo Geniza. These liturgi-cal-exegetical poems, which accompanied the weekly and festival Torah-readings or were commissioned by synagogue communities or by indi-viduals for special occasions, are generally in Hebrew, the language in

---

59   On the halakhic inscription at Reḥov, see ibid., 79–85, and the important articles by Y. Sussmann: "A Halakhic Inscription from the Beth-Shean Valley," *Tarbiz* 43 (1973–74), 88–158; "Additional Notes to 'A Halakhic Inscription from the Beth-Shean Valley'," *Tarbiz* 44 (1974–75), 193–195; "The Boundaries of Eretz Israel," *Tarbiz* 45 (1976), 213–257; "The Inscription in the Synagogue at Rehob," *Qadmoniot* 8/32 (1975), 123–128 (all in Hebrew). Although Sussmann thinks that the inscription was made by an artist not knowledgeable in Hebrew, he argues that the purpose of this fifth–sev-enth century Hebrew inscription was to instruct those who attended the synagogue in the halakhic agricultural obligations that applied in their region (ibid., 128). For this to have been the case, they must have had some understanding of the language of the inscription. The similarities between this text and its parallels in rabbinic sources suggest that this might have been a synagogue within the orbit of rabbinic influence, in which rules governing the practice of Targum might have been fol-lowed. Other, unpublished inscriptions from the same site are in Aramaic.

60   See Z. Ilan and E. Damati, *Meroth: The Ancient Jewish Village* (Tel-Aviv, 1987) (Hebrew, with English summary). On the Hebrew-Aramaic amulet, see J. Naveh, "'A Good Subduing, There Is None Like It': An Ancient Amulet from Ḥorvat Marish in the Galilee," *Tarbiz* 54 (1984–85), 367–382 (Hebrew). On the Aramaic inscription, see also Y. Tsafrir, "On the Word *mny* in a Synagogue Inscription at Meroth: A New In-terpretation," *Qadmoniot* 21/81–82 (1988), 57–58 (Hebrew).

Steven D. Fraade

which they would have been recited in the synagogues. Since to our ears their language may seem strange and artificial, some have asserted that they were mere literary ornaments which need not have been comprehended at all by their audience. However, recent analysis of their language indicates that it would have been well-suited to a Galilean audience which understood both Hebrew and Aramaic, even if not everyone understood the intricate allusions and puns of these learned performances. Not only do these Hebrew poems presume a knowledge of contemporary Galilean Aramaic, but some of their word plays presume a knowledge of both Hebrew and Aramaic.[61] In addition, even though they are in Hebrew, they seem to be closely related, in their language and in the traditions they presume, to the extant Targums which, of course, are in Aramaic.[62] But since these poems, unlike the Targums, were not read in direct juxtaposition with the Torah-reading, they did not need to be distinguished from it but could be read in Hebrew, the dominant language of the liturgy.

If synagogue poetry related to the Torah cycle was composed and recited in Hebrew in the Galilean synagogues, we now know of another type of poetry, from the Galilee of the very same period, which was composed and recited in Aramaic but which served a very different function. An extensive collection of Palestinian Aramaic poetry has been uncovered from the Cairo Geniza whose contents are words of eulogy for the deceased and consolation for their mourners.[63] This gives some

[61] In addition to the works by Ben-Hayyim and Tal cited above, n. 51, see A. Kor, "Yannai's Piyyutim (Liturgic Poems): Evidence to the Hebrew in Eretz-Yisrael during the Byzantine Period" (doctoral dissertation, Tel-Aviv University; Tel-Aviv, 1988) (Hebrew); R. Mirkin, "A Grammatical and Stylistic Examination of the Vocabulary of Yannai," in: *Proceedings of the Fourth World Congress of Judaic Studies*, II (Jerusalem, 1969), 437–441 (Hebrew); J. Yahalom, *The Language of the Ancient Israeli Liturgical Poem* (Jerusalem, 1985).

[62] For a detailed comparison, see A. Kor, "Yannai's Piyyutim." There is one case in which a Hebrew *piyyut* of Yannai (in: *The Liturgical Poems of Rabbi Yannai*, ed. Z. M. Rabinovitz [2 vols.; Jerusalem, 1985–87], I, 216–217) is virtually identical to an Aramaic Targum (Klein, in: *Geniza Manuscripts*, I, 72–75); this has occasioned much speculation as to which derived from which; see Lieberman, "Hazzanut Yannai," 224, 243–244 (Hebrew); M. Zulay, "Studies on Yannai," *The Proceedings of the Institute for the Study of the Hebrew Poem* 2 (1936), 270 (Hebrew); idem, *Zur Liturgie der babylonischen Juden: Geniza Texte* (Stuttgart, 1933), 64–65; Z. M. Rabinovitz, *Halakha and Aggada in Yannai's Liturgical Poems* (Tel-Aviv, 1965), 45–47 (Hebrew); idem, *The Liturgical Poems of Rabbi Yannai*, I, 59.

[63] For preliminary notices, see J. Yahalom, "*Sursi le'ilya'*," in: *Proceedings of the Academy of the Hebrew Language – 1986*, XXXIII (Jerusalem, 1989), 133–137 (Hebrew); J.

confirmation to the saying of R. Jonathan of Beth Guvrin that Aramaic, of all languages, is the best suited to lamentation.[64] The Palestinian Talmud distinguishes between the blessings of the mourners and their consolations in terms of their domains: the former in the synagogue and the latter in the open space of the mourners' "row."[65] From rabbinic literature we know that the language for blessing the mourners was Hebrew; we now know that the language for sharing in their grief was Aramaic.[66]

All of this evidence, as fragmentary as it is, suggests that the language situation in the Jewish Galilee in amoraic and post-amoraic times was much more complex than is generally presumed, having continued to be multilingual long after the Bar-Kokhba revolt. Hebrew, Aramaic, and Greek continued in simultaneous use, albeit to very different extents depending on geographic location and social strata, but even within a given locale and stratum they appear to have been used side by side, but in functionally differentiated ways. This provides a likely linguistic backdrop to the picture of targumic practice that emerges from rabbinic literature of the same setting. As late as the end of the ninth century, according to one testimony uncovered from the Cairo Geniza, an author of a Hebrew grammar, 'Ali ben Yehuda the Nazirite, reports that he would

Yahalom and M. Sokoloff, "Aramaic Piyyutim from the Byzantine Period," *JQR* 75 (1985), 309–321. For the full publication, see *The Poetry of Israel: Poems in Aramaic of Jews of Eretz-Israel*, eds. J. Yahalom and M. Sokoloff (Jerusalem, forthcoming) (Hebrew).

64 See above, n. 40.

65 J Sanhedrin 6, 11, 23d; J Pesaḥim 8, 8, 36d.

66 Two other types of non-rabbinic literature might also be mentioned here. The first is the *hekhalot* texts (in Hebrew), which D. Halperin, *The Faces of the Chariot: Early Jewish Responses to Ezekiel's Vision* (Tübingen, 1988), has argued derive from the "popular" setting of the synagogue; the second is the extensive corpus of Jewish magical texts found in the Cairo Geniza, most of which have not yet been published. According to an oral report by P. Schäfer at the Tenth World Congress of Jewish Studies in Jerusalem on August 22, 1989, these magical texts are in both Hebrew and Aramaic, often mixed in a single text, with instructions to their users (the "simple people," according to Schäfer) often appearing in Hebrew. These texts appear to derive from Palestine from the late Roman or early Byzantine period. For examples, see T-S K1.127, in: J. Naveh and S. Shaked, *Amulets and Magic Bowls: Aramaic Incantations of Late Antiquity* (Jerusalem, 1985), 237–238; T-S K1.143, in : J. Naveh, "A Good Subduing, There is None Like It," 378–379; and T-S K1.18/30, in: L. H. Schiffman and M. D. Swartz, *Hebrew and Aramaic Incantation Texts from the Cairo Geniza: Selected Texts from Taylor-Schechter Box K1* (forthcoming). Note as well a bilingual magical bowl which is inscribed with alternating biblical verses and their Aramaic translations in: S. A. Kaufman, " A Unique Magic Bowl from Nippur," *JNES* 32 (1973), 170–174.

sit in the squares and courtyards of Tiberias listening to the speech of the crowd in both Hebrew and Aramaic.[67] Sitting in a synagogue, our grammarian would have heard mainly Hebrew, but not without its Aramaic accompaniment which, if the rabbinic picture is at all representational, was intended for an audience that was accustomed to switching between the two languages.

Conclusions

Let us then return to that rabbinic picture so that we may understand it once again in its own right. Rabbinic sources conceive of Targum, both in its liturgical and study contexts, not as a substitute for Scripture but as its mediating accompaniment, as a bridge and buffer between written Scripture and its oral reception and elucidation. The status of Targum in both these contexts is rabbinically portrayed as being close to but still less than that of Scripture. We have seen this approximation yet differentiation of status between Targum and Scripture with regard to their recitations, their reciters, their texts, and their languages.

---

[67] See N. Alloni, "Ten Words of Spoken Hebrew in the Tenth Century," *Leshonenu* 32 (1969), 153–172 (Hebrew); idem, *Studies in Medieval Philology and Literature: Collected Papers* (Jerusalem, 1988), II, 303–324 (Hebrew). For a striking example of the continued use of Hebrew in Palestine for private letter writing, at least into the fifth century, see M. Mishor, "A New Edition of the Hebrew Letter: Oxford MS Heb. d. 69 (P)," *Leshonenu* 53/3–4 (1989), 215–264. The evidence presented here suggests, however, that the creative survival of Hebrew was not restricted to southern Palestine (Judea), as is often suggested. My survey of the extant synagogue inscriptions shows no appreciable preponderance of Hebrew over Aramaic inscriptions in the south as compared to the north. Before the discovery of the Bar-Kokhba letters, it was assumed by some that Hebrew had died as a spoken language already in Second Temple times. Those letters provide striking evidence to the contrary, pushing up the date of Hebrew's "death" (see, for example, Kutscher, "Hebrew and Aramaic Letters of Bar-Kosiba," 21–22). Further evidence suggests that even that death announcement was premature. For earlier studies which emphasize the multilingualism of Palestine up to the time of the Bar-Kokhba revolt, see H. Birkeland, *The Language of Jesus* (Oslo, 1954); Ch. Rabin, "Hebrew and Aramaic in the First Century," in: *The Jewish People in the First Century*, II, eds. S. Safrai and M. Stern (Assen and Philadelphia, 1976), 1007–1039; B. Spolsky, "Jewish Multilingualism in the First Century: An Essay in Historical Sociolinguistics," in: *Readings in the Sociology of Jewish Languages*, I, ed. J. A. Fishman (Leiden, 1985), 35–50. For the most recent treatment of Hebrew/Aramaic and Greek bilingualism, with substantial reference to the sociolinguistic literature on bilingualism in the ancient world and in general, see G. H. R. Horsley, *New Documents Illustrating Early Christianity*, V: *Linguistic Essays* (Australia, 1989), 40–50.

To employ a musical metaphor, the performance of Targum may be said to have been neither that of a soloist nor that of an equal partner in a duet, but that of an accompanist to the principal performance of the scriptural recital. The significance of this function should not be underrated. Just as the musical accompanist enunciates and thereby enhances the performance of the soloist through the subtleties of his or her interpretations, so, too, Targum in relation to Scripture. But in both cases, the accompanist must share the stage unobtrusively, that is, without drawing attention away from the principal performer. It is for both of these reasons that the accompanist performs on a different instrument than that of the performer. For the *meturgeman* this different instrument was the Aramaic language. The use of Aramaic as such an instrument served two interrelated functions: first, by translating Scripture into another, but closely related language, the "correct" meaning (i.e., interpretation) of Scripture could be conveyed while remaining close to the cadence of the language of Scripture. Second, by employing a language other than that of Scripture, translation would remain clearly distinguishable from Scripture, just as it was important that the *meturgeman* remain clearly distinguishable from the reader, the former rendering orally what the latter read from a text. If the proximity yet recognizable differences between Hebrew and Aramaic as languages suited this purpose, so did the rabbinic understanding of Aramaic's semi-sacred status. Thus, voices of Torah and Targum, of Hebrew and Aramaic, worked well in the performative ritual of scriptural enunciation and elucidation, even while the two remained visibly and aurally distinct from one another in quality and status.

Much the same can be said of Targum's role in the realm of study and teaching, where it served as the first and bridging link between a fixed scriptural text and its dialectically fluid explication, that is, as the first movement in the shuttle of interpretation. Liminally—and, therefore, somewhat ambiguously—poised between Scripture and rabbinic teaching, Targum was able to partake of something of the quality and status of each. As translation, it followed the text of Scripture and was accorded some of the respect accorded to Scripture. But as interpretation, it gave succinct expression to a received understanding of Scripture—one that not only could be communicated in the course of a Sabbath lection but also could be mastered in the course of a week's study of the same.

The advantage of Targum—its succinct incorporation of rabbinic interpretation into the very fabric of Scripture—poses a serious danger: people might confuse its version of revelation with the original. From

Second Temple times we have, in fact, several biblical paraphrases, both legal and narrative, written in Hebrew which claimed, explicitly or implicitly, to be revealed Scripture.[68] The early rabbis, as we have seen, considered it important to distinguish the text of Torah both from its translation and from its interpretation, in part so as to allow the living elasticity of the latter two, in part so as to maintain the immutability of the former. In the case of midrash this is not a problem, since the very way in which scriptural verses are midrashically cited and set off by rhetorical terminology and attributions to named sages makes fairly evident the line between Scripture and its interpretation, even as both are in Hebrew and even as the two are dialectically interconnected. But in the case of an extensive scriptural paraphrase this line could not as easily be maintained. It is for this reason, at least in part, that the rabbis employed the instrument of Aramaic to distinguish the voice of interpretive paraphrase from that of Scripture, so that the two might be heard and studied as distinct voices in dialogical interrelation to one another, with neither swallowing the other.

Here it needs to be reiterated that Targum as translation never replaced the text or reading of Torah within rabbinic culture, as did the Septuagint in Greek-speaking synagogues and eventually in the Church.[69] Not coincidentally, neither did Aramaic replace Hebrew as the principal language of religious discourse within the former, as Greek and later Latin did among the latter. Rather, targumic translation, both in worship and in study, continued to provide Scripture's ritual and interpretive accompaniment long after Aramaic ceased to be a spoken

[68] Most significant of these is the so-called Temple Scroll from Qumran Cave 11. Similarly, we now have sections of the ancient Hebrew text of the Book of Jubilees. See J. C. Vanderkam and J. T. Milik, "The First *Jubilees* Manuscript from Qumran Cave 4: A Preliminary Publication," *JBL* 110 (1991), 243–270. Of course, within Scripture itself Hebrew to Hebrew interpretive paraphrases exist (notably the books of Chronicles), but by virtue of their inclusion in a single canon they have acquired equal status. Whether the same was the attitude of the Qumran sectarians regarding the canonical status of their rewritten scriptures in relation to the books of Scripture is a matter of scholarly debate, since it is not clear whether all scrolls found in the Qumran "library" are by virtue of their inclusion there of equal canonical status. Compare Z. Ben-Ḥayyim's suggestion ("The Contribution of the Samaritan Inheritance," p. 170) that certain "variants" in the Samaritan Pentateuch reflect an interpretative "translation" of biblical Hebrew into the later idiom of a spoken Samaritan Hebrew which was very close to mishnaic Hebrew.

[69] See above, n. 49, and cf. above, n. 31.

language for Jews.[70] In fact, Aramaic Targums are themselves at times difficult to understand without a knowledge of Hebrew and the Hebrew text of Scripture which they interpret, and often, even when the meaning of the words of a Targum are clear, their interpretive significance can only be grasped in relation to the scriptural text they render.[71] Thus, just as in the live setting of the synagogue the translator and the reader are portrayed as being mutually responsive to one another, so, too, the texts of Targum and Scripture may be conceived of as being mutually interdependent, notwithstanding the important differences in status between them. It may be said that by performatively linking Targum to Torah, and hence Aramaic to Hebrew, the rabbis kept Hebrew alive at a time when, in the multilingual setting of the Galilee, it might have been swallowed by Aramaic. Subsequently, when Aramaic died as a spoken language, this linkage preserved Aramaic when it might have been swallowed by the next vernacular, Arabic.[72]

By bringing together intra-rabbinic and extra-rabbinic evidence, I have not sought to use the latter to establish the representational reliability of the former's portrayal of the practice of Targum in the Galilee of late Roman and Byzantine times. Rather, I have sought to use extra-rabbinic evidence to establish the probability of a multilingual Galilean context, in which the rhetorical and hence transformative force of rabbinical representations of targumic practice would have made sense. If Targum, from the rabbinic perspective, was to be practiced by and for an audience which understood, to whatever extent, both Hebrew and Aramaic, and if that audience were expected to attend both to its Hebrew original and to its Aramaic rendering in their interlinear, responsive reading or recitation of both, then the restless balance of fidelity and freedom in translation[73] was to be achieved in an ongoing dialogue between Scripture and

70 On the question of the continued use of Aramaic Targum long after Aramaic had ceased to be a Jewish vernacular, see the Tosafot to B Berakhot 8a–b; and the responsum of Rav Natronai Gaon to Megillah 21b in *ʾOtzar Ha-geʾonim*, Lewin, pp. 30–31. Similarly, Aramaic continued as a language of sacred discourse in legal, liturgical, and exegetical realms.

71 For this reason, the Aramaic syntax of the "translation parts" of the extant Targums represents a kind of "translation language" different from the non-translational expansions in the same targumim. For these differences, see J. Lund, "A Descriptive Syntax of the Non-translational Passages According to Codex Neofiti I" (M.A. thesis, Hebrew University; Jerusalem, 1981).

72 Of course, the same can be said for the intertwining of Hebrew and Aramaic both in talmudic study and, to a lesser but no less significant extent, in the liturgy.

73 See above, n. 14.

its translation which sought both to draw Scripture's receivers into its text and language, and its text and language into their world.[74]

---

[74] Cf. W. Benjamin's statement (in: Steiner [ed.], *After Babel*, 308), that ideally "literalness and freedom must without strain unite in the translation in the form of the interlinear version. . . . The interlinear version of the Scriptures is the archetype or ideal of all translation." In some of our earliest manuscripts rabbinic Targum is written interlinearly with Hebrew Scripture (see above, n. 31), just as, according to rabbinic rules, it is to be performed, certainly in the synagogue and perhaps in the study, interlinearly as well. For a fuller statement of these conclusions in relation to other models of translation, and in relation to the larger history of Jewish multilingualism, see my forthcoming *Targum and Torah*. I must stress that my focus here has been on how rabbinic literature describes the practice of Targum and not on the actual extant targumic texts that have come down to us. How such texts, both the more literal translations of Targum Onqelos and the freer ones of the other Targums, are to be viewed in relation to this rabbinic picture of Targum in the contexts of both worship and study is a matter for future consideration.

VI. ARCHEOLOGICAL EVIDENCE IN THE GALILEE

The Ancient Synagogues of the Galilee

GIDEON FOERSTER

Throughout the Galilee, to its south and east and including its adjacent valleys, lie the impressive ruins of dozens of ancient synagogues. These remains are significant evidence for the existence of Jewish settlements in the region in the mishnaic and talmudic periods, especially from the third to the seventh centuries C.E. up to the Arab conquest.

In addition to remains of synagogues which have been located and identified *in situ*, inscriptions and architectural fragments found throughout the region have been attributed to synagogues, the exact origins of which are unknown. Literary sources provide still further evidence for the existence of synagogues in the Galilee. All this amounts to about seventy synagogues and a few *batei midrash* (academies). Synagogal remains shed light on the surrounding community as well; only recently have attempts been made to uncover the settlements in which the synagogues were found, e.g., Capernaum, Meiron, Chorazim, and Ḥ. Shemaʿ.

As early as the Second Temple period the Jewish residents of the Galilee built synagogues. Only a few are mentioned in the New Testament (Nazareth[1] and Capernaum[2]) and by Josephus (Tiberias[3]). These certainly were not the only synagogues in the Galilee, and we may also safely assume that similar institutions existed in most of the Jewish

---

1 Matt. 13:54; Mark 6:2; Luke 4:16.
2 Mark 1:21; Luke 7:5; John 6:59.
3 *Ant.* XIX, 6, 3, 300; *War* II, 8, 7, 269; *Life* 11, 54.

settlements in Palestine of this period.[4] Later rabbinic literature mentions a number of synagogues in the Galilee but does not describe them in detail.[5]

Typology and Style of the Galilean Synagogues

The regional and geographical division of the Galilee is reflected in the art and architecture of its synagogues. Those in the Upper Galilee and its outlying areas to the east and south, as well as in the western part of the Golan, may form a distinct architectural and artistic unit. The synagogues of the Lower Galilee, including the Jordan and Beth Shean Valleys, reflect a significantly different artistic and architectural style. This change is both regional and chronological; the latter synagogues were constructed some two hundred years later.

The outstanding remains of the "early synagogues," or the "Galilean" type,[6] are found at the following sites: Bar'am (2), Yesud ha-Ma'alah, Gush Ḥalav, Sasa, Nabratein, Meiron, Ḥ. Shema', Kh. Marus (Meroth), Ḥ. Shura, Kh. Tuba, Chorazim, Capernaum, Ḥ. Veradim, Arbel, and Ḥ. 'Ammudim. Remains of other synagogues in this group whose structures have not yet been uncovered were found at 'Alma,

---

[4] The literary sources mention synagogues outside the Galilee, in Jerusalem as well as at Dor, Caesarea, and elsewhere. We do not know if all these were buildings set aside solely for prayer or for the reading of the Torah; this was possibly the case at Masada, Herodium, Gamla, and perhaps also Chorazim, where a building dating to the first century C.E. is mentioned; see G. Foerster, "The Synagogues at Masada and Herodium," *JJA* 3–4 (1977), 6–11.

[5] Rabbinic literature mentions mainly the synagogue of the Babylonians and the synagogue of Gofna in Sepphoris; thirteen in Tiberias, among them the synagogues of the Tarsians, the Babylonians, the *boule*; and the synagogue at Ḥammath Tiberias. Reference is made to the synagogues around Tiberias, at Ma'on, Kafra, Kefar Ḥittim, nearby Sarongaia, and Sikhnin. Mention is made of synagogues nearby the Galilee, in Beth Shean and Bostra in Syria; See S. Klein (ed.), *Sefer ha-Yishuv*, I (Jerusalem, 1939) (Hebrew). Most of the remains of the above synagogues have not yet been found, while others not mentioned in rabbinic literature have been discovered. Generally, it seems that there was no settlement without a synagogue, and some settlements had more than one.

[6] The only thorough study of the Galilean group of synagogues is that of Kohl and Watzinger, conducted between 1905 and 1907 and published in 1916. See H. Kohl and C. Watzinger, *Antike Synagogen in Galilaea* (Leipzig, 1916). The present writer expanded on this topic in his doctoral dissertation, "Galilean Synagogues and Their Relation to Hellenistic and Roman Art and Architecture" (Hebrew University; Jerusalem, 1972) (Hebrew). A full bibliography up to 1976 is listed in: F. Hüttenmeister and G. Reeg, *Die antiken Synagogen in Israel* (2 vols.; Wiesbaden, 1977).

Dalton, Sifsufa, Peqiʿin, er-Rama, ʿAkhbara, and H. Kefar Hananyah. Outside of this region the "early" or "Galilean" building style has been identified at Danna, Kokhav ha-Yarden, Ramat Issachar, Yafia, Sejera, H. Ofrat, and H. Sumaqa on Mt. Carmel. These remains do not necessarily indicate the existence of synagogues, but such an identification is almost certain. The synagogue at Beth Sheʿarim seems to belong to this group, even though its plan is unclear.[7]

These "Galilean" synagogues are characterized by their monumental ashlars (blocks of hewn stone), particularly in the southern facade facing Jerusalem (see Fig. 1); some of these facades were richly decorated with stone carvings of geometric patterns, floral designs, and animal motifs, others had practically no decoration. These structures are almost always rectangular, sometimes with an attached courtyard. The area of the prayer hall varies from 200–500 sq. m. The size, decoration, and quality of construction are most probably a function of a local community's prosperity and its willingness to provide the necessary funds.

A reconstruction of the plan and interior arrangement of the prayer hall indicates that the roof was supported by two or three rows of stone columns erected on raised pedestals. At times the columns supported a second colonnade, which raised the roof of the hall and possibly allowed for a gallery on the second floor. This plan is called "basilical," although it is doubtful whether it originated in the plan of the Roman basilica (see Fig. 2). Its origin perhaps should be traced to the temples of the Roman period in Syria; two or three rows of stone benches lined the inner walls of the hall.

The center of worship—the Torah ark—was generally fixed in the wall facing Jerusalem, which in these synagogues was usually the wall of the facade. Evidence to corroborate this was found recently at Capernaum (see Fig. 3), Gush Halav, Nabratein, and Kh. Marus (Meroth), where, similar to the finds in the synagogue at Sardis in Asia Minor,[8] the remains of one or two such structures on which the Torah ark apparently stood were found alongside the wall of the entrance. The niche in which the Torah ark (*tevah*) was placed can be reconstructed quite accurately from the architectural elements found at Nabratein[9] (a gable decorated with two lions) (see Fig. 4), as well as from representations on the

---

7 See Appendix for literature on the aforementioned sites.

8 See A. Seager, "The Synagogue at Sardis," in: *Ancient Synagogues Revealed*, ed. L. I. Levine (Jerusalem, 1981), 178–184.

9 E. M. Meyers et al., "The Ark of Nabratein – A First Glance," *BA* 44 (1981), 237–243; see Appendix for literature on this site.

Fig. 1. Facade of Baŕam synagogue. *(Institute of Archeology, Hebrew University of Jerusalem)*

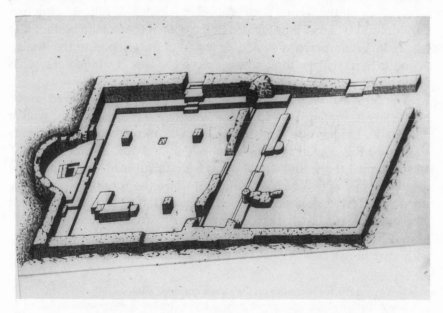

Fig. 2. Basilical plan of Beth Alpha synagogue. *(Institute of Archeology, Hebrew University of Jerusalem)*

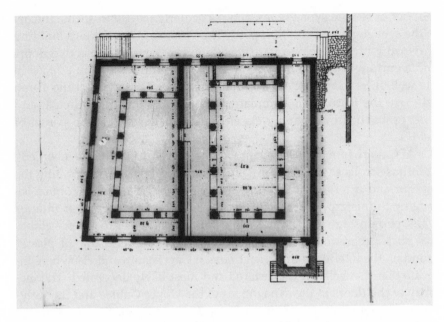

Fig. 3. Plan of Capernaum synagogue. *(Institute of Archeology, Hebrew University of Jerusalem)*

Fig. 4. Stone fragment of Torah shrine from Nabratein synagogue. *(Institute of Archeology, Hebrew University of Jerusalem)*

mosaics of several synagogues, and particularly the Torah shrine (niche) in the synagogue of Dura Europos.[10] The Torah ark appears as a building crowned with a gable or an arch containing a "conch." It has two doors and a curtain (*parokhet*) hanging in front of it, and it stood in a niche in the wall or as a separate structure in front of it. The facade of the Torah ark bore the features of a miniature classical temple, or aedicula, and most probably drew upon the classical aedicula which held the statues of deities.

At Capernaum and Chorazim we find carved friezes with "peopled" acanthus scrolls as well as floral and geometrical designs decorating the interior and exterior walls of the synagogue. The other synagogues belonging to this group bear no clear signs of decoration on their interior walls, perhaps due to their poor state of preservation or to the possibility that such decorations never existed. However, the remnants of plaster found on the interior of the synagogues at Capernaum and elsewhere indicate that the walls were plastered and most likely decorated. The majority of the floors in the synagogues of the Upper Galilee and its outlying areas were built of ashlars and not decorated with the mosaics customary in synagogues in other parts of the Galilee and Palestine. We have no archeological evidence for any other furnishings in the prayer halls, which may have functioned also as *batei midrash*. One may assume that mats covered the floors of the synagogues and worshippers sat on them as well as on stone benches.

*   *   *

The main entrance to the synagogue was set in the wall facing Jerusalem, forcing those who entered the synagogue to make a 180-degree turn to the south if they wished to face the ark. This is, however, a minor problem necessitated by the circumstances, for those who planned synagogues of this type relied upon established tradition and the classical architectural concept which perceived the facade of the Temple as one of its main components. It was thus lavishly decorated and contained the main entrance. The facade in pagan temples generally faced east, the source of light and life; the architects of the "Galilean" synagogues of this group placed the facade to the south, in the direction of holy Jerusalem. However, the facades of the synagogues at Arbel in the Lower Galilee

---

[10] C. Kraeling, *The Excavations at Dura Europos*, VIII: *The Synagogue* (New Haven, 1956).

and H. Sumaqa on the Carmel faced east, and has been explained as perhaps echoing the injunction, "one makes the entrances to synagogues only in the east, for we find that the Sanctuary was open to the east."[11] These synagogues were embellished with Roman decorative art (see Fig. 5) as well as with oriental elements and distinct Jewish symbols, a combination which may be described as an original Jewish creation bearing a discernible regional style. The most richly decorated synagogues were found at Capernaum[12] and Chorazim,[13] the former apparently having influenced the latter. At Capernaum most of the friezes were decorated with acanthus and vine scrolls containing figures of animals (lions, for example), fruit (such as pomegranates and grape clusters), and geometrical patterns. The vine scrolls at Chorazim contain human representations in a vintage scene and at other activities.

The lintels are among the most ornate architectural elements and are a main feature of this group of synagogues. Against the background of the friezes on the lintel and the doorjambs, which were generally done in a formal, classical style, was a series of representations incorporating an interesting combination of ancient oriental tradition and a distinctly classical influence, similar to other decorations in these synagogues. These representations are simple and contain floral or geometric designs, as well as carved figures (some mythological) and animals. Winged victories carrying wreaths were found at Barʿam, er-Rama, and H. Dikke[14] east of the Jordan River, to the north of the Sea of Galilee. Wreaths often appear in the center of synagogue lintels, sometimes supported by cupids (Capernaum) or eagles (Barʿam, Gush Halav,[15] and elsewhere). Closed wreaths having cultic and ritual significance in the pagan iconography were depicted on the lintels at Barʿam, Chorazim, and Capernaum, and, at times, garlands, as at Gush Halav and Capernaum.

Carved eagles were centrally located in many synagogues: an eagle appears on the top of a gable at Chorazim and on the lintels and other decorated parts of the facades at Capernaum, Gush Halav, H. Veradim, Yafia, H. Shemaʿ, and H. Sumaqa. Perhaps the eagle carvings at H. Dikke and Kh. Tuba belong to the gables over the niches or the Torah shrine.[16]

11 See T Megillah 3:22, Lieberman, p. 360.
12 See Appendix, Capernaum.
13 See Appendix, Chorazim.
14 See Appendix, Barʿam and er-Rama; *H. Dikke*: Kohl and Watzinger, *Antike Synagogen*, 112–124; Hüttenmeister and Reeg, *Antiken Synagogen*, I, 103–105.
15 See Appendix, Gush Halav.
16 See Appendix, Kh. Tuba, and above, n. 14.

The eagle, symbol of kingship and sovereignty, once represented the empires of Babylonia, Egypt, and Persia; in the period under discussion, the eagle symbolized Zeus-Jupiter-Baᶜal Shamin, and, above all, mighty Rome. However, for Jews the eagle might also have symbolized God, as allegorized in Deut. 32:11: "As an eagle that stirreth up her nest, hovereth over her young, spreadeth abroad her wings . . . ." The extensive use of the eagle in synagogue decoration illustrates the changed attitude of the Jews toward figural art after the Bar-Kokhba revolt. This stands in stark contrast to the situation in Jerusalem towards the end of Herod's reign, when the appearance of an eagle over a Temple gate led to disturbances and the demand that it be removed.

The lion, who in the Bible symbolizes, among other things, God and the Jewish nation, was also depicted on the lintels and friezes of Capernaum and Chorazim; at H. ᶜAmmudim a pair of lions flank either side of the head of an ox or amphora, a motif reminiscent of oriental art. Three-dimensional statues of lions were found at Chorazim, Capernaum, Barᶜam, Yafia, and H. Sumaqa.[17] These statues were probably placed on either side of the Torah ark, as we find represented on the gable of a Torah ark at Nabratein and on the mosaics of the synagogue at Beth Alpha, for example (see Fig. 6). Mythical creatures, such as griffons, medusas, centaurs, and a capricornus, are represented in the synagogues of Capernaum and Chorazim.

Figures treading grapes in a winepress were carved in the vine scrolls at Chorazim, but it is difficult to identify them since they seem to have been mutilated. The identity of those who destroyed this work of art as well as other figural representations, and when they operated, are unclear. They may have been Jews who strictly adhered to the prohibition against figural art, opposing the liberal spirit expressed during the mishnaic and talmudic periods. Another possibility is that these people were Christians or Muslims who, in various periods, opposed figural representations and are known to have destroyed them.

In addition to the decorations which link synagogal art to classical and oriental art, a few bear distinctly Jewish motifs. For example, a menorah, shofar and incense shovel were carved on a Corinthian capital at Capernaum, and two menorahs were carved on a lintel at Chorazim.[18] A capital with four carved menorahs was found at H. Shura, while the

---

[17] See Appendix, H. Sumaqa.

[18] Z. Yeivin, "Carved Menorahs at Chorazin," *Qadmoniot* 2/7 (1969), 98–99 (Hebrew).

Fig. 5. Architectural fragment from the synagogue in Capernaum depicting two eagles flanked by capricorns. (*Institute of Archeology, Hebrew University of Jerusalem*)

Fig. 6. Mosaic pavement from Beth Alpha synagogue depicting ritual objects. (*Institute of Archeology, Hebrew University of Jerusalem*)

lintels of the main entranceways at Nabratein[19] and H. Shema‘[20] are decorated with menorahs; a relief of a menorah from Peqi‘in probably comes from a synagogue,[21] and menorahs were carved on a lintel at Yafia.[22]

Carvings of the Torah ark and shrine in the form of an aedicula were found at Capernaum, Chorazim, and Peqi‘in. One of the friezes in the synagogue at Capernaum may have been an architectural element of the actual Torah shrine. The frieze is decorated with a shrine resting atop a wagon, reminiscent of the painting at Dura Europos depicting the return of the Ark of the Covenant to Beth Shemesh after having been removed from the Temple of Dagon in Ashdod. If our interpretation is correct, this would be the only depiction of a biblical theme in an early Galilean synagogue.

A number of dedicatory inscriptions, almost all in Hebrew and Aramaic (one is in Greek) were found in these synagogues. Two almost identical dedicatory inscriptions in Hebrew were found, one from the small synagogue at Bar‘am ("Let there be peace in this place and in all places in Israel . . .") and the other from ‘Alma ("Let there be peace on this place and on all the [dwelling] places of the people of Israel . . ."). In each the name of the artisan then follows. Dedicatory inscriptions of individuals, and sometimes of their families, were found at Capernaum, Chorazim, Gush Halav, H. ‘Ammudim, Nabratein, er-Rama,[23] and Kokhav ha-Yarden.[24]

The plans of these Galilean synagogues have much in common. While the building techniques are also similar in their extensive use of large limestone and basalt ashlars and their rich stone carvings, nonetheless exceptions exist, the most notable being at H. Shema‘, in the heart of the Upper Galilee. This is a broadhouse in which the focal point—the platform (*bema*) upon which the ark was placed—was in the center of the long wall facing south, while the two entrances were to the north and west. It is not built of ashlars and is architecturally less impressive than other synagogues in the Galilee, especially in comparison to the synagogue at Meiron, only 500 meters away. No doubt, the community of H. Shema‘ was not as prosperous as that of Meiron. The plan

---

19 See Appendix, Nabratein.
20 See Appendix, H. Shema‘.
21 See Appendix, Peqi‘in.
22 See Appendix, Yafia.
23 See Appendix, er-Rama.
24 See J. Naveh, *On Stone and Mosaic* (Jerusalem, 1978), 70 (Hebrew), who corrects the reading of the inscription .

of the H. Shema‘ synagogue may shed light on the not-so-clear plan of the synagogue at Yafia in the Lower Galilee. It is quite possible that the latter was also a broadhouse, the focal point of which was in the southern wall and the entrance of which was to the west. Synagogues based on the broadhouse plan were excavated at H. Susiya and Eshtemoa in Judea, as well as at Dura Europos in Syria. The focal point of the synagogue at Arbel was in the center of the southern wall facing Jerusalem, where a niche intended for the ark was found. The location of the ark in the synagogue at H. Sumaqa is unknown, but it is also likely to have been in the southern wall.

Mosaic fragments of the pavements were found in the synagogues of Arbel and nearby H. ‘Ammudim in the Lower Galilee. Those in Arbel clearly belong to the building's second phase, but this is uncertain regarding H. ‘Ammudim, where remains of a dedicatory inscription were also found. Many white mosaic tesserae were found in the synagogue of H. Shema‘, but not *in situ*; it is likely that this monochromatic and simple mosaic floor existed in the building's second phase. The synagogue at Yafia, having an unusual orientation, was decorated with rich mosaics, probably even in its first phase. The architectural remains at Yafia seem to preserve the early Galilean style, the mosaics a later style known to us only from the fourth century C.E. onward (see below).

Excavations at the synagogues of Chorazim, Meiron, Gush Halav, Nabratein, H. ‘Ammudim, and H. Sumaqa have shown that all the buildings were constructed in the mid-third century C.E. For the first time we have a chronology for these Galilean structures based on archeological evidence. Before this, Galilean synagogues were dated only by means of stylistic and historical considerations, and were considered products of the second and third centuries C.E. Such considerations proved to be correct, although the date of construction should now be fixed in the third century. The above-noted excavations have also revealed that these buildings underwent many changes—walls were added and floors and other parts of the building were repaired—as a result of extensive use, natural disaster (earthquake) or perhaps manmade destruction. While facades were not altered, the changes in the buildings' interior often had to do with the focal point of the prayer hall and the location of the Torah ark. Such changes and additions are discernible at H. Shema‘, Gush Halav, and Nabratein and will undoubtedly become clearer after further excavation of these sites and others.

The excavators of Capernaum, V. Corbo and S. Loffreda, propose a different and much later date for the synagogue at Capernaum.[25] Based on the pottery and coins found under the floors of the synagogue, they date its construction to the first half of the fifth century, thereby contradicting the generally accepted date of the Galilean synagogues. The political situation in the fifth century as well was not favorable for the construction of such an impressive Jewish structure, at a time when Christianity was gaining power and when, at the same time, an octagonal church was built in an entirely different, Byzantine, style just 40 m. from the synagogue. Corbo and Loffreda did not take into account the building's extensive use, renovations and repairs, and dated it, in their words, according to "the archeological facts" only. In this case, the archeological evidence can and should be interpreted as a phase in the history of the building which may have occurred because of a fundamental repair following the earthquake in Palestine of 363 C.E.[26]

The synagogue at Capernaum is the most ornate of the Galilean synagogues and perhaps the closest in decoration to imperial Roman art.[27] In light of excavations at other synagogues, the foundation of the Capernaum synagogue should thus be dated no later than the mid-third century C.E.

Another important factor directly related to the study of the Galilean synagogues and resulting from the excavations at Chorazim, Capernaum, Meiron, Ḥ. Shemaʿ, and Nabratein is the discovery of the settlements around the synagogue. Several structures, mainly houses with agricultural-"industrial" installations, such as oil and wine presses, were uncovered at these sites.

Jewish settlement in the Galilee following the Bar-Kokhba revolt did not flourish from the outset: only after a period of recuperation and rebuilding, which lasted about one hundred years until the middle of the third century C.E., did Jews begin to build elaborate and impressive synagogues throughout the Galilee. This is corroborated by the discoveries from excavations at many of the above-mentioned sites. It appears that

[25] See Appendix, Capernaum. This evidence does not alter our opinion that the archeological finds of the site should be interpreted differently.

[26] G. Foerster, "The Earthquake on the 19th Iyyar, 363 and Its Historical and Archeological Significance," *Abstracts of the Eighth Archeological Congress* (Jerusalem, 1981), 20; K. W. Russell, "The Earthquake of May 19, A.D. 363," *BASOR* 238 (1980), 47–64.

[27] It must be stressed that there are some later architectural elements which probably replaced earlier ones which went out of use.

this process, which culminated in the foundation of synagogues of monumental proportions, began in small gathering places, private dwellings or specially built structures which bore no distinguishing features of a synagogue. It is therefore difficult to identify them; only thorough excavation of the settlement areas, and perhaps beneath the presently-known synagogue buildings, will give us a clearer picture of this process. In some cases, such as at Gush Ḥalav and Barʿam, more than one synagogue building existed—even though each of these synagogues probably could have accommodated the entire community.

Galilean synagogues are, in general, architecturally and decoratively similar. Their style was drawn from the art and architecture of the surrounding culture and was adapted to Jewish needs, omitting what seemed superfluous and unfitting and adding a number of distinctly Jewish symbols. These monumental structures served the Jewish communities in the Galilee for hundreds of years, from the time of their construction until the abandonment of the settlement following the Arab conquest. Despite the extensive use of these buildings, their form and plan were not significantly altered, except for repairs and some changes in the interior, as mentioned above. East of the Galilee, in the Golan region, remains of about twenty-five synagogues built in a style similar to that of the Galilean synagogues were found, but their date is disputed. Some were probably constructed in the third century C.E. while others definitely should be dated to the fourth to sixth centuries C.E.[28]

The most recently discovered and excavated synagogue, built in the "Galilean" style, is at Kh. Marus, which is identified with Meroth in the Upper Galilee. The date of its foundation is suggested to be the beginning of the fifth century C.E. Its plan, interior arrangement, and exterior are reminiscent of other Galilean synagogues, but it is a far cry from the regional "Galilean" style we have seen in the main group of these synagogues, and certainly later.[29] The suggestion, therefore, that this building may provide evidence for the late date of other Galilean synagogues cannot be substantiated. A mosaic pavement which was part of the original construction was later replaced by a stone pavement. Only one panel

[28] Z. Maʿoz, *Jewish Settlement and the Synagogues of the Golan* (Qatzrin, 1979) (Hebrew).

[29] Z. Ilan, "The Synagogue and *Beth Midrash* of Meroth," in: *Ancient Synagogues in Israel*, ed. R. Hachlili (*BAR International Series* 499; Haifa, 1989), 21–42; Y. Tsafrir, "The Synagogues at Meroth and Capernaum and the Dating of the Galilean Synagogues: A Reconsideration," in: *Eretz Israel*, XX (Jerusalem, 1989), 337–344 (Hebrew), English summary, 207*.

was preserved, and contains, according to the excavators, a representation of David with the weapons he captured from Goliath. This representation is accompanied by a dedicatory inscription in Hebrew. Two further inscriptions in Hebrew contain biblical verses; this type of inscription is rarely found in synagogues but is common in churches. The existence of a *bet midrash* in the complex of this synagogue has been suggested by the excavators.

Typology and Style of Synagogues in the Lower Galilee and Adjacent Valleys Built from the Fourth Century Onward

As we move southward to the Lower Galilee, the Jordan and Beth Shean Valleys, we encounter a completely different artistic and architectural style from that of the Galilean synagogues discussed above. The emphasis on the elaborate exterior of the synagogue building, especially its facade, was now transferred to its interior, which was decorated with ornate mosaics. This basic change in the "late" Galilean synagogues, as opposed to the "early" ones, led to other developments in the planning of the building. When the facade lost its centrality in synagogue decoration it no longer faced Jerusalem, and, as a result, the Torah ark was generally placed in a niche on the back wall which now was in the direction of Jerusalem. In other words, the entrance at this stage was situated opposite the Torah shrine and did not face Jerusalem. The problem that existed in the earlier synagogues, where the main entrance was in the wall facing Jerusalem, was now eliminated. The change in the plan of these synagogues clearly reflects contemporary trends when, for example, greater emphasis was placed on the interior of the building in the Byzantine period, as opposed to the emphasis on the exterior in the Hellenistic-Roman period.

A synagogue of this group from the fourth century C.E. was uncovered in Ḥammath Tiberias.[30] The significance of this building lies in its high quality mosaics, reflecting the finest style of the period and having parallels in Antioch, the capital of Syria. The mosaic in the nave of the synagogue from this period was apparently laid on top of an earlier third-century mosaic. It contains several themes common to the synagogues in the area in later centuries. The mosaic is divided into three panels: a zodiac, whose twelve signs are identified by their Hebrew

---

[30] M. Dothan, *Hammath Tiberias* (Jerusalem, 1983); *EAEHL*, IV, 1178–1184; Hüttenmeister and Reeg, *Antiken Synagogen*, I, 163–172.

Fig. 7. View of mosaic floor from Ḥammath Tiberias synagogue. *(Institute of Archeology, Hebrew University of Jerusalem)*

names, is depicted in the central panel (see Fig. 7). In the center of the zodiac the sun god Helios is represented riding his chariot, with the moon and stars to his sides. The zodiac is set within a square panel, and in the space created between the square and the circle are female personifications of the four seasons, the women bearing symbols of the various seasons along with the Hebrew name for each.

The mosaic panel near the entrance contains a Greek dedicatory inscription naming the contributors to the synagogue. Foremost among them is one Severus, who was raised in the house of the Patriarch. The inscription is set between two lions. The focal point in the southern part of the nave, before the *bema* on which the Torah ark probably stood, is the third mosaic panel depicting a Torah shrine and ark flanked by two menorahs, shofars, incense shovels, lulavs, and ethrogs (see Fig. 8). These ritual objects were used in the Temple, and some of them were probably used in synagogue worship as well. This impressive mosaic features a major theme in Jewish art generally and in synagogues in particular: it symbolizes the continuity of Temple worship and, at the same time, gives expression to the current synagogue ritual.

The three-paneled mosaic in the nave of the Hammath Tiberias synagogue is the earliest of this type known to date; similar mosaics from a later period were found in the synagogues at Beth Shean, Beth Alpha, and Naʿaran in the Jordan Valley. The synagogue at H. Susiya in Judea may have had a similar mosaic. The side aisles of the building at Hammath Tiberias were richly decorated with geometric mosaics and had three dedicatory inscriptions, one in Aramaic and two in Greek. The synagogue was built on the site of an earlier building, from the mid-second century C.E., which was destroyed towards the end of the third century. While the entrance of the early structure was in the south, facing Jerusalem, like the early Galilean synagogues, the entrance to the later building was in the north (and possibly in the east as well), like most of the later synagogues. The synagogue was destroyed in the fifth century C.E. and in its place a much larger building was erected in the late fifth or sixth century. Its plan is basilical, divided into a nave and two aisles by two rows of columns. Only fragments of its mosaics remain among them are representations of vine scrolls and figures of animals. The building was repaired in the seventh century C.E. without many changes. It apparently contained galleries that may possibly have served as a women's section, and a side hall which may have served as a *bet midrash* (see Fig. 9).

Fig. 8. Section of mosaic floor from Ḥammath Tiberias synagogue. *(Institute of Archeology, Hebrew University of Jerusalem)*

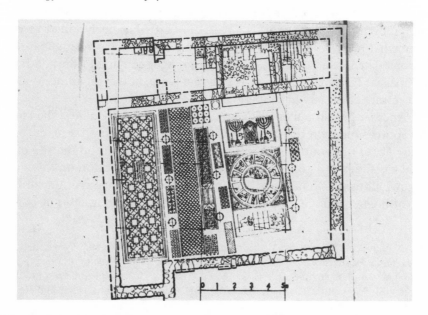

Fig. 9. Plan of Ḥammath Tiberias synagogue. *(Institute of Archeology, Hebrew University of Jerusalem)*

In the early 1920s, another synagogue was uncovered at Hammath Tiberias by N. Slousch.[31] This basilical building, measuring 12 x 12 m., was apparently constructed in the third century. Its entrance was set in the southern wall, facing Jerusalem, however this reconstruction is hypothetical. In its second phase, however, apparently during the Byzantine period, three main entranceways were set in the north. In the building's first phase it had a flagstone floor, upon which a mosaic with a geometric pattern was laid during the second phase. Among the finds of this synagogue are a bas-relief of a menorah and a "Seat of Moses," which is similar to the one found in the synagogue at Chorazim.

In contrast to the two synagogues known to date from Hammath Tiberias, only a few remains have been found in the city of Tiberias itself. Sections of a mosaic with a dedicatory inscription in Greek, a lulav and ethrog, and apparently dating to the sixth century C.E., were discovered in the northern part of ancient Tiberias, in the downtown section of the present-day city.[32] The literary sources mention thirteen synagogues in Tiberias, and only one in Hammath Tiberias, although the two cities were generally considered one during the tannaitic and amoraic periods. The archeological evidence of Tiberias during late antiquity is very fragmentary. Although it was the Jewish center of Palestine for hundreds of years after the destruction of Jerusalem and the Bar-Kokhba revolt, as is well known from the literary sources, only little has been added as yet from what has been uncovered at isolated sites and the synagogue excavations. The small but richly decorated synagogue lying to the south of Tiberias, at Hammath Tiberias, is clear evidence, however, of the wealth and culture of the city in the period of the Patriarchate.

Another Jewish center was Sepphoris, in the Lower Galilee. The literary sources mention that there were eighteen synagogues there, but we know about only one from a fragmentary mosaic found on the site of a local Crusader church. The Aramaic dedicatory inscription on this mosaic mentions one R. Judan b. Nahum who donated money for the building of the synagogue. The plan and date of the building are not clear,

---

[31] N. Slousch, "Les fouilles de Tibériade. A: Première campagne," _Qobetz Receuil Publié par la Société Hebraïque d'Exploration et d'Archéologie Palestiniennes_ 1 (1921), 5–39, and a general plan, 46; ibid., 1/2 (1925), 49–51 (Hebrew); C. H. Vincent, "Les fouilles juives d'El Hammam à Tibériade," _RB_ 31 (1922), 115–122; Hüttenmeister and Reeg, _Antiken Synagogen_, I, 159–163.

[32] L. Roth-Gerson, _The Greek Inscriptions from the Synagogues in Eretz Israel_ (Jerusalem, 1987), 61–64 (Hebrew); _Hadashot Arkheologiyot_ 76 (1980–81), 10–11 (Hebrew).

since only a small part of it has been excavated. A Greek inscription on a lintel found nearby these remains mentions, among others, the head of a synagogue named Judah.[33]

Two synagogues were discovered at Yafia[34] in the hills of Nazareth and at Ḥusifa[35] on the Carmel. The former, probably built in the fourth century C.E., apparently belongs to the "Galilean" tradition even though it is decorated with a mosaic floor; the latter is decorated with a mosaic floor and seems to have been constructed in the fifth or sixth century C.E. The plan of the synagogue at Yafia is not clear due to its poor state of preservation, but it seems that it was a broadhouse with a mosaic floor. In the center of the fragmentary mosaic floor is a circle set within a square frame divided into twelve medallions, which seem to have contained the symbols of the tribes and not the usual zodiacal signs. One of the motifs appearing on the borders of the mosaic is also unusual, an eagle standing on a human head (a mask?).

We do not have a clear picture of the plan of the synagogue at Ḥusifa, but it seems that here, too, one can reconstruct a broadhouse with its focal point—the Torah shrine—on the southern side of the building, facing Jerusalem. The very fragmentary mosaic floor in the nave is divided into several panels; a zodiac is discernible on its eastern side, and a three-line dedicatory inscription in Aramaic borders the zodiac panel on the west. The personifications of the seasons are only partially preserved. The mosaic at the building's entrance had two menorahs depicted on either side of a wreath, containing the Hebrew inscription, "Peace on Israel." A fragmentary mosaic pavement found at Kafr Kanna north of Nazareth contains two dedicatory inscriptions in Aramaic, which indicate the existence of a synagogue here, although the remains are too scanty to reconstruct its plan.[36] Other synagogues in the area, at Beth Sheʿarim and Ḥ. Sumaqa on the Carmel, belong to the Roman period, i.e., the third and fourth centuries C.E. (see above).

---

[33] Hüttenmeister and Reeg, *Antiken Synagogen*, I, 400–418; L. Roth-Gerson, *Greek Inscriptions*, 105–110.

[34] See Appendix, Yafia.

[35] N. Makhouly and M. Avi-Yonah, "A Sixth-Century Synagogue at Isfiya," *QDAP* 3 (1934), 118–131; M. Avi-Yonah, "The Ancient Synagogue of Ḥusifa," in: *Essays and Studies in the Lore of the Holy Land* (Tel-Aviv/Jerusalem, 1964), 11–22 (Hebrew); *EAEHL*, II, 524–526; Hüttenmeister and Reeg, *Antiken Synagogen*, I, 181–184.

[36] Ibid., I, 246–249.

Let us return now to the Jordan and Beth Shean Valleys. At Tel Beth Yeraḥ,[37] south of the Sea of Galilee, lie the ruins of a synagogue whose impressive measurements (22 x 37 m.) rank it the largest of the synagogues hitherto discovered in Palestine. The building plan is "basilical" and includes an apse in the southern wall facing Jerusalem. Although the remains of the floor mosaics are fragmentary, one can detect remnants of vegetal scrolls and figures of animals, perhaps even a man with a horse. The distinctly Jewish symbols of menorah, incense shovel, lulav, and ethrog were carved on a marble pedestal. The building may be dated to the sixth century C.E. A church of apparently the same period was uncovered only 50 m. from the synagogue, and it is likely that the Jewish community lived close to the Christian community of the same settlement, as was the case at several other places.

On the southern bank of the Yarmuq River, some 7.5 km. southeast of the Sea of Galilee, a synagogue was discovered on a prominent site at Ḥammath Gader, which is famous for its thermal baths.[38] In the last phase of the building, the synagogue (13 x 14 m.) had a basilical plan with an apse and *bema* on the southern wall. The building was paved with mosaics in the nave and aisles. Divided into three panels in the nave, its mainly geometric patterns are reminiscent of the Ḥammath Tiberias mosaic, although it has very little figural representation: a dedicatory inscription is flanked by depictions of lions on either side. Several most interesting dedicatory inscriptions in Aramaic appear on the mosaics and contain the names of benefactors and their places of origin. This last phase of the building is dated to the fifth–sixth centuries C.E. Under this building was an earlier phase dated to the fourth century, which had a *bema* attached to its southern wall, but without an apse. It was paved with small flagstones (*opus sectile*) and may even have had an earlier phase in the third century, however this is not clear. A similar development of a rectangular building with a *bema* and an *opus sectile* floor replaced by a mosaic, and with an apse added on, can be seen in the synagogue of Maʿoz Ḥayyim (see below).

---

[37] P. L. Guy, "Beth Yeraḥ," *Bulletin of the Department of Antiquities of the State of Israel* 3 (1951), 32–33; Hüttenmeister and Reeg, *Antiken Synagogen*, I, 72–73.

[38] E. L. Sukenik, *The Ancient Synagogue of el-Hammeh* (Jerusalem, 1935); Hüttenmeister and Reeg, *Antiken Synagogen*, I, 152–159; *Ḥadashot Arkheologiyot* 82 (1983), 11–12 (Hebrew); G. Foerster, "The 'Basilical' Plan of the Synagogue with an Apse and its Chronological Significance in Antiquity," in: *Synagogues in Antiquity*, eds. A. Kasher et al. (Jerusalem, 1987), 173–181 (Hebrew).

In the Beth Shean area, a rich and varied concentration of synagogues has been discovered, two in Beth Shean itself and four in the immediate vicinity: at Beth Alpha, Ma'oz Hayyim, near 'En ha-Natziv, and at Tel Menorah near Kibbutz Tirat Zvi. The synagogues near 'En ha-Natziv and Ma'oz Hayyim were identified as ancient sites known to us from the literary sources. The site adjacent to 'En ha-Natziv is identified with the village of Rehov, mentioned by Eusebius as lying four miles from Beth Shean.[39] The site is also close to Tel Rihab, which has been identified with the biblical Rehov. The site at Ma'oz Hayyim is perhaps to be identified with another village in the Beth Shean area mentioned by Cyril of Scythopolis by the name Baalah.[40] These two synagogues were founded in the third or fourth century C.E.; while their plans are similar in the first phase and they are geographically close to one another, their development is very different.

In both buildings the prayer hall had a rectangular plan and was divided into a nave and two aisles by two rows of columns. In the first phase of the synagogue at Ma'oz Hayyim, a *bema* was placed on the southern side of the building, close to the wall facing Jerusalem; in the second phase the plan was changed and an apse was added in the wall facing Jerusalem, where the Torah ark was most probably placed.[41] In the same phase the flagstone floor was replaced by a mosaic one, a process we have already witnessed in some of the "early" Galilean synagogues but which may be best compared to the development we have noticed at the Hammath Gader synagogue. In the synagogue at Rehov, a mosaic floor was noticeable already in its early phase, although only small fragments of it remain.[42] In all the building phases, the *bema* was placed on the southern side of the prayer hall, without an apse. The mosaic floors in both buildings were only partially preserved, and essentially all that remain are its borders. It would seem that those floors were aniconic, however this is not at all certain since the main iconographic representations

39 Eusebius, *Onomastikon*, Klostermann (Leipzig, 1904), p. 142 .

40 M. Avi-Yonah, *Gazetteer of Roman Palestine* (*Qedem* V; Jerusalem, 1976), 34.

41 See V. Tzaferis, "The Ancient Synagogue near Ma'oz Hayyim," *IEJ* 32 (1982), 215–244; Hüttenmeister and Reeg, *Antiken Synagogen*, I, 307–308.

42 F. Vitto, "Ancient Synagogue at Rehov," *'Atiqot* 7 (1974), 100–104 (Hebrew), English summary, 17–18*; idem, "The Synagogue at Rehov," *Qadmoniot* 8/32 (1975), 119–123 (Hebrew); idem, [short report on the synagogue of Rehov, 1980], *IEJ* 30 (1980), 214–217; idem, "Le décor mural des anciennes synagogues à la lumière de nouvelles découvertes," in: *XVI Internationaler Byzantinistenkongress*, Akten II, 5 (*Jahrbuch der österreichischen-Byzantinistik* 32/5; Vienna, 1981), 361–370; Hüttenmeister and Reeg, *Antiken Synagogen*, I, 369–376.

were usually placed in the center of the floors and in the nave. In the second phase of the prayer hall in the synagogue at Ma'oz Ḥayyim, the meander pattern on the borders of the mosaic close to the apse is embellished with a menorah, bird, and cluster of grapes. It is certainly less impressive than the Torah ark and other Jewish symbols represented on the mosaics of the synagogues at Ḥammath Tiberias and Beth Alpha. The total absence of Jewish symbols at Reḥov is possibly due to the fact that the floor near the *bema* in the synagogue was not preserved.

In the final phase of the Reḥov synagogue (the sixth and seventh centuries C.E.), its narthex, paved with a well preserved mosaic, was added on to the front of the building in the north. In the center of the geometrically patterned floor is the longest mosaic inscription ever found in Israel (see Fig. 10). It contains the agricultural laws concerning the sabbatical year and the setting aside of tithes in the various regions of Eretz-Israel and adjacent areas. Almost the entire text of the inscription appears in rabbinic literature, in the Jerusalem Talmud and several tannaitic sources.[43] Apart from its archeological significance, the inscription contributes greatly to our understanding of the history, geography, literature, halakha, and language of the period. Fragments of plaster preserved in the ruins of the building suggest that the walls of the prayer hall were decorated with painted plaster and dedicatory inscriptions. The ruins of another synagogue, the plan of which is unclear, were found in the southern part of the Beth Shean Valley, at Tel Menorah near Kibbutz Tirat Zvi. A fragment of its mosaic floor preserves representations of two menorahs and a shofar.[44]

At Kibbutz Ḥeftzi-bah, a number of kilometers northwest of Beth Shean, are the ruins of a synagogue known as "the synagogue of Beth Alpha," named after Kh. Beit Ilfa, where the building was discovered.[45] The building was excavated in 1929 and is one of the first and best known synagogues discovered in Israel. It has a typical basilical plan and measures 12.4 x 10.75 m., consists of a nave and two aisles created by two rows of columns, and an apse facing south, towards Jerusalem. An

---

[43] See Y. Sussmann, "A Halakhic Inscription from the Beth-Shean Valley," *Tarbiz* 43 (1973), 88–158 (Hebrew); idem, "The 'Boundaries of Eretz Israel'," *Tarbiz* 45 (1976), 213–257 (Hebrew).

[44] S. Goldschmidt, "Synagogue Remains at the Mound of Kefar Karnaim," in: *Eretz Israel*, XI (Jerusalem, 1973), 39–40 (Hebrew), English summary, 23*; Hüttenmeister and Reeg, *Antiken Synagogen*, I, 435–436.

[45] See E. L. Sukenik, *The Ancient Synagogue of Beth Alpha* (London, 1932); *EAEHL*, I, 187–190; Hüttenmeister and Reeg, *Antiken Synagogen*, I, 44–50.

atrium, through which three entrances led into a narthex and then to the prayer hall, was built in front of the building. This plan (see Fig. 11), which was directly influenced by the plans of contemporary churches, is known, for instance, at Hammath Tiberias, Beth Yeraḥ, Maʿoz Ḥayyim, and Hammath Gader. The building is dated by a mosaic dedicatory inscription, stating that the building was erected during the reign of the Byzantine emperor Justin I or II in the first half of the sixth century C.E.

A well preserved mosaic floor covers the entire hall. The pavement in the aisles is decorated with simple geometric patterns; that of the nave contains iconographic representations and is divided into three panels, similar to the one at Hammath Tiberias 150 years earlier and to one in contemporary Naʿaran in the southern Jordan Valley.[46]

The panel closest to the entrance depicts the Sacrifice of Isaac, a theme of deliverance common in Jewish and Christian art. We have here the most complete biblical representation preserved on a mosaic pavement found to date in a Palestinian synagogue: the figures of Abraham, Isaac, the two servants, the donkey, and the ram, as well as a hand symbolizing the intervention of the angel of God, are all executed in fine detail; phrases from Genesis 22 serve as captions. The mosaic is of early Byzantine style and can be distinguished by its rather naive artistic features.

The second panel, found in the center of the nave, contains a zodiac. At Beth Alpha the figures personifying the seasons in the space between the circle and the square do not align with the signs of the zodiac. In the center of the zodiac we find Helios riding his chariot, with the moon and stars at his sides. The figures are all in frontal view and are completely stiff, lacking any plasticity or depth. This, as well as the "spirituality" expressed by the figures, are a few of the hallmarks of early Byzantine art in the east. Here, too, the zodiacal signs and the seasons are labeled in Hebrew.

The third panel, closest to the apse, depicts a Torah shrine and ark in its center and alongside it two menorahs, two shofars, a lulav, an ethrog, and two lions. On the gable over the Torah ark are two birds, a conch, and the eternal light; the curtain (*parokhet*) is pushed to the sides to afford a view of the ark. The depiction as a whole represents the artist's attempt to concretize the motifs symbolizing the Temple and Temple worship. So, for example, one should interpret the birds on top of the gable of the

---

[46] Ibid., I, 320–334.

Fig. 10. Halakhic inscription from Reḥov synagogue. *(Institute of Archeology, Hebrew University of Jerusalem)*

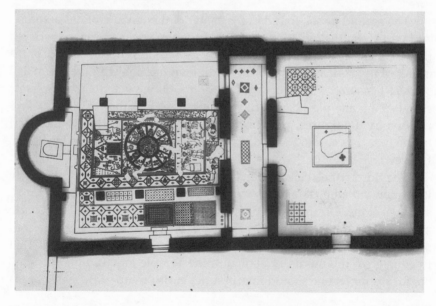

Fig. 11. Plan of Beth Alpha synagogue. *(Institute of Archeology, Hebrew University of Jerusalem)*

Torah ark as symbolizing the cherubs protecting the Ark of the Covenant with their wings.

Although the subjects represented on this floor do not differ from those of other mosaics, its style is unusual and unique in its simplicity and naivete, and no doubt suited the tastes of the small community at Beth Alpha. The two artisans who created the mosaic, Marianus and his son, Hanina, are mentioned in a Greek dedicatory inscription appearing in the northern end of the mosaic floor. These same artisans are also mentioned in the inscription on the mosaic floor of a synagogue at Beth Shean.

Two rather unusual synagogues were uncovered at Beth Shean. One, having the standard basilical plan, must have been a Samaritan building; the other had an unusual plan and decoration.[47] The Samaritan synagogue was found on Tel Etztabah, about 300 m. north of the Byzantine city wall, close to a large sixth-century monastery and the large cemeteries of the city. Its measures 17 x 14.2 m.; its apse faces northwest, not toward Jerusalem; several rooms were attached to the building, and a Samaritan inscription was discovered in one of them. The excavator noted three building phases, the earliest dating to the end of the fourth century C.E., the second to the fifth century C.E., and the last to the sixth and seventh centuries C.E. The differences between the phases are slight and are characterized primarily by repairs and by the addition of rooms to the main structure. The prayer hall was divided into a nave and two colonnades by two rows of columns. The mosaic floor is preserved primarily in the nave and some of the adjacent rooms. It is noteworthy that the mosaic pavement lacks any figural representation and is decorated primarily with geometric patterns and some floral designs. The mosaic floor in the nave is divided into three panels, as at Beth Alpha and Hammath Tiberias. The first panel is mainly geometric. The central one contains a circle in a square, and its design is essentially geometric and does not contain the zodiac, as one might expect. Only the third panel

---

47 N. Zori, "The Ancient Synagogue at Beth-Shean," in: *Eretz Israel*, VIII (Jerusalem, 1967), 149–167 (Hebrew), English summary, 73*; idem, "The House of Kyrios Leontis at Beth-Shean," *IEJ* 16 (1966), 123–134; L. Roussin, "The Beit Leontis Mosaic: An Eschatological Interpretation," *JJA* 8 (1981), 6–19; G. Foerster, "The Survival of Some Classical and Hellenistic Themes in the Iconography of Late Antiquity in Israel," in: *XII Congress of Classical Archaeology, Athens 4–10, September 1983*, Vol. A (Athens, 1985), 132; Hüttenmeister and Reeg, *Antiken Synagogen*, II, 575–577. For an alternative reading of the Samaritan inscription: J. Naveh, "A Greek Dedication in Samaritan Letters," *IEJ* 31 (1981), 220–222.

has some relation to mosaic floors of other synagogues, but with one distinct difference: in this portion of the floor an aedicula decorated with a gable and conch is depicted, with an additional structure in its center between two columns. However, unlike other representations of the Torah shrine, the curtain is not pushed to the sides but conceals the Torah ark. The aedicula is flanked on either side by two menorahs, a shofar, and an incense shovel. The dedicatory inscription in one of the rooms of the building is written in Samaritan letters but its language is Greek. A Greek inscription in another room mentions the artisans Marianus and his son, Ḥanina, who, as already mentioned, were immortalized in the synagogue at Beth Alpha as well. The unusual orientation of the synagogue to the northwest, the absence of figural art, the unusual representation of the Torah ark, the Samaritan inscription, and the location of the building outside the city all lead to the conclusion that this was a synagogue which served the well-known Samaritan community of Beth Shean. Other Samaritan synagogues have been discovered at Shaʿalavim and Ramat Aviv.

The second synagogue at Beth Shean consists of a series of rooms surrounding a courtyard; some of these rooms apparently served nonreligious functions. The northwestern room was paved with a mosaic divided into three panels. The upper panel contains a mythological scene of Odysseus and the Sirens. The central panel contains a dedicatory inscription to Leontis and his brother, Jonathan, who made the mosaic. The inscription itself was surrounded by birds and decorated with a five-branched menorah that was destroyed. The third panel contains a Nilotic landscape: a building with the inscription "Alexandria" and a Nilometer by which the high and low tides are measured; to its right the Nile personified as a bearded god rides a crocodile and holds a trident in his hand. It is interesting to note that these themes are unknown in the iconography of the synagogue. A small room measuring 7 x 7 m. in the southwestern corner of the building served as a prayer room,[48] while the hall described above and other rooms were perhaps used as a hostel for itinerants. The mosaic floor of the prayer room was richly decorated in a style uncommon to the synagogues of this area, but closer to that of the Gaza area. The floor features nine medallions fashioned by vine scrolls growing out of an amphora at the bottom of the mosaic. The central medallion contains a menorah from which an incense burner and ethrog

---

[48] See D. Bahat, "The Synagogue at Beth Shean – Preliminary Report," in: *Ancient Synagogues Revealed*, 82–85; Hüttenmeister and Reeg, *Antiken Synagogen*, I, 53–67.

are suspended, and above it is an inscription reading "Shalom" ("Peace"). The surrounding medallions contain various animals, such as rams and birds; a peacock is centrally placed above the menorah. The border of the mosaic contains scrolls with animals in a hunting scene. The pavement contains two dedicatory inscriptions in Aramaic and one in Greek. In one of the Aramaic inscriptions the members of the Holy Congregation who repaired the synagogue are blessed; the second one blesses an anonymous artisan who worked on the project. The Greek inscription likewise refers to anonymous people whose names, however, are known by God who will always guard them.

Isolated architectural elements of synagogues, the location of which is unknown, were found in the Lower Galilee at Nazareth,[49] Sharona,[50] and Ḥ. Yitzḥaqia.[51] Synagogues at Abelim, Usha, Simonias, and Tivʿon in the Galilee are mentioned in the literary sources but not in this survey.

Summary

The above survey of the impressive remains of some twenty synagogues discovered throughout the Galilee and its adjacent valleys testifies to a generally high level of creativity in planning and construction. Through these buildings the urban and rural Jewish communities have demonstrated their desire, as well as their ability, to enhance and beautify their most important public institution. Jewish builders and artisans who were also members of these communities carried out their work with great dedication. The construction of these synagogues began as early as the Second Temple period and reached its apogee in late antiquity. Even during the fifth and sixth centuries C.E. the high quality of the work was maintained, and both Roman and Byzantine art left their mark on the architecture and decoration of these synagogues. Nonetheless, it must be emphasized that the diverse oriental and Roman architectural and artistic traditions expressed in these synagogue buildings were fashioned into an original Jewish tradition which corresponded to the needs of the communities that created them.

Among the synagogues we have surveyed, those of the early group in the Upper Galilee are the most prominent; their monumental struc-

---

49 Ibid., I, 339–342.

50 G. Foerster, "Some Menorah Reliefs from Galilee," *IEJ* 24 (1974), e.g., 96. Idem, "Remains of Menorot in the Galilee," *ʿAtiqot* 7 (1974), 89 (Hebrew).

51 N. Avigad, "A Collection of Aramaic Inscriptions," *Bulletin of the Israel Exploration Society* 31 (1967), 211–213 (Hebrew).

tures emphasized the decoration on the buildings' exterior. They were constructed primarily during the third century and continued to exist until the Arab conquest. Many changes were made in these synagogues but they did not seriously affect their external appearance. In excavations carried out in recent years in and around these synagogues—at Capernaum, Chorazim, Meiron, Nabratein, and Ḥ. Shemaʿ—private dwellings with agricultural installations were uncovered. In certain cases *miqvaʾot* (ritual baths) were found, too. In Chorazim and Nabratein, public buildings which were not synagogues and the function of which is not clear were also found. The existence of a *bet midrash* in or adjacent to the synagogues at a number of sites has been suggested by a number of scholars.

The art and architecture of the synagogues underwent a fundamental change in the fourth century C.E. This primarily chronological and regional development is evident mainly in the synagogues in the Lower Galilee and in the valleys to the south and west of it; only scanty remains of the "early" Galilean group were also found there, especially at Ramat Issachar. Emphasis was now placed on the interior of the synagogue at the expense of the splendor of the building's exterior. Beautiful mosaic pavements with geometric and floral patterns, as well as figural art, decorated the floors, the most impressive example appearing in the synagogue of Ḥammath Tiberias, one of the earliest associated with this group. The variations in plan and decoration within this group are much greater than that of the early Galilean group, but here, too, they have much in common. Most of the synagogues were influenced to some extent by church architecture, which developed between the fourth and sixth centuries C.E. As in the earlier group of synagogues in the Upper Galilee, here, too, the influence of the art and architecture of the surrounding cultures of the period is clearly evident. At the same time, however, a distinctly original art form which can be labeled Jewish was created. By incorporating Jewish motifs and symbols into late Roman and early Byzantine art forms, the Jews sought to integrate the central institution where they worshipped, studied Torah, and conducted other public functions into their contemporary society.

APPENDIX

Throughout the article I have used the commonly accepted names of sites. The official names as designated by the Schedule of Historical Monuments and Sites of the Israel Department of Antiquities (*Yalqut Hapirsumim* [*Official Gazetteer*], Jerusalem, updated from time to time) appear in parentheses next to the name of the site.

For literature on sites mentioned in this article, see:

ʿAkhbara (ʿAkbara): Hüttenmeister and Reeg, *Antiken Synagogen*, I, 5–7.

ʿAlma: Ibid., I, 9–11.

Ḥ. ʿAmmudim: L. I. Levine, "Excavations at the Synagogue of Horvat ʿAmmudim," *IEJ* 32 (1982), 1–12; D. Adan-Bayewitz, "The Ceramics from the Synagogue of Horvat ʿAmmudim and Their Chronological Implications," *IEJ* 32 (1982), 13–31; D. Chen, "The Ancient Synagogue at Horvat ʿAmmudim: Design and Chronology," *PEQ* 118 (1986), 135–137; Kohl and Watzinger, *Antike Synagogen*, 71–79; Hüttenmeister and Reeg, *Antiken Synagogen*, I, 12–15.

Arbel: N. Avigad, "On the Form of Ancient Synagogues in Galilee," in: *All the Land of Naphtali* (Jerusalem, 1967), 98–100 (Hebrew); Kohl and Watzinger, *Antike Synagogen*, 59–70; Hüttenmeister and Reeg, *Antiken Synagogen*, I, 15–17.

Barʿam (Kefar Barʿam): Kohl and Watzinger, *Antike Synagogen*, 89–100; Hüttenmeister and Reeg, *Antiken Synagogen*, I, 31–38.

Beth Sheʿarim: B. Mazar, *Beth Sheʿarim*, I (Jerusalem, 1973), 22–27; Hüttenmeister and Reeg, *Antiken Synagogen*, I, 68–72.

Capernaum (Kefar Naḥum): V. C. Corbo, *Cafarnao*, I: *Gli edifici della Città* (Jerusalem, 1975); S. Loffreda, *Cafarnao*, II: *La Ceramica* (Jerusalem, 1974); A. Spijkerman, *Cafarnao*, III: *Cat. delle monete della Città* (Jerusalem, 1975); E. Testa, *Cafarnao*, IV: *I Graffiti della Casa di S. Pietro* (Jerusalem, 1972); V. C. Corbo, "Edifici antichi sotto la sinagoga di Cafarnao," in: *Studia Hierosolymitana in Onore di B. Bagatti*, I: *Studi Archeologici* (Jerusalem, 1976), 159–176; idem, "Sotto la Sinagoga di Cafarnao un'insula della Città," *LA* 27 (1977), 156–172; S. Loffreda, "Potsherds from a Sealed Level of the Synagogue at Capharnaum," *LA* 29 (1979), 215–220; idem, "The Late Chronology of the Synagogue of Capernaum," in: *Ancient Synagogues Revealed*, ed. L. I. Levine (Jerusalem, 1981), 52–56; idem, "Documentazione preliminare degli oggetti della XIV campagna di scavi a Cafarnao," *LA* 32

(1982), 409–426; V. C. Corbo, "Ripreso a Cafarnao lo scavo della Città: Relazione preliminare alla XIV campagna," *LA* 32 (1982), 427–446; idem, "Gli ultimigiorno di Cafarnao: Rapporto preliminare dopo la XV campagna di scavo, 6 Giugno–16 Luglio," *LA* 33 (1983), 373–390; idem, "Cafarnao dopo la XIX campagna di scavo," *LA* 36 (1986), 297–308; M. Fischer, "The Corinthian Capitals of the Capernaum Synagogue: A Revision," *Levant* 18 (1986), 131–142; D. Chen, "On the Chronology of the Ancient Synagogue at Capernaum," *ZDPV* 102 (1986), 134–143; V. Tzaferis, *Excavations at Capernaum 1978–1982* (Winona Lake, 1988); Y. Tsafrir, "The Synagogue at Meroth, the Synagogue at Capernaum and the Dating of the Galilean Synagogues: A Reconsideration," in: *Eretz Israel*, XX (Jerusalem, 1989), 337–344 (Hebrew), English summary, 207*; Kohl and Watzinger, *Antike Synagogen*, 4–40; Hüttenmeister and Reeg, *Antiken Synagogen*, I, 260–269.

Chorazim (Korazim): Z. Yeivin, "The Synagogue of Chorazim," in: *All the Land of Naphtali*, 135–138 (Hebrew); idem, "The Excavations at Khorazin, 1962–64," in: *Eretz Israel*, XI (Jerusalem, 1973), 144–157 (Hebrew), English summary, 27*; idem, "Chorazim: A Mishnaic City," *Bulletin of the Anglo-Israel Archaeological Society* (1983–84), 46–48; idem, "Reconstruction of the Southern Interior Wall of the Khorazin Synagogue," in: *Eretz Israel*, XVIII (Jerusalem, 1985), 268–276 (Hebrew), English summary, 74*; Kohl and Watzinger, *Antike Synagogen*, 41–58; Hüttenmeister and Reeg, *Antiken Synagogen*, I, 275–281.

Dalton: Ibid., I, 96–98.

Danna: G. Foerster, "A Menorah on a Lintel from Dana," ʿ*Atiqot* 3 (1966), 66–67 (Hebrew).

Gush Ḥalav: Kohl and Watzinger, *Antike Synagogen*, 107–111; Hüttenmeister and Reeg, *Antiken Synagogen*, I, 144–147; E. M. Meyers et al., "Preliminary Report on the 1977 and 1978 Seasons at Gush Ḥalav (el-Jish)," *BASOR* 233 (1979), 33–58.

Kefar Ḥananyah: Hüttenmeister and Reeg, *Antiken Synagogen*, I, 256–258.

Kokhav ha-Yarden: Ibid., I, 272–274.

Meiron (Meron): Kohl and Watzinger, *Antike Synagogen*, 80–88; Hüttenmeister and Reeg, *Antiken Synagogen*, I, 311–314; E. M. Meyers et al., *Excavations at Ancient Meiron, Upper Galilee, Israel 1971–72, 1974–75, 1977* (Cambridge, MA, 1981); G. Foerster, "Excavations at Ancient Meron" (review article), *IEJ* 37 (1987), 262–269.

Nabratein (Ḥ. Nevoraya): E. M. Meyers, "Preliminary Report on the 1980 Excavations at en-Nabratein, Israel," *BASOR* 244 (1981), 1–25; idem et al., "Second Preliminary Report on the 1981 Excavations at en-Nabratein, Israel," *BASOR* 246 (1982), 35–44; N. Avigad, "The Lintel Inscription from the Ancient Synagogue at Kefar Niburaya," *Bulletin of the Israel Exploration Society* 24 (1960), 136–145 (Hebrew); D. Chen, "The Ancient Synagogue at Nabratein: Design and Chronology," *PEQ* 119 (1987), 44–49; Kohl and Watzinger, *Antike Synagogen*, 101–106; Hüttenmeister and Reeg, *Antiken Synagogen*, I, 343–347.

Ḥ. Ofrat: Ibid., I, 348–349.

Peqiʿin: Ibid., I, 350–354.

er-Rama: Ibid., I, 367–369.

Sasa: *Ḥadashot Arkheologiyot* 28–29 (1969), 4 (Hebrew); Hüttenmeister and Reeg, *Antiken Synagogen*, I, 383.

Ḥ. Shemaʿ: E. M. Meyers et al., *Ancient Synagogue Excavations at Khirbet Shemaʿ, Upper Galilee, Israel 1970–72* (Durham, NC, 1976); Hüttenmeister and Reeg, *Antiken Synagogen*, I, 387–390.

Ḥ. Shura: *Ḥadashot Arkheologiyot* 72 (1979), 41 (Hebrew); Hüttenmeister and Reeg, *Antiken Synagogen*, I, 421–422.

Sifsufa: Ibid., I, 392–393.

Ḥ. Sumaqa: Ibid., I, 419–420; Kohl and Watzinger, *Antike Synagogen*, 135–137; S. Dar and Y. Minzker, "The Synagogue of Ḥurvat Sumaqa," in: *Ancient Synagogues in Israel*, ed. R. Hachlili (*BAR International Series* 499; Haifa, 1989), 17–20.

Kh. Tuba: Hüttenmeister and Reeg, *Antiken Synagogen*, I, 464.

Ḥ. Veradim: Ibid., I, 477–478.

Yafia (Yafa): E. L. Sukenik, "The Ancient Synagogue at Yafa near Nazareth – Preliminary Report," *Rabinowitz Bulletin for the Exploration of Ancient Synagogues* 2 (1951), 6–24; G. Foerster, "On the Mosaic of the Japhia Synagogue," *Bulletin of the Israel Exploration Society* 31 (1967), 218–224 (Hebrew); *EAEHL*, II, 541–543; Hüttenmeister and Reeg, *Antiken Synagogen*, I, 479–482.

Yesud ha-Maʿalah: *Ḥadashot Arkheologiyot* 48–49 (1974), 28 (Hebrew).

Roman Sepphoris in Light of New Archeological Evidence and Recent Research

ERIC M. MEYERS

Sepphoris was a major urban center in the Lower Galilee from the first century C.E. to the Byzantine era. It is located approximately 5 km. northwest of Nazareth and 30 km. east of the Mediterranean, and exactly the same distance from the Sea of Galilee and Tiberias. Standing astride the ancient main east–west highway that linked Acco (Ptolemais) to Tiberias and close to the main north–south junction, Sepphoris' location enabled it throughout its rich history to serve as a major center of trade and commerce and to render military and administrative assistance to its neighbors.

Though fertile lands encircle the city, which rises steeply 115 m. above the surrounding plain, Sepphoris itself derived its water supply from outside the city, from the spring of Sepphoris 2.5 km. to the south and from springs about 6 km. east of the city. Water from the former was carried in containers that were presumably loaded onto donkeys or horses; water from the latter was brought to the city by aqueduct.

Today a large citadel marks the summit of the ancient site. Though it was probably built in Byzantine times, its present configuration is mainly Crusader. To the west, on Franciscan property, the Crusader monument of the Church of St. Anne points to another epoch in Sepphoris' rich history. Until 1948 the existence of the Arab village of Saffuriyeh, with a population then of 13,000, made it difficult for archeological work to be conducted.

Nevertheless, excavation was carried out at the site in 1931, when the University of Michigan, under the direction of L. Waterman, conducted extensive soundings in the theater and on the western summit.[1] Subsequent investigations and publications were inspired by random discoveries. Renewed excavations were sparked by the 1976 survey of the author and J. F. Strange[2] and by the subsequent work of T. Tsuk on the aqueducts.[3] In 1983 Strange organized a new team to conduct further archeological work,[4] and in 1984 the author, together with E. Netzer and C. L. Meyers, established a binational project that led to five major campaigns (herein referred to as the "Joint Expedition").[5]

Though the spate of recent field work at Sepphoris has produced an astonishing array of new material from the late Iron Age until the Crusader era, this paper will deal only with certain aspects of the Roman occupation at Sepphoris. In particular, I will attempt to demonstrate how the archeological record thus far revealed supports the picture of Sepphoris presented by Josephus and some of the rabbinic literature, i.e., that Sepphoris from the first century C.E. onwards was a city inhabited by many well-to-do, aristocratic Jews of a priestly background, and that its success in accommodating an unusually high degree of Hellenization in the second to fourth centuries C.E. could well reflect the inclusion of many rich landowners and other notables in its population. The transfer of the Sanhedrin to Sepphoris at the end of the second century and the location of the patriarchate of R. Judah ha-Nasi there are also to be viewed in this context. Tensions between town and city, rural and urban, especially in the first and perhaps in the beginning of the second century, also contributed to the unique role Sepphoris played in Jewish history in Roman Palestine.

---

[1] L. Waterman, et al., *Preliminary Report of the University of Michigan Excavations at Sepphoris, Palestine in 1931* (Ann Arbor, 1937).

[2] E. Meyers and J. F. Strange, "Survey in Galilee, 1976," *Explor* 3 (1977), 7–18; E. Meyers, J. F. Strange, and D. E. Groh, "The Meiron Excavation Project: Archeological Survey in Galilee and Golan, 1976," *BASOR* 230 (1978), 1–24.

[3] T. Tsuk, "The Aqueducts to Sepphoris," in: *The Aqueducts of Ancient Palestine*, eds. D. Amit, Y. Hirschfeld, J. Patrich (Jerusalem, 1989), 101–108.

[4] J. F. Strange and T. Longstaff, "Notes and News: Sepphoris (Ṣippori)," *IEJ* 34 (1984), 51–52, 269–270; 35 (1985), 297–299; 37 (1987), 278–280.

[5] Idem, "Notes and News: Sepphoris (Ṣippori)," *IEJ* 35 (1985), 295–297; 37 (1987), 275–278; E. M. Meyers, E. Netzer, and C. L. Meyers, "Sepphoris: 'Ornament of All Galilee'," *BA* 49 (1986), 4–19; idem, "Artistry in Stone: The Mosaics of Ancient Sepphoris," *BA* 50 (1987), 223–231.

Josephus, the first-century Jewish historian, provides the earliest literary attestation to Sepphoris.[6] He mentions the site for the first time in reference to Ptolemy Lathyrus' unsuccessful attempt to capture the city during the reign of Alexander Jannaeus (ca. 100 B.C.E.). Numerous Hasmonean coins found during excavation, including coins of Jannaeus, together with other late Hellenistic artifacts and traces of architecture, lend credibility to Josephus' assertion that Sepphoris was already an important Galilean stronghold; he calls it "the strongest city of Galilee."[7] In later times both Antigonus[8] and Herod the Great[9] used Sepphoris as a secure staging platform from which to launch their Galilean careers.

In 57 B.C.E. Gabinius, the proconsul of Syria, divided the Jewish nation into five administrative districts, or councils, called *synedria*: he chose Sepphoris as the Galilean site for one of the councils.[10] For all intents and purposes, Sepphoris had already become the capital of the Galilee by that time. After the death of Herod the Great in 4 B.C.E., a Galilean rebel named Judas son of Ezekias invaded the royal arsenal to seize arms, but the city was so well fortified that the attempt failed.[11] Varus, the legate of Syria, is said to have destroyed the city and sold its inhabitants into slavery in retaliation for this rebellious activity as well as similar uprisings throughout the country.[12] The Joint Expedition, however, has found no trace of violent destruction in the Herodian period. On the contrary, there seems to have been a great degree of continuity between the late Hellenistic and early Roman (Herodian) structures.

Indeed, considering the pro-Roman stance adopted by the citizens of Sepphoris during the First Revolt against Rome, it would be surprising if many inhabitants of Sepphoris supported Judas' defiant and rebellious activities. Varus' quick response, however, led to the rebuilding project of Herod Antipas who, according to Josephus, made the city the "ornament of all Galilee" in the early first century C.E.[13] In 19 C.E. Antipas' impact on the Galilee was broadened when he founded Tiberias on the Sea of Galilee. Antipas himself called Sepphoris *autokratis*,[14] which

---

6 *Ant.* XIII, 12, 5, 338.
7 *War* II, 18, 11, 510f.
8 *Ant.* XIV, 15, 4, 413f.
9 *Ant.* XVIII, 2, 1, 27.
10 *War* I, 8, 5, 170 and *Ant.* XIV, 5, 4, 91.
11 *Ant.* XVII, 10, 5, 271; *War* II, 4, 1, 56.
12 *Ant.* XVII, 10, 9, 289 and *War* II, 5, 1, 69.
13 *Ant.* XVIII, 2, 1, 27.
14 Ibid.

probably indicated its role as a capital city boasting a measure of autonomy.

Although Antipas shifted his administrative base to Tiberias, Sepphoris regained much of its status under the procurator Felix (52–60 C.E.). The royal bank, debt records, and other important archives previously stored in Tiberias were transferred to Sepphoris on the eve of the war.[15] By this time Sepphoris was no longer part of the royal territory of Agrippa II; its new status as archival center brought with it considerable commercial benefit to the city, arousing jealousy in the hearts of many Tiberians, especially that of Justus of Tiberias. It is little wonder that the citizens of Sepphoris were united in their pro-Roman stance[16] and in 67 C.E. were allowed to mint their own coins bearing the legend "City of Peace" (*eirenopolis*). Cestius Gallus, governor of Syria at the time, was no doubt well prepared to reward the local populace for its pro-Roman attitude also after the war.

There can be little doubt that the overwhelming majority or virtually all of the inhabitants of Sepphoris in the first century C.E were Jewish, and that Josephus, commander of the Galilean armed forces until 68 C.E., understood the Sepphoreans' pacifism as a rejection of their fellow-Galileans' anti-Roman sentiments.[17] Josephus himself was excluded from the city,[18] despite the fact that he adopted a pacifistic stance in 68 C.E. when he gave up his command at nearby Jotapata. Sepphoris thus stood strong in its pro-Roman views, arousing the ire of the Galilean peasants and villagers who formed the core of opposition to Roman rule and, as recently contended by Freyne, Horsley, and Hanson, probably also to the Jewish aristocracy of Sepphoris and Tiberias.[19] Such widespread opposition to the direct and indirect rule of the Roman administration on the

15 *Life* 9, 38.
16 *Life* 8, 30; 9, 38; 22, 104; 25, 124; 45, 232; 65, 345–348; 67, 373; 71, 394–395.
17 *War* III, 2, 4, 32; *Life* 65, 348.
18 *Life* 65, 346f.
19 *Life* 67, 375; 68, 384. R. Horsley and J. S. Hanson, *Bandits, Prophets, and Messiahs: Popular Movements at the Time of Jesus* (New York, 1985), passim; R. Horsley, *Jesus and the Spiral of Violence: Popular Jewish Resistance in Roman Palestine* (New York, 1987). I am much indebted to the recent work of S. Freyne on this subject, *Galilee, Jesus and the Gospels* (Philadelphia, 1988), especially Part Two on the social world of the Galilee, 135–175. Freyne's excellent work is the logical sequel to his prior work on the Galilee, *Galilee from Alexander the Great to Hadrian, 323 B.C.E. to 135 C.E.* (Wilmington, 1980). His incisive remarks on Sepphoris in both volumes are a model of sound historical interpretation and stand in bold contrast to some of the remarkable claims about Jesus and Sepphoris that have appeared in print and in the media in recent years.

one hand, and to the urban elite on the other hand, undoubtedly reflects the deep tension that divided city and town in this era.[20] The Roman policy of urbanization[21] ultimately meant that towns and villages were increasingly dependent on the large urban centers. Such tensions were tested to the fullest when Sepphoris adopted its extraordinary policy of pacifism during the First Revolt.

The suggestion of some scholars, therefore, that the failure of the New Testament to mention either Sepphoris or Tiberias is without significance must be questioned.[22] Jesus had every reason to avoid urban centers where the Herodian family and elite were situated. The view espoused by Bösen,[23] that Jesus preached in Sepphoris without success, does not, in our opinion, explain the silence of the gospels, especially since they do not remain silent about other unsuccessful ministries.[24] R. Batey argues that Jesus' preaching indicates knowledge and familiarity with Greek theater, to which Jesus of Nazareth would have had access in nearby Sepphoris.[25] However, Jesus' appearance in Sepphoris is improbable for several reasons: first, Jesus would not have had a sympathetic hearing among the elite, Herodian, and priestly classes, and second, the theater in all probability was not yet constructed.

The considerable first-century remains that have been uncovered in the excavations of the Joint Expedition point to a Torah-true population, judging by the number of ritual baths (*miqva'ot*) in houses and by the strict practice of burial outside the city precincts. The commanding position of Sepphoris on the summit, earning it renown as the strongest city in the Galilee,[26] and the fact that the Jewish population had been there

---

20 So R. McMullen, *Roman Social Relations, 50 B.C. to A.D. 284* (New Haven/London, 1974), 28–56; P. A. Brunt, "Josephus on Social Conflicts in Roman Judaea," *Klio* 59 (1977), 149–153.

21 See M. Avi-Yonah, *The Holy Land: From the Persian to the Arab Conquest (546 B.C.– A.D. 640)* (Grand Rapids, 1977), 127ff.

22 Freyne, *Galilee, Jesus and the Gospels*, 140 and 173.

23 Ibid., esp. p. 140, n. 11, and see W. Bösen, *Galiläa als Lebensraum und Wirkungsfeld Jesu* (Freiburg im Breisgau, 1985), 69–75.

24 Matt. 11:20–24.

25 R. Batey, "Jesus and the Theatre," *NTS* 30 (1984), 563–574. Batey, of course, assumes that the theater at Sepphoris had been completed in Jesus' day (p. 570, n. 35) and enlarged by the second century C.E. At the time Batey wrote the article, J. F. Strange provisionally maintained that the theater was originally built in the second century (p. 573, n. 11), a view espoused by Albright long ago. Batey's views are based also on notions about the proximity of Nazareth to Sepphoris espoused by S. J. Case, "Jesus and Sepphoris," *JBL* 45 (1926), 14–21.

26 *Life* 65, 346; 67, 376.

since Hellenistic times, made it a logical center of Galilean urban culture. The priestly clan of Jedaiah was located there in the second half of the first century and they most likely found a congenial atmosphere. Nevertheless, the extent of their influence on local leadership is not evident in the immediate post-70 period.[27]

If Sepphoris and its associated towns and villages in the Lower Galilee were predominantly Jewish in the first century, it is also quite clear that many newcomers, especially Roman soldiers, moved in after 70. As an outcome of the war against Rome, it became quite clear to the Roman administration that in order to keep order in the province of Syria-Palestine they would have to commit troops or legionnaires to the region of the Galilee; their Galilean base became Legio.[28] During the reign of Hadrian (117–138 C.E.), the "ancient government" of Sepphoris was abolished and a gentile administration was installed; the city became known as "Diocaesarea," i.e., city of Zeus (Dio), the emperor Hadrian adopted the title Zeus Olympios, and a Capitoline temple was apparently built at the site. A milestone bearing the legend "Diocaesarea" and dating to 130 C.E., found on the newly built road from Acco to Tiberias, confirms that these changes occurred during Hadrian's reign.

It is not surprising, then, that some Sepphoreans desirous of regaining a measure of their former independence were active in the Second Revolt against Rome (132–135 C.E.). No doubt the population of the Galilee in general was changing as refugees from the south moved north, some to Sepphoris. Whereas in the first century relations between the upper classes of Sepphoris and the Galileans might have been strained, it is quite clear that matters had changed dramatically by the time of Hadrian. This does not mean, however, that the Sepphoreans played a leading role in the Bar-Kokhba war. Judeo-Roman coins continued to be

---

[27] See the definitive treatment on this subject by S. S. Miller, *Studies in the History and Traditions of Sepphoris* (Leiden, 1984), 62ff. See p. 62, n. 1 for the literature on the twenty-four priestly courses or *mishmarot*. The priestly clan of Jedaiah appears second on the list, which was probably on display in the synagogue in the rabbinic period. See esp. M. Avi-Yonah, "The Caesarea Inscription of the Twenty-four Priestly Courses," in: *The Teacher's Yoke: Studies in Memory of Henry Trantham*, eds. E. J. Vardaman, J. L. Garrett, and J. B. Adair (Waco, 1964), 46–57.

[28] See M. Avi-Yonah, *The Holy Land*, 113, 141ff. Legio became the headquarters of the Sixth Legion, Legio VI Ferrata. With the addition of the Sixth Legion to the Tenth, X (Decima) Fretensis, Judea was raised to the rank of consular province and the name of the province was changed to Syria Palaestina, a revival of a similar expression coined by Herodotus, which today has gained much currency. Herodotus (*Hist.* II, 104:3) speaks of the "Syrians who live in Palestine."

minted at Sepphoris for most of the period between the two wars, but coins bearing the title "Diocaesarea" first appeared under Antoninus Pius (138–161 C.E.). Although there is a fifteen-year cessation of coinage right before the Second Revolt, such a gap was not necessarily related to the existence of rebellious factions in Sepphoris.[29]

Sepphoris became the focal point of Jewish life and learning during the time that the Patriarch R. Judah ha-Nasi resided in Sepphoris (ca. 200–217 C.E.) and when the Sanhedrin, or judicial seat of authority, was transferred there.[30] It was probably at Sepphoris that R. Judah completed his work on the codification and redaction of the Mishnah; such activity was certainly one of the main reasons Sepphoris attracted many other rabbinic leaders who established noted academies there.[31]

In addition to his leadership role in scholarship, R. Judah played a central role in contemporary Palestinian politics; rabbinic literature depicts him as a friend of a Roman emperor—perhaps Antoninus Pius but more probably Caracalla (also known as Antoninus), who reigned from 211 to 217 C.E. A coin from this period provides astonishing testimony to a treaty of friendship between the Roman senate and the Sepphoris council or *boule*, the official governing bodies representing the two peoples. The legend on the coins of Caracalla reads, "Diocaesarea the Holy City, City of Shelter, Autonomous, Loyal, [a treaty of] friendship and alliance between the Holy Council and the Senate of the Roman people,"[32] or a variation thereof.

Although not all scholars interpret the coins of Caracalla minted at Sepphoris as indicative of a treaty of friendship,[33] the data nonetheless tend to support the historicity of the talmudic accounts which idealize the relationship between R. Judah and the Roman emperor. The combination of literary, archeological, and numismatic evidence, while not unique in ancient history, lends great credence to the talmudic view that

---

29 See Y. Meshorer, *City-Coins of Eretz-Israel and the Decapolis in the Roman Period* (Jerusalem, 1985), 36–37.

30 S. S. Miller, "Intercity Relations in Roman Palestine: The Case of Sepphoris and Tiberias," *AJS Review* 12 (1987), 4–6, esp. n. 16.

31 Ibid., 8ff. and idem, *History and Traditions*, 116ff.

32 Idem, "Intercity Relations," 6–7; Y. Meshorer, "Sepphoris and Rome," in: *Greek Numismatics and Archaeology – Essays in Honor of Margaret Thompson*, eds. O. Markholm and N. M. Waggoner (Wetteren, 1976), 159–171.

33 Cf. for example, the remarks of C. M. Kraay, "Jewish Friends and Allies of Rome," *American Numismatic Society Museum Notes* 25 (1980), 53–57, who questions Meshorer's interpretation of the legend, especially the relationship between "Holy Council and the Senate of the Roman people," a phrase Kraay regards as obscure.

members, and possibly a majority, of the *boule* of Sepphoris at the time of R. Judah were Jewish.[34] This may be the only instance of such Jewish political involvement in ancient Roman Palestine. All of this underscores Sepphoris' important economic and political roles in the third century C.E.

It was during the fourth century C.E., however, that Sepphoris underwent some important changes. Both archeological and literary sources attest that after Constantine the Great's official recognition of Christianity (324 C.E.), religion took root in the city in more traditional ways than the Jewish-Christianity that had flourished there earlier. During Constantine's reign (306–337 C.E.), one Joseph of Tiberias received permission to build a church there.[35] By the next century, a bishop of Sepphoris attended the Council of Chalcedon in 451 C.E. By the mid-fourth century, during the reign of Constantius II (337–361 C.E.), Sepphoris is reported as having been the center of anti-Roman activity. The precise details of the so-called Gallus Revolt (351–352 C.E.) are difficult to reconstruct,[36] and although Sepphoris was devastated at about this time, the cause was more likely the great earthquake of 363 C.E., which ended the glory of Roman occupation there. Both the great theater and the splendid villa with its mosaic were buried at this time.

It is quite clear that the Middle Roman period (135–217 C.E.)[37] witnessed dramatic changes in the demography of Sepphoris and of the Lower Galilee generally. As we have already noted, legions of the Roman army were brought into the region to control the territory. The army's needs were not inconsiderable—food, supplies, entertainment, outlets for religious expression—and the facilities made available by the predominantly Jewish population of the Galilee were not adequate; many of the Roman or pagan buildings found there may be attributed to this era. It is

---

[34] So F. Manns, "An Important Jewish-Christian Center: Sepphoris," in: *Essais sur le Judéo-Christianisme* (*Analecta* 12; Jerusalem, 1977), 165–190. The texts on which this assumption is made by Manns are: J Peʾah 1, 1, 16a and J Shabbat 12, 3, 13c, referring to *bouleutai*, and B Sanhedrin 8a, referring to the Jewish majority in the *boule*.

[35] S. Goranson's doctoral dissertation, "Joseph of Tiberias as a Source on Jewish Christian Relations in Fourth-Century Galilee" (Duke University; Durham, NC, 1990), is an attempt to deal systematically with the impact of Christianity and its numerous heresies on contemporaneous Judaism in the Galilee.

[36] B. G. Nathanson, "Jews, Christians, and the Gallus Revolt in Fourth Century Palestine," *BA* 49 (1986), 26–36.

[37] On the variety of terminologies used to describe the Roman period in Palestine, see D. E. Groh, "Jews and Christians in Late Roman Palestine: Towards a New Chronology," *BA* 51 (1988), 80–99.

quite possible that the theater at Sepphoris was constructed in the inter-war period, when many upper class Jews fled Jerusalem to safe places like Sepphoris, where Vespasian had already stationed a Roman garrison. The latter would also have needed pagan temples, which are first attested on coins bearing representations of the Capitoline Triad, Tyche, and various temples from the period of Antoninus Pius (138–161 C.E.).[38]

Significantly, in the inter-war period and during the reign of Trajan (98–117 C.E.) many coins minted in Sepphoris still bore symbols representative of the Jewish population there—the laurel wreath, palm tree, caduceus, and ears of grain[39]—marking the ambient Jewish sense of pride just prior to the Bar-Kokhba revolt (132–135 C.E.). However, the next series of coins minted at Sepphoris, during the reign of Antoninus Pius (138–161 C.E.), already used the pagan name "Diocaesarea" and bore pagan motifs.

With the influx of many new peoples into the Galilee in the second century C.E. (the Middle Roman or Roman II period), it is not surprising that this period is the best represented in the material culture of the site, culminating perhaps with the Roman villa and its Dionysos mosaic situated on the eastern acropolis, adjacent to and south of the theater. By the second century, Sepphoris had become the home of pagans, Jews, and Jewish-Christians. The western domestic area shows major signs of expansion and growth—houses utilizing the contours of their early Roman forebears were developed and enlarged; ritual baths (*miqva'ot*) were introduced to accommodate newcomers and were to be found, as well as cisterns, in virtually every complex and insula. Given the fact that water was difficult to transport to the site, the prevalence of water installations underscored the centrality of ritual purity in the daily lives of the residents. More than twenty such ritual installations have been found in the western area alone. The presence of several bronze figurines,[40] hundreds of second–third century decorated disc lamps,[41] many with presumably pagan symbols on the discs found in this same area, suggests a high degree of Hellenization among the Jewish residents at this time and, together with the rest of the data, suggest a very upper class lifestyle.[42]

---

[38] See Meshorer, *City-Coins of Eretz-Israel*, 36–37.

[39] Ibid.

[40] See above, n. 5 and references there.

[41] Meyers, Netzer, and Meyers, "Sepphoris: 'Ornament of All Galilee'," 4–5.

[42] Though these lamps and lamp fragments are as yet unpublished, they conform well to the standard repertoire of Roman lamps from the period and include every-

From this same period came the *hemi-litrin* leadweight from debris in the east–west street. Inscribed in Greek on both sides, it seems that two generations of market inspectors (*agoranomoi*) are attested, and that Justus, father of Aianos (a name mentioned in Song of Songs Rabbah 6:12), and Simon were apparently both Jewish. A Greek ostracon bearing seven ink-written letters in Hebrew spelling the Greek loanword *epimelos* ("manager" or "overseer") may be dated, according to Y. Naveh and the find's stratigraphic context, to the end of the Hellenistic period, ca. 100 B.C.E.[43] While we find Greek words in Hebrew letters in Sepphoris as early as the Hasmonean period, at the dawn of the Roman era, by the end of the Roman period evidence of Greek language and culture is appreciably greater and is not limited to the fifteen Greek legends preserved on the Dionysos mosaic in the villa. Since all of these examples refer to titles or data that may be associated with officials or official functions of the city—the mosaic legends possibly being associated with the *boule*—we may tentatively suggest that the city of Sepphoris was a melting pot of Greek language and culture for a very long time.

The fact that Sepphoris was at the same time an important center of rabbinic learning, however, leads us to conclude that the mixture of Hebrew, Greek, and Aramaic was symbiotic. Nevertheless, the cosmopolitan world of the Roman city was never too far removed from the village or town of the Galilean peasant, who, for better or for worse—and it would seem for worse much of the time—was dependent on these centers for their economic well-being and growth, supplies, and services.[44] Tensions that were great in the first century C.E. were eased in later antiquity as Christianity spread and paganism flourished. For the bulk of the rabbinic period, however, the village was the likely location of those who desired to preserve a distinctively Jewish lifestyle.[45]

---

thing from a helmeted Athena and erotic lamps to depictions of animals and crustaceans.

43 I would like to thank Professor Y. Naveh for his preliminary remarks on this ostracon, and also S. Goranson for his observations on this matter.

44 See J. Neusner, "The Experience of the City in Late Antique Judaism," in: *Approaches to Ancient Judaism*, V, ed. W. S. Green (Atlanta, 1985), 37–52; S. Applebaum, "Jewish Urban Communities and Greek Influence," *Scripta Classica Israelitica* 5 (1979), 158–177.

45 In this respect, Freyne, *Galilee, Jesus and the Gospel*, 146, n. 27, has adopted the position put forward by me in numerous publications. For a convenient summary of those views, see E. M. Meyers and J. F. Strange, *Archaeology, the Rabbis and Early Christianity* (Nashville, 1981), 45ff.

The Dionysos mosaic was laid at the very apogee of rabbinic activity at Sepphoris, at a time when the theater was functioning and the Mishnah of R. Judah was being redacted and promulgated. These creative bursts in great art and literature most probably were unleashed as a result of complementary synergistic energies. By the beginning of the third century C.E. Sepphoris had become a truly pluralistic center of high culture and rabbinic learning which had absorbed the very best of Semitic and Greek cultures.

The Dionysos mosaic is part of an elaborate Roman villa that adjoins the southern side of the theater of Sepphoris. With a seating capacity of close to 5,000, the theater is by far the most imposing architectural element at the site. It is quite clear from the construction of the villa that the builders carefully considered the site for its location and took great pains to accommodate the awkward topography and steeply rising bedrock in the area, in order to gain one of the finest views in all Palestine as one looked north to the Beth Netofa Valley. The mosaic decorated a banquet hall or *triclinium* in the main room on the villa's first floor. A peristyle courtyard lay to the south, and rooms of all kinds were situated to the east, west, and north. The northwestern corner proved especially interesting with the uncovering of an elaborate bathroom complex.[46]

The mosaic floor of the *triclinium* was laid on bedrock, which had been levelled with small stones and white limestone plaster. Measuring 9.2 x 6.9 m., it is composed of two major sections, one of plain white tiles, the other of decorative and representational panels of multicolored tiles. The multicolored section forms a T-shape and consists of three major parts plus borders. The central section contains fifteen panels of various sizes; surrounding the rectangle is a border of acanthus leaf medallions. Guests sat around on benches or couches along the three undecorated portions of the floor; the beautiful mosaic carpet stood before them in all its splendor to view and discuss.

The panels in the central rectangle all deal with the theme of the life of Dionysos and the rituals or ceremonies that celebrated him in Roman religion. Most famous as the god of the grapevine or wine, Dionysos is understandably connected to feasting, drunkenness, revelry, and ecstatic release. Similarly, such an association can be related to fertility and agriculture and may at times represent the mysterious forces of productivity in nature. Dionysos is often portrayed as patron god of the theater and

---

[46] For the most up-to-date presentation of the Sepphoris material, see E. M. Meyers, E. Netzer, and C. L. Meyers, *Sepphoris and Its Mosaics* (forthcoming).

thus of the dramatic, musical, and poetic arts which were part and parcel of theatrical performances. The proximity of the villa to the theater, therefore, is of great significance, suggesting perhaps that the villa may have served at times as an inn for performers.

The mosaic floor is replete with scenes from all aspects of the mythology and ritual associated with Dionysos: drinking, carousing, preparing wine, ecstasy, music, and various scenes from the god's life story—infancy, childhood, adulthood, conquest, and marriage. The surrounding acanthus medallions depict hunting scenes with many of the animals associated with Dionysos: tigers, goats, deer, and leopards. These lively animals are shown being hunted by naked erotes or cupids armed with bows and arrows and other weapons of the hunt. Interspersed among the medallions are various species of birds. All these elements serve to dramatize the appearance of two female portraits, one in exquisite detail and excellent preservation on the northern edge and one poorly preserved on the southern edge.

Three surrounding panels fill the remaining decorated portions of the mosaic. The best preserved section is the western panel depicting a procession; except for one figure riding an animal, presumably a mule, all others are carrying garlands of flowers, baskets laden with fruit, ducks or roosters. These items appear to be offerings and the procession may be related to the Dionysos cult. On the eastern panel we find a portrayal of a child riding a goat and attended by a woman, as well as a female playing a double flute. These scenes are reminiscent of the mythological motifs appearing elsewhere in the mosaic. The southern border panel, however, is altogether different in character and is apparently a repair from a later stage of use, presumably some time in the first half of the fourth century C.E. The border features a Nilotic scene: a series of figures and animals, including a crocodile, set in the exotic vegetation of the Nile River.

I have gone into a bit of detail concerning the scenes of the mosaic in order to emphasize their obvious pagan content. It is quite probable that important public functions were held in the villa, with its grand courtyard and elegant banquet hall, and that such a building could hardly have been kept secret from the rabbis or prominent Jews who served on the *boule* or city council. During the 1989 season, when the Joint Expedition was unable to complete excavation of most components of the villa, several rooms produced surprises that require further excavation and study. East of the peristyle, for example, and within the villa itself, a water installation very similar to a *miqveh* was uncovered. Since the excavators had previously entertained the possibility of Jewish use of the building, this is not totally implausible. Nonetheless, further clearance and study are necessary before a more definitive suggestion may be put forward.

It should be emphasized, too, that both the theater and the villa are centrally located on the summit and in the city plan in such a way that all access roads would have led to them. The western domestic area briefly described above is just meters away from the villa and no resident of Sepphoris at the time when the theater was functioning could have avoided the hustle and bustle associated with it; most probably people from all walks of life—Jews, Jewish-Christians, and pagans—attended events and spectacles there.[47] People from the surrounding area probably also flocked to Sepphoris on such occasions, either to attend the theater or to hawk their wares. The next nearest theater would have been in Beth Shean, a much larger city and more pagan in character, even though the Beth Shean Valley contained numerous Jewish towns and villages in the Roman period.

Roman Sepphoris was a city of great diversity and much splendor. Although literary sources document a mixed population of Jews, Jewish-Christians, and Romans, archeology has only illuminated the Jewish and Roman (pagan) presence there. By the fourth century, however, that picture changed and Christians were among those who established a definite presence at the site. From a cultural standpoint, the Roman period came to an abrupt end when the great earthquake of 363 C.E. destroyed much of the city. It was then that the villa collapsed, the mosaic was fortuitously buried, and the theater went out of use. It is for this period that a clearer differentiation between Jews and Christians could be discerned in the material culture, such as crosses or Torah shrines stamped on decorated ceramic objects.

The spectre of war with Rome had long since passed as the Byzantine era dawned, although the abortive and complex Gallus Revolt may have marked the last burst of Jewish rebelliousness in 352 C.E. The ruins and excavations of Sepphoris, however, have revealed no signs of a rebellion; it is possible that the great earthquake of 363 C.E. might have covered up any evidence of the so-called Gallus Revolt, which occurred just eleven

---

47 See M. T. Boatwright, "Theaters in the Roman Empire," *BA* 53 (1990), 184–192. Boatwright maintains that theaters outside of Rome were normally used only five to twenty-five times a year; see also J. Kolendo, "La répartition des places aux spectacles et le stratification sociale dans l'empire romain," *Ktema* 6 (1981), 301ff.

years earlier.[48] Because Sepphoris was composed of a mixed population from the second century onward, tensions which once ran high between urban Jewish elite and Galilean peasant diminished with time as a new peace with Rome prevailed, especially during the reign of Caracalla when R. Judah enjoyed prominence.

The archeology of Sepphoris clearly demonstrates that Judaism in this urban metropolis flourished as never before, at a time when Roman paganism was functioning at a high level and nascent Christianity was taking root. That such literary, spiritual, and religious creativity occurred in this flourishing oriental city should come as no surprise. The forces of Hellenization had long since been set loose on Palestinian soil and for centuries had served Jewish particularity. But at Sepphoris, it seems, the urban setting was an especially effective and vibrant catalyst for constructive symbiosis; for most of the Roman period (second–fourth centuries) bitter memories of the two wars with Rome did not stand in the way of accommodation and acculturation. Sepphoris' unique position at the time of the First Revolt, and the special status accorded it as a consequence of its pro-Roman stance, could very well have paved the way for a golden age in the Galilee that was without parallel.

[48] A similar problem in interpretation occurred at ancient Meiron. See E. M. Meyers, J. F. Strange, and C. L. Meyers, *Excavations at Ancient Meiron* (Cambridge, 1981), 158–161.

Overview of the Dionysos mosaic from the *triclinium* in the villa at Sepphoris. Note the central panel, the symposium of Heracles and Dionysos, the later Nilotic scene to the right, and the pastoral scene at lower right. The mysterious lady, possibly Aphrodite, appears in border panel to the left.

Closeup of woman in acanthus medallion in southern border. Called the "Mona Lisa" by the media, her timeless beauty has attracted great attention and underscores the high level of artistry and artisanship of the Sepphoris mosaic, dated to the first third of the third century C.E.

The Roman villa looking north, cleared of the mosaic and still not fully excavated. Note the section under the Dionysos mosaic. The peristyle courtyard may be observed in the foreground.

The western domestic area, looking east to the Citadel. Several ritual baths may be observed, but the main feature is the east–west street with a well-preserved drain.

Closeup of Middle Roman house in the western domestic area, which has utilized earlier elements in its development. Note cave to the right, which served as a ritual bath in the Herodian period.

Six Campaigns at Sepphoris: The University of South Florida Excavations, 1983–1989

JAMES F. STRANGE

This article synthesizes the results of the archeological investigations carried out at ancient Sepphoris from 1983 to 1989 by the University of South Florida and under my direction. A total of six seasons of excavation and two seasons of survey have been completed, plus one season of both excavation and survey.[1] I shall concentrate on the results of the excavations on the hill of Sepphoris, but will also comment on what we believe to be the discovery of ancient Shiḥin northwest of Sepphoris and at the foot of its hill.

The University of South Florida excavations laid out the first probes in 1983 in an area designated as Field I.[2] During the 1983 season the main objective was to determine the nature and type of soil deposits on the top of what researchers have loosely called the "tell." Subsequent seasons focused on Waterman's "basilica," excavated by the University of Michi-

---

[1] Short reports on these seasons have appeared in *IEJ*. See J. F. Strange and T. R. W. Longstaff, "Notes and News," *IEJ* 34 (1984), 51–52, 269–270; 35 (1985), 297–299; 37 (1987), 278–280; J. F. Strange, D. E. Groh, and T. R. W. Longstaff, "Notes and News," *IEJ* 39 (1989), 104–106.

[2] The excavations took place from June 23 to July 23, 1983. The team worked under the sponsorship of the University of South Florida in cooperation with its Program in Jewish Studies, the Institute for Biblical Archaeology of Southwestern University at Memphis, and the Center for Living Bible History in Tampa, Florida. The expedition staff included as Director, James F. Strange of the University of South Florida; Associate Director, Thomas R. W. Longstaff of Colby College; and Administrative Director, Richard Batey of Southwestern University at Memphis. Dennis E. Groh joined the staff of the expedition, also as Associate Director, in 1987.

gan in 1931,[3] then on two trenches east of St. Anne's Orphanage in our Field IV, and most recently on the massive architecture which has come to light east of the top of the hill, in our Field V.

Four teams excavated five 5 x 5 m. trenches ("squares") down to bedrock in 1983. Two trenches were set against the northern and north-western sides of the building used as a school until 1948, usually called the "citadel" or "fort," but for which we prefer the name "fortress." The third was excavated west of the northwestern trench. In these trenches we discovered that Waterman's laconic remark about the depth of fill was correct.[4] There seemed to be more or less one deep Late Roman to Byzantine layer everywhere we dug on top of the tell. As a result of our continuing excavations, however, we could differentiate several accumulations in this thick layer and can now hazard an interpretation as to their uses.

The results of the 1983 probes were as surprising as they were gratifying. The foundations of the fortress were not commensurate with the size and workmanship of its reused stones. The stones in the walls near the northwestern corner, particularly, resemble Herodian masonry. Yet the foundations were made of closely packed stones no larger than 30 cm. and were built directly upon Early Roman quarrying and building operations in and upon bedrock. In and among the stones of the foundations of the fortress the latest pottery and coins date from the mid-fourth century. Therefore, the character of the founding was not as one might expect for large architecture, but resembled a more or less ad hoc arrangement, perhaps not intended to last as long as it obviously did. Also, the conclusion seemed inescapable that the "Crusader fortress" of Sepphoris was originally a Late Roman building measuring about 50 x 50 Roman feet. Whatever purpose it may have served in later periods, this Late Roman building underwent renovation and renewal.

At the level of the top of the founding of the fortress, and at the bottom of its first course of stones, we uncovered a thick, cement-like layer that was eventually to be found everywhere we excavated in Field I, up to and including the 1989 excavations. This layer was certainly contemporary with the founding of the building and seems to have been the surface upon which the workmen stood as they erected the structure and as other workmen dismantled already existing structures in the vicinity.

3 L. Waterman et al., *Preliminary Report of the University of Michigan Excavations at Sepphoris, Palestine, in 1931* (Ann Arbor, 1937), 4–6, 31–34.

4 Ibid., 2: "On an average there are about 2 meters of dirt over the natural surface of the ground . . . . "

West of the fortress, in our third 5 x 5 m. trench, we dug down to the thick, cement-like layer mentioned above. Upon it were accumulations dated to the mid-fourth century and later. Beneath it were slight remains of a house, which were almost wholly cuttings in bedrock, including remnants of a plastered pool, a square opening sealed with plaster, and one cistern mouth. Around the mouth of the cistern stood only a few stones of the house. Upon bedrock the latest remains were mid-fourth century, although pockets of first-century pottery were to be found in the cuttings in bedrock. Therefore, the picture that emerged here was one of dismantling a house almost to bedrock and then laying over the remaining 40 cm. of debris with a thick, cement-like layer which was also found beside the fortress. The dismantling of the house and the building of the cement layer were contemporary, or mid-fourth century. We were puzzled by this sequence of events, but now the picture is clearer.

For example, the digging of a 5 x 5 m. trench just fifteen m. north of the latter square revealed another house dismantled to bedrock in the middle of the fourth century C.E. At the level of bedrock there were only scant remains of foundations and a well-cut entrance to a cistern completely filled with debris. The latest layers all date to the middle of the fourth century C.E., when almost all the stones in the walls of the house were removed.

The cistern in our third 5 x 5 m. square contained a heap of fourth-century debris on its floor when it was last opened and used for refuse. The refuse had collected on an accumulation that was laid in dry conditions, at a time when the cistern was no longer used for water storage. This cistern opened into Chamber 2, a low chamber with several large niches cut into its walls that seemed to have been used for storage. Chamber 2 cut into a second, pre-existing cistern. From this third chamber a tunnel ran to a third pre-existing cistern, i.e., it already existed when both Chamber 2 and the tunnel were cut. In the last chamber an unfinished tunnel led two m. to the south.

The history of these chambers seems to have been as follows: (1) the earliest accumulations on the floors of the cisterns (dipping jars and cooking pots that were lowered on strings to dip water) were from the Early Roman period; (2) in the Middle Roman period the three cisterns were converted to dry storage (which included laying in a plastered floor one m. up in Chamber 3, the cutting of Chamber 2, and the cutting of a tunnel from Chamber 3 to Chamber 4); (3) some time in the Late Roman period these chambers went out of active domestic use and contained refuse; (4) all four chambers and the tunnel were abandoned and sealed off in the Late Roman period. Pottery from the mid-fourth century inside the chambers seems to be associated with casual visitors, perhaps those who were dismantling the house and building the cement-like surface where the house had been.

These chambers were reached by a staircase in the northeastern side of Chamber 2 next to Chamber 1, the first cistern. Unfortunately, the dismantling of the house in Square I/3 in the fourth century C.E. did not allow us to deduce how this entrance fit into the existing architecture. But this was our first clue that there was an underground Sepphoris as well as the city above surface.

Also in 1983 we set trenches inside the walls of the theater discovered by Waterman in 1931. Our intent was to check his stratigraphy and see if we could recover materials from sealed loci in order to date the founding of the theater; although Waterman had dated the theater to the time of Herod Antipas, Albright had looked at the stones and commented that they looked to him to be of second century provenance.[5]

Our first trench was in badly disturbed debris, so we left that area to try another. Our second trench was laid just east of the trench opened by Waterman that exposed the central vomitorium of the structure. We were able to determine with certainty that the founding of the main internal wall took place in the first half of the Early Roman period, however there is nothing in our evidence that would require a date later than Herod Antipas.

The picture of founding and usage suggested by our initial trench in the theater was as follows: (1) founding of the theater in the Early Roman period; (2) renovations of some kind that left significant amounts of Middle Roman debris in the cavea. However, since these layers were not sealed from the top, it is as yet impossible to determine precisely the significance of these layers; (3) abandonment and filling in of the theater in the mid-fourth century. The semi-circular corridor around the back and beneath the third rank of seats remained in use, however, perhaps for storage; (4) final use and abandonment of the corridor in the early fifth century. Many small coins of the early fifth century C.E. found in the accumulation on the floor of the corridor marked the last use of the theater.

Further trenches west of the stage and the presumed *scaena* provided evidence for the first extensive building of the theater in the Early Roman

---

5 W. F. Albright, "Review of Waterman's Preliminary Report on the 1931 Excavations," *Classical Weekly* 21 (1938), 148.

period. We opened a total of seven squares against the northwestern side of the stage and into the remains associated with the theater. Here we disclosed a series of heavy walls constructed with finely cut stones. We also found drains that contained pottery of the first and second centuries C.E. The debris against these constructions contained an overwhelming amount of first-century Roman pottery, but also contained one or more second-century sherds. However, in every concentration of finds the latest pottery, on bedrock, was Early Roman. The latest layers were always in mid-fourth century erosion, the time when the theater went out of use as a theater.

The finds at the northwestern side of the theater, then, tend to support our finds of 1983: (1) the construction of the theater was certainly in the Early Roman period; (2) it continued in use and was probably renovated extensively in the Middle Roman period, or between 70 and 180 C.E. There is some evidence for a major overhaul in the Late Roman period, perhaps in the late third or early fourth century; (3) the theater was abandoned and filled in about the middle of the fourth century C.E. Large amounts of debris from this period washed down the hill into the area just north and west of the stage, which suggests that the buildings on top of the hill also went out of use and no longer held back erosion. It is to this period that we would assign the building of the large wall across the cavea of the theater, which evidently was intended to hold up the fill within the theater; (4) the latest remains are scattered pottery sherds and coins of the fifth century. No wares or other traces of material culture of later periods were to be found here. They could have been eroded away, but it is unlikely that not one sherd or coin would remain if structures of the Byzantine period had been erected here.

In 1984 we surveyed most of the area around Sepphoris in some detail, using a Topcon EDM infra-red survey instrument to gain as much accuracy as possible. We were able to locate about 56 tombs nearly two kms. east of the fortress and one-half km. from the huge underground water reservoir mapped by the Survey of Western Palestine.[6] We were able to add to the map of the area around Sepphoris about 156 traces of human activity, including tombs, storage chambers, olive presses, foundations, and other cuttings in bedrock. We surveyed the route of the aqueduct with an error of less than one part in 10,000, thanks to modern technology. We also located a concentration of these bedrock cuttings,

---

6 C. R. Conder and H. H. Kitchener, *The Survey of Western Palestine*, I: *Galilee* (London, 1881), 331.

chambers, and foundations one km. southwest of Sepphoris, which is mostly likely a small, dependent village of unknown name.

One of L. Waterman's main finds in 1931, and the only architectural feature that he published besides the theater in his preliminary report, was a structure he called "the basilica" or "an old Christian basilica," or even "an early Christian church."[7] S. Yeivin remarked that someone suggested it might be a villa, but he himself did not find the suggestion convincing.[8] M. Avi-Yonah, however, followed this anonymous suggestion.[9] The University of South Florida team set in trenches following the Hebrew University grid, so that the untouched debris at the southern side of the building could be excavated and the details of the architecture could be seen again and redrawn.[10] In this way we hoped to test Waterman's hypothesis that it was a church and the counter-hypothesis that it was a villa.

The results of our excavations were quite clear. All the material remains inside the building were consistent with a private residence or villa: cooking wares, eye make-up paraphernalia, glass unguentaria, jewelry, bone hairpins, bronze clothing pins, needles, loom weights, stoppers, etc. In addition, we recovered a portion of the kitchen, with its oven and associated ash, in the southeastern corner of our easternmost trench.[11]

Beneath almost every room of the villa we uncovered a cistern mouth. In some cases the mouths of the cisterns came to light beneath the lines of walls. For example, the wall between Waterman's Rooms 38 and 39 covered a cistern about two m. deep. Since the latest material in that cistern was Late Roman, the wall had to be contemporary with or postdate that time. (In a second, larger cistern, cut into by the first cistern, we

---

[7] Waterman et al., *Preliminary Report*, 4–5, 32f., and esp. p. vii.

[8] S. Yeivin, "Historical and Archaeological Notes," in: Waterman et al., *Preliminary Report*, 17–34, esp. 32.

[9] M. Avi-Yonah, "Sepphoris," in: *Encyclopedia of Archaeological Excavations in the Holy Land*, eds. M. Avi-Yonah and E. Stern (4 vols.; Jerusalem, 1975–77), IV, 1051–1055.

[10] The only plan of the structure published by Waterman et al., *Preliminary Report*, p. 5, Fig. 2, shows roughly 19 m. of building north-to-south and 15 m. of building east-to-west in a figure 11.7 x 8.4 cm.(!)

[11] Certain finds in the 1931 excavations were also characteristic of a domestic rather than public life. From one cellar, no. 15 found in Room 28 of the "church," came "a large number of household objects...including a group of bone hairpins, one with a bronze-sheet head, a bone kohl stick, two bone ointment spoons, and a bone needle"; Waterman et al., *Preliminary Report*, 33.

found a bronze bowl, a bronze bull, and a tiny bronze incense altar which are most easily interpreted as remains of Serapis worship.) On the other hand, Room 39, which was fully excavated by Waterman, contained a large cistern of its own that was in use when Room 39 was in use, although it does not appear in Waterman's plan.

A second type of chamber found in the villa was cut into bedrock with a stepped entrance down from a paved courtyard or other floor. We found four of these beneath the southwestern rooms of the villa. All these chambers were finely plastered on all surfaces, including the ceiling, and contained pottery of the first and second centuries C.E. It seems clear that these went out of use during or after the second century. We interpret them as *miqva'ot* by analogy with other such chambers excavated at Khirbet Shema' and Meiron;[12] we tentatively date their first cutting and use to the first century.

One of these chambers lay directly in the center of Waterman's Room 43, which was the first room south of the room with the white mosaic (Room 40). At this reading it is not possible to say precisely how this chamber related to Room 43, as the entrance to the putative *miqveh* lay precisely in our southern baulk, yet it seems reasonable to suggest that the *miqveh* was intended to relate to the room.

Four 5 x 5 m. squares in the southwestern part of this villa helped round out the plan and history of the building. West of Waterman's Trench SII, in which the villa appeared, we unearthed a staircase cut into bedrock that led into a total of ten interconnecting underground chambers. For example, as one descended the staircase, which was roofed with a Roman vault, a turn to the left led into a vaulted, plastered chamber lined with benches. Since its floor was lower than the floors of the other chambers, and since a water line could be seen on the wall plaster, it was simple to deduce that this was a pool made by the people who lived in the villa. It is still difficult to interpret precisely what it is, for it could be part of an ordinary bathing complex, and its size (about 3 x 3 m.), with ceilings that allowed one to stand, suggests that several people could use it at once. The back (northern) wall of this chamber was sealed off in antiquity with a secondary wall. A look through a small hole in that wall

---

12   E. M. Meyers, A. T. Kraabel, and J. F. Strange, *Ancient Synagogue Excavations at Khirbet Shema', Israel, 1970–72* (*AASOR* 42; Durham, NC, 1976); E. M. Meyers, J. F. Strange, and C. L. Meyers, *Excavations at Ancient Meiron, Upper Galilee, Israel, 1971–72, 1974–75, 1977* (Cambridge, MA, 1981), 41–44. It is interesting to observe that S. Yeivin, in Waterman et al., *Preliminary Report*, 32, describes these chambers with plaster and steps leading down into them.

revealed yet another long chamber behind the chamber in question, but it is as yet inaccessible to us.

If one turned right at the foot of the stairs, he or she would enter into a vaulted chamber which is virtually a twin of the one described above, except that it had no benches. It also had a hole in its ceiling which was sealed in antiquity as well as niches in two of its walls, namely, on the east and south. The western wall had two very large unfinished niches almost filled with stones. A tunnel led to the east from the southeastern corner to a wall of eroded debris about ten m. away underground. A hole in the floor at the southwestern corner led *down* to a set of three more chambers, the last one of which was not intended to link with the others: workmen had accidently cut into an unfinished chamber in antiquity.

This maze of basements, work areas, storage spaces, pool, and several sumps for storing liquids suggests a villa with a very energetic family or families in residence. The owners had provided themselves with a series of cool and sheltered underground spaces for work and storage. Interior spaces of the villa were often paved with white mosaic with at least one panel of geometric decoration.

The history and phasing of this structure is not yet completely clear, but several observations are in order: (1) the building was already standing in the late first century C.E., though it is not yet possible to say precisely when it was founded. At the moment, the most reasonable, testable hypothesis is that it was founded with the advent of Herod Antipas and his rebuilding of the ruined city after the destruction by Varus. Where the founding of the mosaic floor could be ascertained, it was late first or early second century; (2) the building went through two renovations, in which the walls no longer lined up with the cuttings in bedrock that correlate with the founding and the Middle Roman laying of the mosaic floors; internal walls were shifted to fit the needs of the family that lived there. This much is also plain from Waterman's plan; (3) the building underwent one major renovation in the early fourth century, which, for example, put out of use the staircase that led down to the ten underground chambers. An arch still stood above the staircase, but the family eventually blocked entry entirely; (4) about the middle of the fourth century the building went out of use as a villa. The walls were dismantled almost down to founding by someone seeking building materials. Squatters or other temporary occupants reduced the size of one room in the southwestern side of the building by adding two poorly formed walls of stone in an existing space. These Late Roman people built an oven in the dirt that had accumulated in the stairway down to the underground chambers; (5) this area was provided with a series of white lime and clay floors beginning about one m. above the floor of the villa and resting upon soil debris dating after the middle of the fourth century. There are no structures built above the villa, so the floors, which resemble outdoor courtyard surfaces, must have met a temporary need. In an ash layer associated with the thick, white, limy surface the excavating teams found Late Roman and Early Byzantine pottery with coins of the Constantines and one coin of Julian.

Down the slope on the northern side, the team of the University of South Florida tested the stratification just east of St. Anne's in 1987. Here two squares uncovered Late Roman structures near the surface which were lightly disturbed by modern activities. Yet, even here it was possible to see a consistent picture emerging: (1) the lowest levels reached were partially concealed by later structures which we did not dismantle, however it is possible to say that they represent Early Roman and Middle Roman occupation, presumably houses; (2) in the Late Roman period, a corner of one substantial building with 75 cm.-thick walls appeared here in the southernmost square. Hardly three m. away there appeared a large two m.-thick wall built of two stone faces and filled with stone debris and soil. This wall extended east–west across the entire five m. width of the trench. It is not possible to say at this juncture just what this thick wall was used for, but it could be a terrace wall, some part of a wall for the upper city, or some other precinct wall.[13] It was not designed for defense, as it was no match for any battering ram of the period. Just beside this thick wall the team came upon a piece of cloth in a fourth century C.E. context. This is a rare find in a wet environment such as the Galilee during the winter rains.

The most enigmatic large architectural find—the building found in our Field I just west of the fortress—was gradually uncovered in three seasons: 1987, 1988, and 1989. Our efforts yielded a building with exterior walls more than one m. thick on the east and south. Small rooms about four m. square divide up the interior space. Each room is in actuality a well-plastered pool, though it is difficult to deduce as yet the original depth of any given pool. The bottoms of these pools are not at the

---

13 Waterman excavated across a thick wall of masonry, if the plan can be properly interpreted. This plan, which can be seen in the archives of the Department of Antiquities of Israel and in T. Tsuk, *Sepphoris and Its Site* (Tel-Aviv, 1987), 49 (Hebrew), shows a wall nearly three m. thick standing about 17 m. north of the back wall of the villa.

same elevation within the building and may have originally emptied from one into another.

One tentative interpretation, developed from examination of the architecture that remains, the hydraulic plaster in each pool, and the finds themselves, is that this is a small public bath or a large private bath. As yet there is no sign of a hypocaust, caldarium or apodeuterion, but in general we have eight rectangular pools oriented with the plan of the city. Therefore, our "neutral" designation at the moment is the "pooled building."[14]

The interior of the building on its eastern side had been beautifully appointed with painted plaster, both painted and unpainted plaster mouldings, and bas-reliefs in plaster. The wall plaster has at least two coats: the inner coat was painted with floral motifs and the exterior coat in solid colors. Remains of a badly destroyed mosaic floor appeared out of place in a burnt layer ten cm. above the pool floor in the southeastern corner of the building. Fragments of small-diameter columns, corner columns, and Corinthian capitals bespeak the presence of a second story, perhaps around a colonnade with an unroofed courtyard within.

So far only seven trenches have been opened into the building, so our interpretations are suggestive and tentative. We will test them in our next campaign of excavation. In each case the area of the "pooled building" so far exposed is about 15 x 15 m., or about 225 sq. m. A street is exposed on the east, while on the south there is a very tiny piece of street or plateia to be seen in the side of the trench.

The history and phasing of this building can be reconstructed from its finds: (1) the building was founded early in the Early Roman period; (2) it was in use during the second and third centuries C.E. without modification. During this period, that of Judah the Prince, fragments of oil lamps of the second and third centuries C.E. fell into one of the pools and were not cleaned out; (3) the building was modified somewhat on its eastern side during the Late Roman period, when two cross walls were erected directly upon the eastern pool floor so as to divide the space into smaller units; (4) in the middle of the fourth century C.E. the building went out of use. Signs of burning abound, but the dismantling procedure concealed whatever state the building and its pools were in when they ceased to be used. (But in a trench scarcely five m. north of the northeastern corner of the "pooled building" we found a roof beam burned to

---

[14] It must be mentioned that the finds are also consistent with a nymphaeum or a water filtering installation from which water was fed to other points of the upper city.

charcoal lying on the floor of a house.)[15] Those who put the building out of use proceeded to dismantle the entire structure for building stones. None of the large, presumably cut stones of the exterior walls remains. Likely, they are to be found in the walls of the fortress, just to the east, as that structure was built entirely of previously used stones. Excavation teams found great quantities of destroyed wall plaster, mosaics, bas-reliefs, and one up-ended tub in the debris of the mid-fourth century. Some of the material had been badly burned. It is worth mentioning here that a cistern hardly ten m. south of this building, which had been located by soil interface radar, was partially excavated in 1985.[16] It contained an abundance of melted glass, melted and deformed bronze artifacts, and burnt and scorched stones in and with mid-fourth century coins and pottery. Perhaps this is more of the debris from the "pooled building," though at the moment it is impossible to say; (5) some time after 350 C.E., but probably before 362 C.E. (because of a coin of Julian in a slightly higher layer), workmen constructed a working surface of clay and lime. Our excavations have unearthed this layer at more or less the same height, but primarily on the eastern side of the building. This floor or working surface in general is about two m. above the bottom of the pools on the northeastern side of the building and is also to be found in the trenches at foundation level of the fortress and above the dismantled house between the "pooled building" and the fortress.

When we moved to excavate on the eastern side of the hill of the fortress in 1987, we did not know the extent of the architecture and remains there. Excavations and foot reconnaissance, however, have revealed extensive major architectural remains.

Alongside a cow pen constructed by the present-day moshav, we found about 70 m. of an east–west Roman street paved with successive layers of lime paving. On the southern side of the street and at its eastern extremity we have so far unearthed three ruined vaults with a diameter of 4.2 m. and an internal length of 4.2 m., and a promise of more to come. These vaults went out of use at about 700 C.E., as attested by the post-Reform Umayyad coins in their fill.

[15] This burning was noticed by Yeivin, who called his evidence a "conflagration" and who was inclined to associate it with the Gallus Revolt; Waterman et al., *Preliminary Report*, 31.

[16] R. A. Batey, "Subsurface Interface Radar at Sepphoris, 1985," *Journal of Field Archaeology* 14 (1987), 1–8; J. F. Strange, "Soil Interface Radar," a sidebar in *BA* 49 (1986), 14.

When were they founded? At this moment in time we can only say that there is slim evidence (see below) that they were originally Early Roman in date, but we cannot yet be certain. In any case, we have clear evidence of continuous use and reuse from the Late Roman to the Early Arab periods. The floors inside the vaults were paved with rather poor cobbling late in their history, but we have not yet penetrated those floors to gain the full stratigraphic sequence.

Each vaulted room led into the street through a wide door. The street walls were fully 1.3 m. thick, which suggests that they supported two stories above them. Through the centuries, as the streets were repaved many times, it eventually became necessary for steps to be built so that those inside the vaults could ascend to street level. Around one doorway the users built a curbing in the street around the steps to keep out the troubling winter rains.

At the western extremity of the street the paving yielded only Early Roman wares, however bulldozing for a modern road has cut away later debris layers. A wall on the southern side of the street was founded in the Early Roman period, which suggests that the vaults were also founded then. These rooms had a clear fourth century use.

In our easternmost trench in the street, we have one piece of evidence that those who founded the back wall of the vaulted room on the southern side cut into a pre-existing pool of the Late Hellenistic period. That a pool stood there suggests that we might expect to find the point of entry of the aqueduct into the city in the vicinity of the vaults.

In a flat expanse on the eastern side of the hill, and south of the Roman street discussed above, there stood before 1948 a large threshing floor of the village of Saffuriyeh. In the summer of 1989 we discovered at ground level the top of a heart-shaped column base (for a double column) and a scrap of white mosaic scarcely ten meters away. Excavation in this area yielded dramatic architectural remains very close to the surface.

This building proved to have at least two rows of columns around a rectangular courtyard paved with white mosaics. Between two rows of columns there once stood a fine mosaic of white tesserae. In the mosaic of the aisle between the two rows of columns, two lines about five m. wide and 1.2 m. apart led traffic around the rectangular central courtyard. In the aisle outside the second row of columns we uncovered a carpet of a guilloche around a frame of acanthus leaves and flowers. This design enclosed several black borders. In the center of the rectangular carpet there were probably four registers, but only two have survived. These two registers frame partridges modeled in at least four shades of red and three of yellow, and are fine examples of the mosaicist's artwork. An ancient patch in white tesserae obliterated half of the central rectangle, which we hypothesize originally contained a total of four birds arranged symmetrically along the long axis of the carpet. The two birds now remaining are oriented to the southeast with what we take at present to be the long axis of the building.

Probes beneath a modern dirt road just northwest of the excavated area disclosed more of the mosaic, including the turning of the black bands to the northeast. At the same distance from the outside row of columns, *in situ* but now robbed out, we found a pattern of triangles that mark the edge of a second, as yet unexcavated, carpet.

What is the occupational sequence of this building? (1) in the Early Roman Period some kind of structure had been founded directly beneath the mosaic building. This was only found in one spot so far; (2) workmen laid in the mosaic floor at about 300 C.E. This was the earliest use of the building that we can deduce after one season's work. There is no subsequent floor, but there may be an earlier floor or floors; (3) the building went out of use about mid-fourth century. Most of the building stone in the walls was robbed out then and in the fifth century. Those who carried out the dismantling of walls built fires at irregular intervals on the mosaic floor and trenched along the foundations of walls and stylobates, indicating that they had no special reverence for the structure any more than they did for the "pooled building" on top of the hill; (4) subsequent occupation is not clear, for the remains of the building actually emerge from the ground or are only centimeters beneath modern disturbances. For example, immediately to the north of this building are the remains of an Arab house destroyed after the War of Independence.

Finally, let me add that we believe that we have found the remains of ancient Shihin, a village mentioned often in the same breath with Sepphoris in rabbinic literature. Our surveys on foot and with infra-red optics in 1988 led us to identify an unnamed ruin about 1.5 km. northwest of Sepphoris (map ref. 1760/2415) with ancient Shihin. The main evidence for the identification stems from the many pottery "wasters" found there. That Shihin was a major pottery manufacturing center is well known from the ancient sources.[17] Furthermore, neutron activation

17 The relevant texts are compiled in S. S. Miller, *Studies in the History and Traditions of Sepphoris* (Leiden, 1984), 31. See also Z. Safrai, *The Galilee in the Time of the Mishnah*

analysis of the potsherds and wasters from this village site shows a positive correlation when compared to one of D. Adan-Bayewitz's previously
unidentified groups, the provenance of which he could not prove.[18] In
other words, the sources of most of the common wares of Sepphoris have
now been identified as originating first at Kefar Ḥananya and also at
Shiḥin.

Conclusions

So far our archeological sampling on the hill of Sepphoris has given
us a similar picture wherever we dig. The chronological sequence may
not be borne out everywhere a trench is dug, but it is striking that the in-
ception and close of major occupation so closely parallels what we first
found in 1983.

1) The pre-Antipas city has only turned up in our trenches in scattered
potsherds of the Early Bronze II, Late Bronze II, Iron II, Persian, and
Hellenistic I and II periods. We have not yet found floors or walls to go
with these periods, except in a few limited instances.[19]

2) The city flourished from the first to fourth centuries C.E., but there is a
certain decline traceable in pottery distributions. In other words, if this
one indicator will hold when compared to all other kinds of material evidence, then the Early Roman period was the peak of the city's occupation.

3) There was a major disruption in the city's fortune in the middle of the
fourth century C.E. Since this includes dismantling structures on the site,
construction of the fortress, filling in the theater, and retaining the fill
with a large wall built from architectural fragments, we prefer the inter-

---

and Talmud (Maʿalot, 1981), 44–45, 69–71 (Hebrew); S. Klein, *Beiträge zur Geschichte
und Geographie Galiläas* (Leipzig, 1909), 63–70. The foot survey of ancient Shiḥin was
carried out in 1988 under the supervision of Dr. Thomas R. W. Longstaff. The team
identified more than fifty ancient cuttings, foundations, cisterns and other cavities,
etc.

[18] D. Adan-Bayewitz et al., "On the Identification of Ancient Shikhin: The Ar-
chaeometric Evidence," an unpublished research paper to appear with the formal report of the survey of Shiḥin under the auspices of the University of South Florida Excavations at Sepphoris; D. Adan-Bayewitz, "Manufacture and Trade in the Galilee of
Roman-Byzantine Palestine: A Case Study" (doctoral dissertation, Hebrew University; Jerusalem, 1985).

[19] It should be noted, however, that the Joint Expedition to Sepphoris, directed by
Eric Meyers, Carol Meyers, and Ehud Netzer, has indeed found traces of the earlier
city. Cf. E. M. Meyers, E. Netzer, and C. L. Meyers, "Sepphoris—'Ornament of All
Galilee'," *BA* 49 (1986), 4–19.

pretation that this was due to the Gallus Revolt. Although it is possible that the earthquake of 363 caused extensive damage, it is not evident in our trenches, at least so far.[20] Only further detailed excavation and careful interpretation of finds could tell that story definitively.

One of the major implications from our work of six seasons is that we propose to move the end of the Late Roman period to 363 C.E. This seems to be true especially for Sepphoris, but reflection on the situation in all of Palestine suggests that this would be true anywhere this earthquake provoked at least a temporary *terminus ad quem* of the material culture.[21]

4) The bronze bowl, bull, and incense altar indicate that pagan forms of worship were known and practiced at Sepphoris, though to what extent we cannot yet say.[22] Pagan worship as such should be no surprise, for coins at Sepphoris of Antoninus Pius and Julia Domna depict the deities of Zeus, Hera, Athena, and a city goddess, and the Joint Expedition has published pagan statuettes.[23] The surprise is what such finds might imply about the religious ambience of an otherwise Jewish city that supported the literary and other activities of Judah the Prince.

5) The disturbances at mid-fourth century Sepphoris were not strong enough to destroy the city. Our archeological evidence shows that Sepphoris was a vigorous city well into the Byzantine II period. The latest sustained occupation is to be found in the vaulted chambers on the southern side of the Roman street on the eastern side of the hill. There

[20] On the Gallus Revolt in general, see Z. Frankel, "Der Aufstand in Palästina zur Zeit des Gallus," *MGWJ* 16 (1867), 143–151; idem, *Introduction to the Yerushalmi* (Breslau, 1870), 2–4 (Hebrew); J. Juster, *Les juifs dans l'empire romain: leur condition juridique, économique et sociale* (2 vols.; Paris, 1914), I, 197 and n. 1; B. G. Nathanson, "The 4th Century Jewish 'Revolt' during the Reign of Gallus" (doctoral dissertation, Duke University; Ann Arbor, 1981); idem, "Jews, Christians, and the Gallus Revolt in 4th Century Palestine," *BA* 49 (1986), 26–36. Waterman et al., *Preliminary Report*, 2, suggested that the Crusaders built a citadel about 180 x 90 m. with the fortress in the center. My colleagues and I concur with the idea that this is a citadel, but we suggest that it was built by the soldiers of Gallus who destroyed the buildings in the vicinity.

[21] D. E. Groh, "Jews and Christians in Late Roman Palestine: Towards a New Chronology," *BA* 51 (1988), 80–96.

[22] T. R. W. Longstaff, "Evidence for Pagan Worship at Sepphoris," a paper prepared for the Annual Meeting of the American Schools of Oriental Research, 1988.

[23] Y. Meshorer, *City-Coins of Eretz-Israel and of the Decapolis in the Roman Period* (Jerusalem, 1985), 36–37, coin nos. 91–93; complete coin descriptions, 113; Meyers, Netzer, and Meyers, "Sepphoris—'Ornament of All Galilee'," 4–19.

the latest coins are of the Umayyad period, perhaps just after the time of the reform of 697 C.E.[24]

6) Our surveys of 1982, 1984, and 1988 have indicated to us that around Sepphoris, within 1.5 km. of the fortress, lay at least two dependent villages, one of them is surely Shihin (mentioned in the Jerusalem Talmud and elsewhere), the other is not yet known. There may well be other such localities where ten or so families, or more, pursued a single industry, such as pottery or vintage. This offers us a more nuanced picture of Sepphoris as a center surrounded by a network of small dependent villages and within a larger network of trading villages and towns, a network which may well have made it possible for Sepphoris to develop into the great Jewish intellectual center that it was for so long before suffering eclipse by Tiberias.

---

[24] A. Berman, *Islamic Coins* (Jerusalem, 1976), 9. See p. 26, coin no. 48 for a fals minted at Sepphoris.

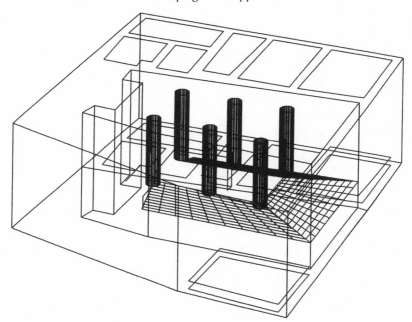

The University of South Florida Excavations at Sepphoris, 1989: reconstruction of the Field I "villa" seen from the south, a "wireframe" perspective view to the north with internal plan.

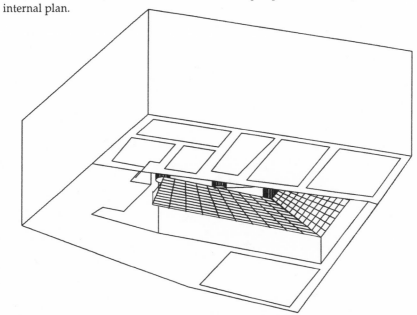

The University of South Florida Excavations at Sepphoris, 1989: reconstruction of the Field I "villa" seen from the south, a perspective view.

Social Aspects of Burial in Beth She'arim: Archeological Finds and Talmudic Sources

ZEEV WEISS

Talmudic lists of public institutions and organizations in a Jewish town regularly omit the cemetery.[1] It is not imaginable that any Jewish settlement, regardless of its size, did not have one. The numerous burial caves discovered in the Galilee are usually attributed to the nearby settlements; moreover, we know of settlements where the cemetery has not yet been found even though one must have existed there.[2]

The absence of the cemetery in these lists and evidence for the existence of cemeteries in many settlements raise the question as to whether the Jewish cemetery was, in fact, a public institution. If so, its character, organization, funding, and functionaries must be defined. On the other hand, if funeral functions were carried out solely by the immediate family of the deceased, may we assume that no organization aided the family in the funerary arrangements? Furthermore, did familial burials customary in Jerusalem on the eve of the destruction of the Second Temple continue during the mishnaic and talmudic periods?

The large Jewish cemetery at Beth She'arim is rich in architectural, epigraphical and artistic finds. We shall attempt to answer the above questions by integrating the Beth She'arim finds with what we know about Jewish cemeteries generally from the talmudic sources.

---

[1] M Nedarim 5:5; T Bava Metzi'a 11:23, Lieberman, pp. 125–126; J Qiddushin 4, 12, 66d; B Sanhedrin 17b.

[2] Z. Yeivin, "Survey of Settlements in Galilee and the Golan from the Period of the Mishnah in the Light of the Sources" (doctoral dissertation, Hebrew University; Jerusalem, 1971), 32–33, 56, 72 (Hebrew).

Familial burial was predominant in the mishnaic and talmudic periods.[3] Burial caves were mostly family-owned, and there was a stringent prohibition of transferring or selling a tomb or even one of the structures adjacent to it.[4] One who was not a family member but who was buried in a family tomb could not purchase his burial plot without the permission of the tomb's owners.[5] People of means hewed burial caves on their own land;[6] others purchased land on which they could hew a tomb[7] or even purchase a prepared one.[8] One could purchase a tomb, or part of one, only if the burial tomb was never used.[9] Inscriptions indicating the names of the owners of specific burial halls can be found on entrance lintels in a number of halls at Beth She'arim (see Ill. 1).[10] Aidesios, who purchased a room in Hall B in Catacomb 12, had inscribed on the right doorpost, "There are in the burial chamber six tombs which belong to Aidesios" (see Ill. 2).[11] From the many grave inscriptions found at Beth She'arim, it is clear that the purchase of a single burial plot in a burial chamber was possible.[12] The purchase of an entire burial hall, a burial room or several burial plots close to one another reflects the desire of family members to be buried close to one another. This type of burial is known to us as familial burial.

[3] Tractate Semahot 14:5–6, Higger, pp. 206–207; B Ketubot 84a. S. Safrai, "Home and Family," in: *The Jewish People in the First Century*, eds. S. Safrai and M. Stern (2 vols.; Assen, 1974–76), II, 779–780. This custom was prevalent in the Greco-Roman world; see E. Rohde, *Psyche*, trans. W. B. Hillis (New York, 1925), 523; D. C. Kurtz and J. Boardman, *Greek Burial Custom* (London, 1971), 143; J. M. C. Toynbee, *Death and Burial in the Roman World* (London, 1971), 74.

[4] Sifre Deuteronomy 188, Finkelstein, p. 227; Tractate Semahot 14:2, 11, Higger, pp. 204 and 207–208, respectively; B Bava Batra 100b.

[5] Tractate Semahot 14:3, Higger, pp. 204–205.

[6] T Oholot 16:11–12, Zuckermandel, p. 614; J Mo'ed Qatan 1, 2, 80b.

[7] M Bava Batra 6:8.

[8] Tractate Semahot 14:3, Higger, pp. 204–205.

[9] Ibid.

[10] M. Schwabe and B. Lifshitz, *Beth She'arim*, II: *The Greek Inscriptions* (Jerusalem, 1974), inscr. nos. 13, 16, 17, 18, 19, 150, 168, 220.

[11] Ibid., inscr. no. 142. Also see nos. 141 and 171. It was also possible to purchase a chamber jointly. See ibid., no. 83; B. Lifshitz, "Greek and Hellenism among the Jews of Roman Palestine," *Eshkolot* 5 (1967), 27 (Hebrew).

[12] N. Avigad, *Beth She'arim*, III: *Report on the Excavations during 1953–1958* (Jerusalem, 1976), 234, 236, 238–239; Schwabe and Lifshitz, *Beth She'arim*, II, inscr. nos. 20, 50, 61, 63, 78, 86, 95. The purchase of a single plot within a burial cave is known from several sites in the Galilee, e.g., Sepphoris; E. L. Sukenik, "Archeological Remains at Sepphoris," *Tarbiz* 3 (1931), 107–108 (Hebrew); A. Druks, "Zippori," *Ḥadashot Arkheologiyot* 84 (1984), 19 (Hebrew).

Ill. 1. An entrance to a burial cave at Beth She'arim, Catacomb 1, Hall G. Inscription on lintel and plaque, in Hebrew and Greek, indicating Yitzḥaq bar Mokim's ownership. *(Institute of Archeology, Hebrew University of Jerusalem)*

Ill. 2. Greek inscription on the right doorpost, indicating Aidesios' ownership of the room. Beth She͑arim, Catacomb 12, Hall B. *(Institute of Archeology, Hebrew University of Jerusalem)*

The midrash commenting on Gen. 49:21 ("Naphtali is a hind let loose") explains, "This teaches that he sped to Egypt like a hind and brought the title deeds of the cave so that he could bury his father,"[13] alluding to the fact that the purchase of a burial plot was made with a title deed. Inscriptions on walls of burial rooms or halls mention the name of the purchaser in order to avoid the burial of a non-family member in a purchased tomb.[14] A number of inscriptions mentioning the purchase of rooms, rather than the burial itself, enable us to assume that the purchase of burial chambers was often made during the lifetime of the head of the family.[15] One inscription from Catacomb 19 at Beth She'arim clearly states: "Justus commanded in his lifetime, on the first of Panemos."[16] Other inscriptions relating to the burial itself rather than to the purchase of the burial plot use burial terminology, e.g., "buried,"[17] "lies"[18] or "rests."[19]

---

13 Genesis Rabbah 97, Theodor-Albeck, p. 1223; see also 98:17, p. 1268, where it says: "brought the book." Regarding a title deed as an interminable document, see Pirqei de-R. Eliezer 39 and also 38. The grave inscription found at Givat ha-Mivtar in Jerusalem clearly states that the cave was bought with a title deed; see V. Tzaferis, "The 'Abba' Burial Cave in Jerusalem," *'Atiqot* 7 (1974), 61–64 (Hebrew); E. S. Rosenthal, "The Givat ha-Mivtar Inscription," *IEJ* 23 (1973), 72–81.

14 B. Mazar, *Beth She'arim, I: Report on the Excavation during 1936–1940* (Jerusalem, 1973), 193.

15 Ibid., 199–200; Schwabe and Lifshitz, *Beth She'arim*, II, inscr. nos. 83, 142, 171–172.

16 Schwabe and Lifshitz, *Beth She'arim*, II, inscr. nos. 190 and also 124. On the purchase of burial places during the lifetime of the purchaser in Jaffa, see S. Klein, *Sefer ha-Yishuv*, I (Jerusalem, 1939), 83, no. 24 (Hebrew). The custom to purchase burial places during the lifetime of the purchaser was also prevalent in the Jewish diaspora of the Roman empire. See M. Schwabe, "A Judeo-Roman Inscription from Bulgaria," BJPES 2 (1934), 18–25 (Hebrew); L. Roth-Gerson, "The Civil and Religious Status of the Jews in Asia Minor from Alexander the Great to Constantine, B.C. 336–A.D. 337" (doctoral dissertation, Hebrew University; Jerusalem, 1972), 134–136. The midrash in Genesis Rabbah 62:3, Theodor-Albeck, p. 675, "R. Samuel b. Naḥman said: Shem and Ever walked before her [Sarah's] bier and saw which cave was vacant for the Patriarch Abraham, and they thereupon buried her in his compartment," may be an example of the purchase of a grave during the lifetime of the purchaser. Quarrying the stone and building the *nefesh* were completed during the lifetime of the person to be buried in the *nefesh*, as understood from J Megillah 3, 1, 73d; B Sanhedrin 48a.

17 Avigad, *Beth She'arim*, III, 234; Schwabe and Lifshitz, *Beth She'arim*, II, inscr. nos. 40, 48, 60.

18 Avigad, *Beth She'arim*, III, 241, 245; Schwabe and Lifshitz, *Beth She'arim*, II, inscr. nos. 66, 153, 155, 159, 182.

19 Avigad, *Beth She'arim*, III, 237, 243; Schwabe and Lifshitz, *Beth She'arim*, II, inscr. nos. 78, 173.

The responsibility of purchasing or hewing a family tomb, as well as bringing the coffin,[20] shrouds,[21] flute players,[22] and mourners[23] to the funeral, fell on the family of the deceased. One may assume that some of the burial inscriptions and decorations were made by family members.[24] The archeological and epigraphic material from Beth She'arim, as well as the talmudic sources, indicate that familial burial was prevalent in the mishnaic and talmudic periods and that there was no public institution run by the community which handled burial and funerary affairs. If that was the case, then who hewed the burial caves, sold them, and dealt with funerary matters?

Talmudic sources make no mention of any organization that dealt with the various functions connected with burial. In Acomonia, in Asia Minor, the funerary needs of the Jewish community were supplied by the "Burial and Benefits Society,"[25] which was responsible for hewing and decorating burial caves. Despite the fact that talmudic sources do not mention a similar organization in Palestine, one may assume that such an organization, like others, existed in the Hellenistic-Roman world. In Rome, the "fossores" were responsible for hewing and selling burial tombs.[26] The excavators of Beth She'arim mention that the building of the cemetery involved the employment of quarrymen, stone pointers, and artisans who decorated the burial halls and sarcophagi.[27]

Although the talmudic sources do not mention an organization which administered cemetery affairs, they do mention several people who worked there. The Mishnah alludes to two functions: "If a man sold someone a place in which to make a tomb [so, too, if a man received from

---

20 M Mo'ed Qatan 1:6; T Shabbat 17:13, Lieberman, pp. 82–83; J Ma'aser Sheni 2, 1, 53c.

21 M Shabbat 23:4; Sifre Deuteronomy 303, Finkelstein, p. 322; J Kil'aim 9, 4, 32a.

22 M Ketubot 4:4.

23 Ibid.; J Berakhot 2, 6, 59.

24 Avigad, *Beth She'arim*, III, p. 254; B. Mazar, "Those Who Buried Their Dead in Beth She'arim," *Eretz Israel*, XVIII (Jerusalem, 1985), 294 (Hebrew).

25 J. Robert, "Epitaphes juives d'Ephèse et de Nicomédie," *Hellenica* 11–12 (1960), 409–412; A. T. Kraabel, "Judaism in Western Asia Minor under the Roman Empire with a Preliminary Study of the Jewish Community at Sardis, Lydia" (doctoral dissertation, Harvard University; Boston, 1968), 109–114.

26 Toynbee, *Death and Burial*, 45. On this organization in the Christian community in Rome, see J. Guyon, "La vénète des tombes à travers l'épigraphie de Rome chrétienne (III–VII siècles): le rôle des fossores, masionarii, praepositi et prêtres," *Mélanges de l'Ecole Française de Rome* 86 (1974), 549–596; J. Stevenson, *The Catacombs – Rediscovered Monuments of Early Christianity* (London, 1978), 7–23.

27 Mazar, *Beth She'arim*, I, 136; Avigad, *Beth She'arim*, III, 137.

someone a place in which to make a tomb] . . . ."[28] The "seller" sold land
for the purpose of hewing a grave and was most likely responsible for
the actual hewing. The "receiver" was the person who actually hewed
the grave and was paid as a contracted laborer. "One who hollowed a
kokh [loculus] in a tomb" and "one who digs a *kokh* in a tomb for a
corpse" were workers who actually hollowed the *kokh*.[29] Hillel the son of
Levi, on whose sarcophagus in Catacomb 20 the inscription clearly states,
"this is the coffin of Rabbi Hillel, the son of Rabbi Levi, who made this
cave," is the only person mentioned by name at Beth She'arim who is
known to have hewn a tomb[30] (see Ill. 3) These people were probably
members of an organization similar to today's *ḥevra' qadisha'*; they probably hewed graves on private lots and sold burial tombs or parts of them,
as was the case at Beth She'arim.

In addition to gravediggers there were buriers,[31] bone collectors,[32]
professional mourners,[33] and flute players.[34] An inscription from the Beth
She'arim synagogue mentions the vocation of two of its members. Rabbi
Samuel was the "the person who prepared the corpse for burial"
(συστέλλον[τος]) and Judah was the actual burier "who laid out the
corpse" (κοιμ[ῶντος]) (see Ill. 4).[35] The sources indicate that these

---

28 M Bava Batra 6:8.

29 Tractate Semaḥot 13:4, Higger, p. 202; B Berakhot 14b.

30 Avigad, *Beth She'arim*, III, 251–252.

31 M Nazir 2:4; J Nazir 2, 4, 52a; B Ta'anit 5b.

32 Genesis Rabbah 89:2, Theodor-Albeck, p. 1087; Tractate Semaḥot 12:7, 9, Higger,
pp. 196–198.

33 M Ketubot 4:4; Tractate Semaḥot 14:7, Higger, p. 206; T Nedarim 2:7, Lieberman,
p. 105; M. Ayali, *A Nomenclature of Workers and Artisans in the Talmudic and Midrashic
Literature* (Israel, 1984), 86 (Hebrew). Regarding the hiring of mourners among Jews
in Roman Palestine in the fourth century C.E., see S. Krauss, "The Jews in the Works
of the Church Fathers," *JQR* 6 (1894), 231. The use of public mourners was prevalent
in the Christian community of Palestine at least until the sixth century C.E.; see Y.
Dan, *The City in Eretz Israel during the Late Roman and Byzantine Periods* (Jerusalem,
1984), 208 (Hebrew)

34 M Ketubot 4:4; M Bava Metzi'a 6:1; T 'Avodah Zarah 6:1, Zuckermandel, p. 469.

35 Schwabe and Lifshitz, *Beth She'arim*, II, 189–190. G. Alon, "Hashkava," *Studies in
Jewish History* (2 vols.; Tel-Aviv, 1957–58), II, 109–110 (Hebrew), rejects Schwabe's interpretation, claiming that *'immutz* in talmudic literature means closing the eyes of
the dead person and that *mashkiv* is not prevalent in talmudic literature. Alon further
suggests that Samuel wrapped the corpse in shrouds and possibly also made the
shrouds, and that Judah was a professional eulogist. It is customary to assume that
professional eulogists existed in Eretz-Israel during the mishnaic and talmudic periods; see M. Ayali, *A Nomenclature of Workers and Artisans*, 90–91; Safrai, "Home and
Family," 778–779; E. Feldman, *Biblical and Post Biblical Defilement and Mourning Law as*

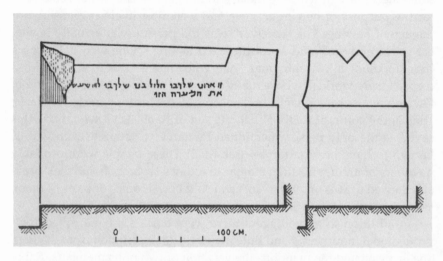

Ill. 3. Sarcophagus, with Hebrew inscription, of Hillel the son of R. Levi. *(Institute of Archeology, Hebrew University of Jerusalem)*

Ill. 4. Greek inscription from Beth She'arim synagogue, citing the names of Samuel and Judah who supplied funerary services. *(Institute of Archeology, Hebrew University of Jerusalem)*

contracted laborers were independent workers employed by anyone in need of their services. One may assume that they were part of a larger organization which supplied funerary services.

Those who could not pay funerary expenses received aid from *havurot*, "societies" which functioned on a voluntary basis, similar to the societies in Jerusalem prior to the destruction of the Second Temple (70 C.E.).[36] The rabbis regarded those who took part in the burial process as people performing a deed of charity and kindness.[37] Abba Sha'ul buried the dead,[38] and the sources say that R. Ḥanina, the son of R. Abbahu, "performed deeds of kindness";[39] while his father thought that he was studying in the Tiberias academy, he was, in fact, voluntarily helping to bury the dead.

The Tosefta says, "one laments and buries the dead of the gentiles for the sake of peace . . . ," implying that in mixed cities Jewish buriers or charitable societies handled the burial of non-Jews as well.[40] The case of a gentile who buried a Jew on the eve of the Sabbath indicates that, when

---

Theology (New York, 1977), 129. A close study of the sources mentioning eulogy and eulogists shows that professional eulogists do not appear in the Palestinian sources but rather only in the Babylonian Talmud, and then only in the discourses of Babylonian rabbis; see B Berakhot 62b; B Taʿanit 5b; B Megillah 6a; B Moʿed Qatan 8a, 25b; B Ḥagigah 15b; B Yevamot 121b; B Nedarim 66b; B Sanhedrin 46b. The *baraita* in B Berakhot 62a is an exception: ". . . Just as the dead are punished, so the professional eulogists are punished. . . ." This *baraita* is not proof of professional eulogy in Palestine because it does not discuss professional eulogists but rather a prevalent custom of praising the deceased: "Praise that applied to him and praise that did not apply to him,"; Tractate Semaḥot 3:6, Higger, p. 112. In Palestine there were no professional eulogists but rather rabbis or others who would eulogize. See T Berakhot 3:24, Lieberman, p. 17; J Horayot 3, 7, 48b; Leviticus Rabbah 20:9, Margulies, pp. 451–452; Lamentations Rabbah 1:9, Buber, p. 39; Ecclesiastes Rabbah 5:11. Thus Alon's suggestion to explain *koimon* as a professional eulogist does not hold when the talmudic sources are taken into consideration. The role of Judah as the person who laid out the corpse, as Schwabe has suggested, makes more sense, for, as we said earlier, there were people who worked as buriers.

36 Tractate Semaḥot 12:5, Higger, p. 195; T Megillah 3:15, Lieberman, p. 357. The activities of the "society" were similar to those of the Collegium Funeraticum in Rome, although in Rome membership in the "society" involved payment; see K. Hopkins, *Death and Renewal* (Cambridge, 1983), 211–217.

37 T Megillah 3:16, Lieberman, p. 357; J Moʿed Qatan 3, 7, 83b; J Ḥagigah 2, 2, 77b.

38 B Niddah 24b.

39 J Pesaḥim 3, 7, 30b; S. Lieberman, *Hayerushalmi Kiphshuto* (Jerusalem, 1934), 425 (Hebrew); J Ḥagigah 1, 7, 76c.

40 T Gittin 3:14, Lieberman, p. 259; J Demai 4, 6, 24a; J Gittin 5, 9, 47c; J ʿAvodah Zarah 1, 3, 39c.

necessary, Jews could use non-Jewish burial societies for the burial of Jews.[41] It is possible that in mixed cities of that period, non-Jewish buriers worked with the Jewish charitable burial societies.

The gravediggers, buriers, and all those who took part in funerary services worked independently of any urban institution or administrative office of the Jewish community. Family members of the deceased used their services to hew caves, purchase entire caves or single burial plots in a burial cave, conduct funeral services, and bury the dead. Even if these workers were affiliated to an organization similar to today's *hevra' qadisha'* or were members of a guild, they still had no official connection to any urban institution. One may assume that, once granted permission by the local authorities, they were free to hew tombs and sell them. Moreover, the familial obligation to bury its deceased members, and the "good deeds" performed by others in this regard, were not connected in any way to the charitable functions of the synagogue.[42]

The existence of private burial societies relieved the general urban as well as Jewish communal institutions from all matters concerning burial. These societies set laws and regulations regarding the environmental rights of the individual, such as determining the location of the cemetery in relation to the city's borders,[43] marking the graves so as to avoid impurity,[44] as well as fixing a number of halakhot concerning buyer-seller relations.[45]

Who was buried in Beth She'arim? The epigraphic evidence indicates that Beth She'arim was the central cemetery for all Jews throughout Palestine and the Diaspora.[46] Beth She'arim attracted many people who

---

[41] J Mo'ed Qatan 3, 5, 82a.

[42] The only hint of a connection between burial and cemetery with the synagogue is found in the words of R. El'azar in Leviticus Rabbah 5:5, Margulies, p. 116: "A man should have a nail or a peg fixed in a synagogue so that he may thereby gain the right to be buried in that place." Margulies cites another version of this midrash, where the word "synagogue" is replaced by "cemetery." The fact that burial and cemeteries are never mentioned among the numerous sources dealing with synagogues leads one to conclude that there was no connection between the two. See also S. W. Baron, *A Social and Religious History of the Jews* (18 vols.; New York, 1952–83), II, 286–287.

[43] M Bava Batra 2:9; T Bava Batra 1:10–11, Lieberman, p. 131; J Nazir 9, 3, 57d; Tractate Semahot 14:9–10, Higger, p. 207.

[44] M Sheqalim 1:1; M Mo'ed Qatan 1:1; J. Mann, "Rabbinic Studies in the Synoptic Gospels," *HUCA* 1 (1924), 351–355.

[45] M Bava Batra 6:7–8; T Bava Batra 6:23, Lieberman, p. 151; J Bava Batra 6, 12, 15c; B Bava Batra 100b–101b.

[46] Schwabe and Lifshitz, *Beth She'arim*, II, 217–222; B. Mazar, "Those Who Buried their Dead," 296–298. The custom of bringing the dead to burial in Palestine is dis-

chose to be buried near the burial site of the Patriarchal family. Both local and Diaspora Jews generally shared caves, although areas in which groups of graves belonged to people from a certain region or origin may be discerned. This is true of the rabbis as well.

In the third and fourth centuries C.E. the rabbis were an elite class in Jewish society of Roman Palestine, as is evident in many instances recorded in talmudic literature.[47] This is also apparent in the Jewish cemetery: special burial caves for the rabbis and their families were found at Beth She'arim, for example in Catacombs 14 and 20 (see Ill. 5),[48] as well as a considerable number of Hebrew and Aramaic grave inscriptions which cite sixteen names with the title "Rabbi." Hall G in Catacomb 1 is similar to the two catacombs mentioned above; it belonged to Mokim and his family and contained seven inscriptions which name people bearing the title "Rabbi,"[49] most of whom were members of Mokim's family (see Ill. 1). Although, as mentioned, familial burials were prevalent in this period, this phenomenon does not necessarily stand in contradiction, as rabbinic circles regarded colleagues as extended family, and their burial caves were called *me'arata' de-rabbanan*, "the burial caves of the rabbis." Thus, in addition to members of Mokim's family in Hall G, one Rabbi Paregoris was also buried there;[50] in the same hall we find the graves of Judah ha-Qatan[51] and Dose,[52] who may have been members

---

cussed by I. Gafni, "Reinterment in the Land of Israel: Notes on the Origin and Development of the Custom," in: *The Jerusalem Cathedra*, ed. L. I. Levine (3 vols.; Jerusalem, 1981–83), I, 96–104.

[47] L. I. Levine, *The Rabbinic Class of Roman Palestine in Late Antiquity* (Jerusalem, 1989), 47–55.

[48] Avigad, *Beth She'arim*, III, 62–65, 114–115; S. J. D. Cohen, "Epigraphical Rabbis," *JQR* 72 (1981), 1–17, states that the title "Rabbi" is not necessarily the title of a scholar but rather of an honorable donor or synagogue functionary. Thus, it is not clear that these catacombs belonged to scholars. The fact that these names are not known to us from talmudic literature is not proof, for one may assume that not all rabbis, or those close to the rabbinic class, were mentioned in the sources; see Levine, *Rabbinic Class*, 49, n. 32.

[49] Mazar, *Beth She'arim*, I, 86, 199–201; Schwabe and Lifshitz, *Beth She'arim*, II, inscr. nos. 18, 20, 31, 41, 43.

[50] Ibid., inscr. no. 31.

[51] Mazar, *Beth She'arim*, I, 200; Schwabe and Lifshitz, *Beth She'arim*, II, inscr. no. 29. This name is similar to the names of Samuel ha-Qatan, ben Qatin, Qatina, Daniel son of R. Qatina; see M. Kosovsky, *Concordance to the Talmud Yerushalmi – Onomasticon* (Jerusalem, 1985), 602 (Hebrew).

[52] Schwabe and Lifshitz, *Beth She'arim*, II, inscr. no. 40. This name is prevalent among the rabbis. See Kosovsky, *Concordance*, 182.

Ill. 5. A view of Catacombs 14 and 20 – burial caves of the rabbis. *(Institute of Archeology, Hebrew University of Jerusalem)*

of the rabbinic class, although they do not bear the title "Rabbi." Such caves often bore the names of their owners, for example *me'arata' de-R. Ḥiyya*, "the burial cave of R. Ḥiyya."[53] When R. Huna the Exilarch was brought to Palestine for burial, the rabbis debated as to where to bury him. In the Jerusalem Talmud the suggestion is made that he be placed "near R. Ḥiyya because he is one of them."[54] R. Huna was, in fact, buried in R. Ḥiyya's cave, together with Judah and Hezekiah, the sons of R. Ḥiyya. R. Ḥaggai volunteered to bring R. Huna to burial, although the other rabbis suspected that he, too, coveted this burial place: "You are looking for an excuse, for you are an old man and you want to go up there and die and be buried there [next to R. Ḥiyya]." The tone of this statement suggests that others, too, may have wanted to be buried there. In any case, it is clear that rabbis chose to be buried near each other.[55]

After the destruction of the Second Temple the rabbis tried to bridge social gaps regarding mourning and burial customs.[56] However, in the third and fourth centuries C.E. we find them formulating halakhot pertaining to mourning and burial which grant themselves a special status. Mourning was prohibited for all during the intermediate days of a festival,[57] but "a sage who died, all are deemed his relations, all tear their garments, all bare [their shoulders], all lament, and all receive a mourners' meal on his account, even in the street of the town."[58] Not only mourning, but also making a coffin in the marketplace,[59] reciting lamen-

---

53 B Bava Metziʿa 85b. The text in B Moʿed Qatan 17a mentions *me'arata' de-ḥasidei* ("the cave of the pious") and *me'arata' de-dayyanei* ("the cave of the judges") in relation to the burial of a disciple or a scholar. It is possible that even these caves, which have a different title, were used for the burial of members of the rabbinic class.

54 J Kilʾaim 9, 4, 32b; J Ketubot 12, 3, 35a; B Moʿed Qatan 25a. This legend and the relationship between the parallels in the talmudic sources are discussed by S. Friedman, "On the Historic Legend in the Babylonian Talmud," in: *The Saul Lieberman Festschrift* (Jerusalem, 1989), 28–46 (Hebrew).

55 The Babylonian Talmud relates a similar situation. R. Elʿazar b. Simeon was concerned that he would not be given a proper burial by the sages: B Bava Metziʿa 84b; PRK 11:23, Mandelbaum, pp. 198–199.

56 T Niddah 9:16–17, Zuckermandel, pp. 651–652; J Sheqalim 2, 7, 47a; B Moʿed Qatan 27a–b.

57 M Moʿed Qatan 3:5–9.

58 T Moʿed Qatan 2:17, Lieberman, pp. 372–373; Tractate Semaḥot 9:1–2, Higger, pp. 168–169.

59 The general laws can be found in M Moʿed Qatan 1:6. The laws concerning rabbis are cited in J Moʿed Qatan 1, 6, 80d: "When R. Ḥananiah, associate of the rabbis, died they made for him a coffin in the marketplace."

tations during the funeral,[60] and holding a mourners' meal,[61] which were normally prohibited during these intermediate days, were allowed in the case of the death of a sage. Participation in the funeral of a sage and lamentations for him were considered a special obligation.[62] Even priests were allowed to participate in the funeral, despite the usual prohibition lest they contract the uncleanliness of a corpse.[63] Lamentations for a rabbi were made in the synagogue;[64] the sources tell us of funerals of rabbis attended by many people.[65] Halakhic discourses were prohibited near the bier of a corpse, and, despite the excuses given in the Talmud, it is clear that some rabbis allowed themselves to behave contrary to this prohibition.[66] Not only sages, but also their sons, enjoyed the benefits of the rabbinic class. Tractate Semaḥot states that, "the sons of rich men are like the children of sages, children of sages are like the children of royalty, and their funeral rites must be attended."[67] The reality as we see it at Beth She'arim, together with the evidence of the talmudic sources, strengthen the assumption that there were burial caves which were restricted to the rabbinic class in the Galilean Jewish cemeteries of the third and fourth centuries C.E.[68]

The uncovering of the Beth She'arim cemetery, where local as well as Diaspora Jews were buried, enables us to study the organization and operation of a Jewish cemetery in the mishnaic and talmudic periods. It has been assumed that burial in Beth She'arim ceased as a result of the Gallus

---

[60] *General laws*: M Mo'ed Qatan 3:9; T Ḥagigah 2:13, Lieberman, p. 386; *laws pertaining to a rabbi*: J Mo'ed Qatan 3, 9, 83d. See S. Lieberman, "Emendations," *Tarbiz* 3 (1932), 453–454 (Hebrew), on the custom of public acclamation.

[61] *General laws*: M Mo'ed Qatan 3:7; *laws pertaining to a rabbi*: J Mo'ed Qatan 3, 9, 83d.

[62] T Mo'ed Qatan 2:17, Lieberman, pp. 372–373; B Shabbat 105b; B Sukkah 29a; B Rosh ha-Shanah 25a; B 'Avodah Zarah 18a.

[63] J Berakhot 2, 3, 4c; J Berakhot 3, 1, 6a; J Nazir 7, 1, 56a.

[64] T Megillah 2:18, Lieberman, p. 353; B Megillah 28b.

[65] J Kil'aim 9, 4, 32b; J Bava Metzi'a 2, 13, 8d.

[66] J Nazir 7, 1, 56a.

[67] Tractate Semaḥot 3:4, Higger, p. 111; B Mo'ed Qatan 24b. On the rights of the sons of sages, see G. Alon, *Jews, Judaism and the Classical World* (Jerusalem, 1977), 436–457.

[68] For additional laws concerning the status of the rabbinic class, see Tractate Semaḥot 10:11, 13 and 11:1, Higger, pp. 183–185 and 186, respectively. Certain laws pertaining to the rabbinic class appear only in the Babylonian Talmud, e.g., B Mo'ed Qatan 25a; B Bava Qamma 17a. It is possible that these laws pertain to the status of the Babylonian rabbis and do not describe the Palestinian reality.

Revolt (352 C.E.).[69] An analysis of the architectural finds and their comparison to other burial sites,[70] as well as new information concerning the extent of the Gallus Revolt,[71] lead to the conclusion that burial at Beth She'arim did not cease then. Rather, Beth She'arim continued to function throughout the fourth and even well into the fifth centuries C.E.

[69] Mazar, *Beth She'arim*, I, 19; Avigad, *Beth She'arim*, III, 3.

[70] For example, see Hall G in Catacomb 1; Mazar, *Beth She'arim*, I, 75–87. Five generations of Mokim's family are buried in this hall. This family came from Tadmor close to the year of the city's destruction (273 C.E.), and it is assumed that the hall was purchased then. If one calculates 25–30 years per generation, this hall was used for at least 120 years, through the end of the fourth century. In addition, Hall I was hewn after the two front rooms in Hall G were used for the burial of two generations of the Mokim family. See Mazar, ibid., 94. Thus, this hall was hewn not before the second third of the fourth century, and, as Mazar explains, was in use until the beginning of the fifth century. Accordingly, Hall J, which is later than Hall I, was hewn only at the end of the fourth or at the beginning of the fifth century. In the Byzantine period, the Jews continued to hew caves similar to those found at Beth She'arim. See U. Dahari, G. Avni and A. Kloner, "The Jewish Necropolis of Beth-Govrin," *Qadmoniot* 20/79–80 (1987), 97–102 (Hebrew); and N. Feig, "Tiv'on," *Hadashot Arkheologiyot* 93 (1989), 29–30 (Hebrew). The fact that the hewing of burial caves of this type existed in the Byzantine period supports the assumption that some of the Beth She'arim caves may very well have been hewn in the Byzantine period.

[71] S. Lieberman, "Palestine in the Third and Fourth Centuries," *JQR* 36 (1946), 336–341; J. G. Gager, "The Gallus Revolt and the Question of Building the Temple in the Time of Julian," in: *Eretz Israel from the Destruction of the Second Temple to the Muslim Conquest*, eds. Z. Baras et al. (2 vols.; Jerusalem, 1982–84), I, 202–208 (Hebrew). In the recent excavations at Sepphoris, where the "Gallus Revolt" broke out, the excavators do not see the destruction of the city as a result of the quelling of this revolt but rather as a continuation of the settlement until the 363 C.E. earthquake and even beyond this date; see E. M. Meyers, E. Netzer and C. L. Meyers, "A Mansion in the Sepphoris Acropolis and its Splendid Mosaic," *Qadmoniot* 21/83–84 (1988), 92 (Hebrew) and idem, "Zippori 1987–1988," *Hadashot Arkheologiyot* 93 (1989), 26–29 (Hebrew).

Contributors

Albert I. Baumgarten, Bar Ilan University

Shaye J. D. Cohen, Brown University

Douglas Edwards, University of Puget Sound

Gideon Foerster, Hebrew University of Jerusalem

Steven D. Fraade, Yale University

Sean Freyne, Trinity College, Dublin

Martin Goodman, Oxford Centre for Graduate Studies

Howard Clark Kee, Boston University

Lee I. Levine, Hebrew University of Jerusalem

Eric C. Meyers, Duke University

Stuart S. Miller, University of Connecticut

Aharon Oppenheimer, Tel-Aviv University

Uriel Rappaport, Haifa University

Gary A. Rendsburg, Cornell University

Zeev Safrai, Bar Ilan University

Anthony J. Saldarini, Boston College

Lawrence H. Schiffman, New York University

Avigdor Shinan, Hebrew University of Jerusalem

James F. Strange, University of South Florida

Zeev Weiss, Hebrew University of Jerusalem

Subject Index

Source Index

Christian and Byzantine Literature